THREE FACES OF IMPERIALISM

THREE FACES OF IMPERIALISM

British and American Approaches
to Asia and Africa
1870–1970

PHILLIP DARBY

YALE UNIVERSITY PRESS · NEW HAVEN AND LONDON · 1987

Designed by Faith Glasgow
Filmset in Monophoto Imprint and printed in
Great Britain by The Bath Press, Avon

Library of Congress Cataloging in Publication Data

Darby, Phillip.
   Three faces of imperialism.

   Bibliography: p.
   Includes index.
   1. Imperialism. 2. Great Britain—Colonies—Africa.
3. Great Britain—Colonies—Asia. 4. United States—
Foreign relations—1945– . I. Title.
JC359.D28 1987   325'.32   86-24665
ISBN 0-300-03748-1

CONTENTS

Acknowledgements   vii

Introduction   1

PART ONE *The Expansion of Empire 1870–1914*

1. Power I   8
2. Moral Responsibility I   31
3. Economic Interest I (written with Grant Parsons)   53

PART TWO *The Inter-War Years*

4. Power II   76
5. Moral Responsibility II   101
6. Economic Interest II   118

PART THREE *The Cold War Era*

Interchapter – The American Experience:
        A Comparative Perspective   142

7. Power III   147
8. Moral Responsibility III   169
9. Economic Interest III (written with Grant Parsons)   190

Conclusion   213

Notes   225

Select Bibliography   256

Index   263

To my mother and the memory of my father

Acknowledgements

It is a pleasure to record the help I have received from friends and colleagues in writing and revising this book. I owe a special debt to those who read all or part of the manuscript. Lord Beloff, Professor David Fieldhouse of Jesus College, Cambridge, and Dr Kosmas Tsokhas of the Australian National University reviewed the work as a whole and made many suggestions of substance. I deeply appreciate their help and encouragement. Professor Gary Hawke of Victoria University of Wellington gave detailed comments on the three economic chapters. Much of the argument in these chapters has been clarified and strengthened, I believe, as a result of his criticisms and recommendations. Professor Richard Neustadt of the J.F. Kennedy School of Government at Harvard provided wise guidance on the American material. He led me to revise my thinking on several points, and generally, I hope, to write with more understanding.

At the University of Melbourne I am grateful for the interest and stimulation of many former students, and especially Grant Parsons, Richard Fuller and Albert Paolini. Chapters 3 and 9 were written jointly with Grant Parsons, and he kept an eye on chapter 6 as well. Without his involvement, the book might not have been completed. I enjoyed innumerable hours of discussion with Richard Fuller about the contribution of imaginative literature, and I have incorporated certain material he made available. Albert Paolini introduced me to some of the writing on American insecurity, and he worked carefully and cheerfully on the revision of the manuscript. I would also like to thank Dr Judith Armstrong for help with various passages and Jan Souter for preparing the typescript.

Much of this book was written at Nuffield College, Oxford, during two periods when I was granted visitors' facilities. I am grateful to the Warden and Fellows for the opportunity to return to college and to be able to work in such a congenial and stimulating environment.

Introduction

This book explores the categories of thought which lay behind British and American imperialism in Asia and Africa in the century from 1870. Imperialism is understood in its broadest sense as denoting domination. As the word is used here, it is not restricted to formal empire and it carries no pejorative implication. It should by now be apparent to all but the most rigid dogmatist that imperialism proceeded on several planes; it presented a number of faces. It was variously – and often at the same time – an exercise in power politics, an expression of moral responsibility and an attempt to secure economic benefit. These three aspects, and their corresponding sets of images, provide the frames of our analysis.

By charting the course of British and American approaches to Asia and Africa, it is hoped that the book will contribute to a fuller understanding of the relationship between the West and the Third World. There is, however, no intention of offering a general explanation of imperialism. For the most part our concern is with the metropoles – with the kinds of thinking and the often unconscious urges which were to lead to domination. But domination is seldom achieved solely through metropolitan capabilities and initiatives. It is now well recognized that imperialism represented interests on both sides of the divide; that it resulted from a meshing of forces. There is a case to be argued that some schools of historical interpretation have over-emphasized the part played by Asians and Africans. There is none for any notion that imperialism can be comprehended simply in terms of the interests and ideas of the dominant power.

This book is written from the viewpoint of international politics broadly understood, meaning that primary attention is paid to those aspects of thinking about Asia and Africa which related to external linkages of some political significance. It is believed that a knowledge of one historical period deepens understanding of another. A familiarity with British approaches to Asia and Africa before the Second World War raises questions and suggests lines of thinking about American approaches in the years after. Both the British and the

American experience put contemporary ideas about the relationship between the West and the Third World in sharper relief. In examining the historical material the hope is to trace some of the continuities and to establish the discontinuities in Western thinking. It is instructive to observe the extent to which apparently novel conceptions are in fact older notions suitably refurbished, or take up themes of an earlier era. No less importantly, we may be able to see new departures for what they are. In this way historical perspective helps sift the transient from the perennial and enables us better to distinguish the immediate triggers of thinking from underlying sources.

The century from about 1870 stands as the epoch of Western domination of Asia and Africa. The ascendancy, first of Great Britain, and later of the United States, deeply marked the life of the underdeveloped world and influenced the approaches of other imperial powers. Inevitably there is some artificiality about fixing an historical era with a beginning and an end. The 1870s have been taken as the starting-point for this study because they saw the beginning of a new surge of imperial expansion and the emergence of a more systematic and self-conscious approach to the underdeveloped world, which was associated with the movement towards formal empire. Our narrative runs beyond the granting of independence to Afro-Asian states down to the late sixties and early seventies, and America's defeat in Vietnam. These years mark a watershed in that the edifice of Western domination, and its intellectual and emotional supports, began to crumble. Ethnocentrism was increasingly recognized and condemned; what might be termed 'imperial will' appeared to be losing ground in the struggle with cultural relativism; much less optimism was felt about what the West could accomplish in Africa and Asia. The fading of the Cold War was accompanied by a growing assertiveness on the part of Third World states, less inclined than ever before to accept their subordination in international politics. The increasing dependence of the West on the economic resources of Asia and Africa, and the greater official recognition of this dependence, was symbolised by the Club of Rome report in 1972 and by the OPEC crisis the following year.

For the purposes of more ordered analysis, the century of Western hegemony in Asia and Africa has been broken into three broad periods. These are: the expansion of empire between 1870 and 1914; the inter-war years which saw the modification and adjustment of many imperial assumptions about the underdeveloped world; and the Cold War era when both the international system and the place of Asia and Africa within it were substantially recast. It must be recognized that at times the material does not neatly fit this periodization. As will be apparent in Chapter 2, much of the thinking about Britain's moral responsibility to dependent peoples took shape well before 1870. As is argued in the interchapter, America's approach to Asia and Africa after the Second World War was influenced by its earlier experience in Latin America and the Philippines.

In the first and second periods our concern is principally with British imperialism; in the third, attention is directed to the imperialism of the United States. This concentration first on Britain, and later on America, reflects the pre-eminence of these powers at different points in time. Until the Second World War Britain played by far the most important role of any Western state in Asia and Africa; during and after the war it was the United States which had most influence. The presumption is that a study of the approach and attitudes of the historically dominant power is likely to illuminate the broader relationship between the West and the Third World. Moreover, during their respective years of overlordship British and American policy-makers shared many assumptions and lines of thinking about the purposes and nature of involvement in Asia and Africa. A comparative analysis is therefore apt, and it draws our attention to points which might otherwise have escaped notice. Yet there are risks in such an exercise because of the manifest differences between the British imperial system and the United States' role in Asia and Africa after 1945. This warning is developed in the interchapter which serves as a short introduction to part three of the book, dealing with America in the era of the Cold War.

Within the chronological framework set by our three periods, individual chapters are devoted to approaches in terms of power, moral responsibility and economic interest. The attempt to break up and analyse historical reality in this tripartite form necessarily involves some abstraction. It is artificial to the extent that seldom do we find individuals or groups thinking of Asia and Africa simply within the confines of one category. It is apparent that the distinction between the three spheres is by no means always clear-cut. Yet, by and large, this division of the material accords with what we know of how people thought and the way in which they organized their mental pictures. Our approach has a larger utility in that power and economic interest are central reference-points in the literature of international relations, upon which the most influential interpretative theories have been built. Moral responsibility has occupied a less prominent place in its own terms. But considered as a form of idealist ideology, there has been sharp debate about its meaning and significance. The structure of this book enables us to see all three approaches in action, as it were, in an historical setting, and the reader may make judgements about their explanatory content.

The chapters on power ask how far the thinking of statesmen and strategists was shaped by doctrines of power politics. This raises the question of the extent to which international politics in Africa and

Asia were understood on the basis of considerations and calculations external to Africa and Asia. The chapters on moral responsibility attempt to assess the nature and significance of ideas that the West had a duty to implant the seeds of progress in the Third World. Almost by definition, progress was understood to be the course followed by Western states, and its most characteristic expression was the commitment to economic development. The chapters on economic interest consider the degree to which Afro-Asia was seen to offer economic benefits to the metropoles, how these benefits might best be realized, and the implications for the indigenous economies. At various points the connections and disjunctions between different conceptions are examined.

It might reasonably be argued that imperialism had other facets, as, for example, the autonomous dynamic of the military establishment and the psychological predispositions of policy-makers. The contention of this book is that power, moral responsibility and economic interests are the key categories, not the only ones. Moreover, very often other impulses or elements were expressed through the concepts and language of power, duty and economics. For this reason some material on the military establishment is discussed in the chapters on power, while psycho-analytical perspectives are treated in the chapters on moral responsibility, and, in the American case, on power.

Our basic concern is with the broad approach of policy-makers to Asia and Africa, not with the making of imperial policy as such. By defining our interest in terms of approaches, emphasis is placed on the importance of background assumptions, patterns of thinking and the mental pictures which were held of other societies. The reference to policy-makers should not be narrowly construed. While those who held power in London and Washington must be the central reference-point, our coverage is necessarily wider and touches all kinds of interests, pressures and opinions which influence official thinking. Very often, in fact, internal considerations of the broadest kind – relating, for example, to the state of the economy or the political climate – left a powerful stamp on thinking about overseas affairs.

To the extent that approaches to the Third World were shaped by views about the external environment, the role of other powers, and Africa and Asia themselves, the material on images and perceptions has a direct relevance. As has often enough been observed, international relations proceed on the basis of what people take to be reality, not reality itself. At times what is taken to be reality is but a fiction of the observer's making. This is perhaps nowhere more apparent than when we look at Western impressions and conceptions of Asia and Africa, and the generalized notions of how much they mattered and in what ways. The importance of images and perceptions in international relations has been increasingly recognised in recent scholarly writing and a considerable literature has developed. A number of works have explored the subject at a conceptual level.[1] Others provide case studies of the images one nation has of another and the influence of such images on policy-making.[2] This literature informs the present study, although the more abstract and theoretical expositions and heavily quantitative approaches were judged of limited utility.

Africa and Asia have been bracketed together, despite obvious differences and despite the heterogeneity of their constituent societies, because there are many areas of commonality in British and American thinking about them, and the differences as seen through Western eyes are themselves revealing. There is some unevenness of treatment. Certain sections are primarily concerned with Asia; in others, African material predominates. The larger category of the Third World has been rejected as the subject of analysis in the belief that approaches to Latin America were often qualitatively different from those to Africa and Asia. In Latin America, Western political control was a product of the first expansion of Europe, not the second. External economic linkages have loomed larger and political doctrines and racial stereotypes smaller than is true of either Africa or Asia. Nor did the Cold War or strategic calculations impinge to anything like the same extent. Indeed, until the advent of dependency theory, a case could be argued that Latin America was to the West a world of its own.

It should go without saying – though in fact cannot – that an exploration of approaches and perceptions is some distance removed from an explanation of policies. Relatively seldom in international politics is it possible to assert that a particular pattern of thinking led to this decision or resulted in that action. The nature of causality is too complex and the evidence usually too limited to permit formulations of this kind. Quite apart from the impact of various external and fortuitous factors, there is no linear process by which ideas determine intentions and intentions find expression in policies. So far as individual decision-makers are concerned, it is extremely difficult to establish exactly what they had in mind – all the more so since their public statements may be calculated to conceal rather than reveal.[3] Insofar as attention is focussed, as it is in this book, on the characteristic patterns of thinking of the time, the most that can be claimed is that here are likely sources of action and probably parameters of policy. As G.R. Elton has argued, the body of ideas current in a society conditions political action but it neither causes nor explains it.[4]

Even greater difficulties surround any attempt to chart the relationship between image and ideas and the conditions of material life. One would like to ask: On what basis did these images emerge? Why were those ideas generally held? Yet the deceptive simplicity of such questions tends to mask the sheer dimensions of the task and the inevitable subjectivity of perspective. This book does not seek to explore the relationship between thought and perception, on the one hand, and underlying economic conditions, on the other. Rather, the view is taken that ideas and images have an importance in their own right – a position increasingly accepted even by Marxists in terms of the relative autonomy or separate development of the cultural order. Implicit in this view is the belief that there is no necessary correlation between the two spheres. While often ideas do reflect existing material interests, they may instead echo interests of an earlier era or indeed be plainly counter-productive. This is not, of course, to suggest that material considerations can be ignored in our analysis. Ideas do not stand independently of interests; nor can they be seen as conceptually distinct. Without some acknowledgement of the interplay between the two realms, it is impossible to understand how ideas change, or the process by which one pattern of thinking is replaced by another.

PART ONE

The Expansion of Empire
1870–1914

One

POWER I

International Relations scholars and historians tend to differ in the
way they approach the role of power in the relations of states. In the
literature of international relations, power so often takes on a logic of
its own and attention is diverted from the purposes for which it is
required. Historians have been much less inclined to treat power as a
clear-cut category or to subject it to the same systematic analysis.
However, their concern with internal circumstances, and often individual decision-makers, inhibits easy assumptions about the explanatory value of the goal of maximizing national power. These general
observations have an applicability to the literature on the second
expansion of Europe. The characterization of the imperialist era as an
age of power politics can obscure the extent to which individual states
pursued different interests. Arguments about the primacy of power
and strategy in the calculations of British policy-makers can lead to the
neglect of other considerations, such as economic benefit, which were
understood to be associated. Here we attempt an intermediate course.
The hope is to catch some of the sharpness of argument of a systems
approach, while at the same time drawing on the evidence of what
statesmen actually thought and what power meant in particular
circumstances.

The object of this chapter is to consider how far British policy-
makers saw Asia and Africa in terms of power politics. To what extent
can their approach be understood as the pursuit of power, prestige and
strategic advantage? What implications did this have both for Britain
and for Asia and Africa? Attention is directed to the relationship
between political concerns and those of an economic and philanthro-
pic nature, but the subject cannot be fully explored here because the
evidentiary material on economics and morality is presented in
chapters 2 and 3. It may be that the question of how far Britain's
concerns were political rather than economic or moral/ideological
admits no general answer, because different sectors within the society
were influenced by different considerations and to some degree
operated on different fronts. To the extent that policy-makers

approached Asia and Africa from a power politics perspective, there is a further question: were the underlying interests – the purposes of policy – located in Africa and Asia or were they anchored in Britain and her relations with the European powers? Put simply, the issue is whether the periphery was seen as an end in itself or merely a means. The perceptions and interests of Great Britain at the height of its Empire raise an especial problem because of the difficulty – even absurdity – of attempting to separate metropolitan and imperial strands.

This chapter, more than any other in the book, takes a wide canvas. Some explication is required of what is meant by power politics. The concept is more open to misunderstanding than is the material relating to our other primary images of moral responsibility and economic interest. A clarification of meaning will sharpen analysis of British diplomatic and strategic perceptions of Africa and Asia in the period of empire. It will, moreover, prepare the ground for our later chapters on Britain in the inter-war years and America in the Cold War era.

It is apparent that Britain cannot be considered in isolation. The interest of British policy-makers in power and strategy outside Europe was necessarily related to the perceived intentions and policies of the European powers. From the 1880s the play of power politics in Africa and Asia was at least in part a consequence of the diplomatic manoeuvring in Europe. Some account is therefore necessary of the changing state of European diplomacy and the patterns of thinking which led to the extension of the European balance of power to the periphery. Contrasts can then be drawn between the position of the European states and that of Britain, and the perceptions of their respective statesmen. It might be added that even a brief account of the European power politics system provides a useful background to our analysis of the United States' approach to Asia after the Second World War. In certain respects there are parallels between the thinking of American policy-makers in the Cold War era and that of continental statesmen in the period of empire.[1]

It is proposed to begin at a general level and to narrow the focus of the chapter as we proceed. First, an outline of the power politics pattern of thought will be given. It is then appropriate to sketch the form such thinking took in Europe in the last two decades of the nineteenth century. Finally, analysis will concentrate on the case of Great Britain.

The fundamentals of power politics have changed remarkably little over the past one hundred years.[2] In essence it provides a way of interpreting world politics; a broad philosophy and a set of maxims which enable states to chart a course *vis-à-vis* other states. It rests on a series of commonsense propositions about the key actors in the system, the bases upon which they act, and the kind of mechanisms and techniques available to them to regulate their relations. Analysis and prescription are an amalgam of the distilled wisdom of certain of the political philosophers and what are taken to be the lessons of diplomatic and military history. In its outward costume, power politics is not much concerned with economics. Predicated as it is on the primacy of the political kingdom, economic factors are assumed to be subordinate and usually derivative as well. Nor, in any substantial way, does power politics address itself to developments occurring within the boundaries of nation states. Traditionally the word 'power' was commonly employed, and, as one writer argues, it signified a 'unity-in-spirit'.[3] Classes, social movements and sectional groups thus remain in the background, incidental to the model.

In large part, then, international politics is a world of its own. The state is the basic unit, the nub of the system. Each state must establish its own security and further its own interests. In the absence of a common authority, conflict, though not necessarily war, is inevitable. The tendency is for states to expand. An area of weakness is an invitation to take possession. Nature abhors a vacuum, it is said – though why this should constitute an axiom of international politics is hardly as self-evident as is often implied. As one state augments its national power, so in turn must the next down the line. Power must be matched by countervailing power. The stability of the system is thus maintained.

While all are agreed on the need for countervailing power, when it comes to spelling this out understandings differ. The key concept is that of the balance of power but, as has often enough been pointed out, it has no fixed meaning.[4] At times it is used to connote an equilibrium of power while at others a preponderance of power is envisaged. According to some formulations, adjustment is by self-regulating processes; in others, it is assumed to be a matter of manipulation by wise statesmen. These and other ambiguities limit the utility of the concept of balance of power as a tool of analysis, but few writers have been able to dispense with it.

To ask what constitutes power is scarcely to move to firmer ground. Power has proved difficult to specify and even more so to measure. Stanley Hoffman has written of the elusiveness of modern power,[5] but it would be mistaken to imagine that earlier generations could dispose of the question in some straightforward way. The ingredients of power have always varied according to adversary and circumstance. Intangible factors like prestige and the quality of statecraft had to be weighed along with the number of divisions or capital ships. What constituted strength from one perspective might represent weakness from another. What, at one point in time, was understood as the successful exercise of power might later be seen as the reverse. Still, the bottom line has never been in doubt. While no one would wish to reduce power simply to military might, in the last resort what carries the day is 'blood and iron'. It is also clear that the very existence of military capability has considerable influence before such a point is reached. These are crucial considerations for the power politics approach. Whatever premium is placed on elements such as national will or economic capability, the preparedness and ability to employ military power go to the heart of the *Realpolitik* structure of thought. While logically it may be possible to abstract the use of force from the power politics system, it has become part of the weave.

In the debates about power politics which have spiralled at intervals since the end of the First World War, critics have charged that the pursuit of national interest through power allows no place for morality and stands in the way of establishing a more harmonious international order. An undercurrent in the literature comes close to reducing power to the law of the jungle. Such interpretations are based on a narrow understanding of power precepts, and take little account of the adjustments and concessions which the real world has required. More than forty years ago, E.H. Carr pointed out that the absence of longer-term purpose represents a major limitation of realist thought, and one which cannot be disposed of simply by arguing that morality is dependent upon power.[6] No doubt this is so. Yet if power politics cannot of itself proffer initiatives of a more positive kind, it can provide the conditions in which they may emerge. Power does not need to be the sole determinant of international action, carrying all other considerations before it. In point of fact, moral considerations – good faith, the minimization of war – always had a place in theory, and the great practitioners of the power politics craft never thought that power alone provided all the answers. In practice, power has always needed to be constrained by values if it is to be translated into action and move events. As we shall see, conceptions of a better global order accompanied the power politics appreciation of British statesmen in their approach to Africa and Asia.

It is also important to recognize that the pursuit of power does not imply a situation of complete disorder in the sense that there are no accepted patterns of behaviour as between states, no conventions or rules as to international conduct.[7] The European state system of the nineteenth century could only operate as it did because there existed a minimum of agreement as to the limits and purposes of interaction, *viz.* that the system must be kept working and that the sovereignty of the major powers must be respected. The interests and values shared by the European states were at their most substantial in the period from 1815 to about 1880 and they underlaid the workings of the Concert of Europe. But even in the last decades of the century – when the Concert was in decline – there remained some restraints on state action and a residual sense of the European collectivity. In such a system, then, it was understood that the search for power took certain forms and that there were limits to its exercise. The point can be made more generally. To characterize states as players presupposes some commonality of interest and the acceptance of agreed procedures or codes of conduct – for example in relation to treaty-making and diplomatic representation. Account must also be taken of the techniques and contrivances – such as alliances and buffer states – which are developed and accepted as aids in the management of power. The persistence of such devices attests to the concern of European states to regulate the course of power politics.

Very little of this sense of commonality and the restraints it engendered extended directly to the non-European states and societies. During the age of imperial expansion, Asia and Africa were regarded as outside the civilized world. Declining indigenous empires, emirates and tribes were not seen as sharing common interests and values with the European states, and hence the exercise of power was not held to be subject to the procedures and constraints appropriate within Europe. That, in some measure, conventions were observed and reckless action was relatively infrequent must be attributed to the relationships between the European states themselves, rather than to any sense of comity between Europe and the outside world.

Considerations of power and political advantage have been mainly the concern of professionals. They were not matters which engaged the attention of laymen except in times of crisis, and even then the response was more likely to be in terms of patriotic zeal than calculations of national interest. Our focus here is on statesmen, supported by diplomats, strategists, a few pro-consuls and other advisers: relatively small and select groups specializing in overseas policy and in many respects detached from the day-to-day life of society. In the British case, on some estimates, 'high policy' was conducted by about fifty or perhaps one hundred individuals.[8] A recurring theme in the literature is the suspicion, bordering at times on contempt, felt by members of the elite for public opinion, especially on matters of foreign policy. Max Beloff writes of a 'certain conscious distrust of democracy', and quotes Lord Esher that 'the English people . . . are children in foreign politics.'[9] Lord Salisbury had a broadly similar view but he nonetheless believed that foreign-policy makers could not stray too far from the currents of public opinion.[10] Two working propositions can be advanced which may help to set the power politics approach in a broader societal perspective. First, the thinking of the foreign-policy elite tended to run along different channels from public opinion, and, as a result, very often the dialogue between statesmen had more points of intellectual correspondence than that between leaders and led. Second, the pursuit of power was conditioned by the exigencies of domestic politics and had to be adjusted and presented in a manner acceptable to public opinion.

The 1880s saw the emergence of what D.K. Fieldhouse has called 'the imperialism of the statesmen'.[11] It was in this decade that European tensions became sharp and protracted, when one crisis overlapped with another, and rivalries in Europe were seen to be tied to developments outside. Although in earlier years Persia, India and China had been factors in European calculations, Asian questions were now more or less continuously on the foreign-policy agenda and their significance was seen to be much greater. For the first time Africa came to occupy a place in European thinking about international politics. Lord Salisbury records: 'When I left the Foreign Office in 1880, nobody thought about Africa. When I returned to it in 1885, the nations in Europe were almost quarrelling with each other as to the various portions of Africa which they could obtain.'[12]

The diplomatic elevation of Africa and Asia was the result of profound changes taking place both in Europe and on the periphery. Outside Europe, the key processes of change were the indigenous responses to European incursions in the form of collaboration and resistance, the disintegrating effects of economic and cultural penetration, and the initiatives of settler societies and men on the spot. The upshot was that problems on the periphery forced the attention of metropolitan capitals and increasingly required decisions about political action. Many of the issues were no longer susceptible to local resolution; nor could they adequately be handled by the traditional instruments of informal control. The dynamic of events on the ground in Africa and Asia could thus be said to lead European statesmen and officials to evaluate in political terms what previously had been regarded as economic or moral concerns, and to see them as raising questions of national rather than merely sectional significance.

At the same time – from about the 1870s – the political and diplomatic scene was changing greatly. The sense of a European community began to splinter in the face of new and aggressive nationalisms. Monarchical solidarity had collapsed. The cultural bonds and intellectual ideals which had been so strong in the first half of the nineteenth century were in decline. People were becoming more fully identified with the state and with national aspirations.[13] Few at the time doubted the drift towards a more fragmented and competitive world and most historians agree that this was the trend. Bismarck's famous dictum that Europe 'is merely a geographical expression' was echoed in other capitals.[14] A novelist of the British Empire caught something of the spirit of the age in the following verse:

> What we have we mean to hold,
> Though pretended friends at home may scowl,

> Though blood be shed,
> And men fall dead, And savage foes around us howl . . .[15]

Forty-five years later, very similar sentiments were summed up more pithily by the historian, Carlton Hayes, when he wrote that all accepted

> . . . the simple plan
> That they should take who have the power
> And they should keep who can.[16]

A number of more specific developments contributed to the growth of tension in the last three decades of the nineteenth century. There were now five great powers – Germany, Britain, France, Austria-Hungary and Russia. Italy aspired to become a sixth, a fact which provoked Bismarck to comment that 'she has such poor teeth and such a large appetite'. The club had been expanded, but it was also less of a club because there was a stronger sense of the distinctive interests of each state. Attempts to underwrite the independence of the powers led to the establishment of formal alliances, a process begun by Bismarck in 1879 with the signing of the Dual Alliance between Germany and Austria-Hungary. Thenceforward, alliance negotiations were central to diplomatic manoeuvring, a development which received wider confirmation with the establishment of the Anglo-Japanese Alliance in 1902. The other distinctive feature of the era was the level of military preparation undertaken by all the major powers. Large standing armies came into existence, and naval construction programmes were accelerated. Compulsory military service became general on the continent, as did the stockpiling of equipment and the expansion of logistical capability. Technological developments in weaponry, leading to much increased range, and doctrinal trends (especially those relating to navalism) forced the pace. By the 1890s Europe had become an armed camp.[17]

In these circumstances European statesmen came to see Africa and Asia in a new light. Increasingly confronted with colonial issues from which it was no longer possible to stand aside, and preoccupied as they now were with calculations of national power, diplomatic advantage and military strategy, territorial claims and counter-claims overseas became instruments in the power struggle in Europe. Such thinking, at its most expansive, was more concerned with abstractions about the imperatives of power and strategy than with estimates of material benefits which might be obtained. The importance of Africa and Asia was therefore extrinsic; what weighed with statesmen were attributes and symbols of significance for European diplomacy. It was for this reason, it might be argued, that in the last decades of the nineteenth century the business of making claims and settling frontiers was seldom accompanied by any substantial economic or even administrative penetration. It was not until later, when other considerations were influential, that the European states became deeply involved in the life of the territories.

It is useful at this stage to set out the power perspective as systematically as possible, exploring its internal logic and the various strands of thinking which it encompassed. It then becomes necessary to qualify the picture by pointing out that statesmen by no means always thought and acted in such well-ordered and mechanistic terms. Moreover, the constructs of power and strategy were neither as self-sufficient nor as geographically contained as some formulations would suggest.

The starting-point of the new diplomacy was the belief that the management of power could no longer be confined to Europe. As the maintenance of the balance in Europe became more complex and the activities and interests of the European states pushed outward, so the chessboard of European diplomacy was extended to Africa and Asia. To varying degrees, developments on the periphery could be manipulated to suit European purposes. Africa and Asia offered a larger arena, more elbow-room, greater flexibility and a range of issues more amenable to negotiation. In short, the process of externalization facilitated internal European stabilization.

This involved four rather different but not conceptually distinct ideas. First, the world outside Europe offered an opportunity for expansion: an outlet for restless energy and emotion which could not safely be employed in Europe as the frontiers became settled and military preparedness increased. This applied especially to France and Russia. After France's defeat in the Franco-Prussian War in 1871, it became an axiom of German policy that France should be encouraged to find provinces in Africa to compensate for those lost in Europe. As Bismarck so graphically put it to the French ambassador in 1879, 'the Tunisian pear is ripe and . . . the time has come for you to pluck it'.[18] Similarly, in the north the German aim was to encourage Russia to move more deeply into Asia, thus diverting her attention from Europe and perhaps carrying the incidental benefit of friction between Russia and Britain. Though there was little to suggest that Russia's actions were much affected by the chancellor's counsel, Bismarck's proddings were continued by Kaiser Wilhelm II when in 1895 he urged his cousin Nicholas II to take up Russia's mission in Asia. It was all very well for the Kaiser to write to 'the Admiral of the Pacific' about defending 'Europa from the inroads of the great Yellow Race' (i.e. the Chinese), but the chances were that Japan, Britain and America would see Russia's involvement in the Far East in very different terms. Displacement was seldom a one-way exercise. An image in one capital was often matched by a counter-image in another. During his apprenticeship in imperial power, Curzon had the perspicacity to see that Russia was playing the game that was being played against her. The essence of Russia's policy, he wrote in 1889, was to 'keep England quiet in Europe by keeping her employed in Asia'. In such ways European statesmen transposed European problems by broadening their vision. What was seen as a diversionary course from one perspective, from another represented the safety valve of the system.

According to other interpretations, what was true of inter-state tensions was equally true of internal tensions. If the stability of the European system could be maintained by a process of externalizing conflict, could not the stability of a society be ensured by externalizing the tensions between ethnic groups and between social classes? Such hopes were openly expressed by imperial advocates such as George Parkin and Friedrich Naumann, and were perceived to lie behind Bismarck's colonial venture. The evidence suggests, however, that on most statesmen's reckoning, internal aims were subsidiary. It is only with the vantage of hindsight and by standing back from the historical detail that the notion that nationalism was forged on the anvil of imperialism, and internal cohesion bought with the returns of empire, derives a superficial plausibility.

Second, overseas claims and possessions could be used as bargaining pieces – credits and debits which made up a state's stock-in-trade in international diplomacy. Some were held to be of vital interest, and as such remained relatively fixed and in the end non-negotiable. The classic cases were the British position in Egypt after 1882 and French supremacy in the Western Mediterranean. Such commitments represented at once positions of strength and sources of weakness, the latter because from time to time their maintenance necessitated concessions and policy adjustments in other areas. This was the meaning of the 'Egyptian lever'. 'Berlin and not Cairo', wrote Sir Evelyn Baring (later to become Lord Cromer), 'is the real centre of Egyptian affairs.' There were other overseas claims and interests, however, which were transferable and expendable, and it was these which gave the system its flexibility. Their value was basically instrumental inasmuch as they represented counters which could be used to strengthen a state's position in Europe or in imperial strategy. This perspective was predominantly a metropolitan one, where interest in and indeed knowledge of Africa and Asia was frequently extremely limited. Periodically it led to sharp disagreements between those at the centre and those on the spot. More than any other line of thinking, this approach reduced Africa and Asia to pieces of real estate, more or less valuable depending on size, geographical position, resources and strategic facilities. The preference of indigenous peoples scarcely came into account.[19] The very phrase 'the partition of the world', used alike by British, French and Germans, connotes the abstract drawing-board nature of the exercise. Lord Salisbury's light-hearted description of the process of partition in Africa is revealing, not least for what is omitted. Referring to his negotiations in 1889 and 1890, he observed that he and the French ambassador had been engaged in the 'task of drawing lines upon maps where no human foot has ever trod. We have been giving away mountains and rivers and lakes to each other, but we have only been hindered by the small impediment that we never knew exactly where those mountains and rivers and lakes were.'[20]

The way in which most colonial questions were subordinated to the requirements of European diplomacy, and in the British case to the demands of imperial strategy, is illustrated by the course of Anglo-German rivalries in East Africa and the Pacific, particularly Samoa, after 1885. Basically Britain was dependent upon German support over Egypt, and Salisbury saw himself as having to pay Bismarck's price in other areas – 'it is our policy to go with him in all matters of secondary importance'. Putting the point more bluntly, he explained: 'I have been using the credit I have got with Bismarck in the Caroline Islands and Zanzibar to get help in Russia and Turkey and Egypt.'[21] Bismarck's colonial diplomacy moved along similar lines. The need for British support in the Mediterranean in the late 1880s required that concessions be made in Africa. Bismarck summed up the situation with the remark, 'England is more important to us than Zanzibar and East Africa.'[22] The settlements eventually reached in both East Africa (1890) and Samoa (1899) were substantially different from what had appeared likely in the mid-1880s, for the simple reason that the diplomatic ledger had changed substantially in the intervening years. While it is not appropriate to pursue the change in circumstances here, both settlements were, in their way, classic examples of the horse-trading which characterized colonial diplomacy in this era. In the former case, Britain won substantial gains in East Africa at the price of making concessions elsewhere in Africa and ceding Heligoland to Germany. In the latter case, Britain withdrew from Samoa and obtained in return certain other island groups, including Tonga with its valuable harbours.

The third way in which Africa and Asia furthered the management of power in Europe was as a signalling-ground for the major powers. Too much should not be made of this point because the difference between using colonial policy as a source of credit and as a signal to another power is only a matter of degree. Nor, of course, can the mainstream of imperial activity and colonial crises be understood in these terms. Still, the management of relations between powers in part depended upon the communication of offers and warnings and some indication in advance of whether support or hospitality might be extended in particular circumstances. Outside Europe a power could more easily test the water because the risks were lower. This is the essence of A.J.P. Taylor's explanation of Bismarck's colonial diplomacy in 1884 and 1885.[23] In Taylor's view – which, it should be said, has been the subject of considerable debate among historians[24] – Bismarck invented or manipulated colonial grievances as a means of changing alliance relationships in Europe. From late 1883 the German chancellor was anxious to establish a rapprochement with France, and this necessitated quarrelling with Britain. Grievances with respect to Angra Pequena, and later south-west Africa and New Guinea, were created for this purpose. Lest France fail to respond sufficiently to German overtures, Bismarck added a second string to his bow. Germany's relationship with Britain could be repaired or consolidated by settling colonial disputes in an accommodating manner. It was this line of policy which became predominant after May 1885. In sum, African real estate represented nothing more than an excuse for disputes or a means of redressing grievances. Either way, the real issues concerned the relations between the powers in Europe.

Finally, overseas possessions might be seen to contribute to a country's standing as a great power. There were two elements here. One was material capability, which could be augmented by the acquisition of overseas bases and harbours, the control of strategic straits and waterways, and the maintenance of external lines of communication. In the early 1880s Ferry spoke of the need for overseas coaling stations. A decade later, British and German strategists analysed the relationship between naval strategy and colonial dependencies in the light of Captain Alfred Mahan's doctrines of sea power and international influence. Overseas possessions also held possibilities as sources of raw materials of economic and military significance, and as suppliers of military manpower. With the important exception of the Indian Army, however, these were things more for the future than of immediate relevance. The second element was sensed or felt, rather than calculated or measured, though it was no less influential for that reason. A nation's standing could not be reduced simply to tonnages of steel and lines of battleships; greatness depended on perception, including self-perception. Overseas possessions conferred prestige.[25] The idea of distance, the splendour of the East, the very vastness of Africa, contributed to the mystique. Not that Portugal or even Holland could thus be numbered among the great, nor Germany excluded on that count; but the impression grew that to be of the first rank a nation needed an overseas estate. The British flaunted it – no one more so than Disraeli, who saw empire in terms of imaginative symbolism. In the absence of opportunities in Europe to enhance their status, the French and the Italians looked further afield. After Bismarck's resignation, even the Germans came to include the colonial world in their search for international prestige. As A.P. Thornton has observed, power 'is neither used nor witnessed without emotion'.[26]

Underlying all of these ideas was the assumption that the utility of the tropical world was determined by the dictates of European diplomacy and strategy. It was an axiom of policy, so fundamental as not to require spelling out, that however attractive gains overseas might be, they could not be allowed to threaten the stability of the European system. It followed that colonial competition between the European states must always stop short of war. Britain stood as something of an exception here, but it was more in theory than in practice. While she acted alone and pushed her luck in places, by and large she 'resolved to share', as Salisbury put it on one occasion. Retreat or withdrawal was thus a necessary adjunct to colonial expansion – witness the Russians at Penjdeh, the French at Fashoda and the British at Port Arthur. Mainly this was a matter of tacit understanding, but ground rules for the avoidance of armed conflict in Africa were laid down at the Berlin Conference in 1884.

It is apparent that the foregoing account passes lightly over alternative viewpoints and exaggerates the pattern-making of European statesmen. By abstracting power politics considerations from their diplomatic context, we have emphasized the logic of power at the expense of the wider picture. Ideas about power and strategy did not stand on their own as a series of well-ordered theoretical constructs which constituted a blueprint for diplomatic action. Nor was power politics as a system of thought as self-contained as is often depicted. To argue that statesmen operated mainly in terms of power does not dispose of the significance of underlying economic concerns or broader cultural influences. Mansergh has gone too far when he writes that, almost without exception, statesmen had no interest in economic or social concerns: 'All their intellectual faculties were absorbed in the fascinating game of power politics.'[27] However much in the background and ill-explored, power politics had an economic dimension. Access to and control of resources was often part and parcel of the strategic imperative, as was denying them to a rival power. The ledger might be assessed in political terms but it was understood that some of the entries were economic. In a similar way calculations of power could seldom be divorced from cultural and racial assumptions. Historians have pointed to the prevalence of concepts such as the pan-Islam menace and the dying pagan empires which derived from the European conviction of racial superiority.[28] William II's ideas about 'the yellow peril' or Nicholas II's habit of referring to the Japanese as 'monkeys' sit uneasily alongside terms like national interest and power capability. For these reasons, the metaphor of the statesmen's map is to a degree misleading.

There are other difficulties about a too mechanistic understanding of statesmen's thinking and action. For all the appeal of interpretations emphasizing prescience and design, it is clear that the course of policy was not always planned; the outcome was sometimes fortuitous. Having observed that the European powers found a safe channel for their exuberance in expansion outside Europe, A.J.P. Taylor goes on: 'They stumbled on this solution by chance, without foresight.'[29] Equally, at times statesmen were carried along by events: they waited to see what would happen. Bismarck's policies in the Angra Pequena dispute in 1884 and German actions in the Moroccan crisis of 1905 are cases in point.[30] Often the short term took precedence over the long. In his memoirs, Grey of Fallodon cautions against ascribing to British ministers elaborate and far-sighted policies when they were guided by immediate considerations.[31] For our purposes it is necessary to strip away the layers of historical interpretation which are often more concerned with analysing the workings of the system than observing through the eye of the statesman. A.J.P. Taylor writes shrewdly that whereas it seemed in the late nineteenth century that the powers had abandoned their disputes in Europe because the prizes elsewhere were so much greater, the truth was the other way round.[32] But is Taylor saying this was the logic of their positions, or is he also implying that this was in fact how they saw things? In the context of his argument the answer is probably the former, but the evidence suggests that in particular cases Taylor's observation is true of statesmen's motivations as well.

The shared understanding that the manoeuvring of the powers outside Europe must not jeopardize the balance in Europe was easier to accept in theory than to ensure in practice. Exporting the frictions of Europe might be the object of the exercise but it proved difficult to stop conflicts overseas having repercussions at home. At times the periphery generated new sources of friction and exacerbated existing ones in Europe. The British occupation of Egypt in 1882 was a running sore which poisoned Anglo-French relations until almost the end of the century. Colonial frictions, especially in West Africa, soured Anglo-German relations and led to the collapse of the Egyptian Conference (the Anglo-French Agreement on Egypt) in July 1884. And so the list can be extended. African and Asian issues compounded the atmosphere of distrust. While none of the disputes led to war between the European states, the Agadir crisis in 1911 came quite close to doing so. Account must be taken also of the Russo-Japanese War and its ramifications for the workings of the European system. Indirectly and in the longer term, it is arguable that the struggle overseas contributed to the slide to the First World War. Nicholas Mansergh has pointed to two aspects of great consequence for Europe's future: Germany's belief that naval strength was indispensable to world power, and the corrosive impact of colonial rivalry on international morality.[33]

Finally, it must be said that the assumption that the Mediterranean, the deserts of Arabia and the chain of mountains running east across Eurasia from the Hindu Kush represented a great political divide, while instructive, is also oversimplified. By and large, on the one side there were those who played the international game, and on the other there were the pieces. Yet the game was played in Europe as well as overseas, and small states and areas of weakness there were grist to the power politics mill. The difference was one of degree and not kind. It was also the case that African and Asian societies were actors in their own right, and entered into the political struggle between the European states. To cite one example, Britain's strategy with respect to the Sudan in the late 1890s was influenced by the growth of Dervish power and the fear of Dervish collaboration with Menelik II of Ethiopia.

With the vantage of hindsight, a number of episodes over these years appear as amber lights, winking notice to Europe that its use of the overseas world for the purposes of power politics could not continue indefinitely. The defeat of the Italian army at Adowa in 1896, the Boxer uprising of 1900, the negotiation of the Anglo-Japanese Alliance in 1902 and the Russian defeat at the hands of the Japanese in 1905 are the key events here. The idea of Africa and Asia as an extended chessboard required considerable modification once the realization set in that some of the pieces were no longer as manoeuvrable as before, and that a few might become players in their own right. Such a realization cannot be said to have occurred in the years before the First World War.

At this point it is necessary to consider in some detail the case of Great Britain. We are now in a position to ask how far British policy-makers approached Africa and Asia along similar lines to the continental states. To what extent were British perceptions shaped by the diplomatic rivalry of the major powers? Did British strategic thinking draw upon different assumptions and take in different interests? How far did Britain's much deeper involvement in the non-European world mean that the categories of power, prestige and strategic advantage by themselves were too simplistic to establish the bases of overseas policy?

There can be no doubt that throughout the period, most British statesmen and officials accepted the broad tenets of power politics. Max Beloff writes that Britain's rulers 'took it for granted that the international world was one of competing powers and that their duty was to make the most of whatever assets were available to them'.[34] Among those assets, military power was ranked highly. Although

Salisbury had no great faith in his military advisers, nor interest in military matters, the influence of strategists was considerable and it increased as perceptions of Britain's vulnerability grew. Some indication is provided by the importance attached to the count of battleship strengths of the principal powers. The natural inclination of British leaders was to place more reliance on military capability in being, than on the assurances of foreign statesmen or even treaty commitments.

The studies of Lord Salisbury, the most influential statesman of the age, bring out the extent to which his diplomacy was conditioned by realism.[35] Interests, the foremost of which was the defence of the Empire, were the nub of the matter. Effective diplomacy required the support of military capability. Prestige was a valuable adjunct. According to a recent biographer, Salisbury had no sympathy with those who brought personal morality into the manner in which British diplomacy ought to be conducted.[36] Yet he believed that certain standards needed to be observed. Good faith he held to be a fundamental principle; another was his rejection of secret diplomacy.

If in many aspects Salisbury was a representative figure of the era, other British statesmen and officials had their own ideas about power and strategy, and the way in which British interests should be advanced. Both Rosebery and Lansdowne were less inhibited than Salisbury by the niceties of diplomatic conduct, and were prepared to act secretly if they considered circumstances so required. Chamberlain, although a vigorous advocate of British power and prestige, was in fact little influenced by the realist tradition with its emphasis on interests and dispassionate calculation. Sentiment, race and a few high-blown notions about the importance of economics were the main elements in his approach to the world.[37] Grey, despite his claim that he never used the phrase 'balance of power',[38] certainly thought in those terms and at various times was involved in attempts to find Germany colonial 'compensation'.[39] Probably the most able – and at the same time, narrow – British practitioner of *Realpolitik* was Sir Percy Anderson, the Foreign Office's African expert until his death in 1896. He wielded enormous influence, especially under Rosebery. In an account of Anderson's African strategy, W.R. Louis argues that he saw the colonial scramble 'mainly as a problem of maintaining British power and prestige'. Louis continues: 'For each move made by Germany or France in Africa, Anderson counter-moved. He had a first-class chessboard mentality.'[40]

The emergence in the 1880s and 1890s of much sharper power politics perceptions, and their transposition to Africa and Asia, was to some degree a consequence of the mounting challenge to Britain's international pre-eminence. British statesmen could no longer assume that Britain's influence would prevail outside Europe and that colonial questions were matters of domestic rather than international dispute.

The rise of European colonial competition was paralleled by the naval construction programmes of rival powers. In 1884 the comfortable assumption of Britain's command of the sea gave way to public agitation in the face of the threatening international system, and thereafter naval scares became a regular feature of British politics. At the same time, British industry and commerce were seen to be threatened by the development of industrialism in Europe, all the more worrying because of its state support and its penetration of overseas markets.[41]

In addition to the impact of the visible decline in Britain's international position, statesmen's perceptions were influenced by the broader currents of thinking about political and social life, which changed so markedly in the last three decades or so of the nineteenth century. One important development was the elevation of the state above humanist principle or individual interest. It became the highest organizational form and the one most likely to advance the collective good. Sir John Seeley at Cambridge wrote that the importance of individuals in history was proportionate to their 'relation to the State'.[42] He saw no incompatibility between political aggregation and liberalism, and tended to the view that there was safety in size. It was also believed that struggle was the natural order of things. The influence of Darwin's writings – and for some, Marx's as well – was to recast the ethics of expansion. Conflict was endemic to all life; the strong must displace the weak. Salisbury developed this theme in his famous speech to the Primrose League in 1898, when he divided the nations of the world into the living and the dying. In his assessment, 'the weak states are becoming weaker and the strong states are becoming stronger'.[43] What Salisbury saw in terms of Darwinian processes, others presented in theories of navalism and geopolitics. It was by studying power in these dimensions, it was argued, that clues to the course of history could be found. In the 1890s, Mahan's writing on the influence of sea power upon history was enthusiastically received in England, and use was made of his stress on the need for overseas bases and colonies. A little later, interest developed in the ideas of Sir Halford Mackinder and Spencer Wilkinson about the relationship between strategy, geography and national cohesion.[44] It would be of very great interest to relate these and other currents of thinking to the underlying material conditions in Britain and overseas. Though clearly beyond the scope of this study, we can at least note that the triumph of industrialism, the growth of materialism, and the development of science and technology led to new attitudes and pressures in British politics. To give an example, in a suggestive passage Arthur Marder points to the role of the armament industry and the coal, iron and allied trades in the 'big navy' movement.[45]

The conclusion thus far must be that from about the 1880s, British statesmen and officials, like their continental counterparts, saw the non-European world largely through the lens of power politics. Beyond this somewhat bland proposition, however, it is the differences in thinking which are striking. Britain's concerns were defensive: to hold on to what she already possessed. The *raison d'etre* of strategy was to deny to European competitors the levers which might be used to prize the Empire apart. Power was needed, not to assert some claim or to exploit new openings, but to close the cracks which threatened the entire imperial structure. Writing in 1877 about the consequences of Britain's occupation of Egypt, Gladstone captured the essence of the situation with his prophetic observation that 'with a great Empire in each of the four corners of the world . . . we may be territorially content, but less than ever at our ease . . .'[46]

Implicit in the idea of a satisfied yet fearful Britain was the realization that the Empire – or at least part of it – mattered in itself. In the course of the nineteenth century, possession of India changed Britain's conception of her own position. India became the eastern base of Britain's global power, and, as such, could never be regarded simply as an object in the diplomatic game between the powers. Few at the turn of the century would have quarrelled with Curzon's statement: 'As long as we rule India we are the greatest power in the world.'[47] More than half a century later, Harold Wilson still felt able to proclaim, 'Our frontiers are on the Himalayas.'[48] Nor could the Cape, the Suez Canal or Britain's position in Egypt be seen as areas of displacement or sources of credit. Indeed, to Cromer in Egypt, and later to Milner in South Africa, the spokes mattered more than the hub itself, India.

Here, then, lies a second difference between British thinking and that of the continental states. For much of the period, the Empire was Britain's primary concern, and her diplomacy in Europe was very largely tied to the advancement of imperial interests. There is substantial agreement among historians that at least until mid-1905 Europe did not figure highly in British calculations. Max Beloff writes that the European balance of power was ignored for forty years.[49] Maurice and Taya Zinkin argue that in the nineteenth century the vacuum created by Britain's safety in Europe was filled by the British Government adopting an Indian policy. They quote, in support, Rosebery's remark of 1892: 'Our great Empire has pulled us out of the European system – our foreign policy has become a colonial policy. But we can never remove ourselves altogether from the European system.'[50] In his account of the events leading to the end of isolation, George Monger emphasizes the hold of the imperial cast of mind, and cites in evidence Britain's approach to the Russo-Japanese War and the Moroccan crisis of 1905.[51] Ian Nish makes a similar point with respect to the Anglo-Japanese Alliance of 1902.[52]

After the turn of the century, the dangers which appeared to threaten the Empire, and the strain placed on Britain's resources, induced policy-makers to become more involved in European affairs. Although the initial motivation was the security of empire, European considerations came to be seen as standing in their own right. The decision in 1906 to hold staff talks with the French and the establishment of the Russian entente in 1907 are indicative of the changing orientation. As part of the process of adjustment, it was held necessary to forgo colonial claims and make concessions overseas. In the Anglo-French Convention of 1904, Britain signed away her interest in Morocco and made colonial adjustments elsewhere in return for a more secure footing in Egypt. The settlement of long-standing colonial disputes cleared the way to a better political relationship with France in Europe. In 1913 Britain initialled an agreement with Germany which provided for the division of the Portuguese territories in Africa, should the Portuguese empire collapse. The idea was to give Germany an alternative to European expansion. In the same year, Britain reversed her policy towards Belgium's annexation of the Congo and extended recognition, thereby conceding that colonial and humanitarian concerns could not be allowed to threaten grand strategy in Europe.[53]

The extent to which Britain's imperial calculations embraced commercial interests is necessarily a matter of interpretation and conjecture. The argument here hinges on how far constructs of power and strategy can be taken at face value, and whether they should be seen as subsuming considerations of economic advantage. Robinson and Gallagher's heavy emphasis on the search for security of the Indian Empire has been criticized, both for its neglect of the economic importance of India to Britain and for exaggerating the influence of the strategic imperative on Britain's overseas designs. V.G. Kiernan writes that the epigram that British Africa was not much more than 'a gigantic footnote to the Indian empire' imposes a duty to explain why India was of such enormous consequence to Britain.[54] Clearly, in Kiernan's view, economic benefit provides a large part of the answer; but he is silent as to whether statesmen perceived the economic basis of their commitment to the defence of India. On this point, enquiry is unlikely to be fruitful because the evidence is limited and there is an artificiality about attempting to dissect such an entrenched world view. Kiernan and other critics contribute more when they argue that the search for strategic security camouflaged or took in other concerns, and was used by business and financial groups to advance their specific interests.[55] A conception of Indian defence which expanded through Cairo, the Cape and Singapore to cover half the world can hardly be understood simply in terms of military mechanics. Security, at this level, encompassed political and economic concerns.

The breadth of meaning attached to the concept of security is most apparent in the thinking about the protection of the lines of communication and naval expansion. Arguments about imperial life-lines turned as much on the flow of trade as on the movement of military units and supplies. On at least one account, the case for controlling the Suez Canal rested on its importance as a commercial route to India, not on its military significance in times of war.[56] Arthur Marder has emphasized the close connection between Britain's dependence on foreign trade and the programmes for naval expansion. Big business supported the case for a large fleet, though it was the defensive role of the navy which was stressed.[57] C.J. Lowe writes to similar effect. The whole pattern of British strategic thinking was bound up with the problems of seaborne commerce. Trade and finance gave Britain 'an enormous vested interest in naval supremacy'.[58] The evidence quite clearly establishes that strategists and their supporters saw interconnections between Britain's prosperity, overseas commerce and the system of imperial defence.

The contention that power and strategy were key considerations in Britain's approach to Africa and Asia requires a further qualification if it is not to over-simplify the picture by suggesting some unitary viewpoint. Power politics perspectives were not based narrowly or solely on the interests of the metropole, because various parts of the Empire were understood to have their own distinctive interests, and at times these were actively pursued by officials on the spot. In this respect the British position was more complicated than that of most of the European states at the time – or, for that matter, the United States after the Second World War. The tendency of many who directed the Empire overseas to view imperial and foreign affairs from the standpoint of the territory in which they were based was matched by Whitehall's reluctance to disregard or overrule the judgement of the officials most concerned.

Above all, this was true of India.[59] India was an empire in its own right, and pursued an imperial policy within its own sphere. Dominance in the Persian Gulf was an Indian interest, not a British interest, and Aden and the protected states were brought into the imperial system by the authorities in Calcutta and Bombay. The regional conception of Indian defence was heavily influenced by geopolitical considerations, which, it can be argued, provide a thread of continuity between the thinking of the Raj and that of the rulers of independent India. Powerful viceroys such as Curzon, and before him Mayo and Lytton, pursued a forward policy with which Whitehall, because of its wider concerns, very often had little sympathy.[60] Something of the same identification with what was taken to be indigenous interests also characterized the approach of Lord Cromer. In the judgement of a recent biographer, he became an Anglo-

Egyptian rather than a British statesman.[61] Egypt was to him the centrepiece. His ideas about imperial defence, which carried such influence with Salisbury and left their mark on the course of British strategy, reflected his preoccupation with Egypt's internal development and regional stability. Lord Salisbury aptly commented: 'If the world were falling to pieces, but Egypt was left intact, Lord Cromer would not ask for more.'[62]

Quite apart from the tendency of officials on the spot to promote what they believed to be the interests of particular territories, local considerations had a more general influence on British thinking. The extent of Britain's involvement in India, Egypt and other parts of the Empire meant that statesmen had to take into account a variety of factors arising from colonial contact. Thus, in the British case, power politics could seldom be addressed solely to the external balance of power; thinking was necessarily conditioned by actual or possible developments within Africa and Asia. One consideration of increasing importance from the 1890s, was the need to placate Moslem opinion, because of the fear that unrest might spread through those parts of the Empire which were predominantly Moslem. This concern invested British policies in India and the Middle East with a wider significance, and had implications for the conduct of Britain's relations with Turkey.[63]

To take another example, the defence of India could not simply be analysed in terms of external machinations. Field-Marshal Roberts, among others, was doubtful about the commitment of the Indian princes, and at various times the possibility of internal revolt was a contingency seriously considered. In the 1870s and 1880s, Salisbury took the view that the greatest danger was not an actual Russian invasion but a programme of subversion: the incitement of domestic unrest and rebellion in India.[64] This touched on a matter upon which great stress was placed – prestige. Earlier in this chapter the connection between prestige and power politics was emphasized, but prestige was no less relevant in the colonial context. Indeed, some British statesmen were concerned with the need for prestige more to facilitate the management of subject races than as a support in diplomatic encounters with rival powers. This was true of Salisbury. His preparedness to go to war in 1877 if Russia permanently occupied Constantinople derived from his fear about the effect this would have on British prestige in the eyes of the Oriental peoples.[65]

Notwithstanding apprehension in some quarters about internal developments in Asia, for the most part the anxieties of British policy-makers stemmed from the ambitions of other great powers. The dangers to Britain's position were seen to lie in the changing alignments and growing strength of the European powers, and, in the Russian case, the programme of railway construction which was believed to have altered the strategic balance. Nowhere was this more apparent than in the Far Eastern crisis in the last years of the century. Britain's preoccupation was with the external, not the internal, dimensions of the crisis.[66] Salisbury attempted to avert partition in the belief that it would be accompanied by desperate struggles between the powers. There was also the fear that an attempt to stem Russia's advances in China could result in Russian pressure on India. The spread of the Boxer movement was thus greeted with relief by some, the hope being that Russia would wear herself out in China.[67] Before that, however, British policy-makers, like their European counterparts, had been taken by surprise by the Boxer upheaval, and for some time they failed to appreciate the gravity of the crisis. The British representative in China was of the opinion that the movement would die down once the drought broke – an early case in the long succession of Western misjudgements about the nature and strength of Asian nationalism, which came to be summed up in the phrase 'but for'.[68]

The conclusion of the Anglo-Japanese Alliance in 1902, landmark though it was, cannot be said to represent a turning-point in British thinking about the nature and source of the dangers which threatened. The rise of Japan as a major power was seen as a case on its own, not as an indication that the relationship between Europe and the non-European world was fundamentally changing. Japan's recent record, especially her role in the relief of the Peking legation in 1900, was taken to show that she had lifted herself out of Asia, as it were, to rank alongside the European states. Yet, at the same time, Japan's ticket of entry to power status was made available by the preoccupation of the major powers with internecine struggle. Britain's major concern after the turn of the century was to establish security against Russia and France, and the immediate problem was Russia's designs in China. Because of the risks in Europe, it became evident that the naval position in the Far East had to be safeguarded by diplomatic means. The United States was a non-starter because of its policy of isolation. The attempt to come to some accommodation with Germany, perhaps in the form of an Anglo-German Far Eastern alliance, proved unproductive. Germany simply was not interested, or at least not at any price that Britain might reasonably consider. Similarly the Russian door was closed to British hopes of a settlement in this direction, or even an understanding about the Far East. Russia approached Japan instead, and Whitehall was left to worry about the possibility of a Russo-Japanese agreement. Checkmated across the European board, Britain turned to Japan. Her concerns were essentially negative. An alliance with Japan was the last card in the British pack if the status quo in the Far East were to be maintained without taking unacceptable risks in Europe.

Taking into account the distinctive perspectives of officials overseas and the considerable influence of internal developments within the Empire, it remains true that ideas about power and strategy formed the core of Britain's approach to Asia and Africa after about 1880. These ideas came together in an understanding of international and imperial affairs which can be broadly labelled as power politics. The statesmen's picture of Asia and Africa was dominated by the great powers and their conflicting interests and ambitions. Military capability was understood to set the limits of effective diplomacy. Given Britain's circumstances, this meant that overseas influence – and indeed the preservation of the Empire itself – depended on the strength of the fleet.

In the struggle between competing powers, the Empire was both the prize to be safeguarded and a source of metropolitan strength. With respect to the latter, India was so important that its loss was unthinkable. Yet there were other overseas territories and claims, the value of which lay precisely in their expendability and hence their usefulness in the bargaining process. To a considerable extent, however, ends and means could not clearly be separated, because thinking was too engrained and organic. The primacy of imperial considerations was indubitable down to about 1905, but thereafter some revaluation took place. The lines of division in Europe were being drawn more tightly, and it could no longer be imagined that the tensions which threatened the system from within could be displaced or externalized by adroit diplomacy overseas. In any case, Africa and Asia offered less scope for adjustment and bargaining than formerly. Partition had been all but completed, and colonial issues had become part of the domestic debate. Administrative structures had been set up and had developed purposes of their own. More interests were thus involved, and the result was less manoeuvrability. To this extent, notions about flexibility were increasingly distanced from actuality.

When we come to examine in more detail the actual policies pursued by British statesmen and reflect on the interests which underlay them, the explanatory content of power and strategy is limited. The emphasis on the pursuit of power in the international context obscures the extent to which it needed to be bedded internally in Africa and Asia through control mechanisms and alliances with indigenous collaborators. The diplomatic influence of the statesmen was in large part contingent on the administrative and political skills of imperial governors and officials. The search for security along the route to India, and indeed beyond, encompassed other concerns and interests, most notably economic ones. Strategy and the protection of trade and commerce went hand in hand.

Viewed in comparative perspective, the analysis of power politics conceptions reveals less about Britain's approach to Asia and Africa than it does about the approach of the European states. In the British case, ideas about the enhancement of power and the pursuit of security stand in more need of qualification; other streams of thinking, relating especially to economic interest and moral responsibility, carried more weight than was usual in Europe. The difference between Britain's approach and that of the continental states must largely be attributed to Britain's much deeper involvement outside Europe. The pulls and pressures from the periphery were too great for statesmen to settle for an understanding of international politics as anchored in Europe, with overseas diplomacy being essentially instrumental. For Great Britain, Asia and Africa mattered in their own right.

Two

MORAL RESPONSIBILITY I

On one plane imperialism sought its justification in a conception of moral responsibility. Alongside the concern to secure diplomatic advantage and the desire for economic benefit, stood a body of thought and belief that advanced peoples had obligations to those less advanced. Societies which had travelled ahead, it was held, had some duty to offer guidance, instruction, and even to rule. The signposts along the way were marked by concepts drawn from politics and economics – trusteeship, colonial development, modernization. Such guides to action were not simply theoretical constructs; they expressed something of the temper of the metropolitan society, or at least sections of it. Imperialism, according to this conception, was primarily a set of moral attitudes.

The object of this chapter is to analyse the content and assumptions of British conceptions of moral responsibility during the period of the second expansion. Our interest lies less in the development of particular policies than in examining the pattern of thinking and exploring its roots. The eclectic and sometimes inconsistent nature of the doctrines of trusteeship inhibit summary judgement about the understanding of the tasks of empire over time and across continents. Even with respect to India, where British conceptions of moral responsibility were most fully developed, one writer describes English ideas as being 'at root confused'.[1] Maurice and Taya Zinkin observe that the debate about Britain's role was never very articulate. 'It tended to proceed by argument over individual issues, rather than by disputation over the philosophy of the whole.'[2] More revealing than the detailed contention between different schools of thinking is the relationship between the idea of trusteeship and the character and psychological predispositions of the imperialists. It is the inner moral impulse which tells us most about this face of imperialism. At various points questions will be raised about how much substance lay behind ideas of moral responsibility and what implications these ideas had for Asia and Africa. The extent to which opinions diverge should be kept in mind. What appears to be cant from one angle is idealism from another; doctrines which, when viewed from certain metropolitan perspectives seem to constrain economic activity overseas, can be interpreted from the perspective of the periphery as the ideology of colonial capitalism.

The cluster of ideas about moral responsibility can fairly readily be distinguished from those about power, notwithstanding the fact that there is an overlap and that both streams of thinking at times influence and emanate from the same people. Whereas the ideas about power are mechanistic and openly directed to securing an advantage, those about moral responsibility are mission-oriented and purport to be concerned with the benefit of others, or at least with mutual benefit. Whereas the one is addressed to external relations – Asia and Africa's place in the world – the other is directed to the internal processes of change. There is a deeper difference between the two approaches which turns on the significance of feelings and belief to the hold of the idea of moral responsibility. A.P. Thornton draws attention to something fundamental when he writes that 'imperialism was a faith and an emotion before it became a political programme'.[3] One can go further and argue that the imperial idea, insofar as it was concerned with moral responsibility, cannot be understood apart from the character and lives of those who promoted it. Imperialism, in this sense, was both a state of mind and a way of life.

It follows that the belief in moral responsibility tended to be most strongly held by people actively involved in the administration and support of India and the colonial territories – pro-consuls, governors, civil officials and military personnel, and of course the India Office and the Colonial Office themselves. In some cases, as for example with Cromer, the responsibilities of imperialism were carefully analysed and set down in writing; in others, understanding lay buried in the approach to work or the rituals of the regiment. Paul Scott reminds us of the expression 'man-bap' – I am your father and your mother – which symbolized the relationship of the Raj to India, the regimental officer to his men, and the district official to the people of his area.[4] For the most part the officials of empire came from the upper middle classes and the middle classes, and their ethos bore the distinctive marks of their class background and rural orientation.[5] A sharper, more critical expression of moral responsibility came from missionaries and church groups, humanitarians and socialists. Imperialism had valuable work to do but its conscience had to be prodded, and often enough its methods needed overhauling. In general, the moral impulse and serious concern with the purposes of empire were restricted to the upper echelons of society and to the educated. Thornton actually argues that the attempt to harmonize the ideals of empire was left to a single class.[6] Parliament rarely took an interest in Indian affairs, much less in colonial issues. There is little to suggest that the masses cared much about the moral responsibility of empire. Jingoism was relatively short-lived and in any case it was not deeply based. Writing in 1913, W.S. Blunt, the radical publicist and critic of imperialism, declared: 'No country in Europe is less inclined than ours to the sacrifice demanded by the needs of an overgrown Empire.'[7] This was perhaps an over-statement, but many imperialists feared Blunt was near the mark.

Before turning to consider the thinking which led many in the British middle classes to see imperialism as a moral responsibility, some introductory comments should be made to establish a rather wider frame of reference. The ideals of empire and their psychological roots need to be seen in relation both to the expansion of British power overseas and to what imperialism meant on the ground. The notion that Britain had some moral duty to intervene in Asia and Africa went back much earlier than the 1870s, and it was not tied to formal empire. Its course can be followed in the extension of the principles of English law to India, the campaigns against the slave trade, the conversionist sentiments of the missions, and the belief that the development of 'legitimate trade' would uplift Africans and Asians from slavery, piracy and degrading idleness. It is apparent that in some instances we are dealing with a response to situations which stemmed from or were accentuated by the processes of European penetration – for example, the development of the slave trade, the abuses of Europeans on the spot and the corrosion of indigenous structures of authority. Thus the legacy of informal imperialism could be invoked to justify the new imperialism. The issue was not one of involvement as against non-involvement, but rather, of what kind of involvement was appropriate. Did not the state have a duty to curb the excesses of its citizens overseas? Was not Britain so placed, materially and morally, as to be obliged to give a lead to the European powers?

Such arguments had been heard before, but in the 1890s they came to be reworked by the group of politicians later known as the liberal imperialists. Like it or not, the expansion of empire had taken place, and the process could not be reversed. Men like Haldane, Asquith and Grey could say that their own hands were clean, but their inheritance was not. In any case, it was scarcely possible to stand aside. Explaining the occupation of the Sudan in 1897, Asquith said of expansion, 'we might control it and direct it . . . we could not arrest it'.[8] Not all liberal imperialists were prepared to go this far. Different views were held about the inevitability and desirability of further territorial extension. Yet it was common ground that the Empire in being was a matter of responsibility. There was a need to be concerned with moral purpose.

Such idealism was often well removed from imperial practice. Other strands of thinking pulled policy in different directions, and in any event the concerns of officialdom were fairly narrow. It can hardly be over-emphasized, therefore, that the doctrines of moral responsibility provide only a skewed and incomplete guide to what was actually happening in Africa and Asia. Their fuller development occurred after imperialism had blazed a trail of brutality, exploitation and cultural dislocation: the elevated sense of mission remained in part a counterpoise to a very different record on the ground. In a memorable passage, Winston Churchill contrasts 'the wonderful cloudland of [imperial] aspiration' with 'the ugly scaffolding of attempt and achievement'. 'The inevitable gap between conquest and dominion becomes filled with the figures of the greedy trader, the inopportune missionary, the ambitious soldier, and the lying speculator, who disquiet the minds of the conquered and excite the sordid appetites of the conquerors.'[9] Joseph Conrad writes more enigmatically but to similar effect in *Heart of Darkness*. He extols the uplifting quality of the imperial idea only to tarnish it by suggesting the image of an idol.

> The conquest of the earth, which mostly means the taking away from those who have a different complexion or slightly flatter noses than ourselves, is not a pretty thing when you look into it too much. What redeems it is the idea only. An idea at the back of it; not a sentimental pretence but an idea; and an unselfish belief in the idea – something you can set up, and bow down before, and offer a sacrifice to . . .

The sting in the last line symbolizes, I believe, not hypocrisy in personal terms, but the moral hollowness that Conrad attributed to imperialism, however much he was reluctant to condemn it unequivocally. This interpretation accords with other passages in his writings where he records his despair with the scramble for loot in the Congo. 'What an end', he observes in one essay, 'to the idealised realities of a boy's daydreams!'[10]

It should also be said that ideas about moral responsibility do not take us far towards explaining the geography of annexation and partition, inasmuch as the main part of the tropical world had been parcelled out before they were of general influence. By the time empire had become an article of faith, it was already very largely an established fact. Even where humanitarian and religious considerations appeared to make the running, they were practically never decisive on their own account. The significance of the belief in moral progress is, in the first instance, social and psychological, not diplomatic. It led individuals, and through them governments, to approach imperialism in a new and broader light. As a result, imperialists saw themselves differently, and they had more success in gaining support from sections of Asian and African societies.

The growth of moral concern enlarged the area of colonial life with which Britain was concerned, and led to a more expansive conception of imperial intervention. Matters such as land tenure and tribal customs, which might earlier and otherwise have been regarded as of purely local significance, became questions of debate and often enough official action as well. Robinson and Gallagher have argued, with respect to Africa, that policy-makers in the 1880s intended nothing more ambitious than building diplomatic fences around the various territories, the point being that they were little concerned with what happened within those fences.[11] But imperialism could not exist simply as an international strategem. It brought into being administrators and critics and a moral constituency, whose concerns were internal as well as external. The idea that Britain had some responsibility for the protection and promotion of what were taken to be indigenous interests meant that, potentially at least, imperialism was directed towards recasting the social order. Its resources were too limited for the task. Yet, over time, the idealism of empire worked as an instrument of internal change – though often in ways very different from the intentions of those who promoted it.

Quite apart from the substantive content of the imperial idea, we need to consider the psychological importance of belief. Seen from this perspective, the ideologies of empire were fundamental to the existence of empire itself. The idealism, however one may judge it, was a necessary adjunct to the maintenance of overseas power and the attempt to extract wealth from colonial possessions. Formal empire could never have gone forward without faith. Those who spent their lives working in and for the Empire needed to believe in a greater purpose in order to believe in themselves. That purpose might appear shallow or mistaken in the eyes of critics, and certainly it proved difficult to translate into a concrete political programme. V.G. Kiernan says simply that the imperial idea was insubstantial.[12] There is much less reason to doubt that it was sincerely, often passionately, held. As J.A. Hobson, with a keener insight than many who followed him, observed, this was 'no case of hypocrisy, or of deliberate conscious simulation of false motives'. He went on: 'It is partly the dupery of imperfectly realized ideas, partly a case of psychical departmentalism.'[13] Few ears were attuned to such incisive words at the time, and imperialists soldiered on, secure in the conviction that they were building a better world. But as the faith failed, empire began to crumble. This is not to underestimate the role of material considerations and overseas pressures. They operated from the outside, as it were, while the erosion of belief corroded power from within. It was the same for the Americans and the Portuguese in the 1970s as it had been for the British in the 1940s and 1950s.

The ideals of imperialism also influenced the thinking and psychology of the colonized.[14] Especially in the period down to the First

World War, many Indians and some Africans in close proximity to the imperial system and its rewards shared the values and aspirations of their rulers. The new order, it has been said, looked like the first step towards a more just and equal world.[15] The ethic of imperialism – and in particular the quest for modernity, as we shall see later – thus took indigenous root. This colonization of the mind was not easily dislodged, and its patterns of thought survived long after the demise of British rule in Asia and Africa. Perhaps there has been a tendency to assume too readily that colonial socialization was more or less complete in the case of westernized Asians and Africans. Recent analysis has suggested that elements of the pre-colonial world view remained intact; that it was often a matter of using westernization for indigenous purposes.[16] These points provide a corrective, yet the dominant pattern was acceptance of the colonial consciousness. It can thus be said that the moral claims and sense of imperial purpose eased Britain's passage into Africa and Asia by attracting local converts. Those who collaborated were seldom motivated by self-interest alone.

The ideology of moral responsibility can hardly be captured in a single formulation. It had different constituent elements, and to some degree its nature changed even in the years before the First World War. Understanding and application varied from area to area, depending on the perceptions of peoples and cultures and the different colonial traditions in particular regions. At one level there were intellectual traditions of great rigour and sophistication, most notably that of the utilitarians who so profoundly influenced the administration of India in the nineteenth century.[17] At another there were the legends and dreams which extended beyond the conscious processes of thought. More often plumbed by novelists and political psychologists than mainstream historians and political scientists, they express some of the romance associated with the imperial undertaking.[18] The idea of Britain as a knight-errant and imperialism as a quest for nobility becomes more persuasive when related to Schumpeter's explanation of the phenomenon in terms of the survival of pre-capitalist social groups imbued with the values of aristocracy.[19] The approach of most officials and soldiers was different again. It was workmanlike, more a matter of good character than of romance or reasoning. The task itself was so large it was often presented in deceptively simple terms. Moreover, many imperialists recoiled from conceptual clarity because their concerns were felt to be innate, instinctive and obvious; part of a world of action and events much removed from abstruse reflection and book learning. Rudyard Kipling understood this well. It was one of the things which forged so strong a link between him and those who worked overseas. Engrained patterns of thought and habits of behaviour had little use for doctrinal adjustments, with the result that theory and practice often cleaved courses of their own.

It follows that no one man spans the period from the 1880s to the beginning of the First World War or catches the changing emphasis of doctrinal evolution. Yet the most expressive and symbolic figure of the era was Viscount Curzon, Viceroy of India from 1898 to 1905.[20] His very personality – serious and highminded, industrious and arrogant, yet with a sense of romance and pageantry – reflects the traditional ethos. His life and career epitomize the stern commitment to integrity, efficiency and the rule of law, which were the dominant themes of the imperial idea at the end of the nineteenth century. Likewise, Curzon's shortcomings made plain the ways in which the imperial task would have to be extended and to some extent redefined in the years ahead. He showed little warmth or sympathy, and gave a sense of loneliness and remoteness from ordinary life. There was his iron will and absolute conviction of purpose, which enabled him to dispense with Indians either as partners or as collaborators in the business of rule. These qualities were already undermining Curzon's viceroyalty before he resigned as a result of his conflict with Kitchener, then Commander-in-Chief in India. Those who followed him, Minto and Morley in India, Lugard and others in Africa, trimmed Britain's sail to a course less imperious, which took more account of local interests and outlooks.

If the imperial idea were to have a text it might appropriately come from Curzon. In high Victorian language, Curzon set out his understanding in a speech delivered in Birmingham in 1908. Extracts from his address could well be entitled 'The Imperialist Manifesto'.

I speak of Empire . . . because I am a convinced and unconquerable imperialist, who by the accident of events has been called upon to spend the whole of his working manhood in the study or service of Empire, and to whom it has come to be a secular religion, embodying the most sacred duty of the present, and the brightest hope for the future . . .

In Empire we have found not merely the key to glory and wealth, but the call to duty, and the means of service to mankind. Empire can only be achieved with satisfaction, or maintained with advantage, provided it has a moral basis. Let us no more forswear Empire than we would abjure our own souls . . .

To the people of the mother state it must be a discipline, an inspiration and a faith. To the people of the circumference, it must be more than a flag or a name, it must give them what they cannot otherwise or elsewhere enjoy; not merely justice or order, or material prosperity, but the sense of partnership in a great idea, the consecrating influence of a lofty purpose.[21]

In one respect these passages represent more than a manifesto: they are in the nature of a creed. Curzon's description of empire as a secular religion echoes his earlier statements that the maintenance of the Indian Empire was a duty 'laid on Englishmen from on high' (1904), and that in India the Almighty had placed the Englishman's 'hand to the greatest of His ploughs' (1905). Curzon was not alone in his transference of the religious impulse to the imperial idea. A number of leading imperialists who had lost belief in Christianity saw empire as a kind of surrogate. This was the case with Lord Milner, Sir James Fitzjames Stephen, the jurist who had such a marked influence on British rule in India, and W.A.S. Hewins, the economist and imperial publicist. There is something of the same feeling in Kipling as well. Others who retained their faith had no difficulty in extending it to make empire an instrument of God's purpose. Such was the spirit in which many of the earlier imperialists approached Britain's role, that the barbs of critics at home and the rise of protest in India could make little impact.

Accepting its religious sense, the belief in moral responsibility can be seen as an expression of power, progress, race and insecurity. Each of these streams of thought and consciousness left its mark on Britain's approach and has a continuing relevance to this study. They thus form the categories of analysis for the remainder of the chapter. It is necessary to enquire in what way they influenced the development of imperial ideology and the extent to which thinking changed over time.

A consciousness of power was intrinsic to Britain's conception of her mission in Africa and Asia. The idealism of imperialism was not something which stemmed from selflessness or other-worldliness. It grew out of Britain's self-perception and the possession of the means to control. The assignment of role, and the implications which were attached to it, bear this out. Imperialists were the actors and initiators. They possessed the attributes of vigour and energy, and shaped the course of events. By comparison, Africans and Asians were essentially objects. Inarticulate, plastic, mostly passive, they were a material from which something could be made. Those who resisted tended to be left out of account because they did not fit the schema. The focus was primarily on those who acted, and the understanding of the imperial process was such that the supposed beneficiaries were in the first instance drained of life and independent purpose. Thus Hannah Arendt can write of British imperialism in terms of dragonslayers who went out to curious lands and naive peoples to slay the dragons which had plagued them for centuries.[22] Edward Said brings to our attention a broader tradition in which the Occident is seen as a hero rescuing the Orient from obscurity, alienation and strangeness.[23] So compelling was this mythology that it captured the imagination not only of imperialists but also of many first- and second-generation nationalists as well. It is apposite to cite an example from outside the British Empire because of the vividness of the imagery. Soetan Sjahrir, later to become a revolutionary and Prime Minister of Indonesia, was deeply influenced by the imperial culture. During his imprisonment in the Indies by the Dutch, he wrote:

For me, the West signifies forceful, dynamic, and active life. It is a sort of Faust that I admire, and I am convinced that only by a utilization of this dynamism of the West can the East be released from its slavery and subjugation. . . .

The East must become Western in the sense that it must acquire as great a vitality and dynamism as the West. Faust must reveal himself to the Eastern man and mind, and that is already going on at present.[24]

For some, the interconnectedness of power and moral responsibility was a basic presupposition of the imperial order and nothing could be achieved unless this was recognized. British rule in India was founded on conquest. Compulsion, not consent, was the only basis upon which India could be brought to civilization. This was the philosophy of Fitzjames Stephen, and it was one which had a strong appeal to many within the Government of India. In a letter to *The Times* in 1878, Stephen pictured the British power in India as a vast bridge over which Indians passed from a dreary, violent land to one that was orderly, peaceful and industrious. Guarded by Englishmen, this bridge rested on two piers, military power and justice, and neither could suffice by itself.[25] It followed, according to this approach, that moral purpose was contingent on a narrow concentration of power and the refusal to be diverted by the appeals of representative institutions.

This line of reasoning gained wider support because of the popular stereotypes of native government. In India – indeed in the East as a whole – despotic rule was taken to be the norm. 'All their great centuries', Baldwin pointed out, 'have been passed under absolute government.'[26] The widely drawn conclusion was that Orientals could not be expected to acknowledge authority unless it was backed by visible power. The belief in the reactionary nature of the Orient thus blunted the idea of radical change. Increasingly, towards the end of the nineteenth century, there was a tendency for British rule in India to become more authoritarian. Force and pageantry were emphasized, on the assumption that Britain needed to act within the Eastern tradition. Curzon was described as an Asiatic Viceroy.[27] Francis Hutchins writes of the attempted orientalization of British rule.[28] In such a climate, moral responsibility appeared not so much directed towards improving the native lot, but rather as the means through which Britain could realize its destiny. In this sense the imperial idea was a celebration of British power.

Critics rightly perceived that here was a chink in the imperialists' armour. Power might momentarily be in vogue, but its costs were real and its time would pass. Writing in 1902, Herbert Spencer drew attention to the feeling of supremacy or predominance which was then manifest in Britain. He went on to make the case that imperial power inevitably constrained the freedom of those who exercised it.[29] L.T.

Hobhouse had a similar message. Imperialism stood for ascendency and it was incompatible with democracy at home.[30] These arguments may not have had much direct effect at the time, but they foreshadowed the growing disjunction between values in Britain and the spirit of domination overseas. With the advent of the Liberal ministry in December 1905, the premium placed on power fell sharply. Thenceforward, power continued, unevenly, to lose ground; but it remained an element in the imperial consciousness through to the end.

At the heart of the belief that British imperialism had a moral responsibility to Asia and Africa was the faith in progress. More than any other word, progress catches the essence of belief of the era. With respect both to the changes in material life and to the optimism of thought and spirit about human prospects, the nineteenth century stands apart from those which immediately preceded it. Material accomplishment and consciousness of advancement were reflected in the emergence of a relationship between the West and the overseas world, qualitatively different from that which had existed earlier. For medieval Europe, as for ancient Greece and Rome, India was a land of wealth, marvel and wisdom.[31] For the European philosophers of the eighteenth century, China was perhaps the most advanced culture in the world.[32] In the view of a Dutch scholar, the period before the nineteenth century 'did not know any superior Occident, nor any self-isolating Orient no longer progressing with it. It knew a mighty East, a rich fabric of a strong, broad weave with a more fragile Western warp thread inserted in it at broad intervals.'[33]

In terms of scholarship, the nineteenth century saw the fullest expression and exploration of the idea of progress since it first appeared in elemental form in classical Greek mythology.[34] Virtually no sphere of thought was untouched by its influence. It came to be seen not only as an ethical good but as a principle of nature – something from which no area of life or quarter of the globe would remain immune. Many of the greatest minds of the age left their mark on its course. J.S. Mill's commitment to the principle of liberty was intertwined with his optimism about human progress. Significantly, however, he was unable to extend this principle to peoples in 'backward states of society' – for them there was nothing but 'implicit obedience to an Akbar or a Charlemagne'.[35] For Marx there were the iron laws of historical development – 'The country that is more developed industrially only shows, to the less developed, the image of its own future'.[36] Darwin's theory of evolution added a new dimension, all the more influential because of his confidence that natural selection worked for the betterment of life. Building on what had gone before, Herbert Spencer carried the idea of progress furthest. Human nature was itself subject to the general law of change. Progress was not a matter of chance or accident, but of necessity, and it searched its way everywhere. He discerned 'the dim outline of a gigantic plan', a systematic movement towards harmony and perfection.[37]

Intrinsic to this thinking was the belief that the West was the embodiment of progress. The greater was the faith in progress, the more manifest was the fact of Western superiority. But each image had its counter-image. Africa served from the beginning as the base from which Western accomplishment could be gauged. The elevation of the West went hand in hand with the downgrading of the East. As Said has put it, 'European culture gained in strength and identity by setting itself off against the Orient as a sort of surrogate and even underground self'.[38] Europe and America's material advancement stood against Asian decadence and African primitivism. Western rationalism was counterposed to Eastern mysticism and superstition; the work ethic to native laziness and fatalism. Whereas Christianity was an agent of moral and economic regeneration, Islam and Hinduism were anchored in the past. There was not much dissent from the Church Missionary Society's description of the Hindu religion as a 'deep and dark grave, in which everything like moral principle, social and domestic happiness, public worth and national energy, lies buried.'[39] Approaches to Islam were more complex, but almost everyone accepted that it was static and that it lived by enslavement and the sword. In sum, the Orient was worn-out, immobile and corrupt. Africa and its peoples were barbaric, indolent and childlike.[40] Such views spanned the political spectrum. Marx and Engels were no less Eurocentric than either of the Mills. So far as Marx was concerned, India, indeed Asia, had long ago ceased to progress. He had little time for what he saw as the torpor of Indian life. He was unimpressed by Hinduism, Indian culture or the 'undignified, stagnatory and vegetative life' of the Indian village. In the opinion of one contemporary scholar, Marx's 'view of the Indian peasant and village life excelled that of the British colonial administrator in its distortion and insulting tone'.[41] For a time, such estimates of the low worth of non-European civilizations were reflected in the thinking of Asians and Africans themselves. Samuel Crowther, a liberated slave who became Bishop of West Africa, declared in 1869:

> . . . to claim Africa for the Africans alone, is to claim for her the right of a continued ignorance to practice cruelty and acts of barbarity as her perpetual inheritance. For it is certain, unless help comes from without, a nation can never rise much above its present state.[42]

In his survey of Indian history, Jawaharlal Nehru comments that the first reaction of educated Indians to the impact of the West 'was one of admiration and acceptance of almost everything Western'.[43]

Given such images of one culture far ahead of all others, imperialism was seen as the means by which the material and intellectual accomplishments of the civilized world could be extended to the uncivilized world. It was the instrument of progress; as Marx put it in the Indian context, England was the 'unconscious tool of history'. Marx had in mind one kind of revolution; most of his contemporaries quite another. Still, nearly all were agreed that the West's role was to rebuild, revitalize and regenerate. What Asia and Africa needed was an injection from outside. There were many separate pieces here – the role of law and efficient administration, the promotion of trade and commerce, the services bringing order and stability, the churches and their evangelical mission – but they came together in a common purpose. Labour and sacrifice were but episodes in the martyrdom of man, observed Winwood Reade. Reade, an unlikely philosopher and African traveller, developed this theme in a book published in 1872, which was reprinted many times and made a deep impression on Cecil Rhodes.[44] Essentially a popularized expression of Darwinism, Reade's work tied together Africa, Europe and, more sketchily, Asia in a universal history, and presented through a series of vivid pictures a past of native barbarism and a future akin to a heavenly commune. It was a book representative of its age – though not everyone was as prepared as Reade to discount the costs of progress in terms of suffering and destruction. Livingstone thought Africans would never be receptive to Christianity and able to move into a better world until commerce and white settlement had destroyed the basis of tribal society. Yet he was not without sympathy for African culture, and he wrote of 'the advance of ruthless colonists' as a 'terrible necessity'. Marx also saw the human hardship and anguish involved in the process of change. He wrote of the destruction of the Indian village as 'sickening' to human feeling, and of the 'brutal interference of the British tax-gatherer and the British soldier'. But such thoughts did not detain him long as he hurried on to unfold vistas of unification, industrialization and regeneration. There were a few, mainly at the fringes of political life, who doubted whether any benefits could be worth the cost. Disraeli once asked, 'Progress to what and from where?' He ventured the thought that Europeans had mistaken comfort for civilization, but it sat uneasily alongside his imperial extravagance and contemporaries no doubt put it down to Disraeli at his rhetoric again.

The furtherance of progress remained the ultimate justification of British imperialism until the end of colonial rule, but the idea was too expansive and the obstacles too formidable for it to serve as a practical guide to policy. Moreover, from well before the turn of the century, thinking began to run along more cautious and conservative channels. Evangelicalism, which had been such a powerful force in favour of westernization, was in decline. In India, the mutiny of 1857 had dashed the more extravagant hopes of reformers, and those in government came to emphasize stability and order as primary goals. In the colonial Empire, the responsibility of rule led to a more sober and restrained appreciation for what could be achieved. Increasingly it thus became accepted that progress could only be furthered by selective change, that the process would be an extended one, and that it was necessary to work through the indigenous structures of authority and cultural patterns.

The ideal of self-government which earlier had been held out as a positive goal now slipped into the distant, unforeseeable future. Indeed, with respect to the Raj, Francis Hutchins argues that a new frame of mind developed which envisaged the possibility of the permanent subjection of India to British rule.[45] Certainly, opinion became increasingly dubious about the appropriateness of parliamentary institutions for non-European peoples. In 1906 Morley, the Secretary of State for India, wrote to Minto, the Viceroy, that he did not 'think it desirable or possible, or even conceivable, to adapt English political institutions to . . . India.'[46] Second thoughts were also becoming widespread about the desirability of a Western education for Indians and other non-Europeans. Not only did such education make little contribution to the needs of colonial societies, but it was seen to foment discontent and political challenge. It was partly for this reason that Curzon attempted to encourage the vernaculars and to change the emphasis from elite to mass education.[47] Later, doubts were raised about the transfer of English law to alien cultures. This applied mainly to Africa, but there was some discussion even about India. After a visit there in 1909, Ramsay Macdonald ventured the thought that 'An attempt should be made to retrace some of our steps towards the methods of justice native to the soil and the people.'[48]

From around the end of the century, then, a new respect for the traditional elements of indigenous societies was apparent. The study of Hindu civilization attracted keener interest and its richness was more widely appreciated. Especially under Curzon, the Raj turned to cultivate the role of the native princes and to draw them into closer association with British rule. The trend to look with increasing favour on pre-colonial structures and traditions began in India and spread to the colonial Empire. There it took firmer root and received doctrinal expression in the principles of indirect rule.

The essence of indirect rule was that progress could proceed only within strict limits and along defined channels. Partly this was a matter of necessity. Empire was run on a shoe-string. Treasury funds were not available for colonial purposes and the various parts of the Empire were expected to be financially self-sufficient. The result was a skeleton colonial service. Lugard pointed out that in 1903–4, each administrative officer in northern Nigeria was responsible for 11,600 square miles and 400,000 head of population.[49] In such circumstances the dangers of a frontal attack on indigenous culture and institutions in the name of progress were plain. Any attempt to build a new social order was likely to result in colonial resistance and endless campaigns of 'pacification', which in turn would increase political opposition to imperialism within Britain. Alliances had to be struck with traditional rulers, and by such means the support of the subject population could be obtained. Likewise, it was held necessary to work within the framework of existing custom, habit and religious belief, except where these directly conflicted with British conceptions of morality and justice.

The recognition that imperialism could proceed only on the basis of finding collaborators was a brake on the process of dislocation and upheaval. The notion of building on a native past, and of colonial development representing a natural continuation of elements in the existing social order, implied not only that progress would be slower but also that it would be different from earlier visions of westernization. To the extent that the administrative structure was to be less centralized and its reach more limited, this could only mean a corresponding reduction in the unification of a territory and in the standardization of life within it.[50] Whatever its shortcomings, bureaucracy was at least a great leveller and it worked to erode traditional patterns. No summary judgement can be passed on the actual record but the evidence strongly suggests that indirect rule held back the process of social change, and to this extent ran counter to the British image of imperialism as an agent of progress. Certainly it worked to perpetuate and enhance the power of traditional rulers. It maintained a high level of tribal consciousness. In some cases it accentuated regional differences.

From a contemporary perspective, perhaps the most striking feature of the British understanding of progress and its transposition to Africa and Asia is its ethnocentrism. The exigencies of colonial control undermined the extreme mono-culturalism of the early utilitarians and the evangelical tradition, but virtually all reformulations of Britain's mission were rooted in Eurocentric assumptions. Even indirect rule carried an ethnocentric stamp, inasmuch as it embodied a low opinion of the indigenous capacity to adapt to Western institutions and to absorb Western values, rather than a high estimate of the worth of indigenous institutions and values. On the Left, George Bernard Shaw, the Fabians and elements in the British Labour Party accepted the worth of empire because they saw it as a way of furthering socialism and the more efficient utilization of resources. While very often concerned with the advancement of native interests, their assurance that they had arrived at the answers to social organization, and that these were relevant to other peoples, merely tapped another stream of European thinking which put the West at the centre of the universe.

Having so characterized British thought, it should be recognized that ethnocentrism is a loaded word. It catches the egoism implicit in externalizing internal patterns and values, but passes over the idealism sometimes involved. Two generations or so later, it is all too easy to discount the strength and sincerity of the belief that empire held the prospect of breaking down barriers of nationalism, poverty and ignorance. Imperialism, for some, was seen to represent the way forward to the common destiny of mankind. This embryonic universalism comes through most strongly in the thinking of Milner and those around him, who were dubbed members of his kindergarten. For them, the peace of the world was best secured not so much by rational discussion or the management of power as by the extension of a common faith. Empire was thus a blueprint for a new international order.[51] John Buchan wrote later, 'we believed that we were laying the basis of a federation of the world'.[52] After such hopes faded, some members of the kindergarten redirected their efforts to schemes for economic reorganization and world peace associated with the League of Nations.

The understanding of progress – and more generally of Britain's moral purpose – was deeply marked by racial consciousness. Certain modes of racist thinking provided a supposedly scientific justification of the unequal relationship between Europeans and non-Europeans. The predisposition to interpret cultural patterns as a function of racial differences reinforced the mental habit of herding peoples into separate enclosures. It also worked to extend the time-span of British overlordship into the far distant future. Racial stereotypes were all the more effective when they were accepted by non-Europeans, in that the European conviction of superiority was augmented by African and Asian negation of their own identity and cultural worth.

The latter part of the nineteenth century saw the emergence of more explicit racist ideas and attitudes in Britain, as in much of the European world, and they passed into popular thinking.[53] The ground was laid in the middle of the century by theorists such as Robert Knox and Arthur Gobineau, who outlined racial typologies with permanent differences between the races. The belief in white superiority was given a powerful impetus and branched out in new and varied directions as a result of the spread of Social Darwinism, with its emphasis upon racial struggle and the survival of the fittest. Confirmation was supposedly forthcoming from a number of different disciplines. Social anthropologists hypothesized a cultural progression with the 'Caucasian' at the top of the evolutionary ladder and the negro at the bottom. Linguists argued on technical grounds that some languages were advanced while others were not, and hence that they could be graded on an hierarchical basis. Similarly, many ethnologists held to the view that humans could be classified according to physical features, and schools of thought debated the relationship between the size and angle of the skull and the brain and intelligence. Although there was much inconsistency and internal disagreement, late nineteenth-century thought about the relationship between Europeans and non-Europeans came increasingly to be anchored in a structure of belief about superior and inferior races.

From here it was a short step to the conclusion that what was natural was also right, and that fitness and election involved duty as well as privilege. In numerous ways, racial notions filtered through Britain's imperial consciousness to influence thinking about moral responsibility. They strengthened the assurance of imperialists. Joseph Chamberlain could boast that 'the British race is the greatest of governing races that the world has ever seen'.[54] Few in Britain at the time would have quarrelled with this assessment. There was also substantial agreement that subject races lacked the qualities of mind and character needed for political and economic advancement – though not everyone was prepared to disparage them on this account. Disraeli, Salisbury and Queen Victoria all took strong exception to the widespread denigration of Indians and their culture.[55] Along with other factors, racial assumptions led to the imperial task being more narrowly defined. Given the unreality of the idea that Africans and Asians could be refashioned in the Western image, what was required was a framework for protection, supervision and gradual development. An associated development was that greater emphasis came to be placed on the need to maintain social distance between the rulers and the ruled. Hence the conventions, taboos and elaborate techniques, designed to maintain the social hierarchy and the racial prestige of the Raj.[56] In one respect, race was seen to require and to justify a deeper involvement overseas. This was in the economic sphere. In his two influential books, *Social Evolution* (1894), and *Control of the Tropics* (1898), Benjamin Kidd argued the case for the economic development of the tropics under European administration. It was expedient to allow the resources of Africa and Asia to remain undeveloped, and nothing could be accomplished so long as they remained 'under the management of races of low social efficiency'. Therefore work would have to be managed by the white man, and the tropics governed as a trust for civilization.

It is important to recognize that ideas about race did not stand on their own. However definitive race was taken to be, the word was used in various senses and it was never clearly differentiated from culture. Thus analysis and argument frequently drew on the cultural characterization, material accomplishment and political sophistication of a people, and on its religion and history. Evidence as to the relative position of a particular group in a racial typography was as likely as not to be drawn from other such quarters. For example, negroes were on the lowest rung of the racial ladder because, among other things, they had no history. The racial dice was in fact loaded with criteria which reflected European ethnocentrism and ignorance.

Seen in this broader context, the centrality of race was reflected in the primacy of the division of the world into Europeans and non-Europeans. This, after all, was fundamental to imperialist thinking and to imperialism as a political phenomenon. Yet it overlaid a more complex scale of racial, cultural and class rankings and by no means obliterated them. Edward Said writes of the absolute demarcation between East and West and of the irreducible distance separating white from coloured, but surely this is to operate too single-mindedly at the international level and to focus too narrowly on the clash of two collectivities.[57] At least in Britain, there was a strong awareness of the divisions within both the society at home and those overseas. This may go some distance towards explaining the emphasis placed on the larger racial divide. Race served to dampen class consciousness, yet at the same time it was necessary to ensure that members of the lower classes working or serving overseas did not degrade the racial prestige of the rulers. Curzon, in particular, was emphatic on the latter point.[58] V.G. Kiernan has aptly pointed out that 'Europeans of superior countries thought of inferior Europeans and non-Europeans in not very different terms.'[59] In many Englishmen's eyes, as one travelled south in Europe one went down the racial scale. The Irish, for that matter, were for long regarded as sub-human, and the British soldier during the Crimean War was seen by his senior officers as not much better. The story has been frequently repeated of Lord Curzon, on seeing British troops bathing in India or France (depending on the version), expressing surprise at the whiteness of their skins.

Earlier in this chapter it was noted that Asian and African cultures were seen to be of very different worth. This was paralleled by – or perhaps more accurately merged with – very different estimates of the qualities of their respective races. By and large there was believed to be a correlation between colour and capability; the lighter the colour of the skin, the greater the ability of a people. It was indicative of much thinking before the First World War that a book on race and empire, published in 1910, had chapters entitled 'The Yellow World', 'The Brown World' and 'The Black Problem'. The brown and yellow races were deemed to be creative, industrious and not far behind the white races, whereas fate had marked the negro down; he was the world's slave.[60]

Significant as these stereotypes were, it would be easy to exaggerate their influence on imperial policy. Without question they reinforced the justification of British imperialism and helped furnish the more detailed assumptions about the needs and potential of African and Asian societies. Yet the images themselves were invariably one-dimensional, often ambiguous or even contradictory, and at times so plainly removed from the dilemmas of trusteeship as to be meaningless. For example while Indian civilization was perceived to be excessively spiritual and non-materialistic, Indians were often depicted as shrewd and grasping. The widely held view that both Africans and Indians were childlike sat uneasily alongside the equally strongly held opinion that the Indians were more advanced. It was thus necessary to postulate that Africans were like very young children, innocent and uncalculating, and hence requiring a much longer period of parental control. It was a good deal more awkward to reconcile the image of Indians as childlike with the equally persistent idea that the East was unchanging. As J.A. Spender pointed out, in what he dubbed the Peter Pan theory of India, this could only lead to the conclusion that these children would never grow up.[61] Many of these images were suggestive of elements in the evolution of British thinking about trusteeship, but nothing more than suggestive.

In summary, ideas about race in the latter part of the nineteenth century showed some prospect of recasting the assumptions of moral responsibility, and indeed the broad structure of thinking about the relationship between Britain and Africa and Asia. In fact, however, race merged with culture, nation, and to some extent class, and became less distinctive as the years passed. It was one element, at times separate, more often intertwined, in an approach to humanity rooted in a consciousness of hierarchy. There were higher and lower forms both in the national and international spheres. The difference between internal and external gradations was a matter of degree, not of kind.

The analysis thus far has emphasized the degree of European assurance, sense of superiority and certainty of purpose in the period of empire. Self-confidence was manifest in terms of power, progress and race, and led to the assumption of Britain's responsibility for the future of large parts of Africa and Asia. Yet the very brashness of imperial attitudes and the outbursts of jingoism raise the question of how far this self-assurance should be taken at face value. One writer refers to 'the sense of guilt and desire for atonement';[62] another to a 'deep-seated uneasiness' about Britain's imperial role.[63] Philip Mason suggests that growing doubt and unease lay behind the racial intolerance and the shrill, arrogant tone of European imperialism in the years from 1880 to 1914.[64] It has frequently been argued that sexual repression and latent homosexuality played an essential part in the psychological processes which impelled individuals to become involved in the building and management of empire.[65] Some formulations are simplistic and ahistorical, but there was certainly an underlying current of masculinity and a persistence about the notion of empire as a means of emotional satisfaction and an outlet for sexual energy. There is a strong presumption that imperialism was tinged by the fact of insecurity, and that doctrines of moral responsibility reflect elements of personal anxiety and social strain. This can be explored most fruitfully through literary insights, which reveal elements of ambivalence and points of tension much less apparent in the usual historical sources. Three themes help broaden our understanding: imperialism as work, as an escape and as self-exploration.

The idea of imperialism as work and of trusteeship as a task to be undertaken runs as powerfully through the literature of the period as through the lives of imperialists like Curzon, Cromer and Milner. In the writings of Kipling, Conrad and Buchan among many others, work, action, duty and commitment are seen as primary and deep-rooted values. Their heroes are invariably men of action engrossed in the tasks before them. Work is not merely an ethical good or a way of coping with the colonial climate and conditions, but a means of psychological adjustment. Alan Sandison has argued that Kipling's fundamental concern was with individual consciousness; that empire provided a setting for the individual's struggle to sustain his identity in a troubling alien world.[66] The declining hold of religion, traditional social hierarchy and conservative values in the face of industrialism, materialism, liberalism and bureaucracy left the individual isolated, insecure and vulnerable. Hence Kim, '. . . alone – one person – in the middle of it all.' Personal fulfilment could be realized and doubts kept at bay only through action in a concrete situation, by being absorbed in the job or playing 'the great game'. But the game was not purposeless as Hannah Arendt would have us believe. It was the ultimate reality because it was life in action. Conrad wrote of himself as having attempted to be 'a sober worker' all his life, partly because of 'an instinctive horror of losing (his) sense of full self-possession'.[67] Kipling and Buchan did not reveal as much about themselves. However, in Buchan's case it is not necessary to draw on self-analysis to see a link between the frenetic activity and endless striving characteristic of his novels and his belief that 'civilization anywhere is a very thin crust'. From this perspective, the exercise of imperial responsibility comes close to being an end in itself. The psychological need to stave off alienation and dispossession was more compelling than the desire to effect change on the ground. A very clear example, though from a later period, is provided in Joyce Cary's novel *Mr Johnson*, where Rudbeck, even as a junior officer, has a passion for roads. He believes 'that to build a road, any road anywhere, is the noblest work a man can do'. His superior, Blore, the District Officer, observes 'It's a great game.'

The second insight afforded by colonial literature is of imperialism as an escape: an escape from the world as it is: the world at home and the adult world. Closely related to the first image, it expresses not only the rejection of the emerging pattern of life in Europe anchored in urbanization, specialization and book learning, but the disillusionment with a society which has failed to live up to the values and ideals held out by parents and taught in the schools and the churches. For Kipling, people were being increasingly insulated from life in the raw – from the struggle with the elements, coping with danger, having to build for themselves. In so many respects his 'great and wonderful world' was on the Grand Trunk Road with its variety, fresh experiences and earthy quality. Morton Cohen writes of Rider Haggard's 'fervour of make believe', and draws attention to his fascination with the supernatural and his yearning for the past, both of which found an outlet in his African novels.[68] Haggard's African writing is in fact a pageant of the heroic and the romantic, and it stands in unstudied opposition to the European present. It is a dream world, all the more powerful and imaginative because Haggard, as a conventional imperialist, was unaware of its sources and implications.

One aspect of central importance was the tendency to draw on the images and ideals of childhood and to project them into adult life virtually frozen and intact. Kipling has been much criticized for his boyishness and his childlike biases, though more recently there has been a recognition that these elements were fused with an awareness of the realities of adulthood. Mannoni has gone so far as to argue that 'no one becomes a real colonial who is not impelled by infantile complexes which were not properly resolved in adolescence'.[69] Hannah Arendt writes of imperialism as 'an accidental opportunity to escape a society in which one had to forget his youth if he wanted to grow up'.[70] Clearly these assessments reflect the perception of reality of the writers and perhaps something of the cynicism of a later generation. The extent to which youthful romanticism was imbedded in British culture is apparent from the way that T.E. Lawrence became a legend in his time. His personality and his life reflect, in enormously magnified form, the visionary and escapist aspects of the imperial venture. There is the link between his youthfulness and his idealism, his rejection of so much of Western civilization as he saw it, his dream of leading a crusade and the fact that in the Bedouin he could find many of the qualities for which he yearned – simplicity, certainty, action and endurance. John Buchan writes revealingly of both his hero and himself when he testifies '. . . I could have followed Lawrence over the edge of the world. I loved him for himself, and also because there seemed to be reborn in him all the lost friends of my youth.'[71]

There is a third theme running through the literature, which sees Europe's outward movement in terms of self-exploration. Most fully associated with Conrad, implicit in the idea of Africa as darkness and the East as mystery, its compass is much wider than our present concern. Certain elements, however, are relevant in that they provide an undercurrent to the predominant conception that the West had the responsibility to ensure development and progress. The eighteenth-century idea of the Noble Savage, too familiar to require discussion here, finds its echo in the late nineteenth-century ambivalence of purpose; the tension between uplifting backward peoples and identifying with their primitive state. More generally, a searching note is struck in some of the literature. There are qualities missing in European civilization, perhaps lost on the march forward, which could be found in the tropics, the desert, and, for the French especially, the islands. Thus the political theme of Europe regenerating a lifeless Asia had its literary and artistic counterpoint in the thought that the less sophisticated world overseas might be able to rejuvenate a greying Europe. It has been suggested that for the novelists of empire, India was to England as the frontier was to America, and that the vastness and space of Africa was symbolic of vision and vitality.[72] There was also the idea that to go outside Europe was to go back in time. In *Heart of Darkness*, as Marlow penetrates deeper into Africa he tells his listeners, 'We were wanderers on a prehistoric earth, on an earth that wore the aspect of an unknown planet . . . we were travelling in the night of first ages.'

What the journey up the Congo River signified for Conrad, the desert did for Kipling:

> If you look long enough across the sands, while a voice in your ear is telling you of the half-buried cities, old as old Time, and wholly unvisited by Sahibs, of districts where white man is unknown . . . you . . . will be conscious of a great desire to take one of the lobbing camels and get away into the desert, away from the last touch of Today, to meet the Past face to face.[73]

In various ways, therefore, the world beyond Europe was seen to offer possibilities of self-knowledge and growth. Alongside the familiar emphasis on the White Man's burden and serving 'captives' needs', were opportunities of psychological, almost spiritual, enrichment. The recollections of colonial life recorded by Charles Allen in *Plain Tales from the Raj* and *Tales from the Dark Continent* provide ample evidence that this feeling was not simply a product of the literary imagination. Such perspectives also enable us better to understand the preference so many colonial officials had for the tribesmen or 'real' Indians as compared with those who had received a Western education or were to some degree 'Europeanized'. The thoughtful reader of Lugard or Swettenham may well be led to conclude that the development of indirect rule was not solely a matter of pragmatism but was influenced by the fascination and attraction of pre-colonial societies. Angus Wilson writes of Kipling being torn between the need to pull India into the present and his 'hatred of anything that threatened the deep and deathly peace of India's ancient mystery'.[74]

It would be fanciful to suppose that the elements of insecurity, escapism and self-exploration changed the complexion of imperial trusteeship. The commitment to order and the stern sense of what Africa and Asia required was dependent upon the fact of British power. The belief in progress, and the need for it to be translated to Africa and Asia, was deeply rooted in the political outlook of the time. Ideas about racial hierarchy helped sustain the self-assurance which led Britain to see itself as the chosen society. In its outward manifestation, moral responsibility drew heavily on those streams of thinking which were part of the public consciousness. Yet, at the same time, the private anxieties and impulses of those most directly involved in the imperial undertaking influenced practice and, in certain respects, doctrine. The underlying insecurity of many of the builders of empire increased the need for ideological justification. Work and duty became almost a religion in order to inhibit questioning. The appeal of the traditional in African and Asian societies took the edge off the urge to reform. The realization that imperial Britain was less sure of its values than outward appearances suggested contributes to our understanding of its arrogance towards the outside world. In the final analysis, the private influences reinforced the public patterns. Trusteeship remained overweening and ethnocentric. The assumption that empire might improve its builders as much as – if not more than – its subjects was yet a further manifestation of European egoism.

Three

ECONOMIC INTEREST I

The relationship between economics and empire remains a subject of easy assumptions and large generalizations. In the popular mind of recent years, probably the dominant image has been economic. One historian writes that in the public estimation, 'Empire was an evil machine to exploit a dependent people by extracting "fat" profits.'[1] Among scholars, opinion is sharply divided, though few would any longer settle for an exclusively economic interpretation. Yet the literature is curiously concentrated on explanation rather than perception. Argument has hinged on the supposed importance of the underdeveloped world as a field for the investment of metropolitan capital or as a market for European industrial output. Much less attention has been paid to the economic ideas and images of the actors. It is striking to reflect that while Lenin's arguments about the nature of imperialism are widely known, only a few historians of the period would be familiar with the thinking of Chamberlain or Salisbury about the relationship between economic interest and imperial expansion.

The purpose of this chapter is to enquire how people at the time thought, what categories of reference they employed, how – if at all – they assessed the likely balance-sheet. A number of associated questions immediately present themselves. What can be said about the roots of thinking – the considerations which led commercial concerns to look upon Africa and Asia with greater interest? How far did different groups have different images? What substance attached to these images? Were they in the nature of surface impressions or the product of sustained interest and enquiry? The discussion of many of the points raised will be necessarily incomplete. The breadth of our focus permits only a skeleton outline, and in any case information about the perceptions of particular groups is surprisingly limited.

The material which shaped economic images and which forms the subject-matter of this chapter is of three kinds. First, there are the theories and models of economic behaviour which encased contemporary thinking and gave meaning and perspective to information about trade, capital and labour. The writings of the classical political economists are central here because they had such a profound influence on both economic analysis and more general opinion.[2] Second, there are the statistical and other data which were available in government records and analysed and discussed by theorists, officials and businessmen. Relevant here are the figures about British and foreign trade, industrial output and the reports of various Royal Commissions, such as those into the depression in trade and industry, and agriculture. From these sources judgements were made about booms and depressions. The third category includes estimates and opinions about specific subjects – as, for example, the resources of Africa or the markets of India. While in some cases appraisal was professional and detailed, very often we are dealing with casual impressions or promotional exercises. Lord Salisbury's 'light soil' of the Sahara, or the widely held stereotype of the 'lazy native', may have had little basis in fact, but they were not necessarily less influential for this reason.

Thinking about economic issues reflected the prevailing assumptions about material progress and Britain's position in the world. The wider satisfactions – and later, apprehensions – of British society influenced the way political economy was employed and interpreted, though changing circumstances did not necessarily lead to doctrinal reformulation. The tradition within which thinking went forward was liberal. National well-being was conceived to be the result of private individuals maximizing their utilities. A minimum of regulation was needed if industry and entrepreneurship were to develop. In the view of the classical economists, however, the state had important functions. A framework of law and order first had to be established and private monopolies eliminated before the market mechanisms should be left to take their course. The involvement of the state was needed, in other words, to ensure that individual interaction worked to promote the greatest public good.[3] This understanding of *laissez-faire* was by no means always shared in political and commercial circles, where often enough the commitment was simply to minimal government.

Making allowance for the divergence of opinion with respect to the role of the state, optimism about the social benefits flowing from the pursuit of individual interest and the system of free enterprise led to a marvellous confidence in the future. Moral improvement went hand in hand with material advancement. Growth was an unquestioned good. Extending these perspectives to the globe came naturally to Victorian Britons. The powerful externalize their own image. Internal growth led as a matter of course to external expansion: like the individual, Britain could both gain and give. It was axiomatic that Britons should enjoy the benefits of tropical products, but if necessary, doctrinal support could be obtained from Benjamin Kidd's contention that a nation with needs which could not be met domestically had the right to draw on unutilized resources outside the civilized world. There was scarcely less doubt that in time backward peoples would be advanced and barren lands made productive. British penetration would pull Africa and Asia into the commerce and civilization of the European world. Few were untouched by these ideas. Even such a stern critic of imperialism as J.A. Hobson accepted that governments of 'civilized Powers' had rights and responsibilities with respect to the development of the tropics and their peoples.[4]

Robinson and Gallagher have reminded us that in practice, early Victorian statesmen were never quite so sanguine as was their theory about what the individual could accomplish overseas without government support.[5] Other peoples' politics posed complications in the form of closed doors and tariff barriers, with the result that even in the first half of the nineteenth century the business of free exchange could not be left simply to merchants and traders. Thereafter, the hold of liberal doctrines was progressively narrowed in response to the changing international environment and the growth of internal pressures. The last decades of the century saw the emergence of much stronger lines of thinking about the necessity for government action in support of commercial penetration. It was not until after the First World War that serious rethinking took place about the necessity for government action to secure African and Asian development.

Against this background of the relationship between economic and political activity, British conceptions tended to be more focussed; to be shaped by particular trains of thought, each with its own sources and perspectives. Three kinds of conceptions are relevant for our purposes, and form the basis of the following sections. These are, first, those derived from an understanding of the nature and needs of the domestic economy; second, those formed by an appreciation of the changing international system; and third, those specifically directed to the economic potential of Africa and Asia. The crucial question is whether these conceptions came together to form an integrated economic appreciation.

(i) *The Needs of the Home Economy*

A concern with the state of the British economy provided the basis of thinking of many in the business community about overseas economic activity in the years after 1870. Their central reference-point was the needs of the home economy, not any realistic appraisal of economic opportunities overseas. Expectations based on steady growth rates were dashed by a series of downturns in the domestic business cycle.

Slumps in the years 1873–9, 1883–6 and 1890–95 were conceived as depressions. The fear that the trade cycles had somehow become linked into a much longer phenomenon led contemporaries to characterize the whole period from 1873 to 1896 as the 'Great Depression'. In large part the pessimism of the time related to the downward movement in prices, which squeezed profits and resulted in a slower rate of growth than before. Concern was most marked in the trade sector. Industrial and financial interests were much less affected.

It is now clear, as far as income was concerned, that the general trend in these decades was one of growth and that service industries and certain manufacturers were doing very well. What caught attention at the time, however, was the fall in prices and the fact that growth was slowing down.[6] The Royal Commissions of the 1870s and 1880s did, of course, collect material which related to incomes as well as prices; but only from exporters running into difficulty, rather than manufacturers serving a booming market for consumer goods in England, and from wheat farmers, rather than pastoral farmers benefiting from the demand for milk. The result was a marked loss of confidence. Increasingly merchants grew to doubt their capacity to operate without the active assistance of government, and comfortable assumptions about British economic supremacy came into question.

The slump of the later 1870s, partly caused by declining exports to Europe and America, took Britain by surprise and found people casting around for explanation and remedy. The writings of the classical political economists over the previous half-century did not seem to provide immediate practical answers to the problems which confronted the British economy. The optimism of the earlier period ill prepared commercial circles for the emerging difficulties and uncertainties. The slump was variously interpreted and different solutions were put forward by different groups. Initially attention was largely directed to internal remedies, but by the last years of the 1870s businessmen were taking an increasing interest in the possibility of developing new overseas markets as a cure for the domestic downturn.

This latter approach hardened and became more general during the slump of the mid-1880s. Although other explanations persisted, the cause of the malaise was most commonly identified as a crisis of overproduction. The belief took shape that too much attention had been directed to increasing production at the expense of stimulating demand. Henceforward a greater effort would have to be made by businessmen to push up the level of demand. In locating the root of the problem in overproduction, commercial opinion broke with classical economics, which was generally understood to embody Say's Law. Despite the debate about detail, Say's Law held that overproduction was impossible – at least in the long run or as an equilibrium position.[7] Classical economists would have said that traders mistook short-term disequilibria for something more, or that overproduction in their line of business meant only that there was a shortage somewhere else and they should produce what people wanted. Traders would then have had to turn to the heretics of the classical era for support, and to arguments which lacked logical consistency until Keynesian thought much later.

Such conceptual considerations do not appear to have troubled British merchants preoccupied with falling profits. Following the lead of the cotton industry, thinking in some quarters now turned outward to the opportunities overseas. As William Hynes has shown, commercial interests increasingly directed their gaze to the hitherto neglected areas of the globe, as a solution to recession at home.[8] Tariff barriers were felt to limit prospects in the settlement colonies, though there was always the possibility of closer commercial cooperation between the various parts of the existing Empire. Influenced by the claims of a vocal lobby of merchants and explorers, more hope was placed in the development of new outlets in the tropical world. The London Chamber of Commerce and its sister bodies in the major manufacturing cities began to look at Asia and Africa in a new light as an area of the world which could be held for free trade. For a time it might be necessary for the government to lend support, and pressures mounted for official action to establish the political conditions in Africa and Asia in which trade could develop.

The recession of the first half of the 1890s produced a similar response. Again, interest grew in the development of new markets overseas and there was a sharp increase in mercantile pressure for government initiatives. Commercial circles were in substantial agreement that overproduction lay at the root of Britain's problem and that the cure would have to be largely external. Ideas for some form of commercial union with the settlement colonies were blocked by colonial businessmen; schemes for imperial preference ran counter to the widely held commitment within Britain to free trade; while the imposition of import duties by the Indian Government limited possibilities in that quarter. In these circumstances hopes were pinned on Africa and the Far East.[9] In 1892 the Journal of the London Chamber of Commerce drew attention to the 'infinite possibilities of Africa', and went on to mention the development of Siam and the southern provinces of China. 'In all this there was . . . the certainty of (economic) revival.'[10]

If economic revival was the immediate concern of British businessmen, an assumption of broader significance can be seen to underlie the pressure to open up Asia and Africa for British trade. The continued belief in *laissez-faire* precluded the possibility of substantial government interference in the home economy in the interests of regulation and stabilization. Governments had neither the predisposition nor the means effectively to control national economic policy. With the level of production left to the calculations of individual entrepreneurs, and the protection of the domestic market largely ruled out-of-court by the ideology of free trade, Asia and Africa became the external fly-wheel of the British economy. As Hynes put it, 'overseas trade was almost the only sphere wherein a state-directed anti-cyclical policy could operate'.[11] Given the climate of the time, this was not simply a matter of economic significance but had far-reaching political implications. If the government could not help to stabilize the economy, a breakdown in the economic system was feared, and this could only lead to deepening class antagonisms and social chaos. Chamberlain, like many European leaders of his time, was acutely conscious of the risk of domestic instability. Tropical and colonial trade thus held out the twin promise of stabilizing the domestic economy and securing the political system.

With the return of economic buoyancy in 1895, the push for African and Asian trade largely subsided. However, before the turn of the century, concern about Britain's overseas economic relations came to be expressed in terms of investment rather than exports, which gave rise to pressures of a different kind. Recent research by Norman Etherington points to a body of capitalist opinion which was concerned to find new fields for the investment of surplus capital.[12] Given the level of imports, the desire to increase overseas investment and the desire to increase British exports amounted to the same thing.[13] The significance of rephrasing the argument would seem to be that the formulation in terms of investment was likely to attract the support of financial interests, which might then lobby alongside manufacturers producing for export. Although the evidence is limited, the import of Etherington's analysis is to flesh out the thesis of Hobson and Lenin. Influential sections of the financial community in Britain came to take a new look at the future of the British economy in the light of the experience of other capitalist states and the changing contours of the international economic system, now increasingly shaped by trusts, protectionism and militaristic imperialism.

Taking their cue from American economic writings, some British analysts feared that the world was moving into a period of global overproduction. This focussed attention on Britain's own situation. Increasingly, concern was expressed about the possibility of a glut of capital in the domestic economy, which would require investors to move overseas in search of new fields. Overproduction thus came to be seen in a different perspective from that which had prevailed in commercial circles during the previous two and a half decades. The problem was no longer to increase demand overseas for industrial production, but to relieve the pressure on capital built up at home. Although well before the mid-1890s there had been an awareness of the opportunities which India and the colonies offered for the employment of surplus capital, there is little to suggest that financial circles were worried about a glut of capital, or systematically advocated the need to find outlets overseas. By and large investors practised what they preached – that capital found its own level, moving out when interest rates at home were low and opportunities abroad looked more attractive.

By the turn of the century, however, financiers and theorists doubted the relevance of the old orthodoxies to the markedly different economic era which appeared to be emerging. Worries about the excess of capital at home and the need for overseas outlets led to ideas that the state should play a larger part in managing the economic system. The favoured solution of some in the 'City' was a policy of imperial consolidation. Britain's economic survival might come to be dependent upon the integration of her various possessions and the establishment of an economic union supported by tariffs and a strong defence force. A number of writers and imperial enthusiasts advocated more vigorous political action in the underdeveloped world, reasoning that with increasing international competition for capital investment, Britain should look to unexplored fields such as China.[14] The Foreign Office, and indeed many merchants, remained unconvinced that the 'new imperialism' was fundamentally different from the 'commercial imperialism' which had developed since 1870, and they showed little inclination to advocate planting the flag in Asia and Africa in the interests of financiers and concessionaires. The editor of the *Statist* dismissed the idea of official British involvement in West Africa and China on the grounds that any economic returns were likely to be meagre and sectional, and not worth the risk of war. The situation was altogether different, however, where substantial opportunities existed for British investment. This was the case in South, central and East Africa because of the importance of gold, along with other interests.[15] Looking further ahead, the imperial lobby argued that unless Britain embarked on imperial planning, she ran the risk of losing a stake in the development of Asia and Africa which would inevitably occur as the United States and Germany aggressively exported their surpluses. For the most part, analyses and recommendations proceeded within the global context and the underdeveloped world was not singled out for detailed treatment. It is pertinent, however, that in tracing the development of this body of thought, Etherington stresses its significance in the southern African context, and asks whether there might not have been a larger vision of economic imperialism behind the policies of Chamberlain and Milner in South Africa.[16]

With respect both to business pressure during the slumps to secure Africa and Asia as British markets, and the subsequent lobbying for tropical investment, further research is needed to establish the government's response.[17] Yet whatever the extent of the causal connection between commercial prompting and government action, there can be no doubt about the increased importance which business-men attached to the underdeveloped world for the British economy. Most businessmen, however, had little interest in Africa and Asia as such, and limited knowledge of the potential of particular regions. The tendency was to lump together those parts of the world where little development had taken place, and to assume that opportunities were available for British exports and investment. The hopes and beliefs of the business sector were largely derivative from the pre-sumed needs of the home economy and the difficulties standing in the way of other external outlets and options. In the absence of a clear understanding of how to cope with the unexpected problem of sustaining the steady growth of the domestic economy, and by a process of elimination, the development of Africa and Asia was the solution which required least adjustment of established doctrine and practice.

(ii) *An Uncertain World Order*

Alongside the keener appreciation of the need for external economic outlets went a new concern about political conditions overseas and the adequacy of informal empire. Fears generated by the uncertain world order thus coincided with apprehensions about a declining domestic economy. The two worked together to push British imperial designs in a new direction. The increasing political discord and the growth of tariff barriers were seen to threaten the established international economic system and Britain's commercial pre-eminence. The most unsettling feature was the industrially invigorated and fiercely nationalistic European states and their expansion into new markets. The result was that British statesmen were led to protect and advance overseas economic interests more actively than in the past, and to experiment with political enclosures which earlier had been rejected as the refuge of the weak.

The broad suppositions handed down from the early and mid-Victorians about the management of Britain's overseas economic interests were clear, if not always consistent or adhered to in practice. The foundation stone was the belief in free trade. Statesmen, economists and businessmen remained committed to the proposition that the nation's prosperity depended on the free flow of goods around the world. Adam Smith had provided the theoretical rationale that free trade was the surest means of economic growth. His arguments meshed neatly both with public confidence in British industry and business, and with its distrust of regulation and restriction. Govern-

ment interference with the processes of supply and demand introduced inefficiencies and dampened individual – and national – energy
and initiative. D.C.M. Platt observes that the rejection of state
intervention remained the usual attitude of mind with respect to
overseas trade and finance long after it had been abandoned with
regard to the domestic economy.[18] Formal empire represented one
form of government interference which, within classical political
economy, was the subject of sharp internal debate. Much of this
debate, which centred on the relationship between free trade and
colonization, was concerned with colonies of settlement and the issue
of emigration. Insofar as argument and analysis were relevant to
Africa and Asia, the movement of opinion was less opposed to formal
empire than before.[19] With respect to India, British political paramountcy was accepted on both political and economic grounds. John
Stuart Mill's position was that, in certain circumstances, free trade
was contingent on the existence of empire.[20] Nonetheless, few economists showed any enthusiasm for colonialism in Africa and Asia,
and in political circles opinion was even more firmly against it. Given
British commercial and technological proficiency, merchants operating in an open market could conquer competition, while political rule
was a drain on consolidated revenue which should be avoided.
Whatever view is taken of the imperialism or anti-imperialism of free
trade, Robinson and Gallagher are convincing when they argue that
Victorian statesmen strongly preferred influence to political possession as a means to national prosperity and world power.[21]

It was evident, however, that historical circumstance had created
two special cases around which distinctive lines of thought had
developed. The first of these cases was the colonies of settlement. In
the view of many statesmen and theorists, colonies such as Canada and
Australia could be seen as extensions of metropolitan Britain: as lively
agencies working to sustain Britain's political and economic supremacy throughout the world. Now part of the established imperial order,
they held the promise of growing commercial returns with limited
political liability. Having tastes and habits similar to those of Britain
herself, the settlement colonies provided markets of a complementary
nature.[22] Economic conceptions were underpinned by racial and
cultural assumptions. It was expected that in time such colonies would
be able to manage their own affairs. These and other considerations
put the settlement colonies in a category apart – though it by no means
followed that any more were wanted.

Businessmen were a good deal less sanguine about the tangible
economic benefits to be obtained. Ideas about kinship and 'Greater
Britain' were all very well but the commercial possibilities of colonial
trade were not such as to induce pragmatic traders to take a keen or
continuing interest in imperial politics. Irritation with protectionist

measures introduced by Canada and the colony of Victoria contrasted with optimistic beliefs in the inevitability of free trade in the tried and tested European markets.[23]

If there was room for argument about the benefits to be derived from colonies of settlement, the case against tropical colonies was overwhelming. Statesmen and businessmen were in agreement that colonial control in Africa and Asia would involve much greater costs and that the social and economic returns associated with European settlement abroad would be notably absent. The tropics were climatically unsuitable for European immigration and it was widely believed that the indigenous people lacked the 'virtues of civilization' necessary for social development.[24]

The second special case was India, which was seen as a world of her own. Clearly she did not fit the mould of the settlement colonies, being unsuited to white colonists, culturally alien and, particularly by mid-century, troubled by racial tensions and political difficulties. Equally, imperial rule and powerful central control sat uncomfortably alongside the Victorian commitment to minimal involvement of the state. In part, the special position of India in British thinking was a reflection of economic self-interest.[25] The acceptance of exceptional political arrangements followed from the importance attached to the economic nexus. Economists, businessmen and statesmen saw India as a safe and expanding market for manufactures and investment, and as a reliable source of raw materials. In the early 1870s, for example, the business sector showed more interest in India than in the settlement colonies. Manchester merchants, in particular, looked to India – though few imagined that their future prosperity was likely to be dependent upon the Indian connection.[26] It was further believed that economic development in India could only go forward given appropriate political conditions and the provision of an administrative framework. Both lines of thinking could claim a pedigree from the writings of the classical political economists. Under British rule, India would be able to develop those resources for which she had comparative advantage. Thus the world as a whole would be enriched.[27] The role of the state in providing an administrative structure and public works was directed to removing the impediments to free trade and economic development.[28]

Strong as they were, none of these economic considerations and justifications was sufficient to accord India her unique status; nor to account for the fact that statesmen and economists alike accepted the inevitability of the imperial relationship – though many were not prepared to see India expand indefinitely on its own initiative. Explanation must rest in the belief that it was not possible to separate the strands of economic interest, political rule and military power which together were indispensable to Britain's imperial position. India was seen as above politics and beyond analysis. As Sir John Seeley was later to write: 'The end of our Indian Empire is perhaps almost as much beyond calculation as the beginning of it. There is no analogy in history for one or the other.'[29]

The sense of optimism and assurance which lay behind the early and mid-Victorian outlook on the world was shaken by overseas developments in the last quarter of the nineteenth century. The crucial decades were the 1880s and 1890s, when external trends compounded internal difficulties to produce a mood of anxiety and apprehension. The central concern related to Europe. Britain's trading position on the continent was believed to be increasingly bleak as a result of accelerated European industrial development and later the effects of the depression there. Alarm was generated, in particular, by German industrial expansion in the eighties and by the revival of French protectionism between the years 1878 and 1892. Worries and resentment were also mounting with respect to the United States and the colonies of settlement. Concern was partly caused by the growth of their own industrial and trading sectors, but even more by the expansion of tariff barriers. At the same time European economic and political penetration of the tropics was gathering momentum. One aspect here was that industrialization, especially in Germany, had made European trading sharply competitive. Another was the extension of political support by European governments to trading activities. Also relevant was the fact that the settlement colonies showed signs of becoming commercial rivals in some regions – for example, the sale of coal to China by Australia.

The upshot of these developments was that commercial interests brought pressure to bear on the government for a more active commercial diplomacy and for official initiatives in support of trade. In the early and mid-1880s British traders were apprehensive that they might find themselves excluded from the Congo basin, or at least severely disadvantaged. Successively, French and Belgian manoeuvring, the attempt to exclude these two states by the British promotion of Portugal's claims, and Germany's colonial diplomacy, provoked political representations. Chambers of Commerce throughout the country criticized the timidity of the Foreign Office and urged the government to adopt more vigorous policies.[30] In West Africa, fear of French designs compounded the worries of trading firms already faced with deteriorating economic prospects because of the disturbed local conditions. Commercial interests were thus led to reappraise their position on the involvement of the state, and the first calls were heard for political intervention.[31] In East Africa, Bismarck's gains were seen to threaten the future of British trade, and mercantile and political interests petitioned the Foreign Office to take commercial interests more fully into their calculations.[32]

Lobbying by merchants stimulated public debate and led to various enquiries and some reconsideration of aspects of established doctrine. In 1885 a Royal Commission was constituted to investigate the increasingly difficult international trade environment. The Commission conducted a questionnaire sent out by the Foreign Office to diplomatic and consular officials in the principal countries with which England did business. The replies vividly testify to the new competitive business world, showing that England's trade situation in Europe was perceived to be under threat, and that outside Europe foreign competition was making a serious impact in places where British trade had previously enjoyed unrivalled dominance. In the Far East, for example, the Germans and Americans were making significant inroads in the trade with China.[33]

Considerable animosity was directed at the methods used by the Germans and French to promote commercial penetration. Indeed, the free trade inheritance was such that attempts by foreign governments to secure trade advantages through diplomatic or official pressure were seen to threaten the international economic order. Still, confronted by persistent foreign perfidy in regions like the Ottoman Empire, West Africa and the Far East, it was necessary to be realistic. In 1886 the London Chamber of Commerce appealed to the Foreign Office for support in Peking. Faced with a situation where German, French and American traders enjoyed official support, what alternative was there if markets were not to be lost?[34] Despite initial Foreign Office reluctance, and under mounting commercial pressure, Lord Salisbury authorized the British Minister at Peking to break with the tradition of official non-intervention. 'In cases where foreign representatives interfere to the detriment of British commercial interests,' he wired, 'you are at liberty to give the latter your support.'[35] Six months earlier he had sent the same instruction to the Minister at Tokyo with respect to British trade in Japan. The seriousness with which Britain's position was viewed was underlined by a much-quoted leader in *The Times* of 1 March 1886. While rejecting a Bismarckian approach, *The Times* argued that it was reasonable to expect the government to help trade. 'To abstain from so doing, in the face of the desperate efforts of Germany and France, is magnificent, but it is notbusiness.'[36]

Complaints about the inactivity of the Foreign Office and, in certain instances, the Colonial Office – and the consequent loss of trade – were voiced from time to time over the remainder of the century. In West Africa they reached a peak in the early 1890s.[37] In East Africa, south-east Asia and China the government was variously urged to plant the flag, to extend British influence, or to establish the political conditions in which trading contracts and concessions could be secured. By the turn of the century, however, fears eased with the gradual return of economic prosperity at home and the solidification of territorial interests on the periphery.

Much has been written about Whitehall's response to the pressures from commercial interests during these years. In the earlier literature it was often too readily assumed that commercial lobbying had been effective, or at least that there was a coincidence of view between government and business. A more sober assessment would now seem in order. Alarm at discrimination and protection had to wrestle with official caution and bureaucratic tradition. With respect to British diplomacy in China, for example, it has been argued that even after Salisbury's directive of 1886, 'old attitudes died both very hard and very slowly'.[38] In general, Whitehall's response was to adjust rather than overhaul traditional policies. The lock on more sweeping change was the commitment to *laissez-faire* which remained deeply engrained in ruling circles. Still, the nature of the doctrine was such that on each occasion when an extension of government was proposed, an argument could be advanced that the step was consistent with a proper understanding of the boundaries between public and private activity. As a result, the scope of *laissez-faire* was somewhat narrowed in the late nineteenth century. Two broad propositions can be advanced.

First, statesmen and officials devoted more attention to trade with the underdeveloped world than had been the case before 1880. The higher visibility of Asian and, to a lesser extent, African commerce followed naturally from the fact of foreign economic competition and penetration. It was also a function of the deteriorating trading prospects in Europe, America and the settlement colonies, to which must be added the effects of the economic downturns at home. In short, markets in the 'semi-civilized' parts of the globe were seen as more important and less secure than before. The extent to which they were seen in terms of potential growth admits no certain answer. Joseph Chamberlain, of course, was one who believed that determined action had to be taken not only to protect Britain's existing tropical trade but also to ensure that the door to new markets was not closed by foreign governments. In his view, the neglected estates of the tropical world must be developed; the state was required to act in the interests of posterity.[39] Chamberlain aside, there is at least a strong presumption that the deep unease about foreign commercial penetration of the underdeveloped world was influenced by future possibilities, in addition to the protection of existing interests.

Secondly, in the last two decades of the nineteenth century it was recognized that British commerce on the periphery required more political support than before. The broad principle remained intact that it was not the business of the crown to promote private commerce, and that individual initiative would best flourish with minimum government influence. It was conceded, however, that changed circumstances threw up special cases. Diplomatic action could appropriately be taken to secure equality of treatment between British and foreign merchants and manufacturers; confronted by 'unfair' foreign competition, 'free trade' yielded place to 'fair trade'. One initiative of the 1880s was the improvement in the gathering and circulation of information about overseas trade by the Board of Trade.[40] Another was the policy of counter-concession adopted in China, in response to French commercial diplomacy directed to obtaining railway concessions.[41] More difficult to pin down, anxiety about the possibility of being excluded from African and Asian markets by the actions of foreign governments helped shape the diplomacy of imperialism. Obvious instances are the diplomatic jostling on the Congo in 1883 and 1884, and British action in West Africa in the nineties because of the threat of French control on the Middle Niger. Accepting the primacy of the strategic imperative, a strong case can be put that Robinson and Gallagher underplayed the economic influences on British policy.[42]

It is not proposed to pursue this point here because an explanation of the course of policy falls clearly outside the purposes of this book. Our central contention is simply that the 1880s saw the emergence of a different mood on the part of statesmen toward developments on the periphery. More issues of a political nature were being generated by overseas economic concerns. Considerations of power and strategy could less easily be disentangled from matters of trade and commerce. As in the case of China, economic activity might pre-determine political influence; conversely, the diplomatic advances of a rival state could result in the door being closed to British trade. Men like Chamberlain and Curzon saw clearly that the two realms could not be separated. But it was not only a matter of changing thought; it was also a matter of different reflexes. External stimuli produced reactions of a defensive and protective kind. In a climate of uncertainty about the future of international politics and characterized by mistrust of foreign initiatives, Asia and Africa loomed larger in British appreciations of the international economy. Yet as Forbes Munro has argued in a broader context, Britain's approach tended to lose contact with the very real problems on the periphery of the international economy and become a mere reflection of neuroses at its unstable centre.[43]

(iii) *The Economic Potential of Africa and Asia*

Accepting that Asia and Africa figured more prominently than before in British thinking because of the uncertainties of the global order, we need to ask how much attention was actually paid to the economic potential of these continents, and what kind of returns, if any, were envisaged. The generality of these questions makes it necessary to proceed with some caution. Broadly speaking, three very different groups within British society took a positive view of economic prospects in the underdeveloped world: manufacturers and business-men under threat because of domestic recession and increased competition in established markets; visionaries and enthusiasts for empire for whom economic considerations were of secondary consequence; and merchants already engaged in a specific trade in Asia or Africa who, for various reasons, found that trade becoming more difficult or less profitable. In some cases the tendency was to look to Africa and Asia as a whole or without much differentiation; in others, attention was concentrated on a particular region or country. There is an additional problem about attempting to establish a general perspective, and that is the limited nature of the assembled evidence as to the perceptions of different groups and the depth of their concern. Recent studies have substantially increased our knowledge of the attitudes of Manchester merchants to commercial prospects in Africa; we know much less about opinion in industrial and financial circles or about the evaluation of statesmen.

Despite the difficulties presented by the differences in focus and the unevenness of the material, a number of themes emerge which are of great interest. One is immediately struck by the impressionistic nature of British conceptions, and the looseness of argument. Except for the case of India, there was remarkably little in the way of sustained enquiry. Nor was there much attempt to collate the available material and to sift fact or reasonable supposition from hope or fanciful speculation. In 1894 Joseph Chamberlain declared in Birmingham: 'What is wanted for Uganda is what Birmingham has got – an improvement scheme.' A railway from the coast would bring to that population 'our iron, and our clothes, and our cotton, and even our jewellery, because I believe the savages are not at all insensible to the delights of personal adornment.'[44] Of course information was often inadequate, but the tendency was for it to be used in support of rehearsed positions or highly particularized interests. The most optimistic assessments of markets and resources in the underdeveloped world were usually made by those on the spot, either local merchants or travellers and adventurers. Business groups at home were likely to be sceptical and to emphasize the potential difficulties and risks of tropical enterprises. Apart from Chamberlain, few statesmen appeared moved by the general economic prospects of the periphery; much less did they attempt to grapple with the issues in a systematic manner. There was a wariness of taking reports at face value, and a continued reluctance to be saddled with administrative and financial burdens in pursuit of speculative returns. Probably more influential than arguments about specific interests was the fear of future exclusion – it was good politics to keep the door open to as much of Africa and Asia as possible. This broad picture of course requires adjustment and qualification closer to the ground, and this can best be done by examining the separate patterns of thinking with respect to Africa, China and India.

Until the 1880s, when political considerations merged with economic ones, Britain's interest in economic involvement in Africa north of the Zambesi River was very limited. In West Africa there was the trade in palm oil, palm kernels, groundnuts, and, much less important, gold and timber. For the most part this trade was specialized, tied to Liverpool and not of general economic significance. Cotton-growing had proved disappointing. The first plantations of cocoa, coffee and rubber were in the process of being established, but much remained experimental. In East Africa British merchants were engaged in a smaller but more broadly based trade in ivory, wild rubber, cloves, copra, hides and skins. It was not until the first decade of the twentieth century that plantation commodities, such as cotton, coffee and rubber, were introduced from other parts of the world. In general merchants were satisfied with the existing trading arrangements and had no need to attract attention or to press for political support. Statesmen were unconcerned. Interest quickened from about the middle of the decade as a result of pressures from traders for assistance because of unsettled local conditions and foreign initiatives. At about the same time, reports flowed back to Britain from explorers, publicists and travellers about untapped markets, reserves of raw materials and the prospects for the cultivation of tropical products. In 1884, for example, H.M. Stanley gave a glowing account of the economic potentialities of the Congo basin, telling his Manchester audience that if every female inhabitant of the vast basin bought only one Sunday dress made of Lancashire cloth, an export of 300 million yards would result.[45] But enthusiasm on the part of promoters did not connote measured judgement. Nor did it necessarily win converts. Very often reports were based on shadowy notions and unrealistic expectations. Occasionally metropolitan business interests were attracted, but more usually they remained cynical. The attention given to Africa by London, Manchester or Glasgow tended to reflect the pressures brought to bear by people on the spot rather than any calculation of the dividends likely to be obtained.

By the 1890s West Africa was receiving modest but fairly constant attention. However, this was not because statesmen or businessmen had some general conception of its economic future; it was largely a consequence of a variety of pressures and processes to which some response had to be made. The established spheres and patterns of trading were being disturbed by the introduction of regular shipping, increased penetration of the interior because of the falling price of raw materials, and tribal conflict. West African merchants became more vocal in their demands for various initiatives, including the construction of railways.[46] Chambers of Commerce extended their support. At times Whitehall acted apparently in response to these pressures, but there is little to suggest it was convinced by optimistic estimates of future economic prospects. Although the importance of the commodity trade was acknowledged, it was hardly considered a sufficient basis for political action.[47] Outside opinion was more mixed. A commercial geographer, for instance, expressed the view that despite the obvious difficulties, with a little Englishman's 'pluck', new fields of enterprise could be rendered productive.[48]

The picture is not substantially different in East Africa. In the early nineties there were similar pressures for political action, particularly in connection with the annexation of Uganda. Chambers of Commerce throughout Britain urged the government to retain the territory and thus secure a valuable market at a time when exports were falling. Yet, as in earlier years, capitalists showed no inclination to risk funds. When in 1896 the decision was taken to construct a railway to Uganda, neither the government nor the opposition expected much in the way of commercial advantage.[49] Indeed, it has been argued that the search for export staples occurred later and stemmed largely from the need to increase colonial revenue and to find traffic for the railway.[50] With the exception of cotton in Uganda, the economic returns from East Africa were of little consequence until after the First World War. Writing in 1920, Leonard Woolf felt able to conclude: 'The prophecies of the economic imperialist with regard to the East Coast of Africa have proved completely false. British possessions there are of negligible importance to British industry, whether as sources of supply for raw material or as markets for manufactures.'[51]

Unlike the case of Africa, the British image of China was in the first instance economic. The vastness of the country, the size of its population and the exotic nature of its commerce gave rise to the 'China dream'. In large part, the political debate about British policy was an attempt to determine how much substance attached to this dream and at what political cost. It was Chinese commodities, not markets, which initially interested British merchants.[52] Throughout the nineteenth century tea and silk were the staples of trade, and they came to be supplemented by a variety of primary products. Cotton manufactures were the most important British export, though in the last two decades of the century a range of consumption goods were shipped to China. The allure of much wider market opportunities was strong, and it persisted despite the fact that actual returns were often disappointing. In the 1880s and later, finance increasingly featured in British thinking, with investors conscious of China's small public debt and her need for railways and public utilities. Even the enthusiasts had to concede, however, that the realization of China's potentialities was dependent upon vigorous action on the part of the British government. It should also be said that the China trade, directly with Britain and indirectly through India, provided Britain with a substantial surplus of international receipts over payments, which was of importance to her international trading position.[53]

The last quarter of the nineteenth century saw the emergence of new hopes, frustrations and pressures with respect to the China trade. By this stage the number of treaty ports extracted from a reluctant imperial government had been expanded, and the process of inland penetration was under way. For many years local traders had lobbied the Foreign Office for assistance in securing more favourable conditions of trade. The long-standing view of the old China hands was that trade prospects were hampered by restrictive treaties and the corruption of local officials. To these dissatisfactions was added a growing concern with the variability in quality of products for export, and the rise of Chinese middlemen. In the 1880s increasing local difficulties led merchants to press the Chambers of Commerce in London and Manchester to obtain government assistance in the construction of railways to facilitate trade and open up the interior.[54] These efforts met with some success. In 1883 the London Chamber supported and publicized the reports of the explorer, A.R. Colquhoun, of untapped markets in the south-west. In 1884 and 1885 merchants in London and Manchester privately raised funds to proceed with the survey of a possible railway from the interior to Burma.[55] It would be mistaken, however, to take particular episodes where interest was substantial as evidence either of the general view of British business or of high hopes on the part of the government. Nathan Pelcovits has gone so far as to characterize the years 1873 to 1890 as the period of apathy, excepting only the various schemes for an overland railway to Rangoon.[56] Barrie Radcliffe has argued that discussion of the commercial prospects of China was spasmodic and not widespread. Again we find the theme developed that increased attention was more a consequence of the campaigns of the traders than a response to an overwhelming belief in the importance of the China trade.[57] While statesmen and officials were clearly aware of the value of trade with China, they were never convinced by the extravagant claims of local merchants. A detailed report in 1869 by Sir Louis Mallet, Under-Secretary of the Board of Trade, was accepted by Whitehall as the best available assessment, and set the guidelines of thinking for the remainder of the century. According to the report, the China trade was relatively small, confined to a few largely unimportant products, and was certainly inferior to trade with 'more civilized' countries where political and cultural obstacles were less evident.[58] In the view of the Foreign Office, to accede to the demands of the China lobby would be to establish a second oriental empire along the lines of India. This was roundly rejected. Evidence built up over time suggested that any long-term economic returns were outweighed by the risks of political conflict.

The last years of the century saw a return of the debate of thirty years earlier about the relationship between commercial penetration and political support. This was the period when the economic partition of China was accomplished, when the key issues related to the negotiation and financing of railway concessions, and when diplomatic issues were increasingly intertwined with those of trade and investment. Both the government and the China Association were slow to appreciate the implications of the changed situation, preferring the traditional open-door policy to exclusive rights in national spheres.[59] When in 1898 the government broke new ground by obtaining a lease of Wei-hai-Wei, it acted in response to the German occupation of Kiao-chau and to the activities of the Russians, the French and the Japanese. New methods were seen to be necessary to protect Britain's existing commercial stake and safeguard her broader political interests. The government's action was strictly limited, however, and fell far short of the hopes of the China Association for some acceptance of responsibility for establishing the broader political and fiscal conditions in which commerce might develop with greater vigour.[60] Nor were the concessions negotiated by government representatives taken up with any enthusiasm by British financiers. Metropolitan capital was decidedly lukewarm about the China prospect, at least in the absence of government guarantees.[61] In the face of official determination to adhere to a policy of limited liability, and the general unresponsiveness of opinion at home, the hopes of the China lobby gradually faded. The economic returns might still be significant, both sectionally and nationally, but after the turn of the century the idea of a Chinese El Dorado had dissipated.

The question of the economic benefit of India to Britain posed difficulties of a different order from the cases of Africa or China, or indeed any other part of the underdeveloped world. With Britain immersed in the execution of policy – much of it of a long-term nature – and well aware of the detailed terrain of the economic landscape, policy-makers were hardly likely to be persuaded by visionary prospects or to settle for a few maxims of hard-headed prudence. An enquiry into India's profitability was at once too large and too narrow for statesmen or even scholars to tackle in any seriousness. It was too large because its implications far outran the political options; it was too narrow because it left out of account the non-economic elements which permeated thinking. One crucial fact which distinguished India from the remainder of the underdeveloped world was the wealth of information Britain had about the requirements for Indian development and the obstacles in its path. There were reports and statistics on such diverse subjects as railway development, famine relief, trade, irrigation and finance. In 1889 the writer of an unofficial report on Indian administration expressed satisfaction with the achievement of registering and recording information on matters such as the movement of prices, and the conditions and prospects of crops. 'The results of all these observations and registrations are published either weekly or monthly, and there is thus given to the public, to traders, and to the Government, early and accurate information of much practical value which was not available in any shape thirty years ago.'[62]

If there were many difficulties and little incentive to draw up a ledger sheet, it nonetheless seems clear that there was a general understanding that India was of great economic importance to Britain.[63] By the 1880s India attracted almost one fifth of Britain's entire overseas investment, accounted for 19 per cent of her total exports, and was the hub of a regional trading system.[64] Both as a source of raw cotton and as a market for cotton manufactures, India was of crucial importance to Manchester. In the years down to the First World War trading patterns diversified somewhat. Britain's share of Indian exports declined from 53 per cent in 1870 to 25 per cent in 1910. She retained her position as by far the most important supplier of Indian imports, though her percentage of the total fell from 83 per cent in 1870 to 62 per cent in 1910.[65] India played a key role in strengthening Britain's position in the international financial system. To simplify greatly, India had a surplus of international receipts over payments in its trading with the United States. Thus in 1880 Britain settled more than one-third of her deficits with Europe and the United States through India.[66] The figures establish that in this respect India became progressively more important in the years down to the First World War. However, as Max Beloff points out, by the turn of the century most of the major political figures justified Britain's rule in terms of the benefits it could bring to India, rather than the rewards that might accrue to Britain.[67] To what extent India was seen at the time as likely to produce ever-increasing returns, cannot be established with any certainty. The assumptions which underlaid policy were decidedly positive – that modernity and development would break down the isolation and self-sufficiency of the Indian village, and that the application of British experience and technology would enable her undoubted economic potential to be realized. The policies of the Raj were after all predicated on the optimism of early Victorian liberalism. Yet at the same time the obstacles to development rooted in the culture, and in the form of famine and population pressure, came to be more fully recognized. The irony was that as the process of economic rationalization went forward, political and social difficulties increased. The emergence of Indian nationalism may not have threatened the structure of British power but it increased the costs of extracting benefit and deepened doubts about the longer term. There was also the cotton industry's fear of Indian competition. This led the Manchester Chamber of Commerce to set up an enquiry in 1887 into the growth of the Bombay spinning industry and its exports of yarn to China and Japan, which was published in 1888 under the title *Bombay and Lancashire Cotton Spinning Inquiry*.[68]

What can be said with confidence is that so far as India was concerned, the British were too deeply involved and knew too much to have any notion that the subcontinent could be made in any short space of time to yield up economic returns of a different order from those in the past. The parameters of policy were set; the expectations relatively inelastic. Britain was not dealing with untapped markets or hitherto unexploited resources. She was confronted with an economic system which could not easily be made responsive to Britain's changing needs in the light of the domestic economy or the international system.

In large part, British interest in the economic potential of Asia and Africa and the heightened expectation of commercial returns must be explained in terms external to Asia and Africa. Comfortable assumptions about Britain's economic future, based on confidence in the domestic economy and the benefits of free trade, were increasingly questioned in the last decades of the nineteenth century. For many, analysis began with the belief that the continuance of economic prosperity at home was coming to depend more and more upon the expansion of overseas trade, and later, and to a lesser extent, upon the export of capital. Yet in a changing international environment characterized by uncertainty, strong competition and tariff barriers, external economic opportunities were seen to be narrowing and options increasingly precluded. In this situation Asia and Africa figured more prominently in commercial calculations, and pressure increased that they be secured for the benefit of British trade and enterprise. Only at this point was attention directed to the actual returns which might realistically be expected. Even then, British perceptions were largely impressionistic and derivative.

We are left, therefore, with three sets of images – the needs of the domestic economy, the nature of the international system, and the prospects of Asia and Africa – which came together as a matter of logical progression. But underneath the surface order and apparent meshing of approaches, the material was often disparate and the integration forced. Different groups had different perceptions. Optimism in one quarter was matched by pessimism in another.

Hard-headed pragmatism sat alongside wishful speculation. In the end, much of the unevenness of British thinking must be related to the continuing hold of *laissez-faire* assumptions and the absence of machinery for formulating national economic policy.

PART TWO

The Inter-War Years

Four

POWER II

The First World War is usually taken as a watershed in the evolution of relations between the West and the non-European world. The tendency has been to emphasize the distinctive features of the pre-war and post-war eras. In most simplified form, the period down to 1914 has been presented in terms of the establishment and consolidation of European domination of Asia and Africa, while the period after 1919 has been examined from the standpoint of the erosion of that dominance. Similarly, the ascendancy of *Realpolitik* before the war has been contrasted with the retreat from power politics after the war, an interpretation which in the colonial context has sometimes been strengthened by focussing on the internal rather than external aspects of European imperialism. The significance of the Great War rests in the fact that it brought to a close an international political system and moral order determined by the great powers within Europe. The argument further runs that it lowered European self-esteem and bled the physical capability of the great powers. Moreover, Europe's moral and material superiority could never again be accepted as self-evident by those outside.

As more historical evidence has become available, the emphasis has shifted. The continuities, both in policy and in perspective, are now more apparent. The impact of the Great War was not necessarily less than earlier thought, but less immediately politically significant. Thus the time-scale has lengthened. Max Beloff has in fact argued that in the British case it was only after the Second World War that the survivors of 1914–18 came into their own.[1] Charles Mowat has contrasted the changing spirit in society and the arts with that in the political realm, where the older generation remained in the saddle and the tendency was to look backwards.[2] There are good grounds for thinking, therefore, that if the First World War represents a great historical divide it does so more from the vantage of hindsight than from the standpoint of the participants in the 1920s and 1930s; its significance rests more in underlying trends than in the actual course of events in these years. The object of this section is to enquire how far the international system as it affected Africa and Asia had changed from pre-war days, and more specifically, what were the assumptions and calculations of British policy-makers with respect to the non-European world. To what extent did ideas about power shape British appreciation of Asia and Africa during the inter-war years? Contrariwise, what new elements emerged after 1918 which changed, checked or moderated traditional precepts of power?

A number of difficulties stand in the way of an attempt to discern broad patterns over the period, and inevitably invest analysis with a degree of artificiality. For one thing there are large gaps in Western thinking about Asia and Africa's place in international politics during the inter-war years. Aside from the 'Far Eastern problem', the non-European world did not impinge on the global system in any sustained way, and it was not seen to require systematic attention from this perspective. For Great Britain, while problems of imperial policy received constant attention, much of the concern was of a specialized nature, and in any case imperial affairs were by no means fully related to international affairs. Africa was largely left to the Colonial Office and for much of the period it continued to operate in a sphere of its own. With respect to the Middle East in the years between 1922 and 1935, for the most part policy-makers felt confident they had secured Britain's position against both external and internal threats, and thinking was concentrated on the mechanics of management.[3] For all the preoccupation with the devolution of responsibility in India, it is remarkable how little the debate extended to the wider international implications of constitutional change. In this regard Churchill's opposition to constitutional reform after 1929 stands out, because he saw concessions in India as undercutting Britain's global position. He was incensed that the Conservative leadership could not appreciate that any weakening of the imperial structure was a threat to British power.[4] The general surveys of international relations over the period did not attempt to establish the position of Asia and Africa in the framework of international diplomacy. With the exception, again, of the Far East, scattered references to events and incidents on these continents gave little sense of continuity and took only passing notice of indigenous developments. E.H. Carr's *International Relations Between the Wars* had one chapter devoted to the Far Eastern crisis and, apart from that, Asia and Africa were condensed into a short chapter entitled 'The Non-European World', which was written largely in terms of its significance to the struggle in Europe. R. Palme Dutt's *World Politics 1918–1936* came closest to relating the predominant patterns of global manouevring to the largely submerged tangle of relations between Europe and the non-European worlds. His attempt to link the conflict between the 'have' and 'have not' powers with the colonial order anticipated some of the analysis of a later period, but it had little in common with mainstream scholarly writing of the period.

This relative neglect of Africa and Asia by statesmen and diplomatic scholars is not surprising in the light of the concern about European alignments, the role of the USSR and the rise of Nazism. It must also be attributed to the compartmentalization of thinking about overseas affairs. International politics was narrowly understood, and for most purposes colonial questions fell outside its purview. Attention was directed to relations between the great powers – the challenge of Germany and Japan, the question of American involvement or non-involvement – and the hopes pinned on attempts to construct a more peaceful international order. The latter, which centred on the League of Nations but included the various disarmament initiatives, were effectively tied to the interests of the great powers and took limited account of the non-European world except for the case of Japan.[5] The greatest part of Africa and Asia remained enclosed within the European imperial systems. After the peace settlements, comparatively few crises erupted in the colonial world which became matters of international diplomacy. Territorial questions had been settled; tensions were internal rather than external, and there was limited scope for manoeuvrability. In these circumstances it is necessary to guard against the temptation to impute a solidity of thought which did not exist at the time.

A second difficulty lies in the fact that during the inter-war years Africa and Asia did not constitute categories of reference or analysis from the viewpoint of Western policy-makers. These continents were not seen as having any coherence either in international diplomacy or in strategic thinking. Earlier, during the period of expansion, European statesmen had tended to think in collective terms such as Asia, the East, the Orient and Africa, if only for the negative reason that these areas lay outside the comity of nations. In the meantime interests had deepened, the international system had diversified, and particular regions had developed distinctive features of their own. After the Second World War, with the recognition of the international significance of Afro-Asian nationalism and especially during the Cold War when developments on the periphery were viewed in the light of their supposed significance to the central balance, Africa and Asia again became useful units of reference. In the years between the wars, however, neither the political subordination of Asia and Africa to Europe nor the fact of economic backwardness were sufficient to give these areas a distinctive identity in world affairs. Broadly speaking, Asia and Africa were tied into international politics through the operation of three separate systems, the European, the imperial and the Far Eastern, which in varying degrees overlapped and interacted.

The European system was fundamentally concerned with the

stability of the centre. Africa and Asia were relevant insofar as they could contribute to the peace of Europe. *In extremis* this meant that colonial territories were hostages to the maintenance of an external status quo, which was not necessarily in the interests of their people. The imperial system proceeded on the assumption of the centrality of the British Empire in world affairs, and was anchored in Britain, India and the white Dominions. The security of the Empire remained tied to the protection of these territories and the safeguarding of the lines of communication between them. But over time conceptions broadened so that much of Asia and Africa came to be seen as related to the task. The structure of imperial defence also contributed to the security of the Dutch, Portuguese, Belgian and even French colonial empires. It thus provided the underpinning of Europe's overseas domination. The Far Eastern system essentially describes Japan's quest for expansion, first in China and later in south-east Asia, and the response this produced from states anxious to preserve so far as possible the existing economic and diplomatic patterns. Its repercussions were global as well as local, because Japanese power threatened America's position in the Pacific, British maritime strategy, and the security of Australia and New Zealand. The three systems came together in sharpest form for Great Britain. Thus British policy-makers, more than those of any other state, were faced with the problems associated with Asia and Africa's incomplete incorporation into the international system.

It follows from the preceding remarks that no one set of ideas provides a means of interpreting Western thinking about Asia and Africa in international politics during the inter-war period. The situation of the non-European world – in but not of the international system – was too complex for this. When we come to look at thinking about world politics as a whole, the position was quite different. The management of the international system was a subject of the first importance. While there was considerable uncertainty and conjecture about how to proceed, a good deal of common ground existed about the format of discussion. The First World War was seen to reveal the bankruptcy of the European power politics system. Liberal thinking, personified by Woodrow Wilson at the Paris Peace Conference, attempted to steer a course in the direction of open diplomacy, collective security and disarmament, leaving behind the secret man-oeuvring of elites and heavy reliance on the military factor. The lines of analysis were thus set by the debate between the internationalists and the traditionalists – or as they were later dubbed, utopians and realists. Power or the rejection of power was the nub of the issue. The most penetrating attempt to interpret the inter-war era using power as the reference-point was made by E.H. Carr in *The Twenty Years Crisis 1919–1939*. As he saw it, power was the underlying international reality then, as in all other periods, but its management was obstructed by liberal universalist ideology. In fact the doctrine of the harmony of interests, which was fundamental to utopian thought, was a rationalization on the part of privileged groups who equated their continued predominance with a generally acceptable international order. The commitment to peace and the belief in international morality represented the interest of the satisfied powers in the maintenance of the existing system – not some collective good shared by all states. Hence the years after 1931 which saw the return of power politics could more usefully be interpreted in terms of the end of the monopoly of power enjoyed by the forces of the status quo.

There are obvious difficulties about relating this theoretical exposition to the diplomatic detail of the period. It is equally apparent that scholarly opinion was often far removed from the assumptions of policy-makers. Even with respect to diplomacy between the great powers, the internationalist/traditionalist dichotomy obscures the uncertainty and disorder of much thinking about the post-1918 international system and the tension between hope and cynicism on the part of statesmen and advisers. The evidence suggests that internationalism and faith in the League of Nations made substantial headway in informed and articulate circles in Britain, but much less among those in government. The main strength of the realist tradition lay in the Foreign Office and the service ministries.[6] However, even in the Foreign Office, realism lost ground in the 1930s with the rise of a generation more middle class than before and influenced by its experience of the First World War.[7] It must be said, however, that attempts in the literature to characterize individuals and sections of the overseas policy-making establishment in terms of moralism and traditionalism, although suggestive, are not fully convincing. The categories are too clear-cut and often the jump is too easily made from public statement to private assessment. In the view of one historian, every British politician and official in 1935 claimed belief in the League of Nations, though what this meant in practical terms is harder to define.[8] Corelli Barnett's contention that Sir Robert Vansittart, who became Permanent Under-Secretary of the Foreign Office in January 1930, 'was as emotional and romantic in his idealism as any' scarcely carries conviction.[9] Many of his other sketches of the idealism of particular policy-makers take little account of the streaks of hard-headed pragmatism and an awareness of limited options. In the Ethiopian crisis Sir Samuel Hoare was said to have cynically disregarded the League, and yet later he was to be criticized for his political naivety. According to a recent assessment, 'whether he shared the somewhat mystical faith of some of his contemporaries in that institution is doubtful, but he was shrewd enough to realise the value of League approval'.[10]

With respect to Western thinking about Asia and Africa, the relevance of the realist/moralist dichotomy is less and its capacity to mislead proportionately greater. The liberal idea of a new international-al order had limited meaning and made little headway outside Europe, because its presuppositions were almost exclusively Western and its purpose was to secure the stability of the Western world. Ideas about self-determination and open diplomacy spilled over to Asia and Africa, undermining elements of the old diplomacy; but they failed to hold out any coherent alternative design.[11] The brief of the League of Nations was global but its dynamic was European. Significantly it floundered on non-European questions – Manchuria and Abyssinia – partly, at least, because they were non-European and therefore seen to be of secondary importance.[12]

The realist side also had less clarity and consistency outside Europe than within. Elements of uncertainty about the nature and workings of diplomacy at the centre were greatly magnified when it came to Western thinking about Asia and Africa, because the ends of policy were often cloudy and the threats diverse and not readily calculable. A particular problem stemmed from the fact that, to a much greater extent than before the war, the challenges to British power overseas came from within Oriental societies rather than from other states. For the most part, these challenges were met by adjusting the methods of control – what one historian has termed the 'fancy footwork' school of imperial history[13] – within the framework of formal empire. There is reason to doubt how far power politics doctrines, by their very nature, could have provided clear guidance to Western policy-makers, given the interplay between external and internal politics on the periphery and the multifaceted nature of the commitments and ties of the metropoles. Looking back after the Second World War, there may well have been unwarranted optimism on this score.

For a state to ground its policies in *Realpolitik*, a certain sharpness is required with respect to evaluating interests and capabilities, and there must be a capacity to adjust the one to the other. The tight logic of theory looks decidedly out of place when compared with the loose understandings and relationships of the time. The extent and nature of metropolitan interests overseas was hardly a matter of precise calculation, and inevitably involved assessments of the broadest and most subjective kind. American advocates of power precepts were continually hampered by the confusion within the United States as to its national interests in Asia and the Pacific. In the early thirties, the navy in particular saw this as a major impediment to strategic planning.[14] In the British case it was possible to find interests all over the globe, but who could define the British interest in India? And what would be the consequence if some committee did so? The question of capabilities was also far from straightforward. Japan's

economic diplomacy in the twenties, and the difficulties presented by
the rise of nationalism in China, the Middle East and elsewhere, ruled
out an approach based solely in terms of military inventories. Inevitably it was an area of some confusion, and there was often a
disjunction between military estimates and political appreciations.
Akira Iriye has referred to the bifurcation in the United States and
Japan between foreign policy and military thinking as they related to
the Far East.[15] In Britain the ten-year rule was proclaimed in 1919,
which laid down that the British Empire would not be engaged in any
great war for the next ten years. In the circumstances of the time,
military capability came to be seen as something relatively fixed, at
least in the short term. On the one hand, policy-makers were
confronted with a political climate less prepared than ever before to
see military power as the basis of security, and with defence expenditure as the most obvious target for economies in public spending; on
the other, a kaleidoscope of threats and problems which, seen through
the eyes of British strategists, spanned half the world.

In addition, it is necessary to remember the friction and mutual
suspicions between the United States and Great Britain which stood
in the way of collaboration and more effective military planning in the
Far East. Realist thinking has always been at its weakest with regard to
relations between allies. But whether America was an ally was a moot
point. What more difficult situation could be imagined than that in
which one section of the British policy-making establishment
approached the United States with distrust while another was committed to the doctrine of the special relationship between the two
countries?[16] The situation was one in which Britain's leaders found
themselves with little capacity to adjust policies in the light of changed
circumstances. Accumulated but ill-defined interests, engrained
habits of thinking, and domestic constraints combined to limit
flexibility and narrow options. Even asking fundamental questions
was not practical politics. The understandable temptation was for
the political leadership to allow affairs to take their course in the
hope that the situation would become clearer and the prospects
brighter.[17]

Analysis in terms of power was further complicated by hopes about
empire and fears about race. For some, empire represented an
alternative approach to international politics which, although drawing
on ideas about power, could not be reduced simply to power. Others
concerned with events outside Europe saw the possibility of race
becoming a key factor in international relations. Neither perspective
received detailed consideration in the mainstream writings about
international politics at the time.[18] This was because international
relations had become a separate and distinct field of study at the end of
the First World War largely in response to the widespread belief that

power politics had failed to keep the peace, and it remained tied to the debate stemming from this contention.[19]

Especially in the early post-war years, the British Empire constituted a challenge to modes of thinking about world politics anchored in the pursuit of national power. There were, of course, those in Britain who saw the Empire as a storehouse of power, a means of shoring up Britain's declining position in world affairs. The same image was even more influential in the outside world. Woodrow Wilson, for example, regarded the representation of the Dominions at the Paris Peace Conference as an attempt to rig British voting rights. During the Second World War, F.D. Roosevelt conceived the Empire as a system for the extraction of resources and thus a threat to world peace. There was another view, however, which saw the Empire as a collectivity which looked beyond national horizons or material interest narrowly defined. According to the thinking of Milner, his kindergarten and their organ, *The Round Table*, empire was a partnership which might at once combine an alliance with a series of family relationships. In some respects the aspirations of the Round Table movement were given a fillip by the contributions of the Dominions, India and the colonies to the war effort, and by the wartime propaganda which held out a vision of the democratic unity of the Empire. In fullest form, these ideas opened up new directions in thinking about world politics; the Empire was a microcosm of the frictions and difficulties which existed between different communities, and a pilot study of how they might most productively be tackled. In 1918 Lionel Curtis described the British Commonwealth as 'a genuine League of Nations and a good deal more. It is a league and more than a League, a State and less than a state'. As Sir Keith Hancock, writing later, put it, 'We are one, and we are many'. After the early twenties, when hopes of organic unity, a single fleet, and a sharing of the burdens of imperial defence had been dashed, the Empire could still be seen as a unique system of consultation and collaboration. Clearly the relations between Britain and the Dominions did not fit the general mould of foreign relations and they could not be comprehended purely in terms of power. There was more uncertainty about how India and the colonial Empire fitted into the scheme. Most commonly the relationship with India was seen as a half-way house, combining elements of partnership with a large measure of coercion. The colonial territories attracted only limited attention – Britain being chiefly concerned with their economic possibilities and the Dominions with matters of security and immigration – and it was too early to predict what pattern might emerge. From the viewpoint of the Colonial Office they might eventually become participants in the imperial system on a cooperative basis. Yet if some advocates of colonial development had their way, the future of the territories would be to secure the interests of the metropole, and perhaps the Dominions as well.[20]

Whatever the long term might hold, however, Britain's approach to India and the colonial Empire during the inter-war years could not adequately be summed up in the language of interests and power. Habit, a lack of analytical thinking, the responsibilities of trusteeship, and undertones of the partnership with the Dominions combined to rule out such a possibility. *Pax Britannica* proceeded in the interests of peace and stability, though it was arguable for whose benefit. After the war the British army returned to policing the beats of empire with almost obvious relief. The Chiefs of Staff continued to see empire as their principal role, despite the differing assessment of the Foreign Office, and only reluctantly in the thirties came to accept a continental commitment.[21] Yet the fact of the matter was, so Michael Howard tells us, that the characteristics which made the Empire seem so strong in 1919 were in almost every respect elements of weakness rather than of strength.[22] Correlli Barnett has gone so far as to argue that in the inter-war years the Empire had become a high trust rather than merely a source of wealth and power. India was a liability not an asset; colonial policy was an essay in altruism (in sharp contrast to that of the French, the Dutch and the Belgians); the Empire stood as an immense structure of entanglement because the English 'had failed to see it and deal with it in terms of English power'.[23] These themes, while not without some basis, cannot be sustained. It is the contention of this chapter and the next that, while the British did not see the Empire solely in terms of power and exploit it to the full, romantic idealism was seldom dominant and at times was tainted with self-interest. The exercise of power was often constrained either by the absence of available capability or by the need to conserve it. In many respects the Empire was less pliable than before. The difficulties and costs of exploiting overseas territories and resources for metropolitan purposes were becoming greater.

Along with the mystique of empire, ideas and fears about race jostled Western power precepts, sometimes reinforcing and occasionally displacing considerations of power politics. W. Roger Louis, writing of the early post-war period, has commented that the issue of race rested at the heart of power politics in the Far East.[24] In Lord Vansittart's view, much of the talk in the thirties about action in support of non-Europeans was hypocritical. As to the possibility of fighting the Japanese over Manchuria or the Italians over Abyssinia, he bluntly observed: 'nobody in Britain thought seriously of sacrificing her sons for yellow men. In such matters unavowed racialism prevailed.'[25] Christopher Thorne has asserted that the Pacific War of 1941–5, seen within a perspective of a hundred years or more, was in one of its vital aspects a racial war.[26] Hugh Tinker, in his impressionistic survey of race and international order, inclines to interpret the inter-war years in terms of a deepening division of the world along racial lines.[27]

It is difficult to evaluate such wide-ranging claims. Writing more than forty years ago in the context of the treatment of Indians in South Africa and Kenya, Sir Keith Hancock observed a disposition in European and even Indian imaginations 'to leap from immediate grievances, fears, and ambitions, into vague and vast visions of a momentous contest between East and West, of which all Africa was the stage'.[28] Systematic scholarly enquiry into race in international politics has been a curiously neglected field. On the basis of the available material, one is inclined to suggest that in the years between the wars race presented a fundamental challenge to the structure and workings of international relations, but that in the end it failed to cleave its own path and was largely subsumed into and hidden by other and more traditional approaches. Even if race cannot stand as an independent category, however, racial prejudice and considerations of colour often enough influenced policy-making in the inter-war period.

The failure of the Japanese attempt to insert the racial equality clause in the Covenant of the League of Nations, even when softened by omitting the word 'race', was the most blatant case of racism shaping Western policy. The vehement opposition of the Australian Prime Minister, W.M. Hughes, supported by the Prime Minister of New Zealand, W.F. Massey, was instrumental in securing British opposition and American abstention, the former in the interests of empire unity, and the latter because of fear of the response in Congress and on the west coast to an outburst in the plenary session by Hughes. Race also played a part in the British decision not to renew the Anglo-Japanese alliance. In Washington, Balfour eventually capitulated to American opinion, which was seen to be interlaced with racial fears, despite the argument of Curzon (among others) that failure to renew would revive the old position in the Far East of 'the white man against the dark man or the yellow man'. It is significant that during these years a number of influential books expounding racial theses were published, particularly in the United States. These works vividly depicted the Japanese threat, warned of the dangers of miscegenation and Oriental immigration, and contributed to a climate of racial fear.[29] Lloyd George told the 1921 Imperial Conference that in a world increasingly threatened by division along lines of race, the British Empire was a saving fact. 'Our foreign policy', he declared, 'can never range itself in any sense upon the difference of race and civilisation between East and West.'[30]

But in fact the Empire had its own racial problems and divisions. At that very conference Field-Marshal Smuts had dissented from a declaration that there was an incongruity between the position of

India as an equal member of the British Empire and the existence of
disabilities for Indians in some other parts of the Empire. Earlier, the
exclusion of or discrimination against Indians by the Dominions had
led to proposals – by the India Office, the Aga Khan and the East
Africa India Congress – for Tanganyika to be given to India as a
colony.[31] This was never a serious possibility, and the treatment of the
Indian community in South Africa and Kenya remained a source of
tension in imperial affairs throughout the next decade. The Indian
government took a number of initiatives over the issue, and after 1927
stationed an agent in South Africa to watch over Indian interests.
More fundamental was the question of India's self-government and
international status, because it went to the heart of the meaning of
empire. Behind the various enactments and proposals, the debate was
riddled with racial assumptions and prejudices. R.F. Holland has
argued that Commonwealth membership had become for many a
synonym for white supremacy.[32] A German historian, commenting on
Hancock's *Survey of British Commonwealth Affairs*, contended that
empire's community consisted in the community of race among its
ruling class.[33] Hancock argues vigorously that his critic is mistaken,
but his reply is concerned with rejecting a narrow national interpretation of English rule rather than tackling the question of colour. There
were many Englishmen, Milner and Churchill to cite two, who would
have been in substantial agreement with the German critic.

Although at times race served as a general index to confirm and
deepen the gulf between Africa and Asia and the West, it also worked
to complement and reinforce more specific lines of thinking related to
power politics. This applied to the stereotypes of the Japanese and
Chinese. In the Japanese case the racial factor gave a sinister twist to
images of power, modernity and militarism. Japan was the Prussia or
Germany of the East, and there seemed to be an insidious quality
about her statecraft and people which made it natural after Pearl
Harbour to characterize her behaviour as treacherous. Yet however
much Western thinking was shaped by fear and distrust, Japan
commanded respect and was always taken seriously. Attitudes to
China were very different. Her lack of power and inability to 'put her
house in order' entitled her to little respect, and dovetailed with the
image of the Chinese as wretched and helpless. At best China was seen
as a ward (Woodrow Wilson); at worst as an inert mass (Curzon). The
power politics conception of China as 'the sick man of Asia' had its
popular echo in a degree of sympathy and moral concern. This later
came to be harnessed in wartime propaganda when parallels were
drawn between China and the European democracies. In such ways
the threads of power and race interwove in a complex and uneven
design.

Against this background of variegated perspectives towards the non-European world, we now turn to examine the ideas of British policy-makers about the pursuit of power in Asia and Africa. How much of the old structure of thought survived the First World War and the liberal challenge to which it gave rise? What continuities can be discerned between the diplomacy of imperialism and that of the inter-war years?

The first thing to be said is that some continuity was ensured by the overseas military campaigns of the Allies and the secret agreements made between the European states and Japan during the course of the war. The occupation of the German colonies and the hopes and fears of the European powers surrounding Middle Eastern strategy – and hence spoils which might accrue from the destruction of the Ottoman Empire – were par for the power politics course. Likewise, the wartime agreements about the future disposition of the colonies and territories concerned evidenced no expectation on the part of states-men that anything different could be expected. Italy was induced to enter the war by the Treaty of London in 1915, which promised colonial compensation should Britain and France increase their African territories at the expense of Germany. The Sykes-Picot agreement of 1916 designated spheres of influence in the Arab world and was one of a number of undertakings made with respect to the Middle East. Russia secured concessions in Asia Minor, which subsequently lapsed, and understandings were reached between Britain and France concerning the future of certain German colonies in Africa. In 1917, in return for a Japanese commitment to send destroyers to the Mediterranean, the Allies agreed to support Japan's claim to Shantung and the German islands in the Pacific north of the Equator. In addition, there were discussions between Britain and the Dominions about territorial questions, and Australia, New Zealand and South Africa made plain their determination to retain the former German colonial possessions in the Pacific and in south-west Africa. The claims through conquest and the practices of diplomatic bargaining over Africa and Asia during the war thus ran true to the traditions of the second expansion. The only differences apparent were that the colonies of settlement had become players in their own right, and Japan's actions, especially her Twenty-One Demands presented to China in 1915, showed more clearly than ever that she understood how the game was played and was prepared to play it hard.

Two considerations were uppermost in British colonial calculations. One was that the acquisition of enemy territories might serve as useful bargaining counters at a later stage. According to Maurice Hankey, Secretary to the British Cabinet, Lloyd George 'wanted assets to bargain with against those of the enemy'.[34] Among others, the Under-Secretary of State for India was concerned with bargaining-power to secure colonial exchanges with France.[35] There was also a school of thought which held that colonial concessions might be a necessary price to secure a lasting peace in Europe. Second, enemy territory overseas was seen to be of intrinsic strategic importance, both in the sense of providing bases, troops and resources during the continuance of the war or in any future conflict, and in the negative sense of denying such advantages to the enemy. It was widely believed that the advent of wireless and the development of submarines and air power had increased the values of overseas toeholds. As always, Britain was preoccupied with the Empire's lines of communication. W. Roger Louis, in his definitive study of British policy, concludes that the 'powerful theme of *Africa and the Victorians* is even more true of British statesmen of the First World War period than for those of the partition era'.[36]

At the Paris Peace Conference, where the fate of the former Turkish territories and German colonies was settled, the scales were heavily tilted by the facts of military occupation and the cynicism of the majority of the assembled statesmen about the prospects of internationalism. Woodrow Wilson and liberal opinion could change the course of the power politics stream but certainly not stop its flow. In any case Wilson's ideas were vague and general, and he believed that these questions were of secondary importance to the European settlement. The mandate solution was regarded by British statesmen as a satisfactory compromise. Having regard to both domestic and international pressures, it was the best that could be obtained, and the system was not seen to represent any threat to the security of the Empire. The dissatisfaction of Australia, New Zealand and South Africa was unfortunate but American enmity on colonial affairs would have been of much graver consequence.[37] Throughout, the negotiations were approached in a hard-headed manner. With respect to the Middle East settlement, Jukka Nevakivi observes that although Lloyd George had only a vague personal interest in the area, the 'politician in him was always awake, anxious to bring something home in turn for English blood and sterling spent . . .'[38] In November 1921 the fate of Wei-hei-Wei, the British treaty port in China, was discussed by ministers as part of an attempt to settle outstanding aspects of the peace settlement in the Far East. The report of the meeting by a cabinet official indicates how little thinking had changed since pre-war times, and is worth quoting at length. Balfour was anxious for views on whether he could barter the port away.

Churchill was willing to barter it away as part of a big solution of the Chinese problem but not otherwise and he was angered at the way our position was being weakened at Washington. 'We gave away Heligoland in this light-hearted fashion, we gave Corfu away and bitterly rued it. We gave Java away, a brilliant tropical garden.' The P.M.: 'We have got many of these tropical gardens and they are full of serpents.' . . . 'Why', asked Churchill, 'should we melt down the moral capital collected by our forebears to please a lot of pacifists?' 'In the interests of a lot of decrepit mandarins,' chimed in Curzon. Churchill: 'I would send a telegram beginning: "Nothing for nothing and precious little for twopence"' and this became the decision.[39]

Subsequent ministries were not disposed to analyse Britain's options in such a tough and forthright manner. The two Labour governments took a different approach to overseas affairs, placing hope in the authority of the League of Nations, the spirit of conciliation and the possibilities of disarmament. Few Conservatives shared the faith of Ramsay Macdonald and Arthur Henderson that much could be accomplished by working along these lines, but for the most part they declined to say so publicly. The widespread support throughout the country for the League of Nations and a more enlightened diplomacy, and the campaigns of pacifist groups, appear to have changed the tone of political discourse about diplomacy and defence. Nevertheless, in their approach to the place of Asia and Africa in international politics, most British statesmen continued to think in traditional categories.

The conservatism of their evaluative lenses is apparent from the assumptions which surfaced from time to time about who were the actors, what benefits might be derived from colonial territories, and the relationship between Asian and African issues and broader European or global concerns. Throughout, the pre-eminence of great powers was accepted as a matter of course. The Washington Conference of 1921–2 stabilized the situation in the Far East on the basis of the paramountcy of Britain, the United States, Japan and, to a lesser extent, France. China was subordinated to this regional design. Japan was conceded wide rights of action and expansion. Balfour and Cromer took the view, advanced earlier by Grey, that if Japan was locked out of America and the Dominions, the door in China must be kept ajar – 'A nation of that sort must have a safety-valve somewhere.'[40] The naval limitation treaty owed little to pacifism or idealism. In the words of one historian of British policy, it came about 'because the statesmen of the Powers, approaching the problem as shrewd, hard-headed realists, had discovered a method by which all concerned might at the same time reduce their capital fleets and increase their security'.[41] When Britain signed the Kellogg Pact for the renunciation of war as an instrument of national policy in 1928, it sweepingly excepted the defence of the Empire and regions of the world where it had 'a special and vital interest'. In line with the *Realpolitik* tradition, small powers were largely discounted. Italy and

Belgium's colonial claims received little consideration at the Peace Conference. George Beer, an adviser to Wilson, reflected a widespread opinion when he noted in his diary that these small nations bored him.[42] Areas of instability were seen to constitute a threat to the system. In the case of China, what caught attention was not the development of nationalism but the extent of disorder. An official at the Foreign Office explained that little could be done to modify the unequal treaties until a central government emerged with which negotiations could proceed.[43] Arnold Toynbee expressed the thinking of many of his contemporaries when he wrote with respect to Turkey that 'primitive organisms do not suffer the same shock as more complicated ones'.[44] The comment had a more general applicability, as did his admission in 1923 that 'We do not primarily think of Turkey as the home of fellow human beings.'[45]

No less than in pre-war years, statesmen and officials saw the Empire as a source of prestige and the basis of British influence in the world. Its abandonment was therefore unthinkable. Whether it actually contributed to Britain's military capability was less certain. As a study group of the Royal Institute of International Affairs pointed out, insistence upon the advantages to be derived from control of strategic points tended to obscure the liabilities involved.[46] Similarly, constant reiteration of the benefits in times of war of colonial food supplies and raw materials, for example steel alloys and rubber, overshadowed the diplomatic and strategic costs involved. In the circumstances of the time, thinking was more often a rationalization of the existing situation than an attempt to assess the ledger. In the French case, the contribution of colonial troops during the war (nearly two million men, of whom about a third were combatants), the supply of raw materials, and the campaigns of Albert Sarraut, Minister of the Colonies from 1920–24, led to the colonies being more fully incorporated in metropolitian military and economic designs.[47] Colonial troops were an integral part of the French defence forces, and compulsory military service existed for overseas subjects as well as for the French at home. No such systematic development took place within the British Empire. With certain exceptions, colonial forces were not available outside the colony of recruitment. The position with respect to the Indian Army was of course different. Although it was paid for by the Government of India, from the middle of the nineteenth century it had been the real strategic reserve of the British Empire in the East. During the inter-war years, its role was clarified but not fundamentally changed. Despite the opposition of Indian nationalists, more concrete arrangements were made for both India and the Indian Army to contribute to the general system of imperial defence, a process for which the Indian government provided financial support in the thirties.[48]

In many respects the Empire was more vulnerable than before the war, especially in the East, because of the growth of Japanese naval power. Writing in 1936, Admiral Sir Ernle Chatfield, the First Sea Lord, conceded: 'It is even open to doubt whether it is in reality strategically defensible.'[49] The economic constraints in Britain were such that attempts by the Services to obtain more resources were strenuously resisted. At various times the possibility of a non-aggression pact with Japan was floated, but it raised too many difficulties for action to be taken. It cannot now be doubted that the growing insecurity of the Empire was narrowing Britain's international options and putting her overseas interests at risk. Firm decisions were required about increasing resources or reducing commitments. There were a few at the time who saw this, but the policymaking establishment proved incapable of confronting the situation in this way. As the strategy and construction of the Singapore naval base makes plain, policy was an amalgam of hope, compromise and short-term expediency.[50]

The proposals canvassed in the latter half of the thirties for a redistribution of colonies or of colonial advantages in favour of Germany provide a concrete illustration of the hold of traditional power precepts, and of the way they came to the political surface in times of crisis. The willingness in London to consider bargaining with colonial territory is reminiscent of pre-war imperial diplomacy which led to an agreement being initialled in 1913 between Britain and Germany for the division of Portugal's African colonies. The essence of the matter, as Vansittart put it, was that German expansion was inevitable and a choice had to be made between Europe and Africa. He advocated settling for Africa, 'in regions with which we were always well able to dispense.'[51] In the belief that colonial questions might be part of a general settlement, and later at least a means of buying time, a number of schemes were considered by the Cabinet for a reshuffle of central African territories in conjunction with France. These included concessions in West Africa and the return to Germany of Tanganyika.[52] Although the main opposition to these proposals was based on ethical considerations and the belief that Hitler could not be bought in this way, objections were also advanced on strategic grounds. Earlier arguments about the risks of a German presence in Africa were revived and invested with new force by the rise of air power, the fear of the submarine and the fact of the German-Italian alliance.[53] By the last months of 1938, hopes that Germany might be diverted by gains in Africa had been abandoned in most quarters as unrealistic. Yet what is significant is that until that time the idea of a colonial settlement in Africa generated wide support among British statesmen and officials.

Thus far it has been argued that many of the background assumptions relating to the non-European world were power-oriented and represented a continuation of pre-war thinking. At the same time, pressure from home and abroad was directed to liberal reform of the international system. Within the policy-making establishment there was some support for armament reductions and the League of Nations, both on the pragmatic ground that Britain's position *vis-à-vis* other states might be strengthened, and, less commonly, in the hope that international relations might proceed on a more harmonious basis. The question must now be posed as to the extent to which Britain's approach to imperial and international issues in Asia and Africa can be characterized in terms of power politics. The gist of much of the literature is to suggest that, remembering the constraints under which policy-makers operated, there was more *Realpolitik* than liberal hopefulness. There are, however, some sharp differences of opinion. According to Correlli Barnett, during the inter-war years romantic idealism displaced the brokerage of power: in the colonial Empire Britain was influenced by duty; in India it was love; in the Far East a combination of softness and sentiment were predominant.[54] Although in some respects Barnett's study catches the changing temper of the period, there would be little support for such an extreme interpretation. In John Darwin's view, policy-makers were shrewd, tough-minded realists determined to maintain British power but by different methods. Restricting his analysis to Britain's relations with Egypt, India and the Dominions, Darwin argues that the directors of empire were confident of the cultural, economic and strategic ties they had created, and were thus able to stage-manage the move from formal rule to informal influence.[55] The extent of the disagreement between the two historians is illustrated by their interpretation of the Government of India Act of 1935. For Barnett it was 'yet another blend of appeasement and caution'.[56] In Darwin's assessment, it 'clearly signalled London's determination that India should be held within the imperial system'.[57]

The contention that policy-makers acted from strength and according to the dictates of geopolitics is strongest with respect to Egypt. Britain's interests in the Middle East had always been tied to imperial communications, and there had never been any question either about the necessity of holding the area or of its subordination to the strategic requirements of the Empire as a whole. In his detailed study of the years 1918–22, Darwin concludes that the old objectives of pre-war imperial policy kept pride of place in the calculations of policy-makers in the aftermath of war.[58] His more impressionistic account of British perceptions during the remainder of the period carries conviction insofar as it relates to the primacy of strategic considerations and the determination to preserve British predominance. It was with respect to the Middle East that the views of the Service chiefs and the old guard at the Foreign Office carried most weight – though the ranks of the latter were thinning during the thirties.[59]

With regard to India the thesis about Britain's determination to hold firm and to extract the maximum geopolitical and strategic returns is generally persuasive, although overdrawn. A number of key policy-makers certainly saw the constitutional reforms of 1919 and 1935 as a way of reshaping Indian politics, diverting nationalism to the provinces and securing the centre. Such action, it was calculated, would ensure India's subordination to Britain's imperial purposes. In 1934 Baldwin himself defended the forthcoming Government of India Act by arguing that through devolution, 'you have a good chance of keeping the whole subcontinent of India in the Empire for ever'.[60] As already observed, the role of the Indian Army in imperial defence was reiterated in the twenties and thirties, and towards the end of the period India's strategic value was seen to have substantially increased.[61] It has further been argued that the transfer of power was not an end in itself. Even after the Second World War, by which time independence was accepted as inevitable, the aim of policy-makers was to maintain India within the imperial defence system and to use the economic and military resources of an undivided India to advance British strategic interests.[62] For all the strength of these arguments, however, Darwin's case is overstated. In a recent critique of interpretations cast in terms of self-interest and collaboration, Gowher Rizvi reminds us of the stream of thinking which envisaged gradual progress towards self-government. The guardians of empire, he argues, 'had a different vision of their role than that posited by most of their latter-day interpreters'.[63] It might also be said that Darwin's interpretation makes insufficient allowance for London's uncertainty and hesitation, or for the extent to which thinking changed as options narrowed. Moreover, it leaves out of account the influence of the electorate. Private designs had to contend with public perceptions, and over time the conservative standpoint was undercut by progressive opinion.

When it comes to the Far East, it must be doubtful whether any general propositions about the place of power in British thinking can do justice to the difficulties of Britain's position or the relationship between the various considerations which weighed with policy-makers. Britain's failure to renew the Anglo-Japanese Alliance in 1921 has been interpreted as a departure from her traditional reliance on the balance of power and as opting for American goodwill at the price of Japanese hostility.[64] Clearly there is much force in this argument. Yet the issue was not seen as representing such a clear-cut choice at the time;[65] the preference of the British public could not be discounted, and was it so unreasonable to assume that Japan would be deterred from reckless action because of America's involvement and potential power? Much later, Sir Robert Craigie, Britain's highly respected ambassador in Tokyo, believed that the Japanese would be deterred from attacking Singapore by the realization that the United States might send a powerful battle fleet to Honolulu.[66] If, overall, Britain's policies in the Far East ran counter to the dictates of power politics, it must be said that especially in the early post-war years, much of the thinking was hard-edged and pragmatic. It was in this spirit that in 1921 the cabinet decided that the alliance should in principle be renewed. Later developments led to a change of course.

Much the same point can be made with respect to the Singapore base. The decision taken in 1921 to create the base rested on the need for Great Britain, as an imperial power, to maintain naval mobility and to protect British territories and trade east of Suez.[67] These arguments, which were reiterated by the Admiralty and the Foreign Office in their subsequent defence of the scheme, appeared compelling to statesmen of a traditional cast of mind. They ran into difficulties with changes in Britain's leadership and economic position. The Labour governments of 1924 and 1929–31 had hopes that security could be established through non-military initiatives. Throughout, the resources were not made available – and perhaps were not available – for the fleet and other requirements of the Singapore naval strategy. It is beyond dispute that as the Japanese threat increased, and as the construction both of ships and of the base was retarded, the Singapore strategy ran counter to realist precepts. What is less clear is whether realism could offer British policy-makers a way out of the dilemma. If in the final analysis the Treasury was correct, and Britain was over-committed, would it have been realistic to begin dismantling the Empire, and if so, how?

Where expenditure was not so central, British governments had less difficulty in following a power politics course. In the Manchurian crisis which burst in late 1931, the government recognized that Britain was in no position to call for strong action in the League of Nations or to press for sanctions. In adopting a conciliatory approach to Japanese aggression, pragmatism in Whitehall prevailed over popular sentiment. Calculations of economic interest may also have played a part, as there was substantial approval in business circles of Japanese involvement in Manchuria – encouraged by expectations that British capital might be required to develop the region.

Similarly, in the Abyssinian crisis of 1935, government policy was the result of a careful calculation of British interests. Early optimism and wishful thinking about the League of Nations gave way to the ill-fated Hoare-Laval plan which proposed conceding large parts of Abyssinia to the Italians, despite the British government's public commitment to the cause of collective security within the League of Nations. The key role in pushing the government to adopt a more expedient approach was played by Vansittart at the Foreign Office, and the Chiefs of Staff.[68] Well before the crisis erupted, Vansittart's position was that, given the European situation, Britain could not afford to alienate Italy, that concessions were required somewhere, and that the sacrifice of Abyssinia counted for less than the loss of Austria's independence.[69] It has been argued that Vansittart's thinking was influenced by his dislike of Abyssinia as an economically and socially backward colonial country.[70] Certainly throughout these years Vansittart – and probably the Foreign Office generally – had slight regard for Africa except as a source of potential credit in Europe. Stanley Baldwin's position appears to have been very similar. His biographers write that 'Africa, as for so many of his Victorian generation, was essentially subordinate to European affairs, in degree and kind'.[71] The Chiefs of Staff were in agreement that Britain must avoid war with Italy, but for rather different reasons. Apart from the immediate costs of victory, which were assessed at four capital ships and considerable exhaustion, a hostile Italy would imperil communications and substantially weaken Britain's position in the Middle East and Far East. From this viewpoint, support for Abyssinia was ruled out by a naval strategy which was tied to the defence of imperial interests.

Reviewing the material we have considered, the question of the priority accorded to power in British thinking about imperial and other non-European issues can be answered only in the most general terms. Power considerations counted for more than might have been expected, either from interpretations of Britain's overall orientation to international affairs or from the traditional perspectives on decolonization. Certainly, ideas about power politics by no means always prevailed. Invariably they were challenged by alternative conceptions of international politics. However, belief in power and distrust of the League of Nations was characteristic of the political Right, and right-wing Toryism held the reins of government after 1931.

Although the main lines of *Realpolitik* thinking in the inter-war years harked back to the diplomacy of imperialism, the management of overseas power also involved novel elements which stemmed from changes at home, in the non-European world and in the workings of the international system generally. These new developments complicated the pursuit of power and deprived it of the sharpness of earlier years. They also set limits to the maintenance of European domination overseas, and foreshadowed the problems and constraints which were to trouble Western policy-makers in the years after the Second World War.

While it was still appropriate to speak of patterns of diplomacy over rather than in Africa and Asia, these patterns were becoming increasingly ragged because of the changed constellation of external actors, the variety of their approaches, and the declining capabilities of the European states. Japan had emerged as the major power in the Far East, but her pan-Asianist thinking, the extent of her economic leverage, and the racial factor strained the categories and techniques of power politics. Equally clearly, the United States had to be included in calculations about East Asia, but how could diplomacy proceed on a sensible course when confronted by a player who was not prepared to play according to the rules, and indeed for much of the time was not prepared to play at all? The Soviet Union presented further difficulties with its Far Eastern initiatives, its denunciation of the old imperial system and especially the unequal treaties, and the unsettling effect of the language of Marxism-Leninism. In addition there were the Dominions, with an increasing recognition of the distinctiveness of their own national interests, and, in the case of Australia, New Zealand and South Africa, with firm views about the management of parts of the non-European world. Paradoxically, certain of the indigenous states – China, the Philippines and Abyssinia – found they had interests in involving the metropoles in their security. The same point can be made for certain factions in the colonial world, though for reasons of domestic political expediency. It is a considerable misrepresentation of the historical record to picture Africa and Asia united in determination to expel the external powers.

The upshot was that the affairs of Asia could no longer be conducted from afar with the same shared understanding and habits of mutual accommodation. The play of power politics was seldom far below the surface, but its course was more erratic than before because of the lack of common assumptions between the players and the erosion of agreed procedures and diplomatic techniques. These observations apply pre-eminently to the Far East;[72] they have some relevance to western Asia and the Middle East; much less to Africa. The fact was that the question of America and the problem of Japan cast long shadows. One of the preoccupations of empire for British strategists and statesmen was that developments almost anywhere had repercussions down the imperial line. This global mentality, forever concerned with relationships and implications in so many spheres and areas, passed to the United States after the Second World War, and the Americans faithfully adhered to its traditions in the fifties and sixties.

The conduct of orderly diplomacy on the basis of power politics had also become more complex because of the social processes taking place within Asia itself. Among many other factors, the impact of the First World War and Woodrow Wilson's declaratory diplomacy accelerated internal changes, deepened grievances, and gave Asian and Arab nationalism an increasingly external orientation. The extension of European political thought and practice overseas was working to ensure that the structures of Asian and African societies developed along familiar lines, but the effect was to undercut the old bases of European dominance. If China was to count in international councils it had to be united under a strong government; if Egypt was to secure any kind of independence it had to put up leaders who could command some domestic support and yet deal with Britain on British terms. Prodded and provoked by the West, nationalism dug deeper into indigenous societies. How deep it went was by no means clear to British policy-makers, however, and the question remains a bone of historiographical contention today. At the same time nationalism lashed out more vigorously at metropolitan policies. Clearly it constituted a challenge to the old order, but not necessarily one that would always work to Britain's disadvantage. In the Far East, China's self-assertion led the West to pull back and to agree to treaty revision. Broadly, in the years down to 1931, nationalism was seen as a threat to Britain's position; thereafter it was viewed with more sympathy and as having its uses *vis-à-vis* Japan. In the Middle East Britain found it politic to attempt some accommodation with Arab nationalism, and she secured her strategic interests through devolution and the setting up of various levers of control. As Vansittart put it, the task was to encourage 'practical and realistic younger nationalists . . . who seem to recognize the inevitability of the British connexion'.[73] With respect to nationalism in India, there were substantial differences of opinion. Churchill had no doubt that Congress leaders were unrepresentative and untrustworthy. Birkenhead and Winterton thought it ridiculous to imagine that Indian nationalists would follow the path taken by the Dominions. In the middle ground, Chamberlain took the position that Indians were like 'spoiled, wilful, naughty' children who had to be prevented from injuring themselves.[74] The optimistic school of thought was summed up by Hoare when he argued that the 'real danger in India is not Congress or Communism, or misgovernment; it is irresponsibility'.[75] It was the optimists who made the running. A mixture of reforms, promises and limited international status staved off the day when fundamental decisions would have to be taken. Only Africa remained as yet relatively undisturbed by the forces of indigenous change.

In their attempt to maintain Britain's position overseas, policy-makers showed a clear preference for indirect leverage over outright assertion. Military action was avoided if at all possible, and the collaborative net was cast wider. Compared with the pre-war situation, the difference was one of degree. In general it was becoming harder to separate the management of international diplomacy over Asia and the Middle East from the manipulation of power within indigenous societies. Even where formal responsibility for internal affairs was cast off, Britain could not remain detached from local

politics. In Lawrence Durrell's novel *Mountolive*, Pursewarden
warns:

> . . . why are we thinking up these absurd constructs to add to our own
> discomfiture – specially as it is clear to me that we have lost the basic power
> to act which alone would ensure that our influence remained paramount
> here? . . . How long will fair words and courtly sentiments prevail against
> the massive discontents these people feel? One can trust a treaty king only
> as long as he can trust his people. How long remains before a flashpoint is
> reached?[76]

Even among those who approached involvement in Asia and Africa
along traditional lines, military power was less directly related to the
pursuit of diplomatic objectives than was the case during the period of
the second expansion. In general, British policy-makers were less
willing than before to resort to force, and increasingly military power
was viewed as a general backstay of diplomacy rather than as a specific
instrument of coercion. For one thing the forces were over-stretched,
and from the mid-thirties the European situation inhibited undue
action elsewhere. For another, attitudes to the employment of force
had changed substantially since the First World War, and largely in
response to it. Writing in 1928, a Foreign Office official declared that
Britain's China policy was based upon 'a strong and widely held belief
that from every point of view forcible intervention in the affairs of
China cannot safely or decently be contemplated'.[77] With respect to
the Japanese invasion of Manchuria, a contemporary historian
observed that while the episode would have been judged satisfactory
in its results by pre-war standards, it was certainly not according to
the viewpoint of the thirties.[78]

One is left with the impression that as often as not, policy-makers
were concerned with images of power which shaded off into considerations of prestige and status. Perhaps more than in any other period,
those who determined imperial policy attached great significance to
form and to questions such as with whom one dealt and how; their
attention was directed to the trappings of military power rather than to
considerations of what so many frigates could actually do in a
particular situation. The newly appointed British Ambassador to
Tokyo reached Japan in 1920 in a light cruiser because the Foreign
Office believed that his 'arrival in a warship should add considerably
to his prestige with the Japanese'.[79] Such a view was representative of
much thinking in these years about how the West ought to act in the
Orient. Writing in 1923 about the perfect traveller, E.M. Forster
recommended a touch of the regal and a glint of outward armour
because 'diffidence will not succeed in the East'.[80] An historian of
British policy in the Middle East has observed that the Empire was
largely dependent upon the myth of invincible power, rather than

upon the reality of its exercise.[81] A classic illustration is the construction and role of the Singapore base. While it would be an exaggeration to describe British policy over Singapore as an exercise in bluff, this was certainly the case with Churchill's despatch of the *Prince of Wales* and *Repulse* to the Far East in 1941. Here was a clear attempt to use military capability to strengthen Britain's diplomatic position without much account being paid to strategic realities.

Finally, attention must be drawn to the constraints and sensitivities of public opinion. Although the way was paved by the basic social changes and developments in communications which had been occurring since the latter part of the nineteenth century, the First World War was the crucial event in the emergence of public opinion as a political force. Thereafter, the views of the electorate weighed almost continuously on policy-makers, generally working to induce caution, restraint and often indecision. Majority opinion was set against anything that smacked of the old diplomacy or involved the exercise of naked force. 1914 spelt the end of the jingoism which had so often characterized public reaction to overseas crises. Instead there was an air of indifference or at least detachment from unending problems in distant places. Occasionally issues arose outside Europe upon which the public held strong views which complicated policy-making – the most notable being the Italian invasion of Abyssinia. During that crisis, it has been argued, the separation between those who proclaimed ideas about morality and law, and those who held responsibility and thought in terms of power and armaments, was dangerously wide.[82] For the most part, however, the checks and restraints set by public opinion on action in Asia and Africa were indirect and derivative; they were a spin-off from the public's approach to the central issues of the League of Nations, militarism and public expenditure. Thus over Abyssinia the national government believed it had to appear to support the League of Nations for reasons of domestic opinion.[83] Generally, the electorate's hostility to military expenditure and mobilization for the forces induced a more conciliatory non-European posture. Michael Howard has emphasized the readiness with which British governments during the inter-war period tailored overseas policies to the mood of the electorate, in substantial contrast to the pattern of political decision-making before the war.[84] The demand for economic retrenchment strengthened the hand of the Treasury in the formulation of overseas policy. Indeed, in the debate about the construction of the Singapore base, the Treasury featured significantly in key decisions and showed no hesitation in advancing arguments on broad strategic policy and on weapons requirements.[85] One of the most distinctive features of the inter-war years, then, is the extent to which domestic politics affected overseas perceptions and options. Less and less could power politics have a life of its own.

Surveying the period as a whole, ideas about management of power cannot be said to have provided a coherent frame of reference with which policy-makers could approach the non-European world. Thinking was too uncertain in the aftermath of the Great War, and overseas questions and problems too diverse to allow some tidy reformulation of the pre-war diplomacy of imperialism. Britain's approach was further clouded by the challenge of liberal internationalism, by ideas concerning race, and by assumptions about empire as an end in itself. Nonetheless, considerations of power featured prominently and persistently. At times attention was directed to nuts and bolts issues rather than to matters of engineering. British policy-makers proved adept at overhauling the apparatus of dominance in the Middle East, for example, but they were much less comfortable enquiring into the purposes of the structure of imperial power. New trends which affected the workings of the old diplomacy caused some hesitation and adjustment. By the end of the thirties they might have been expected to lead to a redefinition of the relationships between the West and the overseas world. As it happened, however, the war and America's conversion to global strategy ensured a new chapter in the subordination of Asia and Africa to the play of an external system of power politics.

Five

MORAL RESPONSIBILITY II

In the years between the wars, morality provided much of the vocabulary of Western discussion of Asia and Africa. The future of these areas and the policies to be adopted towards them could not be considered without recourse to ideas about responsibility and guidance. Over and above the differences between the colonial empires, or even between those territories which were colonies and those which were not, was the assumption that Asia and Africa, excepting only Japan, were in a position of dependence, their peoples in need of some external support. The fact was that in these years the metropoles were having to wrestle with questions of social and economic change on the periphery which, in varying degrees, were a consequence of the second expansion of Europe. Positions initially taken for reasons of external advantage came to acquire an internal complexity; approaches which earlier had been seen as natural and right increasingly posed ethical dilemmas for which no simple solutions were available. Moral pretensions also sprouted vigorously in an international climate of heady idealism. The promptings of nationalism in Asia and the sensitivities of public opinion in Britain and America brought new considerations into focus. Even those unmoved by progressive ideas about the claims of the colonial world found more need than before for moral justification because of the ideological challenges of America and the Soviet Union.

In a number of respects, Western perceptions of moral responsibility in the inter-war period branched in new directions and became more specific and functionally oriented. In large part, however, the beliefs and images of the late nineteenth century continued to sustain the sense of moral commitment of policy-makers and colonial officials. Whatever hopes – or fears – might be held for the future, the assumption of the time was that responsibility flowed from inequality. There were those who had the capability to conduct their own affairs and those who as yet did not; societies which had arrived and societies which were still at various stages along the way. Although assumptions about racial and cultural superiority could no longer be taken for granted, the facts of power and the belief in progress continued to set the limits within which thinking proceeded.

The chapter begins by considering the implications for Asia and Africa of the attempts to organize the conduct of international relations on the basis of moral principles. To what extent did the non-European world feature in such designs, and how did it fare? Then, turning to the British case, attention is directed to the body of thinking specifically concerned with Asia and Africa. In the light of the changing context of colonial policy-making, how far did earlier thinking continue undisturbed and how far was it adjusted and redirected? The final section explores the declining faith in imperial purposes and the doubts about the possibility of Western improvement of the non-Western world which are expressed in much of the literature of the period.

It is a sobering commentary on liberal attempts in the inter-war years to place international relations on a more enlightened and harmonious footing, to observe the limited account taken of the non-European world and the interests of its peoples. The growth of the peace movement and the family of theories and proposals associated with the establishment of the League of Nations, the promotion of new norms of international behaviour and the pursuit of disarmament cannot be said to have contributed in any substantial way to rethinking the nature of the relationship between the West and its colonial dependencies. The moral imperative was not only Western – indeed largely Anglo-Saxon – in origin but decidedly Eurocentric in ambit and perspective. The basic concern was to secure the stability of the relations between the powers – which meant the metropoles plus Japan – and the overseas world was incidental to this design. At times it benefitted from the wash, but it was usually seen as a resource with which to consolidate the position at the centre.

Of course there were radical critics and publicists who took a close interest in the non-European world and whose economic analyses led them to challenge established colonial orthodoxies. Men such as E.D. Morel, J.A. Hobson and Norman Angell held strong views on the need for international action to promote the interests of African and Asian peoples. Under their influence the Union of Democratic Control, founded in 1914, attempted to combine the campaign against militarism and the old diplomacy with reform of the colonial system.[1] Free trade and the open door, it was argued, would both advance native interests and check the operation of the balance of power.[2] Various proposals were floated to safeguard against 'collective colonialism' and unrestricted capitalist penetration, though in many cases their political feasibility was open to question.[3] Despite its influence on the Labour Party in those early years, the Union of Democratic Control was unrepresentative of mainstream internationalist opinion, and after 1924 it increasingly lost ground to the League of Nations Union which was of a decidedly Eurocentric cast of mind.[4]

It must also be said that to the extent to which liberal internationalism helped shape international relations between the wars, it bore the stamp of power politics. Whatever their persuasion, most moralists came to some accommodation with great-power diplomacy. Indeed F.H. Hinsley observes that many of the proposals advanced by organized internationalist groups favoured the great powers.[5] The adjustment to the facts of international power can be seen in the establishment and working of the mandate system, and in the structure of the League of Nations itself. Although there were some British and continental socialists who saw the Paris Peace Conference as providing an opportunity to overhaul and reform the colonial empires under the aegis of an international body, the Conference restricted its attention to the matter of former enemy territories, and even this was a low priority compared with the issues in Europe. Similarly Woodrow Wilson's formula of self-determination, which at an early stage Balfour interpreted as applying to civilized communities only,[6] was progressively diluted until it became, in the words of one historian, 'the principle of implied collective self-determination'.[7] Despite the fact that almost all parties saw the mandate system as a compromise, it accurately reflected the gradualist, reformist and paternalistic assumptions of the liberal world-view insofar as it extended to Asia and Africa.[8] Certainly some new ground was broken. Wilson succeeded in blocking annexation, establishing the principle of international accountability and the supervision of the Permanent Mandates Commission, and obtaining some recognition for the idea of eventual self-government. Still, one factor in Wilson's thinking – and it was shared by many liberals, though not by Colonel Edward House, Wilson's key adviser – was the belief that imperialism was a cause of war and that it was thus necessary to remove the competitive and irrational atavistic elements from European involvement in backward areas. By imperialism Wilson understood formal political rule, and it is significant that he never questioned his basic assumption that America's commercial and moral expansion into China contributed to the welfare of the Chinese people.[9]

More generally, what stands out is the extent to which the mandate system followed earlier lines of diplomatic practice and liberal imperial theory. Wilson's initial thought that the mandates might be administered by small states yielded to the facts of occupation, which meant in nearly all cases administration by great powers or by regional states in league with great powers. Both Article 22 of the Covenant and the three different classes of mandates testified to the continued acceptance of an hierarchical ordering of human communities, with different rights according to their degree of advancement. The precedent of international control by treaty was established by the Berlin Act of 1885. Given the Belgian record in the Congo, there was little ground for optimism with respect to either of its twin purposes – the promotion of free trade and native welfare. The principle of the open door, as set out in the charters of the 'B' class mandates, seemed more likely than before to be effective in securing equality of external economic opportunity, but there was no evidentiary basis for the assumption of indigenous benefit. The principle of the sacred trust, which derived from British imperial theory, was likewise more an expression of intent than a means of ensuring systematic social and economic change. Commenting on the operation of the system, H. Duncan Hall observes that the League of Nations managed to some extent to keep the mandates out of the forefront of world politics.[10] This may be taken to suggest that their insulation from international politics was at the expense of sustained interest in their future development. The fact that in the thirties a good deal of the discussion about Germany's lost colonies was cast in the phraseology of the 'have' and 'have-not' states[11] indicates the continuance of traditional ideas about the value of colonies in terms of prestige, markets and raw materials for the metropoles.

In other areas also, much of the inter-war thinking with respect to internationalism and a more peaceful global order reflected European interests at the expense of non-European ones. The historian of the League of Nations Union records that that body paid little attention to Asia in the years before the Manchurian crisis.[12] The same point stands for Africa until the Abyssinian conflict, except for the fear expressed from time to time about a possible 'Negro' threat to the civilized world. Writing in 1926 of the French recruitment of colonial troops, G. Lowes Dickinson, a Cambridge classicist and a leader of the League of Nations Union, raised the possibility that these black troops might overwhelm Europe 'as the barbarians once overwhelmed the Roman Empire'.[13] A strong case can be argued that the structure and workings of the League of Nations itself was tied to the interests of the satisfied Western States. Palme Dutt's accusation that its founders planned the League as an instrument of imperialist domination over subject peoples and that it had a counter-revolutionary role, although exaggerated, is not without substance.[14] In the early thirties Asian opinion was profoundly sceptical about the League, and calls were made for an Asian League and an African one as well.[15] That the League was Eurocentric is undeniable, though this was probably inevitable. Clearly the great powers exercised a determining influence – a point accepted and even welcomed by many internationalists and peace groups[16] – and it became commonplace to observe that Britain and France saw the League primarily as an institution for the maintenance of European security.[17]

A similar Eurocentric and great-power bias infused the various disarmament schemes and proposals in the years between the wars. The Washington Conference of 1921–22 froze the situation in the Far East on the basis of the interests of the major Western powers plus Japan, and over the head of China. The central concern of the powers was to redefine their relations with one another, and the problems of China were therefore a subordinate consideration. China was not accorded full international status and the powers were not prepared to pledge themselves unequivocally to her equality and independence.[18] Writing of the background to the Disarmament Conference which began in February 1932, Gathorne-Hardy stresses the extent to which the European nations believed the post-war security system was built on too wide a basis. Their peoples, he said, 'showed no enthusiasm for the idea of crusading for peace in the remoter ends of the earth'.[19] In May 1933, when prospects of a successful outcome looked bleak, the editor of the League of Nations Union's *Headway* counselled his readers that if the League's 'writ does not run at the other end of Asia that is no proof that its writ does not run in Europe'.[20] At the same time Hugh Wilson, the American representative at the Conference, wrote back to Washington that if the United States wished to strengthen peace machinery, it should restrict its attention to the European region. This position was substantially accepted by the head of the United States Delegation to the Disarmament Conference, but shortly afterwards America retreated into isolationism.[21] A rather different and perhaps more arguable example of the extent to which security thinking was only incidentally, if at all, concerned with non-European peoples is provided by President Roosevelt's ideas in 1936 and 1937 about the neutralization of the Pacific.[22] Had they been realized, the effect might well have been to underwrite the continued dominance of the external powers and to subordinate indigenous political interests in the Pacific and south-east Asia to outside security interests.[23]

The one clear case where liberal opinion came down firmly in support of a non-European cause was that of the Italian invasion of Abyssinia in 1935. In Britain, public indignation at the Hoare-Laval plan expressed not only the rejection of the old diplomacy but widespread sympathy for the Abyssinian cause. Duff Cooper wrote that he had 'never witnessed so devastating a wave of public opinion'.[24] Yet in the face of the obvious diplomatic difficulties of Britain's position, its force was fairly quickly spent. Europe again became the preoccupation, faith in internationalization was dented, and some League supporters even came to the view that it was necessary to make coercive clauses of the Covenant in Europe by repealing them elsewhere.[25] While the Abyssinian crisis demonstrated the extent of public feeling about the particular episode, it can hardly be taken as evidence of any sustained interest in or concern about the non-European world.

For a small minority of metropolitan policy-makers and informed outsiders, the moral challenge of determining appropriate policies towards Asia and Africa constituted a subject in its right, not something that tagged at the heels of liberal internationalist attempts to reform the world system. For many who worked overseas – administrators, soldiers, missionaries and the like – conceptions of duty and responsibility were part of their approach to daily life. It is this body of thought and perception to which we now turn and it will be considered in the context of Britain's relationship with the dependent Empire. The key development of the inter-war years was the growing specificity of thought with respect to moral responsibility and the emergence of new ideas about how that responsibility should properly be exercised. This was partly in response to much stronger pressures within government that the colonial Empire should be managed to Britain's economic, and at times political, advantage. The relatively untroubled cast of mind of pre-war days gave way to an increasing awareness of the perplexities of the imperial relationship and of the moral dilemmas it posed. What previously had been accepted almost as a matter of faith increasingly became material for debate; where before discussion had so often been in well-rounded terms, now the issues and implications were drawn out in sharper form. In many ways the arguments in the twenties and thirties were relevant to the post-colonial period, and especially to the role of the United States, but they became a largely forgotten chapter.

In several respects the context of British colonial policy-making had changed since the pre-war period, and was in the process of changing more substantially still. First, it was increasingly difficult simply to express broad declarations of moral earnestness without confronting practical difficulties and contending pressures, and making choices. The political situation overseas had hardened. In India the tempo of nationalist agitation had speeded up, and the issue of self-government was no longer a remote ideal but a demand almost continuously on the political agenda. Earlier pledges or understandings were cast in a different light by recent political developments and changing moral perspectives. One such case was the long-standing obligations to the Indian princes, which were irreconcilable with the devolution of power to the Indian people and the requirements of Indian unity. In Africa nationalism had not yet reached the surface, but the claims of the European and Indian communities as against the interests of the African natives led to a conflict between the principle of trusteeship on the one hand, and on the other the conventions regarding the granting of responsible government to European communities overseas and the claim for equal rights as between Indians and Europeans. With respect to Kenya, what Sir Keith Hancock called the 'white ideal' still influenced the British government during the war years and immediately after, and the assumption was that colonial autonomy would come in due course.[26] Yet in 1923 the White Paper on Indians in Kenya asserted that 'the interests of the African natives must be paramount'. Reflecting on the speed of change and the difficulty of resolving different problems in a common setting, Sir Keith Hancock asked how the settlers could 'be expected to understand that their idea of empire, which in 1915 was accounted noble, and in 1920 was still a respectable orthodoxy, must be deemed in 1923 to be tainted with sin?'[27]

Secondly, there was the growth of world opinion about the position of and policies towards colonial dependencies. Inevitably nebulous and uneven, it nonetheless worked to push imperialism on the moral defensive. Increasingly, arguments about the benefits of colonial tutelage had to be spelt out in greater detail and assertions were weighed against performance. The establishment of the mandate system provided a focal point for thinking and prescription. Lord Irwin (later Earl of Halifax), Viceroy from 1926 to 1931, took the view that the effect of the idea of self-determination was to create a very much stronger claim for the wards, rather than the trustees, to be the deciding party.[28] Writing generally of the period from 1919 to 1947, Michael Edwardes has gone so far as to argue that in the Indian case, successive concessions were made not so much to Indians as to the newly enfranchized classes in England and to world opinion.[29] This interpretation echoes the assessment of many of the British in India but it must be regarded as highly doubtful. There is little to suggest that world opinion over India significantly influenced London much before the war. Nor did India figure prominently in public thinking at home – least of all, perhaps, on the part of women. Still, in December 1931, looking to the longer term, Gandhi made the observation that he wanted to develop world opinion so that England would be 'ashamed to do the wrong thing'.[30] From 1936 until at least 1938, the question of the return of German colonies attracted wide attention, and according to the *Official History of Colonial Developmment* it led to 'deep heart-searching'. If the refusal to return German colonies was to be acceptable to world opinion, it had to have a sound moral basis.[31] It was during the war years, however, that overseas opinion weighed most heavily with British policy-makers. Lord Hailey, speaking to an American audience in 1943, put world opinion as of the first importance among factors to be considered in determining the future of colonies.[32] Seen through British eyes at the time, world opinion came down largely to American opinion. The evidence makes plain the degree to which American anti-colonialism jolted British complacency and strengthened the hand of those anxious to pursue more progressive colonial policies.[33]

Within Britain itself, empire was coming to be seen in a rather different light. In the twenties, anti-imperialism emerged as a body of thought of some political significance and gained limited expression in Labour Party statements about India's right to self-government. Men such as Leonard Woolf, Norman Leys, and later, Leonard Barnes and W.M. Macmillan were active in Labour Party committees, and many had had personal experience either in India or in the colonies. Mostly moralists themselves, they were concerned to expose the shortcomings of existing thinking and practice, and hasten the process of colonial advancement. The growing radicalism and intellectual influence of critics on the Left sharpened debate, though it remained largely an in-house affair. Their indirect influence was probably greater inasmuch as their arguments helped tarnish the image of empire. While sustained interest in imperial affairs had always been restricted to a minority of the British public, it seems clear that between the wars the intensity of feeling and sense of excitement about empire was waning within the society as a whole. This theme will be developed in the final section of the chapter but it helps to explain the more muted moral tone of official approaches to colonial affairs.

Although the changing international and domestic environment had a growing influence on reinterpreting the tasks of trusteeship, it left the basic presuppositions of thought largely undisturbed. The sense of obligation for the protection and progress of the dependent territories remained distinctively imperial, not something exercised on behalf of an anonymous internationalism. It derived its moral force from a belief in British virtues and traditions. The values which characterized the Colonial Service during the twenties and thirties represented a continuation of those which had underpinned the thinking of imperialists such as Milner and Philip Kerr during the war years and before. Robert Heussler remarks that the men of the Colonial Service 'stood by their own, i.e. British standards'.[34] From time to time during the inter-war period, the idea was floated of international control or even international administration of colonial dependencies. During and immediately after the war liberal opinion favoured the extension of the mandate system to the colonial dependencies, particularly in Africa, and the principle won some acceptance in Labour Party pronouncements.[35] The hope was to secure more adequate promotion of native rights and to undercut economic imperialism through the operation of free trade – though Leonard Woolf feared that the old system would probably continue to operate under a new name.[36] The idea was revived and won wider support in the latter half of the thirties, especially on the part of those who had come to accept the justice of Germany's colonial claims, or at least entertained the hope that concessions in Africa would further European stability. By then, however, there was no necessary correlation between support for the internationalization of colonial dependencies and a concern for African welfare. Moral considerations could be found both for and against such proposals, as the global situation was less conducive than at any stage since the First World War for cooperative ventures in internationalism. In any case much of the debate had only a tenuous connection with the interests of African peoples. Writing in 1938, even such a forthright critic of national imperialism as W.M. Macmillan conceded that the 'chicken of internationalism has not cracked the hard shell of nationalism which obviously covered the mandate system at its institution'.[37] With the failure of appeasement, ideas about internationalization were abandoned.[38] In some respects, then, the approach of war pushed colonial liberalism into the background and had the effect of reinvigorating faith in the distinctively national nature of the colonial undertaking.[39] On the other hand, influential figures in the colonial establishment had come to accept the inevitability or desirability of some widening of international action and accountability. Both Lord Lugard and Margery Perham favoured the extension of two of the principles of the mandate system – the open door and the prohibition of military exploitation of natives – to all colonies. Margery Perham cautioned against exaggerated hopes by pointing out that the system was regulative, not creative, in its function.[40] Lord Hailey advocated an experiment with regional councils or commissions dealing with groups of colonies to facilitate consultation and coordinate policy.[41] After the war this more internationally oriented understanding of colonial responsibility increasingly eroded the traditional conception rooted in British nationalism and imperialism.

Another substantial and revealing continuity in British thought in the inter-war period is the extent to which ideas about moral responsibility remained tied to political development rather than self-government. The ideal of self-government was of course accepted as the ultimate objective of British policy but, so far as the mainstream of thinking was concerned, a much greater sense of moral commitment and emotional fervour attached to the journey than to the arrival. Independence might be inevitable, but it was far in the future and there was little inclination to hurry it along. What held attention was how much remained to be accomplished rather than such progess as had been made. Something of an exception may be made for the Left and circles within the Labour Party, though even here there was a good deal of paternalism, and independence was practically never regarded as a moral absolute. In the Indian case the promise of 'the progressive realization of responsible government', held out in August 1917 and shaped by the exigencies of the First War, had to wait until March 1942, and the exigencies of the Second, for confirmation that this meant complete independence. In the interim, progress was uneven and final intentions obscure.

It must be doubtful whether any single interpretation can catch the measure of changing and conflicting conceptions of moral responsibility over this period, especially taking into consideration the strands of pragmatism and feelings of resignation and inevitability. On one account, once the writing was on the wall, the long-standing sense of obligation came to be replaced by the politics of expediency. Michael Edwardes writes that after 1918,

> Britain's moral responsibility for the welfare of the Indian people was of no consequence, for the questions now were not concerned with what sort of government suited India, but with how and when power was to be transferred to the Indians, and with the quickest and most reasonable way of satisfying all the pressure groups as well as, if possible, the conscience of the British.[42]

There are insights here but the interpretation proceeds on the basis of a particular and older conception of Britain's moral purpose. For others, moral responsibility flowed along rather narrower channels than before, focussed as it was on the need to maintain the unity of the country in a situation of uneven political development. The first step in devolving power, the Montagu-Chelmsford constitution of 1919, had greatly intensified the tensions within the Indian Empire – the key set of tensions being between the Muslim communities and the Hindu majority. In part, the constitutional negotiations of succeeding years represented an attempt to reconcile greater autonomy with political unity.[43] Then there was the concern to fulfil obligations to particular groups – the princes, the Muslims, the tribes and the Harijans. The commitment to the princes, expressed partly in treaties going back to the days of the East India Company, was given a new moral force by the support extended by the rulers in the First World War.[44] The princes, so the argument ran, could not simply be handed over to a new government responsible to an Indian legislature.[45] Gratitude to the Muslims for their support of the war effort in 1939 and 1940 contributed to the Muslim community being given in August 1940 what has been described as a 'veto' over India's constitutional progress.[46] As Congress saw things, these were the latest strategems in the traditional policy of divide and rule. Yet for many in Britain or still in the service of the Raj, the obligations were deeply felt. Temporizing had a moral imprint.

Reflecting broadly on the material about the transfer of power two impressions recur. The first is that moral concerns appear to have receded into the background when finally the decision was taken to grant independence to India. This is not to question the sincerity of Attlee's commitment to Indian independence but to emphasize the narrowing of options and the primacy of political calculations. Faced in 1946 with the prospect of administrative collapse in India, the claims of minorities no longer held London's attention and the case for the earliest possible withdrawal of British forces proved irresistible. The government's overriding objective was to avoid an ignominious withdrawal, and, associated with this aim, to secure India's participation in the Commonwealth defence system. The determination to protect Britain's strategic interests helps to explain why so little thought was given to any continuing moral obligation to the defence of India after independence. In the crucial years from 1942 to 1947 British policy-makings were intent on maintaining, so far as possible, the existing defence nexus, not adjusting to the requirements of a post-colonial order.[47] Secondly, as self-rule for the Indian sub-continent moved from being a matter of philosophical speculation to the political drawing-board, so the focus of moral concern shifted from India to Africa.

The increased attention devoted to Britain's task in Africa can be seen as a post-war variant of the long-established preference of British policy-makers and officials for the less developed as compared with the more Westernized communities outside Europe.[48] This cultural bias now took on a continental dimension. A number of rather different considerations appear to have contributed to the redirection of moral concern. One was surely the sense of challenge associated with the 'primitiveness' of Africa. Its need for external assistance was taken to be manifest; the opportunities for constructive work almost unlimited. Britain's future in Africa appeared all the brighter when set against the disillusionment felt in some quarters with the course of events and policy in India. Charles Allen has commented that as the demands for home rule in India grew, so its attraction for those seeking a career overseas diminished.[49] In Africa, on the other hand, the time-scale was open-ended and career prospects seemed assured. In December 1917 the Labour Party memorandum on war aims put the African peoples in a special category and rejected the possibility of self-government or self-determination.[50] Twenty years later a study group of the Royal Institute of International Affairs still felt able to assert that complete independence could not be expected 'under any foreseeable conditions'.[51] On all counts, Africa's colonial future was reckoned in generations.

Both directly and indirectly, some of the ethos of the Raj found its way to Africa. Two of the great figures in the history of British colonialism in Africa had had earlier experience in India: Lord Lugard began his career as a soldier in the North West Frontier Province; Lord Hailey had been Governor of the Punjab and the United Provinces. *Tales from the Dark Continent* records the influence of family backgrounds connected with the Indian Army and the Indian Civil Service on a number of men who entered the Colonial Service and worked in Africa between the wars. Sir James Robertson, who served in various parts of Africa and became Governor-General of Nigeria, recalls that he was 'brought up to think of carrying on the tradition of going to India'.[52] Both his father and grandfather had been in India, but in the troubled conditions of the early twenties he entered the Sudan Political Service instead.

The crucial shift in British thinking about Asia and Africa was the progressive re-interpretation of the idea of trusteeship from an essentially protective and negative set of injunctions to a commitment, more potential than actual, to the processes of internal change.[53] This shift took place in a piecemeal fashion over a number of years, and its design was not shaped, and its full significance perhaps not grasped, until after the Second World War. One index of the extent of rethinking was the growing criticism, especially in the thirties, of the principles and practices of indirect rule. With respect to Nigeria, for example, complaints were voiced about the increased autocracy, exploitation and corruption of native rule, and the contempt shown on all sides for the educated African. Prodded by liberal and radical critics, official thinking slowly and hesitantly moved in the direction of a more systematic and far-reaching approach to economic and social advancement. The welfare of indigenes could not be left to the vagaries of an undirected external capitalism and a series of checks and curbs on the traditional native leadership; it was the task of the colonial administration to prise open the door to development.

This was coming to be seen as having two aspects. The first was the need for more central management of society: in place of the hope of natural growth was the idea of planned development. The second was the acceptance of the desirability of a wider involvement of the administration in the life of the society, as reflected by the stress coming to be placed on education and the concern with welfare. As yet these were little more than ideas and they met with considerable resistance within the colonial establishment. There was also the problem of resources. Colonial initiatives would require metropolitan funding, but the principle that the colonial endeavour should be self-supporting was deeply entrenched. The establishment of the Colonial Development Fund in 1929 represented a break with tradition but not more than £1 million a year was to be available for fifty territories with a population of sixty million. Moreover, the provision of funds for the development of colonial agriculture and industry was expected to promote 'commerce with or industry in the United Kingdom' and thus reduce unemployment – an exercise in moralism with a large slab of inbuilt self-interest.[54] The real watershed was the Colonial Development and Welfare Act of 1940.

Extending our gaze to 1947, and thus taking into account the impact of the war, American pressures, and the ideological perspectives of the

Attlee government (and especially those of Arthur Creech Jones, the Colonial Secretary), the extent of the change in British thinking is little short of revolutionary. The preservation of traditional patterns had been abandoned for modernity, indirect rule for active intervention, the tribal rulers for the educated elite. At least such was the doctrine; practice could hardly keep in step.

With the vantage of hindsight, certain themes emerge with respect to the nature and consequences of Britain's understanding of the tasks before it in Africa and Asia during the years between the wars. In large part it was moral conceptions, first about welfare, and later about development, which propelled Britain into a much deeper involvement in the life of its colonial dependencies than anything previously entertained. D.A. Low writes of the 'second colonial occupation of Africa'.[55] Paradoxically it can be argued that paternalism and obligation, more than economic interest or power calculations, lay behind the regulation and reorganization of indigenous affairs which some dependency theorists have seen as establishing the bases of post-colonial dominance. According to the perspective of the time, however, intervention was seen as a necessary part of the process of promoting political and economic development and it was increasingly accepted as the only responsible course.

Along the same lines, the reformulation, in the thirties, of the concept of trusteeship in terms of social welfare and economic progress can be seen to contain the seeds of the commitment to development which was to become so central a part of the Western approach to Asia and Africa after the Second World War. The moral obligation then being reshaped was cast in terms which could endure beyond the transfer of power, though as yet there was little sign of the colonial 'guilt' which was powerfully to reinforce it. The crash programmes in agriculture and public works and the provision of public services which Britain implemented in Africa in the late forties provide a case study of trusteeship understood as development. However, as D.A. Low remarks, the new directions in thinking were mostly too late to influence British rule in India.[56]

The changing content of ideas about trusteeship both reflected and contributed to a deeper change in the emotional bases of British thinking about the relationship between the metropoles and the non-European world. During the inter-war years generalized conceptions of the civilizing mission increasingly gave way to an emphasis on superior knowledge, technology and skills.[57] The cultural and racial underpinnings of Western superiority were being slimmed or at least made less visible; the new supports fashioned from the material of economics, science and political theory appeared more neutral because they dealt with things which were presumed to be transferable. Whether in fact they were substantially less Eurocentric is open to argument. The idea of mission, which suggested a natural unfolding of the non-European future in the light of the European past, was to some degree superseded by a growing commitment to empirical enquiry in Africa and Asia. Influential figures such as General Smuts, Sir Stafford Cripps and Lord Hailey drew attention to the absence of hard facts and social statistics, and their efforts bore fruit in the substantial increase during the thirties of research projects, commissions of enquiry and surveys of various kinds.[58] Lord Hailey's *An African Survey*, first published in 1938, is the pre-eminent example.[59] Partly as a result of more systematic enquiry and the findings of anthropologists such as Malinowski at the London School of Economics, racial and cultural stereotypes of the innate backwardness of African peoples became less common and less influential.

To this point our discussion of moral responsibility has proceeded at what is customarily understood as the political level. It has been concerned with political doctrines and theories, the thinking and action of political actors, and the changing political context both at home and abroad. The picture which has emerged is of an internationalism taking limited account of the interests of the non-European world, of national imperialism proving stronger than global reformism, and of the British colonial elite reformulating the tasks of trusteeship in accordance with its own distinctive experience and guided by its own moral lights. There has been little to suggest any early or substantial recasting of the imperial relationship. The custodians of empire displayed a surprising confidence in their ability to stave off new challenges and to fulfil their chosen purposes.

This picture, however, is incomplete. Beneath the political surface there were currents of doubt and anxiety. Changing values and perspectives within British society made the imperial venture appear less secure, less effective and less rewarding. This dimension is caught in the literature of the period which both expresses and reinforces a pessimism about the accomplishments and prospects of imperialism. Colonial novels of the inter-war years thus deepen our understanding of the psychology of dominance and provide a corrective to the diplomatic and archival material.[60]

The first message which emerges from the literature is a growing disillusionment about what Europe could accomplish in Africa and Asia. It is a striking commentary on our present theme that at the time when Curzon was proposing to secure British paramountcy in Persia, and the search for Indian security led the cabinet to attempt to consolidate Britain's strategic monopoly in the Middle East, E.M. Forster was reaching the conclusion that there was nothing more to be done in India: empire was a failure. A decade later, and more angrily, George Orwell wrote the same in *Burmese Days*. Thus we have counterposed a macro and a micro view of British dominance: imperialism from the perspective of geopolitical power, displaying a confidence that it could be adjusted, shored up and even extended; and imperialism viewed from within, where the representatives of different societies collided and misunderstood or exploited each other. According to this latter view, we are left in no doubt that imperialism would fall apart.

No less striking is the contrast between the official optimism about imperialism as an instrument of economic and social progress, and the conviction of many of the novelists that it was nothing of the kind. The idea that Britain could serve as a powerhouse of development and that European patterns were transferable was naive, misguided, even absurd. Evelyn Waugh satirized the liberal conviction in *Black Mischief*: native soldiers issued with boots for the first time eat them as extra rations, and a local chief sees modernity in terms of being 'refined in our cruelty to animals'. Flory in *Burmese Days* expresses Orwell's cynicism: 'we'll have wrecked the whole Burmese national culture . . . we're only rubbing our dirt on to them.' As Susanne Howe observes of the novels about India, they are a record of a great defeat. 'India could hold out the longest . . . (it was) the ultimate waste of spiritual energy.'[61] It is unnecessary to chronicle the cases in colonial fiction where Westernization is shown to be superficial, where European implants grow in strangely different ways, and where the apparently Europeanized characters are shown as fragmented and unattractive and become the subject of ridicule. There is much here of relevance to a later era. Many of the barbs of the novelists of the twenties and thirties were to be rehoned in the sixties and seventies by critics of development theory and Western ethnocentrism.

Alongside doubts about the benefits supposedly conferred by imperialism on its colonies went a questioning of what it meant for its principals. Despite the fact that the architecture of dominance remained intact, the colonial novelists of the inter-war years saw the exercise of influence in more complex terms. The directors of empire might continue to direct but they were by no means always in control. In some circumstances the indigenous client or collaborator could manipulate the patron. Thus in very different ways Orwell's U Po Kyin and Cary's Mr Johnson determined the workings of the system. U Po Kyin exploits the imperial factor to realize his own ends. He is admitted to the Club, gains promotion in the imperial service, makes large sums through bribery and, as his final triumph, is presented with an award at a durbar in Rangoon. Mr Johnson succeeds in getting Rudbeck to shoot him, thereby short-circuiting the process of British justice and robbing the gallows.

Both in the novels and in the personal and historical narratives of the period, considerable emphasis is placed on the survival of patterns of behaviour on the periphery which had become obsolete at home. The maintenance of empire is seen to be dependent upon prestige. Hence the insistence on 'the pukka Sahib code', 'an unbreakable system of taboos' (Orwell) and 'a thousand rules made to support it that are not needed in more civilized places' (Cary). The view we are led to is that the exaggerated reliance on form and ritual reflects the declining power of the metropole and the fact that its agents are less sure of themselves and their role than before. Those on the ground are caught, pincer-like, between the needs and expectations of imperialism and those of its colonial subjects. George Orwell tells the story of how, as a police officer in Burma, he was called to deal with an elephant which had gone wild. The animal was by then harmless but Orwell felt compelled to shoot it because the huge crowd expected it of him. At this moment he grasped 'the hollowness, the futility of the white man's dominion in the East. Here was I . . . seemingly the leading actor of the piece; but in reality I was only an absurd puppet pushed to and fro by the will of those yellow faces behind.'[62] John Galsworthy in *Flowering Wilderness* has his hero renounce Christianity (and his integrity as an Englishman) at pistol point but at the cost of social ostracism and personal crisis.

Partly because the system in its state of increasing fragility requires its agents to act a part, imperialism is seen as morally degenerating for the imperialists. The extent varies among characters and authors. In Paul Scott's *The Day of the Scorpion*, Hari Kumar simply observes that 'in India the English stop being unconsciously English and become consciously English.' E.M. Forster attacks the 'herd instinct' and the immediate withdrawal behind racial lines when any native question presents itself: rationality is lost and Europeans are described as 'putting aside their normal personalities and sinking themselves in their community'. More reluctantly he comes to the view that empire stands in the way of personal fulfilment: the Raj is a rock upon which the friendship of Fielding and Aziz founders. A much stronger statement comes from Orwell, perhaps because of the tension of a man who, like many of his characters, is simultaneously dominator and dominated.[63] Reflecting on his situation, Flory finds empire 'a stifling, stultifying world in which to live . . . Your whole life is a life of lies.' The key word in the lengthy passage setting out Flory's thoughts is 'poison' – empire infects and spreads. Far from developing character, as in the earlier period, empire has become morally corrosive.

More generally, the novels of the inter-war years bring out the changing political ideals of the period and suggest that imperialism is being undermined from within. The scaffolding of empire no longer holds the eye; perspective is close to the ground. The novelist's concern has moved beyond myth, the heroic and martyrdom; the actors are cut on a smaller scale. The sense of mission ordained from on high has given way to a more pragmatic recognition of jobs to be done – the maintenance of local order, the building of roads and bridges. Raw violence has been replaced by the occasional riot or feuding over admission to the Club. Joyce Cary's novels are interesting in this regard because he feeds into them some of his respect and feeling for the old pre-consular era (especially Bewsher in *An American Visitor*), yet he is in no doubt that imperial rule must make a more positive contribution to colonial development.[64] The central point which emerges, then, is that imperialism as an idea and ideal by which to set one's sights was rapidly losing ground; faith was crumbling in the face of the challenge of liberalism.

The final word must come from Paul Scott, expressed through the character of the historian, Guy Perron, in *A Division of the Spoils*:

> For at least a hundred years, India has formed part of England's idea about herself and for the same period India has been forced into a position of being a reflection of that idea. Up to say 1900 the part India played in our idea about ourselves was the part played by anything we possessed which we believed it was right to possess (like a special relationship with God). Since 1900, certainly since 1918, the reverse has obtained. The part played since then by India in the idea of Englishness has been that of something we feel it does us no credit to have. Our idea about ourselves will now not accommodate any idea about India except the idea of returning it to the Indians in order to prove that we are English and have demonstrably English ideas. . . . Getting rid of India will cause us at home no qualm of conscience because it will be like getting rid of what is no longer reflected in any mirror of ourselves.[65]

Six

Economic Interest II

Interest in the economic relationship between Britain and the under-developed world during the inter-war years has been relatively restricted. For the most part, the material has been the preserve of imperial historians. Recently it has attracted study by some dependency theorists, though their concern has been largely with consequences rather than intentions. Students of international relations have paid much less attention to the subject than they have to the economics of Britain's participation in the second expansion or America's involvement in the Third World since the Second World War. It may be that interest is limited because academic contention has been so much less sharp than with respect to the other periods. Indeed, among specialist opinion there has been substantial agreement about the main lines of thinking and perception.

An explanation of the extent of scholarly agreement in an area characterized by so little common ground between various schools of thought would surely begin by acknowledging the influence of Sir Keith Hancock's magisterial *Survey of British Commonwealth Affairs, Problems of Economic Policy, 1918–1939*, which was published in two parts in 1940 and 1942.[1] In a recent assessment of the contribution of this work, David Fieldhouse has concluded that Hancock's analysis has never been seriously challenged.[2] That Hancock's work was not narrowly or technically economic but set in a larger political and normative context, and that it was concerned to outline broad patterns of thought more than to trace the course of particular policies, makes it of especial value to scholars interested in the contemporary relationship between the West and the Third World, and the historical processes by which that relationship was set. It is therefore ironic to reflect that while the *Survey* succeeded in establishing categories and themes which won wide acceptance, by laying out the field so definitively, it may unwittingly have contributed to the neglect of wider interest in the perceptions and problems of the period.

In the inter-war years economic issues bulked large in British thinking about overseas affairs, including imperial affairs. This economic orientation is one of the distinctive features of Britain's approach to Asia and Africa in the decades between the wars. During the period of expansion, considerations of power and prestige most often attracted the attention of statesmen and played the largest part in shaping their general appreciations of the overseas world. Even if India constituted the economic bedrock upon which so much else was built, the understanding of India's economic importance was of the most general nature and it was often implicit rather than explicit. When we turn to the case of the United States after the Second World War, we find that the dominant image of Asia and Africa was political; as will be argued in later chapters, America's approach was shaped in large part by doctrines of power and strategy.[3] Between the wars, however, economic interests were constantly in the foreground. This was particularly true of Great Britain because of the changed position of her domestic economy. In the eyes of the British policy-makers, America was the first priority, followed in most years by Europe, but concern extended across the globe. Politicians ignored trade and finance at their peril; overseas economic conferences attracted a blaze of publicity; diaries, memoirs and the public record attest to the extent to which even the imperial system was discussed and analysed in economic terms.

In several respects the attention directed to imperial economic affairs represented less of a break with tradition than might on the surface be imagined. For one thing, excepting India, Asia and Africa did not figure prominently in British conceptions of the imperial economic system. The Dominions were held to be of the greatest importance, and the problems and possibilities of integrating their interests with those of the metropole played the largest part in setting the course of British thinking. India came next in priority, though discussion was more specialized and the number of discussants more restricted. The colonial Empire was a poor third. In Ian Drummond's judgement, British policy-makers 'worried very little about the dependent empire'.[4] Certainly it did not feature significantly in the general appraisal of tariffs and trading patterns, as at the various imperial conferences (most notably the Imperial Economic Conference in Ottawa in 1932). Even in some circles which might have been expected to stress the interests and potentialities of the colonies, the evidence suggests a lukewarm approach. Writing in 1938, W.M. Macmillan lamented the neglect of the colonial world in the deliberations of the Round Table Group. He went on: 'It is under such guidance that for most of our national leaders co-operation with the Dominions has now become the chief end of political wisdom, the place of the dependent Empire in the new scheme of things falling more and more completely out of sight.'[5]

Nor should the general economic orientation to overseas affairs be taken to indicate sustained and systematic analysis of economic issues. Doctrine was often uncertain, motives mixed and the need for reliable information at times disregarded. With the vantage of hindsight, it is easy to point to the inadequacies of economic analysis, and the hesitancy and superficiality about concepts and policies.[6] Yet uncertainty and elements of confusion could hardly have been avoided in a period in which the old orthodoxies of international trade were crumbling, and their replacements in the form of protectionism and self-sufficiency were very largely outside the experience of British policy-makers.[7] It must also be said that what purported to be economic evaluation or prescription was sometimes nothing of the kind; political reasoning masqueraded as economic analysis or brandished economic slogans. At various points in the chapter the theme will be developed that arguments about tariffs or colonial development were often as much a means of mobilizing party and electorate as they were directed to securing economic ends. Many of the societies which advocated imperial economic planning and development were primarily influenced by the mystique of empire.[8] Lord Beaverbrook's crusade for empire free trade in the early thirties is better understood in terms of political idealism than economic calculation. Beaverbrook was an imperialist, and A.J.P. Taylor tells us that at bottom his conception of imperial unity was sentimental.[9] He made up the Empire Crusade as he went along, broadening his imperial conception from the Dominions to the colonies, in which initially he had little interest.[10]

Reviewing the period down to the First World War, it has been argued that information about the economic conditions and potential of the underdeveloped world was often inadequate, and that not much attempt was made to collate the material which was available.[11] To a considerable extent this characterization holds good for the inter-war years, although the situation improved in the mid- and late thirties. Writing of the early thirties, B.R. Tomlinson observes that the degree of ignorance in official circles about the Indian economy was 'horrendous'.[12] Sir Philip Cunliffe-Lister (later Lord Swinton) records that on his appointment as Secretary of State for the Colonies in November 1931 there was an extraordinary absence of detailed knowledge about the economics of the colonies. His account is worth quoting at length.

> No one had ever attempted to make an economic survey of the Colonies; there was no Economic Department. In general terms, of course, it was known what the different Colonies produced; but no serious attempt had been made to assess their total production of different commodities or the relation of Colonial capacity and production to world production and consumption. There were no records or statistics of the amount which different countries took from the Colonies, the relative importance of these

markets, or where the imports to the Colonies came from. There was no assessment of the actualities much less the potentialities of mutual trade. Commodities had never been considered as commodities . . . Knowledge of market conditions and trends was wholly lacking.[13]

More generally it has been argued that remarkably little economic information was transferred from one part of the Empire to another, and that when considered in the context of the international economy the parochialism of colonial policy was more striking still.[14] There is thus a strong presumption that, more often than not, the direction and drift of economic thinking preceded the collection and collation of appropriate data.

Following the lines of our analysis of the period 1870 to 1914, this chapter is concerned to trace the evolution of Britain's conceptions of its economic relationship with Asia and Africa down to the Second World War. As before, the key signposts are the benefits Britain might obtain, the contribution it could make to colonial development, and the relationship between the two. Interest is fixed on the main streams of thought and perception, not the evolution of specific policies or the theoretical disputation of professional economists. Emphasis is placed on those ideas and images of significance for international politics. British thinking about South Africa – which was extensive – is considered only insofar as it was relevant to the remainder of the continent. Our enquiry proceeds by ordering the material into three blocks or sets of images, which form separate sections. The first considers the place of Asia and Africa in the imperial and international economic systems. It traces the movement from free trade to protectionism and thus sets the context for the following sections. The second takes as its theme the tropical Empire as a support system for the British economy, and considers in more detail the benefits it was thought the metropole could obtain. The third section focusses on the economic aspects of the imperial trust and explores the changing concepts of colonial development.

(i) *Enclosing The Imperial Economic Order*

In large part the inter-war years can be interpreted in terms of a struggle between two competing conceptions of how Britain's overseas economic interests could be best advanced: the one, a vision of an interlocking and inwardly oriented imperial system, and the other, a commitment to the 'Great Commercial Republic of the World'. The former saw Britain's relationship with the Empire as natural, and advocated a system of imperial preferences which would build on the links rooted in history and sentiment and extend the ties of capital and currency. The latter adhered to the tradition of free trade and put its faith in the open economy and the largest measure of *laissez-faire*. Until 1930, support for imperial initiatives was limited. The 1932 Imperial Economic Conference in Ottawa marked the high point of the pull of imperial economy, though even then its hold owed much to the push of circumstances at home and abroad. Over the next few years the difficulties and disappointments of making empire the cornerstone of Britain's overseas fortunes led to reassessment and partial retreat. It is within this framework that the more sharply focussed ideas about the economics of Asia and Africa – what kinds of development should be encouraged and what kinds of benefits expected – must be considered.

The conception of an imperial future drew its inspiration from Joseph Chamberlain, and the core of its economic doctrine from the Birmingham school. It was carried forward by Lord Milner and the economist W.A.S. Hewins. L.S. Amery became its principal advocate between the wars. According to this view, Britain faced growing difficulties in the world economy both because of declining industrial growth at home and because foreign states erected barriers against British commerce and allowed themselves to be guided by considerations of narrow self-interest. Unable to retreat into national self-sufficiency, but unduly buffeted in the global arena, it was therefore necessary to establish an intermediate economic order. This order was to be anchored in Britain's relations with the Dominions. Its essential components were 'men, money and markets' – a phrase coined by Amery and launched by Stanley Bruce in 1923, which provided the categories for Hancock's analysis of the imperial economic system.[15] In short, through migration, the export of capital and the establishment of tariff preferences, Britain was to promote the flow of resources from the Empire and secure sheltered markets for her manufactures.

India figured only marginally in this scheme of thinking, in part perhaps because the 'men' element in the Amery trilogy did not apply to India, which was hardly a likely destination for surplus Britons. In any case, it quickly became apparent that as far as India was concerned, there were more costs than benefits in a general system of preference. What was in India's interests was not necessarily in Britain's interests and very often the two were in conflict. Moreover, in 1919 an understanding was established that Britain should not interfere in Indian fiscal affairs – the fiscal autonomy convention. Thenceforward the Government of India, not the United Kingdom government, effectively became the arbiter on matters relating to taxes and tariffs.[16] To a considerable extent, therefore, it was accepted that India had to be left to follow its own course, which was one of increasing protectionism.[17] The situation with respect to the colonial

Empire was more encouraging. With the exception of those territories within the Congo Basin, which were debarred from granting fiscal preferences by international convention, the colonies could be required to conform to an Empire economic design. As recognition grew of the distinctiveness of Dominion interests, and the fact that Dominion politicians could not be expected – much less forced – to subscribe to a common economic blueprint, the assumed pliability of the colonies became more important.[18] In addition, the problem of indigenous industrialization, which complicated India's situation, was not seen to be relevant. The colonies would be suppliers of resources and primary products, and take manufactures in return.[19] The complementarity of metropolitan and overseas imperial interests was at times argued but more often assumed. It was also forgotten when, according to the most self-interested formulation of the imperial economy, the colonies were held to be imperial estates.[20]

For many of its advocates and supporters the broad conception was as much political as economic. A few like Cunliffe-Lister might examine the ledger book with the dispassionate eye of the accountant, but for men such as Amery and Hewins empire was a good in itself as well as a system of mutual economic advantage. The words 'dream', 'ideal' and 'vision' recur both in writing at the time and in subsequent analysis. In his introduction to a publication of the Empire Economic Union, Amery argued that the conception of empire economic unity 'is one that appeals equally to our practical sense and to our instinctive idealism'.[21] On the Labour side, J.H. Thomas took much the same approach. On his appointment as Secretary of State for the Colonies in 1924, his first words to his staff at the Colonial Office were reported to be: 'I've been sent here to see that there's no mucking about with the British Empire'.[22]

The commitment to the 'Great Commercial Republic' was established orthodoxy until the 1930s. It was stronger than the case for an imperial economy in doctrinal terms, and had the support of most economists.[23] All the old arguments were rehearsed about the advantages of the free movement of capital and labour, open markets and the minimal role of the state. Despite the fact that for several decades Britain's share of the world trade had been falling and in the thirties international specialization diminished, tradition was on the side of free trade. It had been the dominant ideology since the middle of the nineteenth century, and part of its continuing hold lay in its association with Britain's ascent to economic pre-eminence. It lost its traditional political mouthpiece with the decline of the Liberal Party but it gained a new ally with the rise of the Labour Party, which in general supported free trade.

The need for a global outlook was ranged against the ideal of empire self-sufficiency and the immediate campaign for the extension of imperial preference. It was necessary to weigh the opportunity costs of such provincialism, bearing in mind that economic conditions would sooner or later return to normal. Above all, account had to be taken of the damage likely to be done to foreign markets, which were still of great importance to Britain and to other empire countries as well.[24] Arguments from the perspective of Britain's interests meshed with others from the perspective of colonial interests. Lugard left no doubt about his conviction that the obligations of imperial trusteeship were best fulfilled by adherence to the principles of equal access and maximum competition. In 1916 when economic liberalism was eroded by the pressures of the war, Lugard declared his belief 'that the very foundations of the British Empire rest on its tolerance and the "Open Door" which it has always afforded to all the world.'[25] Later he dismissed the mercantilist thinking of the Empire Resources Committee with the observation that 'these schemes of interference imposed by a bureaucracy unhinged by its exercises of power are too opposed to the genius of the English people to last.'[26]

It is unnecessary here to provide an historical account of the struggle between these two conceptions in the years between the wars. The process which led to the adoption of a general tariff coupled with imperial preference in 1931 and 1932, and the subsequent measure of disillusionment, have been fully reviewed in the literature, and the main lines are clear.[27] A number of points require spelling out, however, because they bear directly on the way Asia and Africa were perceived and the nature of the images held. In retrospect, and in the light of the difficulties and changing directions of Britain's overseas trade, it is surprising what limited headway was made by those who argued for an imperial economy. Generally India and the colonies remained in the economic background. Comparatively few individuals or groups considered it feasible, or were prepared, to countenance approaches designed to extract the maximum economic advantage from India and the dependent Empire. The constraints of liberalism were congruent with the more hard-nosed preferences of the business sector. With a few exceptions, manufacturing and industrial interests until the depression adhered to the belief that a multilateral trading system offered the brightest prospects. Hancock's memorable summing up over forty years ago remains undisputed today: 'The walls of the free trade citadel had been breached here and there, but they still stood impressively throughout the nineteen-twenties.'[28]

In the presentation of their case, the advocates of an imperial economy made maximum use of various developments at home and abroad which might propel thinking in new directions. The most important were the requirements of prosecuting the war, the need to combat domestic unemployment and the growth of foreign tariffs. None directly related to Asia and Africa. Yet it was these issues which visionaries were able to exploit to gain a wider hearing and more political clout than otherwise would have been possible. In his section entitled 'Economics of Siege', Hancock analyses the war-time mentality and the way it provided fertile soil for the growth of heady schemes of imperial self-sufficiency and colonial exploitation. For the most part such ideas died back after the war.[29] Nearly all scholars have stressed the significance of high unemployment in Britain to the increased attention directed to imperial preference and colonial development.[30] With unemployment acute in 1921 and 1922, and approximately one million people out of work each year from 1925 to 1929, politicians had to take great care before rejecting imperial remedies irrespective of assessments about their economic viability. The increase in tariffs, especially manufacturing tariffs, throughout the world in the twenties provided valuable ammunition for those who called for a change of direction. The argument was now more persuasive that internationalism was dead and that Britain trailed the field. It proved difficult to rebut when in 1930 the Smoot Hawley Tariff Act became United States law, thus bringing an end to the short-lived tariff truce of the late 1920s.

In the cut-and-thrust of the political debate, much of the thinking with respect to the colonial world – and indeed the Empire as a whole – did not run deep. Very often Africa and Asia figured by default. The assumption was that empire development and trade might fill the gap opened by developments in other quarters. The colonies could write off the British war debt; generate employment at home; help make up the leeway caused by foreign tariffs. At various points, also, issues of imperial economics became intertwined with the struggle between political parties and conflicts about the Conservative leadership. Thus in the 1923 general election, Baldwin's commitment to imperial preference was in part influenced by his belief that it was sound electoral strategy. It was necessary to pre-empt Lloyd George, who was supposedly thinking along similar lines. Reportedly the cabinet favoured a rapid election, reasoning that 'the more the country understood the policy the less it was thought they would like it.'[31] The electoral rebuff suffered led Baldwin to change course on empire preference, convinced that the electorate remained committed to free trade. Beaverbrook's subsequent Empire Crusade was an attempt to put the Conservative Party back on the preference rails, but it may also have been influenced by his desire to topple Baldwin.

The great depression of 1930–32 dramatically changed the environment of British economic thinking. Business opinion, even in those sectors such as shipping and banking which had remained committed to free trade throughout the twenties, agitated for change. In 1930 the General Council of the Federation of British Industries came out in favour of industrial protection and imperial preference. The general

public had become more empire-minded, partly as a result of propaganda campaigns by various imperial societies and Beaverbrook's
Empire Crusade. Pressure from the Dominions was also important.
Dominion ministers were highly critical of Britain's agricultural free
trade. The British market held out the prospect of substantial gains
for Canada, Australia and New Zealand – and it was difficult to brush
this aside when London had no alternative anti-depression strategy to
offer. Within the government, the current of thinking moved correspondingly. At the turn of the decade Ramsay MacDonald commented: 'The day is coming when we may have to give up orthodox
free trade as we inherited it from our fathers.'[32] In 1931 the national
government was returned on a platform of considering every remedy,
'not excluding tariffs'. The need for a new approach to Britain's
economic ills was now widely accepted. Against this background,
Hancock writes of the move from free trade to imperial preference in
1931 and 1932 as 'an almost reflex action'.[33] Drummond argues that at
Ottawa, policy emerged *de facto*: British delegates sailed off to
Quebec with an open brief; they had a long list of questions but few
answers.[34] While the significance of the Ottawa conference is undoubted, it is scarcely less clear that Britain's image of an imperial
economy had limited content. Conceptions of what could be accomplished through imperial preference were ragged, and co-existed along
with very different ideas about overseas economic relations. Walter
Runciman, President of the Board of Trade, for example, planned to
use the Ottawa agreements as a launching-pad for a programme of
trade bargaining with foreign countries.[35]

The assessment that thinking in 1931 and 1932 about imperial
preference was often loose, and bore the marks of what Hancock called
'the crisis atmosphere',[36] derives support from the way in which the
British government turned back on Ottawa from about 1935. Increasingly, attention was directed to the home economy at the expense
of overseas trade and investment.[37] More important in the present
context is the movement towards multilateralism which occurred in
the late thirties. A number of factors were relevant here. There was
the difficulty of moving from rhetoric to implementation, which was
soon evidenced in the bargaining over specific commodities. It was
equally apparent that in many instances, empire markets would need
to be more substantially supplemented by foreign markets than had
been previously conceded. In others, imperial preference came to be
seen as beside the point. There was also the need to adjust economic
policies in the light of wider political interests, especially with respect
to the maintenance of friendly relations with the United States.[38]
While in some measure the retreat from Ottawa can be understood in
terms of developments occurring and evidence becoming available
after 1932, it nonetheless indicates the extent to which economic

analysis was mixed with political pragmatism and imperial romance in the years 1930 to 1932.

(ii) *The Tropical Empire as a Support System*

In the inter-war years British thinking about Africa and Asia was preoccupied with those parts within the Empire. The China market, it is true, remained a matter of concern: for instance, in August 1930 the Labour government appointed a committee to investigate the trade situation; but little emerged by way of recommendation or prospect.[39] Some consideration was also given to developments within the other colonial Empires, especially what the Dutch were doing in the East Indies. Overall, however, much less interest was taken in Africa and Asia as a whole than during the period before the war. Attention was more concentrated, it might be argued, because the ground had to be more carefully cultivated if worthwhile returns were to be obtained. The day was over when easy pickings could be had by scratching the surface everywhere.

This section considers in more detail the ideas and images of those who believed that the British economy could be shored up by an increasing reliance on, and development of, the economic potentialities of the Empire. Imperial visionaries and the various societies which campaigned for empire preference obviously come within this category, but it also includes at a number of points a broad range of politicians, public figures and business interests. In many cases the background to thinking was the assumption that Britain was in economic decline. She had lost her old predominance in international trade; industry was no longer competitive with foreign rivals; unemployment was rife. In a letter to the Prime Minister in November 1925, Hewins wrote that before the war there had been a steady decline in the relative position of Great Britain, that the war had temporarily suspended the operation of more permanent factors, but that these had been resumed since the war. He went on: 'We cannot expect to restore to Great Britain, standing alone, the predominance she enjoyed in the markets of the world years ago. But we may, by an Empire policy, hope to give an increasingly dominant position to the trade of the British Empire.'[40]

Here, then, was the first prong of attack. The loss of overseas markets, especially in Europe and Latin America, was plain for all to see. Given the dependence on export production of much of British industry, the solution lay in finding new external outlets. One avenue was the colonial Empire, where Britain could establish easier and more secure entry than elsewhere. A report on the colonial Empire, prepared in 1931 by the Research Committee of the Empire Economic

Union, drew attention to its 'vast importance' and to 'potentialities only dimly realised at the moment'.[41] Where possible, there should be reciprocal imperial preference. Where this was ruled out by treaty restrictions, unreciprocated preferences made sense because the greater prosperity of the territories would automatically reflect itself in a large increase in the purchase of British goods.[42] A particular problem was posed by the rapid penetration of colonial markets by cheap Japanese textiles. Here the solution would have to be quotas. The decision was taken in 1934, although only after considerable debate, and it was never implemented across the board. According to Cunliffe-Lister the decision was welcomed by the colonies, but there is no evidence that this was so.[43] It is in fact unlikely that at a time of hardship they were keen to pay more for textiles in the interests of British manufacturers. Runciman asserted later that the quotas 'had saved Nigeria for the Lancashire trade'.[44] It could also be argued that they helped alert Japan to the economic advantages of colonies and strengthened the hand of those who advocated that Japan establish an empire of her own.[45]

The second prong of attack was to stress the importance of the colonial world as a supplier of resources and raw materials for British industry. Hancock has charted the growth and decline of the movement to make the Empire independent of foreign imports during and after the First World War.[46] At the forefront of the propaganda campaign was an unofficial body established in 1916, the Empire Resources Development Committee, whose proposals were specifically directed to the colonial territories because they were seen as unlikely to secure self-government and more open to political direction.[47] After grandiose hopes for empire self-sufficiency faded, imperial advocates continued to emphasize the advantage of colonial over foreign supplies. Many remained unconvinced. William Lever, for example, had no doubt about the importance of the tropical world both as a source of supply and as a market for low-grade soaps, but his vision was not contained by the geography of empire. Obstructed by colonial officials in West Africa, he showed no hesitation in negotiating concessions in the Congo.[48] There were times, however, when business and political opinion was persuaded of the advantages of empire production. A clear illustration is provided by the support given to empire cotton production in the early twenties, as a consequence of the difficulties then being experienced in obtaining American supplies. Industry in Lancashire, including the cotton unions, took a keen interest in the Gezira scheme in the Sudan, and in the prospects in Kenya and Uganda.[49] It was partly on this basis that substantial loans were extended to the Sudan and to Kenya and Uganda.[50] At least in the short term, all three territories were regarded as sources of supply more than as markets for British goods.

Empire production was seen to have an additional advantage, in that in certain cases it related directly to the problem of Britain's adverse balance of payments with the United States. In view of the American debt, Amery argued to the cabinet in 1925, it was necessary to develop sources of supply from the colonial Empire.[51] The production of tobacco and cotton in Africa meant that imports from America would be reduced, thus saving scarce dollars. Of immediate significance were the dollars brought in by Malaya's exports of tin and rubber to the United States. Between the wars these were of the same order as the entire exports from Great Britain to the United States. The result was that Malaya was justifiably regarded as a 'dollar arsenal'.[52]

The development of colonial production of minerals and vegetable resources led to state involvement, both imperial and local, in schemes for restricted output and organized marketing which went beyond the traditionally accepted role of government in the market-place. The first experiments took place in the twenties, most notably the preferential export duty on West African palm kernels and the Stevenson plan for rubber restriction in Malaya. These attempts to lift commodity prices through political means were largely unsuccessful.[53] The slump in exports and prices of primary products at the end of the decade led to more extensive and ambitious schemes for controlling commodity production, and the beginning of a more or less systematic development of marketing regulation aimed at securing high prices and stable demand. Collaboration with the Dutch in the East Indies produced international commodity agreements with respect to tin and rubber, which hinged on output limitations. Others were negotiated for sugar and tea.[54] In Africa the growth of interest in orderly marketing was reflected in the introduction of measures with regard to government quality control, licensing of traders, and production quotas and zoning arrangements.[55] These initiatives are of longer-term significance because they pointed the way to some of the key features of commodity politics in Africa and Asia after the Second World War. The international commodity agreements of the thirties provided a precedent for Third World attempts in the sixties and seventies to maximize economic returns and derive political leverage through the establishment of mineral and food cartels. Interest in orderly marketing led to the development of marketing boards during and after the war, which later became a general and permanent feature of the development strategy of the independent states.

More immediately relevant for our purposes is the thinking which lay behind policies of commodity control. Despite elements of similarity with some of the earlier conceptions of imperial visionaries, for the most part thought developed in response to the crisis conditions caused by glut and depressed prices.[56] All parties involved had some stake in a recovery of export earnings. The British government was concerned that the colonies should not become a burden on the imperial exchequer, and in the case of Malaya there was the interest in American dollars. The colonial governments needed local revenues and were fearful of civil disorder resulting from labour reductions in the plantation industry and the squeeze on indigenous producers. Even consumers had a longer-term interest in rationalization as a stable price was preferred to a wildly fluctuating one.[57] Drummond is therefore right to emphasize the mixed motives which lay behind all the plans for commodity control.[58] Clearly, commodity management cannot simply be attributed to a narrow preoccupation with self-interest on the part of the metropoles, regardless of the consequences on other parties.

With respect to investment, the colonial Empire was seen to occupy a somewhat special position. For a variety of historical and institutional reasons, capital tended to flow more readily within the Empire than to foreign countries. In the view of advocates of imperial economic unity, this was something to be built on. The Empire Economic Union, for example, thought preferential inducements to the flow of capital into the Empire might be made to play an important part in a general imperial policy.[59] A central consideration was that investment in the colonial Empire was more likely to result in the purchase of British goods and equipment and could more readily be steered in this direction. To some degree, official thinking moved along similar lines. Examining the record of the twenties and thirties, Hancock observes an increasing governmental concern with the location of British investment and a desire for its proceeds to be spent on the products of British industry.[60]

The latter point is illustrated by the background to the loans and grants made to African colonies for developmental purposes in the 1920s.[61] In large part their political attraction lay in their presumed capacity to generate exports of capital goods and thus increase employment at home. Hence they were promoted by imperial lobbyists as a weapon in the battle against unemployment; they were resisted by the Treasury on the ground that this was wishful thinking. The Colonial Office was caught in the middle, profoundly uneasy because it feared that assistance on this basis was likely to skew development to suit the interests of the metropole regardless of colonial needs. At the political level, thinking was often superficial and heavily influenced by electoral calculations. In the early and mid-twenties much of the appeal of railway construction in Kenya and Uganda was tied to the hope that jobs would be created at home. It was the same a few years later with perspectives towards the Colonial Development Act. The mood of the time was summed up by the approach of J.H. Thomas, the Minister of Employment in the Labour government. According to his biographer: 'The projects that seethed in his mind ranged from a bridge over the Zambesi river to a traffic circus at the Elephant and Castle.'[62]

In each of the areas we have considered there was less optimism about the prospects in India than about those in the colonial Empire. Britain's colonial future had barely been charted, whereas in India the problems and constraints of extracting economic advantage were increasingly severe and increasingly apparent. This was because the two economies were less complementary than before and because it was accepted that there were strict limits to the extent to which India could be pushed to serve imperial economic purposes. Tomlinson has argued that the benefits which Britain could obtain from her rule in India were diminishing and that the costs were increasing.[63] This is probably how most contemporaries assessed the situation. Essentially Britain's approach was defensive: how to preserve, so far as possible, its most important interests. These were the maintenance of the Indian Army at minimum cost to Britain, the honouring of the sterling debt and the payment of the 'home charge' (the salaries, pensions and training costs of those in the service of the Raj). As a result, the central issue of thinking and policy was public finance.[64]

On the general question of the extent to which the currency arrangements of the Empire were seen as a means of improving Britain's fiscal position, the evidence is unclear and incomplete. The considerations were complex, and understanding at the time was limited. The sterling area emerged more or less by accident and was not controlled by London. Drummond makes the point that although Britain benefitted when sterling balances increased, little is known of the role of British authorities, much less their motives.[65] Elsewhere the same writer concludes that exploitation, or something like it, appears in connection with colonial currency boards, though 'nobody yet knows whether anybody planned things this way.'[66] Overall it seems safe to assume that the management and manipulation of currency did not feature significantly in British thinking about the advantages of empire.

Co-existing with the belief in the economic potentialities of the tropical Empire was some recognition of attendant limits and risks. Quite apart from the opportunity costs stressed by free traders, occasional elements of doubt arose directly from the imperial undertaking itself. Tomlinson writes of a concern that the economic weakness of the periphery might pull down the centre – as was the case with respect to India in the thirties.[67] During the financial crisis of 1931, the British government feared that a falling rupee and the possibilities of India's default on her sterling debt could endanger the pound and the Empire's financial reputation.[68] There was also the worry that if Britain attempted to push its economic interests too strenuously, such action could be counter-productive economically and put the political structure at risk. Account had to be taken of the possibility of civil unrest and organized retaliation. In India there was the rise of the civil disobedience movement and the boycott of British goods in the early thirties under Congress leadership. It had to be admitted there was a limit to how far trade could proceed on a basis of coercion. Lancashire's attempt to prevent the raising of Indian cotton duties in 1930 met with the argument by the Viceroy that: 'There is a strong underlying desire among Indians today for protection, and if we starve it altogether we shall create a dangerous political situation.'[69] Towards the end of the period, and looking further ahead, some commercial interests sounded notes of pessimism. What future could British firms expect on the Indian sub-continent? Was it not inevitable that the Ceylonese, for example, would take more control of the island's resources?[70] Such doubts grew stronger and more persistent during the course of the war.

(iii) *The Imperial Trust and Colonial Development*

Alongside neo-mercantilist approaches to the colonial relationship was a body of thought concerned not so much with the benefits to be derived by the metropole as with safeguarding and advancing the interests of the colonies. Although most individuals and groups accepted in principle that both sides should gain from economic development and exchange, as we have seen, by no means all were prepared to take too seriously the interests of African and Asian societies. Here we are concerned primarily with those who did. Compared with the years before the First World War, much more thought was given to the economic aspects of imperial trusteeship and the obligations it imposed. In the thirties particularly, ideas about colonial development became sharper and had more content.

The most important area of scrutiny and rethinking concerned the assumption handed down from the nineteenth century that the growth of trade and commerce between Britain and the underdeveloped world would prove mutually beneficial. There had always been dissenters on the Left, but with certain modifications the general proposition had been widely accepted and was easily inherited. The orthodox doctrine was that of free trade, the argument being that through the open economy and free competition, international specialization would maximize returns for all.[71] Amery's alternative conception, inherited from Chamberlain (see p. 122) but with a rider about the promotion of the interests of the periphery, predicated the complementarity of

Britain's need for the outlets for manufactures and equipment and the colonies' requirement for inputs to develop their agricultural and mineral potential. Despite the differences between the two approaches, both envisaged the future of the underdeveloped world largely in non-industrial terms,[72] and neither was much concerned with the particular conflicts and problems arising from the economic penetration of traditional societies. These became more pressing and more apparent in the years between the wars.

Even in the twenties some doubts were expressed that the open economy might not necessarily promote the best interests of the colonial society. Lillian Knowles, while generally optimistic, drew attention to the difficulties arising from the encroachments on native land, the impermanence of the planter and the importation of foreign labour.[73] Sterner critics worried about the trend towards monopoly in expatriate commerce, and the exploitation of native labour. In general, however, those most concerned with the interests of the indigenes continued to place their faith in the open economy, even if – and to some extent because – the rate of economic change was likely to be slower than under a system of state direction. Rapid economic progress could all too easily lead to the disintegration of the traditional society. This was a key consideration in Lugard's thinking. Moreover, proposals by men like Milner and Amery for greater involvement by the imperial government and more centralized planning were seen to carry the risk that colonial interests might be subordinated to those of the metropole. The Colonial Office was usually suspicious of such approaches, and sometimes hostile.[74] The small lobby concerned with native rights was similarly critical. A related concern was that some schemes for colonial development and assistance were directed to rich colonies, like Ceylon, which could contribute to the imperial economy, not to those which were poor.[75]

The erosion of the preference for the open economy began in earnest in the 1930s. The dislocation of the international trading system and the dramatic fall in the price of primary products reduced the credibility of the traditional reliance on market forces. At the same time pressure was mounting for a more positive and expansive interpretation of the trusteeship ideal.[76] Hesitantly and unevenly ideas emerged that, much more than in the past, the state would have to intervene in colonial economic life. Tariffs, import quotas and marketing mechanisms might have a constructive part to play. Colonial development could no longer be left simply to local initiative and private enterprise. In such ways the ground was prepared for an enlarged role for the imperial centre and the colonial state.

With respect to India, thinking about the role of market forces and that of government involved somewhat different considerations. For one thing, the special position of the Government of India in relation

to the British government meant that Britain's capacity to direct
India's economic course was much less than was the case with respect
to the colonies. Further, India had already achieved significant
industrialization and its fuller development was accepted as being
dependent upon some measure of protection. This thinking lay
behind the establishment of a Tariff Board in 1923, empowered to
recommend protective tariffs for a limited period in the case of
industries which were likely to be viable in the longer term without
them.[77] Thenceforth protectionism developed on a broader basis. On
the general question of the role of the state in economic affairs, there
was something of a disjunction between thinking and practice.
Government influence and control over the economy increased substantially during the inter-war years. Yet much official thinking clung
to the ideal of the free market. Theoretical arguments in defence of
laissez-faire were supported by the political consideration that it
enabled the government to keep a low profile.[78] Writing in 1929, Vera
Anstey cautioned against exaggerating the power of government,
though she conceded that in India the part played by the government
in economic life was necessarily greater than in most other countries.[79]
A few adopted a radically different position. Sir George Schuster, the
Finance Member of the Government of India in the early thirties,
argued for much more vigorous economic planning at the centre, and
even raised the possibility of a five year plan.[80] However, the
expansion of government action which occurred was mainly a consequence of the war and changes in the internal economy resulting
from the disturbed conditions of the inter-war years.[81]

There can be no doubt that the development ideal was stronger and
more compelling with respect to the colonial world than with respect
to India. In the latter case it was essentially a matter of holding the
ring: uncertainties about the time-scale, the position of the Indian
Government and the strictly limited means compared with the
magnitude of the problem, all combined to focus thinking on short-
term and circumscribed objectives. B.R. Tomlinson has argued that
on financial matters Britain's interest was neither positive nor
dynamic.[82] In the judgement of another historian, the metropole 'only
troubled itself very late and rather feebly about agriculture'.[83] It was
thus in regard to the colonial territories that awareness grew that not
all forms of development were necessarily in the interests of the
indigenous people, and that reliance on market forces was no longer a
sufficient basis of approach. Yet as A.G. Hopkins has emphasized in
his study of West Africa, this awareness did not generate any coherent
body of opinion about how to proceed. On the ground, colonial
administrations, far from imposing themselves on events, tended to
respond to concrete issues as they arose.[84] Keeping Hopkins' assessment in mind, it is now necessary to place the ideas and responses of

policy-makers in the broader context of approaches to African and Asian development – what was required, how it might be provided, and the kind of society envisaged.

The first need, it was recognized, was overseas capital. It was held that the largest part would have to come from private enterprise and that this would ensure its most efficient utilization. Some were concerned about the risk of exploitation and were anxious to devise means by which foreign capital could be kept under control.[85] Leonard Barnes, for example, thought a solution might be found in the establishment of an International Board of Colonial Investment under the aegis of the League of Nations.[86] Herbert Frankel pointed out that too much capital from abroad led to a gap between capital equipment and the customary means of production and consumption, which could have undesirable effects on development.[87] Except with respect to mining ventures, however, this was seldom a problem in these years. Instead, the problem was how to increase the flow of capital from abroad.

From the start it had been accepted that the state would have to shoulder the largest responsibility for the establishment of a transport and communication system. In general, private enterprise could not anticipate returns in a reasonable period of time. But once a framework for commercial activity had been established, private enterprise could be expected to carry forward the processes of development, and it would do so in a natural and non-hurried manner.[88] As far as the Colonial Office was concerned, the model for development was the West African experience.[89] Various factors, however, led to some modification of this ideal and mounting pressure for more state involvement and a system of imperial funding. The flow of overseas capital sharply diminished and the rates of interest increased; local revenues were cut as a result of the fall in price of primary products; then there was the problem of poor colonies unable to attract much private capital and reluctant to be hindered with loan interest. To these must be added the heavy political pressures to use overseas investment as a means of combating unemployment at home. All of these issues figured in the debates about colonial loans in the twenties, and in that leading to the passing of the Colonial Development Act of 1929. It was not until 1940, however, that the Colonial Development and Welfare Act of that year inaugurated a programme of public investment on a significant scale and clearly tied to the development interests of the recipient countries.[90]

In striking contrast to the conventional wisdom of the post-World War Two period, shortage of labour in the inter-war years was held to be a major impediment to tropical development. The problem was regarded as at its most serious in Africa in the twenties, when it was widely agreed that the labour force was insufficient for the calls made upon it.[91] Throughout the tropical world, however, it was felt that native indolence and inefficiency constrained capital development. The root of the problem, it was commonly explained, lay in racial characteristics and static social values. Anstey observed of India that the 'most desired luxuries are the opportunity to lie in the shade and sleep and smoke, or to squat by the side of the road and chatter.'[92] According to another view, the cause was to be found in malnutrition and ill-health. Knowles, for example, attributed lack of initiative and enterprise to hook-worm and the debilitating influence of malaria.[93] As the possibility that laziness might be curable gained ground, and the problems associated with the importation of labour became more evident, ideas circulated that attention should be directed to diet, health and welfare. Thus development began to take on a broader meaning and the role of the state was enhanced. It should be emphasized, however, that until the Second World War such ideas were in their infancy and their implementation embryonic.

Almost inevitably the question springs to mind as to what kind and degree of development was envisaged by the small constituency actively interested. Yet it is doubtful if a general answer can be given. Indeed, some sort of blueprint for change could hardly be expected, remembering how hesitant was the departure from the traditional ideal of 'natural' development, and taking into account the extent to which perspective varied from region to region. Instead of some conception of a future colonial order, the literature suggests a series of assumptions and preferences which took firmer shape in the course of debate, with adjustments being made as circumstances changed. Those most committed to peasant society tended to be vague about what kind of economic progress they would welcome. Those who looked forward to substantial economic and technological change were likely to be uncertain (or uninterested) as to what this meant for the colonial society at large.

India aside, it is clear that industrialization featured only marginally in British thinking. The issue provoked little discussion, largely no doubt because it was still assumed that the economic future of colonial territories lay in the expansion of primary production, and few proposals were made for industrial development. Occasionally ministers expressed doubts that industrialization would benefit colonial peoples, and made it clear that there was little prospect of imperial support.[94] In general the Colonial Office was of much the same view, although the limited industrialization already under way in Singapore and Hong Kong appears to have been viewed with some sympathy. At one stage a paper was submitted that colonial industrialization should not be discouraged. The Treasury expressed its general opposition to the Colonial Office's position. The question was not considered by the cabinet.[95] Basically, industrialization was a non-issue; it could be argued, however, that this was because of the negative nature of metropolitan presumptions.

The development of mining provoked much greater interest. Most usually it was seen as a mixed blessing. On the one hand, it brought money and technology into territories lacking both. It could also have a multiplier effect in that it led to the growth of railways and ports, and these in turn made possible the development of large-scale agriculture.[96] Thus even if mining enterprises were wasting assets, they could help create the conditions for more broadly based development in the longer term. Frankel summed up the predominant view when he wrote in 1938 that mining had been the touchstone of economic development in most of Africa.[97] On the other hand, it had to be conceded that mining produced labour problems and was socially destructive. Critics, especially on the Left, pointed to the drain on village manpower and to the evils of the migratory labour system and the importation of labour. The problem, it was acknowledged, was how to ensure control of the industry so that it could serve the wider interests of colonial development.[98]

On all sides there was agreement that, for the most part, Asia and Africa's future lay with the development of its agricultural resources. The key question was whether agriculture should follow the course of peasant production or large-scale plantations. A related question was the extent to which agriculture should be geared to export production. Even the advocates of peasant agriculture accepted that some proportion of native production would go overseas. How else would funds be obtained to promote initial development in the form of public works and services? In some cases the financial imperative lay behind attempts to introduce new forms of native production. According to an historian of Ugandan agriculture, people 'were urged to grow cotton in order that they might be able to pay taxes'.[99] Accepting, however, that the tax revenues might be used to finance public investment, too much emphasis should not be placed on the distinction between a fiscal and a developmental concern.

In the years after the war, commercial interests and much agricultural opinion were increasingly attracted by the plantation model. Overseas demand for tropical products was growing and prices were high. There was much evidence to the effect that plantations produced a superior product and that yields per acre were substantially, and sometimes dramatically, in excess of those produced by traditional methods. In addition, plantations brought in capital and new technology, together with the management to use them. By no means were all convinced. The Colonial Office and many administrators overseas expressed doubts about the wisdom of the plantation economy, and at times were flatly opposed. Peasant production was often cheaper and more efficient, they argued, and account had to be taken of the labour demands of plantations on the economy as a whole. Even more important were the corrosive effects of the system on native society, especially tribal morality and discipline. The creation of a landless proletariat was incompatible with the imperial trust.[100] In general, though, the case for plantations made the running for most of the twenties, and there were strong pressures for the establishment or extension of plantations in many colonial territories. In some, these were resisted. The most notable case was West Africa, where Lugard and his successor, Sir Hugh Clifford, denied entry to Lord Leverhulme and other planting interests.[101]

In the thirties the current of thinking moved against the plantation economy. Those most concerned with the interests of colonial societies came to stress the costs and distortion both of monoculture and of heavy dependence on export production. The impact of the depression was crucial here. Between 1928 and 1932 most African and Asian countries suffered seriously in international trade. There were major falls in exports and prices, and recovery was slow and hesitant.[102] The loss of income from exporting led to substantial cuts in public spending and had a serious effect on economic activity generally. Investment in plantations largely dried up and an increasing number of existing plantations were abandoned as unviable. It was apparent that the established approach to development had run into deep difficulties.[103] One approach was to experiment with production limitations and organized marketing.[104] There was also a trend to emphasize the advantages of peasant over plantation production. As one authority put it in 1933:

> . . . it seems somewhat dangerous in this world of economic nationalism and currency disorganization to subject primitive peoples too exclusively to the dominance of world factors over which neither they nor their government can possibly exercise any effective control. It is submitted, in other words, that far more attention should be paid to African rural economy on a whole.[105]

Some change in this direction can be seen in the actual policies pursued by colonial authorities, especially in East Africa and Malaya.[106]

The growth of concern about conservation in the thirties contributed to the turn against the monoculture of the plantation and, to a lesser extent, the more intensive exploitation of peasant production. Influenced by the American experience, the idea of mixed farming – especially the alternation between cropping and non-tillage – and the need to practice methods of soil conservation were taken up by the Colonial Agricultural Service.[107] Science was thus seen as lending its support to a 'hasten slowly' approach which dovetailed neatly with the general preference of many old colonial hands.[108] Another theme of the thirties was the need to tie agriculture to the nutritional requirements of native people. In 1936 the International African Institute devoted a complete issue of its journal to the problem of nutrition.[109] In the same year, the Colonial Office asked all colonial governments for a survey of the nutritional status of their populations and the steps being taken to improve it.[110] On the basis of the West Indian experience, W.M. Macmillan added his voice to those who argued for a greater emphasis on food crops for local consumption.[111] By the time Hancock wrote the second part of his *Survey*, he was able to conclude that opinion had swung from favouring an agricultural system organized for export to a less specialized one, more largely concerned with satisfying local needs.[112]

To take stock of the position with respect to imperial trusteeship: two trends in thought can be said to have emerged and gained support during the inter-war years. The first was that development which advantaged the metropole did not necessarily advantage the colonial society. Secondly, development could no longer be left simply to the ordinary processes of capitalist penetration and exchange. More thought was thus directed to the kind of development preferred. This was coming to be seen in terms of a modified and more prosperous peasant society with some central planning and state involvement. It was further believed that greater use would have to be made of science and technical knowledge. What was required was a more systematic and professional approach than in the past.

Advocates of an imperial economy were in agreement that tropical development could not be left to the natural workings of the international market-place. Their preoccupation with the benefits which could be secured for Britain and the Empire meant that they had arrived at this conclusion much earlier and held to it more strongly. According to their conception, however, economic change in the colonies would be more far-reaching and would proceed more rapidly. This could be accomplished only through a vigorous involvement of the state, both at the centre and at the periphery. If the colonial world was to realize its potential and make a full contribution to the imperial venture, it was inevitable that many elements of the indigenous economy and culture would be replaced by Western imports.

The thinking of both groups, it is clear, had more content than was the case in the period before the First World War. The ideas about costs and benefits were more fully developed; the images of economic change were much sharper. Yet it is also true that both the advocates of an imperial economy and those who promoted colonial development had difficulty in gaining wider interest and support. The tropical and colonial worlds featured in the public mind only at times of slump at home and when other overseas opportunities looked bleak. The economics of empire were matters of specialized pleading, not general concern.

If interest at the time was limited, it is hardly surprising that after the Second World War the ideas and experimentation with respect to colonial development in the twenties and thirties received scant attention outside a small circle, very largely restricted to the United Kingdom. For the Americans who picked up the torch of development in the late forties, the British experience of the inter-war years was an unknown chapter. Yet the sophistication of much of the analysis of the colonial development lobby and its critics was considerable. The question of the complementarity of interests, the concern about export dependence, and the debate about the advantages of plantation as compared with native production were directly relevant to the problems of American policy in the fifties and sixties, and foreshadowed in many respects the radical critique of the 1970s.

PART THREE

The Cold War Era

Interchapter

THE AMERICAN EXPERIENCE: A COMPARATIVE PERSPECTIVE

It is a basic presupposition of this book that comparisons can be drawn between the approaches to Asia and Africa of Great Britain and the United States. The hope is that insights and perspectives may emerge which will contribute to a better understanding of both the British and the American experience, the broader relationship between the West and the Third World, and the influence of dominance on thought and behaviour. Before turning to examine the approach of the United States after the Second World War, we need to be aware of the differences in the position and circumstances of the two countries. The cause of comparative analysis is not served by passing lightly over those features of the American experience which diverge substantially from the case of Great Britain in the period of empire and in the inter-war years.

Probably at no stage in United States history have Asia and Africa represented a natural unit of reference for America's policy-makers and people. In the years before the Second World War, such a grouping was too expansive to make sense given America's interests and capabilities; in the period after, it was too limited to accord with geopolitical and economic appreciations of the world scene. It must therefore be recognized that, from Washington's standpoint, there is some artificiality about where the bounds of our enquiry are set. To a much lesser extent, the same point can be made from London's perspective. For the most part, the Empire was a more usual category of reference than Asia or Africa or the coupling together of the two continents. That a subject or area of interest is delimited differently from the way it would have been at the time, in no way invalidates enquiry. At times it is appropriate to ask questions or to proceed along lines influenced, for example, by later or more general perceptions. Asia and Africa became a recognized and significant grouping in international politics, and they were seen as such in Washington. It is true that the larger category of the Third World found more favour with American policy-makers and scholars. The inclusion of Latin

America in the present study, however, would have changed the scope and nature of the project.[1]

For the century and a half before the Second World War, when Americans thought of the non-European world, what came to mind were those parts in which they had special interests or with which they had particular ties. Latin America was of foremost concern. It was considered to be of such importance that it was designated as a hemisphere apart by the Monroe Doctrine and its various accretions and corollaries.[2] In Asia, American diplomacy and public interest was restricted to the East. There was what was taken to be the special relationship with China, signified by the Open Door initiative of 1899 and the years of missionary activity. There was the encounter with Japan, where early hope and assurance gave way to fear and animosity. And there was the colonial experience in the Philippines from 1898 to 1946. For the rest, Asia impinged little on America's consciousness. In the view of one scholar, vagueness about Asia was 'the natural condition even of the educated American'.[3] Africa was even more remote, and American contacts fewer. The United States played a key part in the establishment of Liberia in 1822, and its delegates participated in the Berlin Conference of 1884–5. But, such occasional episodes apart, Africa remained a closed book until well after the Second World War.

Rather different interpretations of American diplomacy in the non-European world can be advanced by focussing on the imperialism of Theodore Roosevelt, the idealism of Woodrow Wilson, or the westward movement of the frontier in search of new markets and materials. Even proceeding along lines such as these, however, the conclusion must be reached that United States interest in Asia was limited, spasmodic and uneven, and in Africa it was minimal. For the most part, initiatives and rhetoric were grounded in America's own experience, their content too insubstantial and overly general to be said to represent an approach to Asia and Africa. Much of the indiscriminate moralizing about the need for self-determination and the evils of colonialism, for example, was faciliated by America's remoteness from the actual issues (as equally was true, at a later stage, of much European and British moralizing to the United States over Vietnam).

After 1945 America's involvement in Asia grew rapidly. Interest in Africa was notional rather than actual. It was not until J.F. Kennedy became President that much attention was paid to the continent, and that failed to last. The theme will be developed in chapters 7 to 9 that in the post-war period American interest in both Asia and Africa was externally derived and narrowly directed. The United States was not so much pulled in by interests or events in Asia and Africa as pushed to become involved by its understanding of the global conflict with the

Soviet Union. Its points of contact were as limited as its concerns were
selective. All this stands in partial, though substantial, contrast with
the British case.

There is, of course, an even greater contrast when we compare the
nature of the two imperial systems. The British ruled over vast areas
in Asia and Africa. They made laws; they administered; they had men
on the spot. Their approach, their ideas and perceptions, were
influenced by the fact of responsibility. American imperialism has
been of a different order. Since the Philippines became independent,
the United States has not had to accept the degree of responsibility
which fell on an imperial power in the formal sense.[4] Certainly troops
were despatched in crises, but rule remained in local hands. The
influence and coercion that the United States sought to exercise was
mostly external and informal. It was a matter of advising rather than
deciding; of sending in technicians not administrators. Often the
instruments of influence were less overtly national than before.

Account must also be taken of the difference between Britain and
the United States as world powers. In some considerable measure,
Britain's power derived from her position in Asia and Africa. As we
have seen, the whole of the Indian Army, the chain of strategic bases,
and the economic resources and prestige of the Empire were recognized as contributing to capability and influence. American power
existed largely independently of Asia and Africa; its bases were
overwhelmingly internal. This may help to explain why America's
approach was less circumspect than Britain's, and why so little
sensitivity was shown to political interests and issues within and
between Asian and African countries. Writing in 1952, D.W. Brogan
drew attention to what he called 'the illusion of American
omnipotence'.[5] This catches something of the attitude of mind
although it goes too far. For all the optimism, most Americans
accepted that there were limits to what the United States could do in
Asia; the point is rather that the limits were set too widely and the
earlier experience of the colonial powers discounted too readily.

In partial explanation it is necessary to look at the impact of the
domestic political environment. A reminder is perhaps timely that
images of the external world are shaped at home. America's approach
to Asia and Africa encapsulated features of its society and politics
which were often misunderstood or even incomprehensible abroad. In
comparison with that of Britain, the approach of the United States
was more heavily influenced by the attitude and assumptions of the
public at large, and it more visibly carried the stamp of domestic
political processes.

In the United States the belief was widely shared that the country's
involvement overseas, like the state's involvement in society, should
be responsive to public opinion. This meant that Washington was

especially sensitive to popular attitudes and prejudices, and it led policy-makers and advocates to present issues and policies in terms or language with which the electorate would be sympathetic. At no stage was this more apparent than during the Cold War. The nature of the debate and the way in which material was presented was also influenced by the separation of powers and the machinery of policy-making. Here we need to note that although ultimate constitutional responsibility for foreign relations resides with the President, his power in practice is shared with Congress. The President is therefore required to bargain and persuade. Congress can obstruct, force changes in, and effectively nullify foreign policy. But Congress cannot itself conduct foreign policy. Within the executive branch, under the President, the responsibility for foreign affairs is shared between the State Department, various other departments and agencies such as the Departments of Defense and Commerce, and the White House Office advisers.[6] Perhaps inevitably, there has been a tendency for these bodies to speak publicly with different voices. It is thus of the nature of the American system that there is a fuller airing of different points of view and that positions are more often exaggerated or disguised for the purposes of bargaining than is true of most Western countries.

In one respect the debate with which we are concerned was unusual. Especially in the early post-war years there was less special pleading than might be imagined, by individuals and groups inside or outside government with a particular interest or a specific stake in Asia or Africa. Compared with Britain, there were fewer pressure groups or natural constituencies primarily concerned with Afro-Asian issues. In the years immediately after the war, the China lobby was, of course, a force to be reckoned with. Throughout, the Services were heavily involved. Until the sixties, however, their interest tended to be general and not tied to the non-European world. Much the same can be said of scholars and businessmen. Within the State Department, until 1958 African affairs were dealt with mainly by officials whose province was Western Europe or the Middle East.[7] Over time, the position changed. As American involvement broadened, the number of interested parties increased. The development of aid programmes brought into being a bureaucracy with its own interests and specialized knowledge. Government funding contributed to the growth of academic expertise, especially in languages and area studies. Within the defence establishment, counter-insurgency became a subject in its own right and encouraged some geographical re-orientation. Late in the day, businessmen began to look more closely at Asia and even Africa in search of economic opportunities, but this process was scarcely under way before the late sixties.

The nature of the American system and culture appear to have compounded the problems the United States had in determining its approach to Asia and Africa. The relative openness of the political system and the populist tradition encouraged discussion in large categories and well-rounded terms. The emphasis placed on the dangers of communism or the sins of colonialism provided little incentive to ask questions of a more specific and searching nature. Given her limited experience and knowledge of Africa and Asia, it is scarcely surprising that many of America's images were distorted and that so much of her thinking was determined by events elsewhere.

Seven

POWER III

Until well into the 1960s when the revisionist historians provoked
rethinking, the Cold War was understood very largely as a manifestation of power politics. The maintenance of the balance of power was a
constant and recurring theme in Western speeches and official documents. The main body of scholarly writing was in a similar vein – in
marked contrast to the literature on international politics in the
inter-war years. For most of the period, the preoccupation was with
the central balance between America and the Soviet Union, but the
central balance was seen as affecting the course of diplomacy almost
everywhere. Events in the Third World were thus interpreted in the
light of the conflict between the First and the Second. This broad
picture stands in need of some qualification. The dominance of Cold
War stereotypes and the concentration of attention on the position and
policies of the United States have tended to obscure the differences in
approach within the Western world. One major area of difference
related to Asia and Africa. British and European policy-makers never
subscribed to the American view that the significance of these
continents in international politics derived primarily from the global
struggle. To a substantial extent perspectives proceeded on different
national bases, however parallel policies may have appeared to run.

The traditional imperial powers had interests and obligations which
had developed over a century and more, and their relationship with
the colonies or successor states could hardly be reduced to a manifestation of the central balance. Doctrines and habits of mind which were a
legacy of empire prevented any recasting of a frame of reference which
was more complex and historically specific. To varying degrees the
imperial states attempted to shore up their positions by clothing their
Afro-Asian involvement with the rhetoric of the Cold War. The
Malayan 'emergency', the first Indo-China war, and the counter-
insurgency campaigns in Angola and Mozambique were presented as
contributions to the global position of the West, but this was more by
way of rationalization and justification.[1] The United States, on the
other hand, entered the post-war era with far fewer entanglements in

Asia and Africa and without any detailed familiarity with developments in the colonial world. The way was thus open for American
policy-makers to define an approach to Asia and Africa which
accorded with their larger global appreciation. Paradoxically the
United States became heir to the European tradition of *Realpolitik*,
though it drew on and developed this body of thought according to its
own unique history and circumstances.

The object of this chapter is to explore the ways in which
balance-of-power precepts shaped American perceptions of Asia and
Africa and in turn set the course of policy during the years of the Cold
War. First, American ideas about power politics need to be set in the
political and intellectual context of the time. Attention then will be
directed to the form which these ideas took and to why they endured
for so long with so little challenge. This brings us to the question of
the implications of American ideas about the power struggle for her
understanding of developments in Asia and Africa, and their relationship to United States interests. Finally, some comparative comments will be made about American power politics conceptions during
the Cold War and those of European statesmen in the late nineteenth
century.

The question immediately arises as to when American policy-makers
came to be decisively influenced by balance-of-power considerations
in their approach to the areas outside Europe. In many respects it was
an incremental process and no single event or development can be said
to mark an absolute turning-point. John Gaddis has established that
the containment of the Soviet Union was much in the minds of
Washington officials from 1941 onwards, though the material he
considers relates mainly to Europe.[2] The most powerful advocate of
power precepts for the world outside Europe was the Navy. On the
basis of calculations of overseas security, the General Board of the
Navy favoured the continued existence of the British Empire, and
resisted the arguments for international control of the Japanese
mandated islands in the Pacific.[3] Oceanic issues were analysed within
a global strategic framework. The conclusion reached was that the
islands should be placed permanently in American hands. It is beyond
doubt that during the war years constructs of the balance of power
gained wider currency in Washington. It is difficult to go beyond this
rather bland proposition because the claims of power politics had to
co-exist and compete with the ideals of universalism, as publicly
promoted, for example, by Wendell Willkie, the Republican presidential candidate in 1940.[4] Bearing in mind Roosevelt's dominance of
United States diplomacy, there is also the problem posed by the
uncertainty of many of his positions and the contending strands within
his thinking. His sensitivity to security and power considerations sat

uneasily alongside his convictions about international trusteeship and the evils of colonialism.

A power orientation was increasingly apparent during the early Truman period, in part, it has been said, because of the much greater influence of the State Department and foreign-policy professionals with the new administration.[5] American concern then largely related to Europe, but in the winter of 1945–6 Truman saw Soviet pressures on Iran and Turkey as an immediate threat to the global balance of power, and in the longer term as putting the Middle East at risk.[6] By 1947 the balance of power had supplanted universalism, though it was mainly conceived in relation to Europe. It was indicative of administration thinking over the next two years that George Kennan argued that priorities had to be established. With the exception of Japan, his areas of vital interest lay in the Western hemisphere, and it was here, he argued, that the United States must concentrate its efforts.[7]

Washington's thinking about security in Asia had no clear or consistent design, but with respect to this region, too, ideas about power and the need for some kind of balance gained ground. The problem was of a different order from that in Europe because of the lack of confidence in Chiang Kai-Shek, the absence of other allies, and the perceived limitations of American capability. At the same time Republican attacks on the administration's passivity and the activities of the China lobby created a climate of opinion at home which was profoundly unsympathetic to diplomatic pragmatism. Nonetheless, hopes were held that China might follow a Titoist course, and steps were taken to bring about a situation in which the United States might be able to capitalize on a split between China and the Soviet Union. So far as south-east Asia was concerned, there was a reluctance to get involved – all the more pronounced since on one line of reasoning United States action could be counter-productive. Within the south-east Asian division of the State Department it was believed that nationalism was a force against communism, and there were even hopes that an accommodation might be reached with Ho Chi Minh.[8] Thinking along such lines was undercut by events, the growing influence of the Defense Department in Washington, and the pressure of public opinion. The European precedent was becoming more compelling; the arguments for considering Asia as a special case no longer held the same attention. The fall of China in 1949 was of unquestionable significance in tightening the casings of American *Realpolitik* thinking, and extending its geographical reach. United States' recognition of the Associated States of Vietnam, Cambodia and Laos, and the decision to extend military and economic aid to the French in Indo-China demonstrated the increasing predominance of global over regional and local issues. The militarization of policy was accompanied by, and to some extent was the result of, a bitter internal debate, bureaucratic shortcomings and considerable confusion.[9] The process was carried further by the Korean War. In the view of most analysts, the administration's response to the Korean War marked the globalization of the strategy of containment.[10]

It is necessary at this point to sketch a working outline of the power politics pattern of thought as it developed in the United States during the post-war years. The basic fact of international life was taken to be the power struggle between the Soviet Union and the United States. The Soviet Union, acting at times through a compliant China, was bent on an expansionist course, and the United States had no choice but to contain Soviet moves by the development of a system of countervailing power. Blocked initially by America's nuclear monopoly and subsequently by the balance of terror, the Soviet Union resorted to indirect action outside Europe, often using as its instrument local communist parties under its control. Thus America was led, first in the Far East, and later in the Middle East, to extend the policy of containment originally designed for Europe. Analyses and strategies for these areas developed within the confines of a geopolitical model which took bipolarity as its central reference-point. The link between the central and the regional and local was established by a number of ancillary doctrines and concepts, most notably the indivisibility of peace, the domino theory, and the various formulations of the purposes and methods of limited guerilla war. Yet, as we shall see, the logic of power politics was warped or displaced by other influences which arose from within American society and the policy-making process.

The transformation in America's outlook on the world which occurred between the late thirties and the late forties comprised at least three elements of great significance to the way in which the United States was later to approach developments in Asia and Africa. The first was the movement from isolationism to globalism: the replacement of the belief that America could and should insulate itself from overseas events by the conviction that America must attempt to shape the course of events, and that what happened in one theatre could not be isolated from what happened in another. The second was the shift from internationalism and the hopes pinned on collective persuasion, to an appreciation of international leverage which hinged on the efficacy of power. Third, and closely related, was the sea-change in attitudes toward military capability, with force coming to be seen as a means of maintaining peace rather than a cause of war.

It is evident that these clipped propositions compress historical trends over time and are themselves the subject of considerable debate. Scholars of decidedly different casts of mind have emphasized what they take to be apparent or underlying continuities. According to Hans Morgenthau, the United States has pursued a consistent foreign policy, the pattern of which has been shaped by its determination to preserve American dominance in the Western hemisphere and the balance of power in Europe.[11] Robert Osgood has interpreted the isolationism of the thirties as but part of a much longer tradition of attempting to keep the political affairs of the United States as independent as possible from the affairs of other nations.[12] He argues further that during the crisis years before Pearl Harbour, the great mass of Americans came to recognize their dependence on the distribution of overseas power.[13] Revisionist historians such as Kolko and Magdoff have traced or asserted a fundamental continuity in terms of the economic motif – that the world must be kept open and made safe for American capitalism.[14] These larger issues of historical interpretation fall outside our present concern. Whatever conclusions are reached about consistency and continuity with respect to policy and motive, it is beyond argument that the windows through which the world was viewed were substantially different at the end of the forties from those of a decade earlier.

The explanation of this change in outlook is to be found both in the lessons derived from the pre-war experience and in the immediate political landscape. By the beginning of the Second World War a number of the key concepts and symbols of progressive diplomacy had been discredited. Isolationism, appeasement, Munich and Pearl Harbour were taken to be the heritage of the thirties, and over time made a deep impression on the American memory. It became an axiom of American diplomacy that there must be 'no more Munichs'. Stalin was regularly equated with Hitler, and both Truman and Johnson recalled the folly of appeasement in order to justify their military action in Korea and Vietnam.[15] Chester Bowles observed that the Kennedy administration could not bear to be thought 'soft'. 'Everyone carried the Munich model around in his head.'[16] In the popular mind the belief took shape that overseas events did matter to the United States; that concession merely whetted the appetite of aggression. Senator Arthur Vandenberg, a leading advocate of isolationism in the thirties, was converted to a tough-minded interventionist. Reflecting on the Japanese attack on Pearl Harbour in 1941, he wrote later: 'In my own mind, my convictions regarding international cooperation and collective security for peace took firm form on the afternoon of the Pearl Harbour attack. That day ended isolationism for any realist.'[17] Truman was convinced that the war was the result of United States isolationism. Men such as George Kennan and James Forrestal were adamant that the United States must never again neglect military capability. Despite the assessment of a few liberals like Henry Wallace, Secretary of Commerce and former Vice-President, who remained set against balance-of-power manipulations, Churchill increasingly assumed the status of mentor as well as hero. His historical

understanding and his maxims on power were cited frequently by
writers such as Bernard Brodie, Hans Morgenthau and later Henry
Kissinger. According to David Halberstam, the national security
officials during the war held a view more parallel to that of Churchill
than Roosevelt. 'The lesson of history from Munich to Berlin was
basic, they decided: one had to stand up, to be stern, to be tough.'[18]

One development of some consequence here was the shift in
scholarly thinking which began to take place in the thirties. The
liberal optimism of the internationalists increasingly came under
challenge from those with a more cynical understanding of the
international environment. Reinhold Niebuhr, the Protestant theolo-
gian, starkly presented the latter viewpoint when he indicted moralists
for failing to understand 'the brutal character of the behavior of all
human collectives, and the power of self-interest and collective egoism
in all inter-group relations'.[19] Niebuhr, whom George Kennan described as 'the father of all of us', exerted a profound influence on
informed opinion and endowed the pursuit of power with a respecta-
bility which it might not otherwise have had. The thesis which
Niebuhr developed with a broad philosophical sweep was subsequently elaborated by scholars in the field of international relations.
Frederick L. Schuman, Nicholas Spykman and Hans Morgenthau,
among others, were concerned to base scholarly thinking about
international politics on the primacy of power considerations. The
new realism, as this approach came to be known, drew heavily on
traditional writings about power politics and it had an historical bent.
A renewed interest was taken in geopolitics, and strategic matters
began to attract some attention – most notably on the part of Edward
Mead Earle. The climate of opinion was also shaped by the writings of
publicists who addressed themselves to the immediate issues of
America's relationship to Europe, the war and interventionism, but
who approached these questions from a background of history and
ethics. In this respect Hamilton Fish Armstrong, Max Lerner and,
above all, Walter Lippmann can be seen to have been influential in
encouraging rethinking about America's role in the world.[20]

It was Soviet action in Europe after the Second World War,
however, which played the decisive part in converting American
policy-makers to a power approach to international politics, and in so
changing public opinion as to enable this to take concrete form. Soviet
gains and rethinking about the intentions of her leadership directed
attention to the configuration of power. In the assessment of the
Truman administration, the Soviet Union had substantial military
capability immediately available; the states of Western Europe had
been gravely weakened. The existence of a power vacuum in Europe
confronted the United States with a new and threatening situation.
Historically, so the argument ran, the nexus between American

security and the balance of power in Europe had been obscured by the
existence of an external counter-weight. As Henry Kissinger was later
to put it, America had been able to shelter behind *Pax Britannica*,
and he quotes with approval Lord Bryce's observation in 1888 that
America had been sailing 'on a summer sea'.[21] In the late forties,
however, only the United States could provide a system of countervailing power. It was one thing for this conclusion to be reached by
America's leaders; it was another to gain acceptance in Congress and
widespread public support. Events in Greece, Czechoslovakia, Berlin,
and later, China and Korea made the difference. Truman remarked
after he left office that without Moscow's 'crazy' moves 'we never
would have had our foreign policy . . . we never could have got a thing
from Congress.'[22] Thus it was the shock of post-war developments,
coming on top of a reappraisal already under way about the nature of
international politics, which enabled the administration to lead America in a new direction via the Truman Doctrine, the Marshall Plan and
the strategy of containment.

There is no need here to rehearse the details of these policy
initiatives. What is relevant is the form taken by American thinking
about power politics, and some explanation of its persistence throughout the Cold War years. In the formative early post-war period,
America's attention was concentrated on the situation in Europe in the
face of the Soviet threat. The ideas that took hold bore the stamp of
that preoccupation. The political terrain was made up of nation states
in which there was no fundamental clash between leaders and led, and
which had a clear and shared sense of external threat. Regarding the
Soviet Union, the view developed that there was limited scope for
negotiation and accommodation, and that threats would need to be
handled through deterrence. The interests of all parties were thought
to be easily definable and the objectives of policy relatively clear. Thus
the power politics approach which emerged was Eurocentric in that its
categories of reference were drawn from the established state system
with its settled patterns of interaction. It is a central theme of this
chapter that the power politics model remained within this mould
after it was extended to Asia and the Middle East, and that there was
no fundamental change under the Eisenhower and Kennedy administrations. In the interim, however, two distinctively American elements were added which made the pattern of thinking even more
potentially distorting as a guide to what was happening outside
Europe. Later a third element was influential – although how far it
had its roots in American culture is arguable.

The first element was ideological. The rival power structure was
invested with the image of anti-Christ, and Russian interests equated
ipso facto with the spread of communism. A hard-headed approach to
the place of power in international politics ran counter to American

traditions, and yet widespread domestic support for foreign-policy initiatives was a matter of particular significance in the United States. The policy-makers of the Truman administration – mostly of a decidedly elitist cast of mind – found it politic to present the calculations of power in the language of ideology. The classic case was Acheson's attempt to win congressional support for the American commitment to Greece and Turkey in 1947 by invoking images of an ideological chasm and a great crusade.[23] Apparently Truman accepted the need for such presentation; Vandenberg, who was chairman of the Senate Foreign Relations Committee and whose support was crucial to the administration, insisted. Later there was the official vision of communism as 'a vast monolithic system', and the rejection of national communism. Although the evidence indicates that in private Dulles (Secretary of State under Eisenhower) knew better, this kind of representation was seen to be functional, especially in terms of gaining support for defence programmes.[24] It is clear that ideology became more than simply a device for gaining public backing; it infused itself with power and became part of the furniture of policy-maker's minds. The result was that although American perceptions remained rooted in power, they had an extravagance and a crudity quite different from the pragmatic approach of an earlier generation of European states-men. As Halberstam comments: 'There was stunningly little debate or sophistication of the levels of anti-communism.[25]

The second distinctive feature of America's approach was its increasingly military bias. At the outset no such imbalance existed, as is apparent from the priority accorded to European economic recovery in the form of the Marshall Plan, and the preparedness of James Forrestal, the Secretary of Defense, to take short-term military risks to restore economic security. From about 1950, however, American strategic doctrine came to overshadow political and economic assess-ments, developing within a cocoon of thought preoccupied with general war and deterrence theory. In part this can be attributed to the international climate of the time and the belief that war was imminent – which, after all, had a powerful effect on other governments as, for example, Attlee's in Britain. But it should also be related to the legacy of isolationism, an impatience with the complexities of power politics, and what Bernard Brodie has called 'the wish for total solutions'.[26] What is notable is the extent to which analysis of America's role in the world took place in a strategic format, and the degree to which perceptions, and in turn policies, evolved from the debate about military mechanics. This is a recurring theme in the literature on American defence policy, and is perhaps the conclusion of most far-reaching significance to be drawn from the *Pentagon Papers*. It is not possible here to give a full account of the way in which strategic doctrine and the process of defence decision-making disproportionately influenced the evolution of American diplomacy – and most especially American involvement in Asia. However, a few illustrations of the issues involved will help to flesh out the argument.

The military's right to assign strategic value to various territories and areas of the world clearly provided the foundation of much of the power of the defence establishment during the period of the Cold War.[27] This was augmented by their control of certain kinds of information, the preparation of contingency plans and the presentation of options.[28] The process of defence budgeting and the rivalry between the Services had a direct influence on the forces and weaponry available, and thereby on the political choices open to Washington. Similarly, financial considerations often left their mark on the development of doctrine. This can be seen most clearly in the Republican 'New Look' of 1953, and more generally in the strongly held belief that, in deciding its military posture, the United States should so far as possible rely on technology and fire-power rather than manpower.[29] The impact of civilian strategists in the Pentagon on America's overseas orientation has been frequently criticized, especially for the way their disciplinary backgrounds resulted in a narrow concentration on logic, predictability and cost effectiveness.[30] By working along these lines, Alexander George and Richard Smoke have developed a general critique of deterrence in American foreign policy.[31] They argue that the tendency has been to employ strategic deterrence as the paradigm case for thinking about deterrence across the board. The extension of such theorizing about nuclear war to encompass conventional limited war and lower levels of violence involved serious misunderstandings and led policy-makers to pursue inappropriate policies.

In summary, it can be said that under the influence of defence doctrines and patterns of decision-making, more emphasis was placed on means than ends, on the instruments of coercion than the interests they were intended to further, and on internal factors than external. All too often there was an over-reliance on the use or threat of military power at the expense of diplomatic initiatives or the offer of inducements.[32] Correspondingly, political assessments – for example, of Third World aspirations and sensitivities, the nature of regional relationships or the extent of American interests – were neglected or undervalued. With regard to the Soviet Union, there was a consistent tendency to pay more heed to capability rather than intention.[33] In the light of more general material, it might also be suggested that the predisposition of strategists led to an incuriosity about the outside world, the causes of conflicts and America's adversaries.[34]

Alongside the influence of anti-communist ideology and the excessively military orientation, thinking about power politics appears to have been influenced by a sense of self-doubt and a need to confirm

and demonstrate personal and national capacity. We can begin with
Senator Fulbright's thesis about the arrogance of American power.
There is a generality – in places even a lack of clarity – about his
diagnosis, because of his caution with the material. In essence he
argues that, judging from the historical record, powerful states tend to
express their power, to be excessively involved in foreign affairs, and
to develop a sense of mission. Fulbright attributes this to 'a deficiency
rather than an excess of national self-confidence. In America's case the
evidence of a lack of self-confidence is our apparent need for constant
proof and re-assurance . . .'[35] In the first decade or so of the Cold War
this cannot be demonstrated in any positivist fashion. Truman and
Eisenhower were both secure in themselves and in their presidencies.
There was widespread support for an activist foreign policy, and
general confidence in the nation's military capability. Yet within
American society there were also currents of a different order. The
paranoia about the domestic influence of communism can hardly be
explained simply in terms of the external threat presented by the
Soviet Union. To many conservatives the root problem lay in the
spread of collectivism which threatened the traditional American way
of life.[36] Attention might also be directed to the strain arising from the
position of negroes, and to the feelings of powerlessness and alienation
which David Riesman and others saw as arising from structural
changes in American life.[37]

It has been suggested that in the fifties, foreign policy served as a
means of rationalizing and externalizing the currents of tension and
anxiety within American society.[38] While the notion of displacement
lends itself to over-use, it helps to account for the sweeping nature of
American conceptions and the extravagance of presentation. Containment was directed internally as well as externally. The apocalyptic
description of the communist threat overseas expressed something of a
different insecurity felt at home; the rhetoric of 'rollback' of Soviet
power, 'liberation' and 'massive retaliation' helped to satisfy the
impulse for action and initiative which had limited domestic outlets.
Clearly, however, this material needs more searching examination
than it has so far received. A later, though more limited illustration of
displacement is J.F. Kennedy's attack, during the 1960 campaign, on
the Eisenhower administration's neglect of Africa. Reportedly, Kennedy exploited America's need to develop an African policy because it
was a way of winning support from American blacks without alienat-
ing Southern whites.[39]

The argument takes a rather different form when we come to
consider American involvement in Vietnam. The material of immediate interest here is concerned with the personal insecurity of America's
leaders and their predilection for demonstrating masculine vigour. It
may be, in fact, that the war crystallized many of the doubts and

anxieties within American society, and that certain personal similarities between Presidents Kennedy, Johnson and Nixon were not simply fortuitous. Bruce Mazlish notes the extent to which the three men shared a need to compete, to win at any cost, and always to appear 'strong'. He ventures the thought that: 'Our choosing of this triumvirate of recent Presidents at least suggests a correlation between their psychic needs and those of a broad segment of the American population.'[40]

Only in strictly limited respects, however, can Kennedy be bracketed together with Johnson and Nixon. Kennedy's biographers bring out his fear of failure, and his almost childlike admiration for physical daring and male heroism.[41] In office his natural inclination was to see overseas affairs in terms of challenge and he was intent on proving his 'toughness' and 'guts'.[42] On one analysis, Kennedy suffered from a neurosis, meaning that an underlying anxiety produced a compulsion to dominate and an urge to reckless action.[43] This view lacks balance and it cannot be accepted. It leaves out of account Kennedy's confidence in office, his preparedness to compromise, and, to paraphrase Richard Neustadt, his enjoyment of himself. In a passage which offers clues on how to identify the insecure, Neustadt contrasts Kennedy with Johnson and Nixon. Kennedy, Neustadt writes, 'watched himself with wry detachment; his sense of humor was a sign of his perspective. Perspective is precisely what these others lacked. Their solemnity about themselves was of a piece with their intensely personal reactions to frustration.'[44]

Frustration certainly takes us some distance towards understanding the response of Johnson and Nixon to Vietnam. It was, however, a frustration which fed on personal insecurity, one aspect of which was the concern with masculinity. It is well recognized that Johnson was insecure – 'profoundly so', in the judgement of Harry McPherson, Johnson's special assistant from 1965 to 1969.[45] He was especially unsure of himself in foreign affairs where both his knowledge and his interest were limited. He once confessed that he often confused Algeria and Nigeria because they both ended in 'geria'. Johnson was at his most vulnerable over Vietnam where events were so much at variance with his political experience and beyond his power to control. Haunted by the fear of being called 'coward' or 'weakling', he became obsessed with the need for action, will and strength. The sexual symbolism of Johnson's language reveals something of his approach – though less of his actual conduct of policy. He often spoke in the first person of 'shoving' or 'ramming' the bombs up Ho Chi Minh's 'ass', or alternatively, of having the Vietnam War pushed up his rump – 'they'll push Vietnam up my ass everytime! Vietnam! Vietnam! Vietnam! Right up my ass.'[46] The most vivid account of Johnson's personalization of the war in terms of his own sexuality comes from a former aide, who describes an informal discussion after a cabinet meeting in 1967:

> . . . soon LBJ was waving his arms and fulminating about his war. Who
> the hell was Ho Chi Minh, anyway, that he thought he could push America
> around? Then the President did an astonishing thing; he unzipped his
> trousers, dangled a given appendage, and asked his shocked associates:
> 'Has Ho Chi Minh got anything like that?'[47]

Nixon lacked Johnson's commanding presence and swashbuckling
manner, but for all the differences between the two men there are also
obvious parallels. James Barber argues that Nixon was moved by an
endless struggle to control – to control himself, others, but 'above all,
to control doubt . . . doubts about his manliness'.[48] Nixon's fears
about his personal adequacy, his masculinity, and allegedly even
impotence, expressed themselves in a craving to test himself and in the
belief that he was being tested by others. Hence in Vietnam Nixon
wanted not only to be seen as tough, but as tougher than his
predecessor – 'the only question is whether we have the will to use
[our] power, . . . What distinguishes me from Johnson is that I have
the will in spades.'[49]

These lines of Nixon's illustrate the way in which the insecurity of
some American leaders misshaped their approach to overseas conflicts. The personal became so intertwined with the national, that very
often the need to appear resolute and to act with strength overshadowed the issues and interests involved. There was, of course, some
correspondence between the kind of action which satisfied the psychological needs of American policy-makers and the presumed requirements of power politics. This no doubt helps explain why many of the
presidential statements about strategy in Vietnam did not cause more
alarm in official circles at the time. There were also crucial differences. Personal insecurity gave rise to an exaggerated emphasis on
strength and action and will, to the neglect of interest in compromise
and accommodation. It led to an over-valuation of the utility of
military power, at the expense of diplomatic initiatives and a search
for shared interests. In such ways, insecurity worked to reinforce the
biases already set by the elevation of strategic concerns and the
preoccupation with adversarial relationships. The result was that
some elements of power politics, such as coercion and prestige, were
greatly magnified; others, like the need for flexibility and open
communication, were largely discounted.

The argument so far has been concerned to establish the main lines of
American thinking and their relation to the architecture of American
diplomacy. America's view of the world was constructed around her
understanding of the central balance. This understanding was guided

by doctrines of power politics – albeit of a particular kind. Once charted, the ends of American policy became fixed, and argument was mainly addressed to the question of means. For two decades containment set the limits within which options could be considered; for only a slightly shorter period, the domino theory was taken to define the geopolitics of south-east Asia. It is now necessary to consider in more detail the implications of this approach for America's understanding of Asia and Africa.

The visibility of an area and the priority to be accorded to it followed largely from its presumed significance to the global power configuration. This was determined not simply by its location and resources, or even by the extent of the United States stake, but also by the value supposedly attached to it by the Soviet Union. Such an approach substantially broadened the ambit of United States security interests and, potentially at least, changed the way in which America looked at overseas developments. Whereas, earlier, security had been defined in the hemispheric terms of the Monroe Doctrine, it was now understoood to be global in scope. It also meant that the concept of national security was more fluid and subjective, in that it placed the linkage between a particular country or region and the United States in the much broader context of the relationship between the central adversaries.

The result was that, seen through the eyes of American policy-makers, Asia and Africa in effect broke into those parts which were threatened by Soviet expansionism, those which were important in resisting Soviet expansion, and those which had no bearing on the power struggle at the centre. In south-east Asia the threat was taken to be established beyond doubt. It was believed that the loss of an area of such strategic importance, with its rich natural resources and large population, would tilt the balance of power eastward. The mechanics of the process were left largely undefined. Until 1965, however, the region did not receive the sustained attention that might have been expected, given America's strategic appraisal. The position in the Middle East was regarded as broadly similar, except that America's economic stake was larger and the need to maintain Western access to oil made the strategic interest more direct. As was made clear in the debate over the Eisenhower Doctrine in 1957 (see p. 162–3), it was feared that if the Middle East were lost the door would be open to Soviet domination of Africa and the Indian sub-continent, and that Europe itself would be in peril. Japan and, to a lesser extent, the Indian sub-continent, figured in terms of potential counterweights to the Soviet Union and China. The rapid elevation of Japan to the status of ally caused initial misgivings in parts of Asia and in Australia, which remained fearful about the possibility of a revival of Japanese militarism. American ideas about the role India could play were more modest, but they contributed to the difficulties and frictions between New Delhi and Washington.

Africa was largely neglected. In the fifties America's strategic toeholds in the form of air and port facilities, and its interest in maintaining access to the economic resources of the centre and south, were not of sufficient weight to warrant close attention in the absence of a Russian counter-move. In addition, there was a tendency for policy-makers to regard the continent as a European sphere of influence. A former United States ambassador to Guinea has noted the influence of the concept of 'Eurafrica', which for a time intrigued even the perceptive Adlai Stevenson.[50] Until the Congo crisis of 1961, therefore, Africa did not directly impinge on the central balance. One result was that the continent received only a tiny proportion of America's foreign-aid budget – under 3 per cent in 1959. It has been reported that the implicit military stand-off of the super-powers in Africa was put on a firmer basis in 1962, when Kennedy and Khrushchev reached an understanding that the two powers would maintain a 'military moratorium' on Africa.[51] The disengagement of the super-powers was shattered when the Angolan crisis broke in 1975. Kissinger's position was simply that, although Africa was irrelevant in itself, it had become important as a setting for Cuban-Soviet involvement.[52]

An adjunct of this global perspective was that when Asia or Africa came into view, the focus was on external aspects at the expense of internal. Most usually analysis of events and trends was in diplomatic and strategic terms, and the dynamics of change were taken to be exogenous rather than indigenous. This was especially marked with America's understanding of communism and Asian nationalism. In the early Cold War years nationalism was frequently taken to be communism in another guise, and communism itself but an ideological expression of Soviet interests. The failure of United States policy-makers to distinguish the persistence and variety of national and local interests because of their belief in the homogeneity of communist power is now well established. It is strikingly illustrated by Dean Rusk's description of China in 1951. In the view of the Assistant Secretary of State, 'The Peiping regime may be a colonial Russian government . . . It is not the government of China. It does not pass the first test. It is not Chinese.'[53] In Korea the administration was in no doubt that the Soviet Union lay behind every move made by China and North Korea. Even where formal independence was conceded, radicalism was assumed to indicate susceptibility to Soviet designs. An example was President Nasser of Egypt. 'If he was not a communist,' Eisenhower subsequently admitted, 'he certainly succeeded in making us very suspicious of him.'[54] In the sixties, when the Sino-Soviet split forced reassessment of the image of a monolithic world communism, China commonly came to be presented as the main threat in south-east Asia. There was, however, a good deal of confusion – and sleight of hand – as to whether China or the Soviet Union was the prime mover, and about the meaning of national communism. Despite these areas of uncertainty or ambivalence, communism remained the enemy – indeed, in Nixon's view, it was more dangerous than ever – and it continued to overshadow national and regional appreciations.

Afro-Asian nationalism developed on a number of different levels, and was therefore open to a variety of interpretations. In the broadest terms it could be seen either as an historically conditioned response to the external environment or as a manifestation of internal social change. The American understanding fell very largely into the former category. For much of the period nationalism was considered to be a passing phase, closely tied to the colonial experience: in time the new states would make a choice between the West and the communist world. In the interim, non-alignment, 'peace areas' and radical rhetoric were seen to play into the hands of the Soviet Union. Hence the challenge of American policy was to redirect nationalism. The Philippines was seen as a model case and Ramon Magsaysay was held up as an ideal Asian leader. Significantly, Magsaysay found it politic to reject the term 'Philippine nationalism'. He spoke instead of 'positive nationalism', based on a 'special relationship' with the United States.[55] The Kennedy administration was less negative and less simplistic in its approach to nationalism than its Republican predecessors though very often its actions failed to live up to its theory. Generally scholarly attention was riveted on the role of elites, educated overseas, unable to realize their ambitions, and therefore striking back at the West with ideological weapons derived from the West. Much less attention was paid to the domestic roots of nationalism, and to the possibility that it represented an attempt to reshape the economic and social structure of Third World societies.

American perceptions of guerilla war followed a similar pattern. In the fifties and for most of the sixties, interpretation was set by the strategic dimensions of the Cold War, with the result that guerilla war was seen as a tactic adopted by the communist bloc because direct expansion was barred by the nuclear balance. Thus revolutionary leaders were cast as agents or instruments of Moscow's purposes, and enquiry focussed on the extension of aid and support and the provision of sanctuaries. Despite Kennedy's deep personal interest in guerilla conflict, and the expansion of United States counter-insurgency capability under his administration, America's understanding remained essentially strategic. It was not much before the end of the decade that guerilla war was brought within the tradition of thinking about revolution, and serious consideration was given to its internal causes.[56] In many respects the global interrelationships thus perceived were figments of the Western imagination. Few scholars would now accept the view, for example, that in Vietnam or the Middle East the sources of insurrection were largely external. But in other respects the picture was not too distorted, because often guerilla groups saw themselves as the carriers of communist ideology while incumbent regimes presented themselves as representatives of Western liberalism. Given the climate of the time, and irrespective of external involvement, guerilla war was important for international politics because of the anticipated significance of changes in the ideological commitment of Third World regimes. And to some extent it was a self-fulfilling prophecy. If a state or national movement showed left-wing leanings it was given short shrift by Washington and snapped up by Moscow: witness Cuba.

The global perspective toward communism, nationalism and guerilla warfare greatly compounded America's difficulty in understanding developments in Asia and, to a lesser extent, Africa. It gave rise to an implicit assumption that the key questions of American policy should be addressed by those familiar with the wider issues of international politics and strategy rather than by the student of local politics and social change; matters of geopolitics were for the generalist, not the regional specialist who might not see the wood for the trees. It is significant that Dulles, as Secretary of State, was widely regarded as a 'one-man band', and that he relied on departmental officers to produce 'facts' to support his positions, rather than for ideas.[57]

The dominance of the generalist over the specialist was a consistent feature of American involvement in Vietnam. When in 1963 the chairman of an Interdepartmental Working Group on Vietnam expressed pessimism about the prospects of Diem and Nhu, and ventured the thought that perhaps the United States should disengage, Dean Rusk closed discussion by saying that America would not leave Vietnam until the war was over and won. McNamara agreed.[58] Daniel Ellsberg, special assistant to John McNaughton, Assistant Secretary of Defense, later revealed that until 1969 he remained unfamiliar with the earlier history of the French struggle against Ho Chi Minh.[59] Michael Forrestal, a member of the White House national security staff, recalled that in 1963 it was very difficult to find anyone in the government who knew anything about Buddhism in South Vietnam.[60] Washington's lack of interest in Vietnamese history and culture followed naturally from its belief that the course of national affairs had to be seen in the larger international context. Senator Gale McGee explained in 1968: 'To understand Vietnam, it is necessary to understand that the issue is not Vietnam.'[61]

Much the same thinking appears to have lain behind the formulation of the Eisenhower Doctrine in 1957. Preoccupied with the danger of Soviet penetration, Eisenhower and Dulles discounted the hold of Arab nationalism and showed little sensitivity to the position of the Arab states themselves. There was considerable resistance to the administration's plan in Congress, in part because it had been brought forward without the advice or knowledge of any interested or affected party.[62] Much later, Kissinger showed little hesitation in ignoring the advice of Africanists in the State Department over Angola.[63] Such action can be related to the 'need-not-to-know' syndrome.[64] The classic case was surely the diplomatic isolation of China in the fifties. By the middle of the decade direct contact had virtually ceased, American writing had dried to a trickle and news-reporting was second-hand.[65] American policy-makers were thus able to proceed on the basis of their ideological preconceptions, untroubled by any fear of contradiction on the basis of what was happening in China.

A further implication of the globalist perspective was that the United States came to the view that an injection of outside resources might consolidate the internal position of Third World states and regions, and thus incline the balance in the West's favour. Such resources could take the form of economic and military aid, combat assistance or diplomatic reassurance – the latter being one of the aims of the Eisenhower Doctrine. This supposition derived both from an understanding of power which overweighted its tangible components, and from the belief that it was inputs by the other side which were responsible for destabilization.

One is left with the impression that, seen through American eyes, the Third World was lacking in substance. There was a certain emptiness about the societies of Asia and Africa; their political life and culture, if not compliant, were hardly pictured as presenting serious obstacles to external designs. Hence they were open to manipulation by the communist powers and, conversely, they could be pushed and shaped to serve American purposes. The tendency was to view the areas outside Europe as vacuums in international politics – Eisenhower in fact made reference to a power vacuum in the Middle East in his presentation of the case for an American commitment to the region in January 1957.[66] Implicitly at least, this characterization advanced on the basis of power politics criteria spilled over to influence thinking about internal matters – about leadership, social structure and culture. Its impact was all the greater because it ran in parallel with more long-standing features of America's outlook, such as the relative lack of content of existing images of Asia and Africa, assumptions about economic and cultural backwardness, and the fact of racial prejudice.

On the basis of his interviews with 181 Americans, representative of leadership types, Harold Isaacs has written that, for the great majority, ideas about the Chinese were not firmly fixed; they floated relatively freely and thus could be buffeted into changing shapes by passing circumstances.[67] He goes on to show how the broadly favourable pre-war American image of the Chinese was transformed after the communist victory in China and during the Korean War. For a time, those who strongly admired the Chinese were able to take refuge in the notion of the 'un-Chineseness' of the new regime. For most, however, there was a reworking of the untrustworthy Oriental stereotype. The image of the Chinese as unaggressive and ineffectual was replaced by that of a threatening foe, moving as a 'human sea' or 'yellow tide'.[68] In a similar way the widespread use of the term 'gooks' by GIs during both the Korean and Vietnam Wars can be seen as a means by which the Asian enemy was not only divorced from his culture but robbed of his humanity as well.

The changing American images of China are but a striking illustration of the imagined plasticity of all Third World societies and cultures. Edward Said notes how readily 'the Arab' seems to accommodate the transformation into which he is continually being forced.[69] After the 1973 war, the Arab was no longer pictured as a hopeless nomad but as disruptive and menacing. Probably the most vivid description of change wrought by external action was that given by General MacArthur when assessing the American impact on Japan at the end of the Second World War. In MacArthur's view, total defeat left a vacuum in Japan.

> And into this vacuum flowed the democratic way of life. The American combat soldier came . . . They saw and felt his spiritual quality . . . A spiritual revolution ensured almost overnight, tore asunder a theory and practice of life built upon 2,000 years of history and tradition and legend.[70]

It was a short step from underestimating the strength of historical and internal factors in the Third World to assuming that some Third World states could be assigned a part in America's geopolitical design. Propelled forward by the logic of globalism, successive administrations worked from the premise that the balance of power had to take in Asian and, later, Middle Eastern states; that there was a need for regional anchors of American power and quasi-independent centres of diplomacy which were susceptible to American bidding. Thus began the search for regional counterweights around the rim of China and the Soviet Union – the main candidates being Japan, India, Pakistan and later Iran – and the attempt to mould the power configuration of the periphery to suit American needs at the centre. This process was accompanied by the negotiation of security pacts and bilateral alliances, the establishment of military bases and the extension of military aid. A key element here was the American assumption of an identity of interest with the client state on the larger issues, when in fact the shared interest was often specific or illusory. The classic case was Pakistan, linked to the United States through SEATO and

CENTO, but whose primary interest related not to the fear of communism but to insurance with respect to India. Another element was the reluctance to admonish or take action against a leadership set on an expansionist course, for fear it might go Moscow or Peking's way. A clear example is America's approach to Indonesia during its confrontation with Malaysia in the early sixties. Similarly, there was the tendency for United States policy-makers to describe military juntas as democracies and to overlook domestic repression if a regime was thought useful in holding the line against communism.

It is clear that the United States belief that events on the periphery must necessarily be subordinate to the central struggle was not shared in many Asian capitals, but for the most part America heard what it wanted to hear and passed lightly over the rest.[71] On one assessment, where the United States attempted to manipulate intra-Asian power relationships, this 'fostered artificial imbalances, encouraged other external intervention, and frustrated the evolution of solidly based regional power patterns rooted in local realities'.[72] This is perhaps too strong an indictment of American policies but it identifies the opportunity costs involved. Certainly America's alliances with Third World countries proved increasingly domestically disruptive – as was the case in Pakistan, Thailand and the Philippines – and their relevance to the central balance became more and more questionable.

A final consequence of the globalist perspective was the tendency for the United States to become locked into positions in Asia, even where the issues and interest were of secondary importance, because all the world was watching. The periphery became a signalling-ground and America was constantly fearful that the Soviet Union or NATO allies might receive the wrong message as to America's will and resolve. The *Pentagon Papers* establish in the clearest terms the importance of prestige and credibility to the course of American involvement in Vietnam.[73] As America's concern with the direct geopolitical relevance of south-east Asia to the central balance abated, this psycho-symbolic dimension gained ground. An obvious illustration is the changing rationale of the domino theory. By the time of the despatch of ground troops to Vietnam, the meaning of the domino theory came to rest not on military mechanics but on the credibility of the United States' commitment. As Assistant Secretary of Defense John McNaughton put it in a memorandum to Robert McNamara in March 1965, American war aims in Vietnam were 70 per cent to avoid a humiliating US defeat, 20 per cent to keep South Vietnamese territory from Chinese hands, and 10 per cent to permit the people of South Vietnam to enjoy a better, freer way of life.[74] Thus intervention in Vietnam can be seen as a consequence of the American understanding that failure to act in a specific theatre endangered the structure of American global power. The predisposition toward action impelled

policy-makers to take risks. J. and G. Kolko point to Dulles' belief
that the United States could not retreat from challenges where
American interests were minimal, without threatening the future of
American power where its interests were primary.[75] They continue:
'Such a vision, which men like Acheson and Nitze held with a greater
rigor than even Dulles, was in its first phases both ideological and
strategic, making the taking of uncanny and dangerous risks an
integral aspect of American foreign policy.'[76]

Earlier in this chapter it was argued that the United States became
heir to the European tradition of *Realpolitik*, though with significant
differences. The point may be developed a little further. By way of
conclusion, let us consider America's understanding of the place of
Asia and Africa in the international system, in relation to that of the
European states during the second expansion. The risk of distortion
must be set against the sense of perspective which may be gained.
Despite the obvious and substantial changes in the international
environment over the intervening decades, there are broad similarities
between the two approaches. In both cases there was relative ignorance of and lack of interest in the societies of Asia and Africa and the
social processes at work in those societies. In both, images of the
non-European world reflected the concerns of international politics
which were tied to the clash between great powers. In broadly similar
ways there was the subordination of the periphery to the requirements
of diplomacy at the centre, understood in terms of maintaining a
balance or gaining an edge.

There should be nothing very surprising about this correspondence
of approach, given a starting-point anchored in power politics. The
pre-eminent facts of international life were, after all, similar in the two
periods. On the one hand there was limited room for manoeuvre at the
centre – the existing positions of the great powers had to be regarded
as more or less fixed. The advent of nuclear weapons and the
establishment of the NATO and Warsaw pacts after the Second World
War can be compared with the hardening of the alliance systems, the
militarization and the growth of tension in Europe in the last two
decades of the nineteenth century. On the other, the periphery was
not seen as a force to be reckoned with. Lacking conventional power,
and, initially, political organization of a kind that would be recognized, African and Asian countries were accorded little status in
international politics. Raymond Aron has observed that until the two
world wars, the Eurocentred system treated as equals only those states
outside Europe capable of imposing respect for their existence and
their rights by force.[77] The granting of independence did not radically
change the position. With the partial exception of the doctrines of
non-alignment, the new states were unable to impress their own

distinctive problems and perspectives on the outside world.[78]

It is apparent, however, that in the years after the Second World War the United States did not approach the overseas world from a basis of abstract calculations of power and self-conscious pragmatism. Nor could the international system as it impinged on Asia and Africa be said to operate simply along such lines. Much more than in the past, ideological conceptions influenced the patterns of power politics. The ideas of men like Henry Stimson, the wartime Secretary of War, and James Forrestal, Secretary of the Navy and later Secretary of Defense, that ideology needed to be kept out of international politics were swept aside with the onset of the Cold War.[79] They probably had no hope of realization in any case because of America's diplomatic tradition and the powerful constraints of public opinion. It must also be said that statesmen were a good deal less free than before to act in the light of power precepts because of changes in the external environment. The emergence of the new states of Africa and Asia limited the manoeuvreability of outside powers. The opportunities for horse-trading were more limited. New instruments and techniques of leverage had to be developed – for example, incentives in the form of economic and military aid. In short, the periphery could not so easily be organized to suit external purposes.

Ideological conceptions were important in two respects: they changed the nature of interaction between the principal adversaries and they limited options on the periphery. On the first point, the ideological division between the United States and the Soviet Union resulted in little faith being placed in the efficacy of negotiation. The diplomatic stand-off of the Cold War was a far cry from the shared assumptions and relatively open patterns of communication character-istic of great-power diplomacy at the end of the nineteenth century. The diplomatic isolation of China, proceeding as it did on the implicit assumption that China had no stake in the existing system and that no accommodation was possible, broke sharply with European prece-dent. With respect to the second point, Asia and Africa were not seen as an undifferentiated mass. Many of the states and social movements flew ideological flags – Marxist or liberal-capitalist – and these were held to be significant in international politics. Equally, some Third World states, for their own reasons, were pro-Russian or pro-Western and this introduced presumptions of support or opposition. Ideologic-al orientation on the periphery thus generated various pressures which narrowed the range of external options. The result was that the international system had less flexibility than before.

Alongside and related to ideological considerations, power politics thinking was conditioned by assumptions about the economic conflict between East and West. Perhaps less than ever before could a clear distinction be maintained between political and economic concerns in

international politics. While European statesmen often enough acted
on the basis of economic calculations, their understanding of the
international order was primarily political. Only to a limited extent
were the economic aspects of relations between states related to ideas
about power and power politics.

In the post-war world the connection between the two realms was
close and few doubted it. One does not have to accept the revisionist
thesis that the elaboration of the Russian threat and the manipulation
of power and strategy were means to sustain a capitalist political
economy, to be persuaded by the evidence that policy-makers were
keenly aware of the interrelationship between America's political and
economic interests overseas. This theme will be developed more fully
in Chapter 9, but it can be foreshadowed here by referring to the case
of the Japanese mandated islands. William Roger Louis asks whether
the United States estimate of security included making the world – or
in this particular context, the Pacific and Far East – safe for American
trade and investment. He concludes: 'The American wartime officials
would probably have given a generally affirmative answer to that
question.'[80] Whether policy-makers would have said the same publicly
in later years is doubtful, but the evidence suggests strongly that in
their thinking security had an economic dimension.

Eight

MORAL RESPONSIBILITY III

The commitment to high moral principle has been the central and most persistent feature of the ideology of American foreign policy. Deeply embedded in the political culture, it has given the public pronouncement of American leaders a distinctive tone. In 1919 Woodrow Wilson told his fellow countrymen that America was 'the only idealistic nation in the world'.[1] Nearly half a century later President Johnson declared that 'America's only interests in the world today are those we regard as inseparable from our moral duties to mankind.'[2] A large literature has grown up on the role of moral affirmation in American foreign policy. Among the most notable contributions were the writings of Reinhold Niebuhr, Hans Morgenthau and George Kennan, which took as their theme the way idealism had obstructed the pursuit of national interest. Since the mid-1960s and under the influence of the revisionist historians, a more cynical approach has been evident. The tendency has been to see principle as frequently running in parallel with economic interest but at the same time to point out that often there was a wide gap between rhetoric and practice.

The writing about the place and meaning of morality in American foreign policy goes much beyond the purposes of this chapter. By their very nature, moral perspectives are most usually expressed in universalist terms and the literature is therefore of the broadest scope. Most studies range globally and draw on historical material from before the Second World War. Many attempt to trace the influence of idealism on particular lines of policy and to make assessments using the yardstick of national self-interest. Our concern here is more limited. It relates to those aspects of the moral impulse which affected post-war American thinking about Asia and Africa, and helped shape perception of what was happening there and what the future might hold.

We begin by attempting to characterize the nature of America's moral response to the new states, and some comparisons are drawn with the earlier British doctrines of moral responsibility which evolved within the framework of formal empire. The enquiry then proceeds thematically. What are the roots of the American predisposition for approaching overseas policy in terms of high moral purpose? What form has America's moralism taken insofar as it has related to Asia and Africa? What significance has it had with respect to America's understanding? The chapter concludes with some observations on the relationship between moralism and insecurity.

It is perhaps a truism to observe the extent to which America's moral conceptions arose from and remained tied to the domestic political culture. Yet what is significant is how little these conceptions were influenced by an appreciation of conditions and events overseas. External developments affected which elements were projected at particular times, and they had some impact on doctrinal form, but the corpus of ideas and sentiments was throughout derived from America's own experience and history. Morality probably always draws its strength from inner conviction, but in the ordinary course it is conditioned by external circumstance and the process of interaction. In the British case, for example, the understanding of other societies, and especially of India, was of undoubted importance in the shaping of the doctrines of moral responsibility. For the United States, however, the focus was overwhelmingly internal and it was on this basis that ideas developed about American exceptionalism and American innocence, and about how America offered an example to the world. Writing in 1847, Albert Gallatin invoked an image which has retained its hold on succeeding generations: 'Your mission is to improve the state of the world, to be the "model republic", . . . to be a model for all other governments and for all other less-favoured nations.'[3] One aspect of this self-image has been the implicit rejection of other forms of political and social organization, or at the very least an indifference to alternative historical experiences. This self-indulgence, which we label as ethnocentrism, has been a characteristic feature of American idealism with respect to the outside world. A second and related feature is that American idealism has not been tied to any specific notion of responsibility. The moral impulse has floated freely. It was abstract and non-territorial; not something which developed within the framework of particular international relationships or which was directed toward specific peoples or countries. A partial exception must be made for America's traditional approach to China, which had a distinctive content and moral tone. Until 1949 American thinking about China represented a half-way house between an indiscriminate internationalism and the focussed concern of formal imperialism.

Both of these points contribute to a fuller understanding of the almost religious quality of America's external orientation. The words 'crusade' and 'evangelism' have featured prominently in writing about American diplomacy. The point is not only that the United States has been committed to reforming ideals but that its approach has been characterized by moral fervour, the conviction that it has the answers, and a reluctance to compromise. An evangelical strand has been present in the foreign policy ideologies of other states – Britain during the late nineteenth century, Portugal in the last decade of her African empire – but it has seldom been dominant and in most instances has been tied to a particular class or constituency. In the British case, for example, Raghavan Iyer points out that evangelism appealed especially to non-official bodies and societies – though at times they were able to modify or change official doctrine.[4] The position in America has been substantially different. While evangelical zeal has fluctuated according to domestic leadership and overseas events, it is deeply embedded in the culture and has become part of the mental make-up of the people. The populist tradition has ensured its expression at the political level more often and more directly than has been the case in any other Western country.

As a result of the themes of revisionist historians and dependency theorists, and the disclosures about the Vietnam War, the ideals championed by the United States may not now be seen as having much moral force. Indeed, to present these ideals in the Third World context as moral conceptions may be taken as another of the ironies of American history. Yet until the late sixties what was remarkable was the faith shared by so many Americans that the lights which had guided their course at home were relevant to other societies. In its public expression, the American creed began with the commitment to political liberty. The greatest danger to liberty was seen to be posed by the tendency of governments to enlarge their powers at the expense of the individual. The ideal was thus freely elected democratic governments which would ensure freedom of speech and religion, and the rule of law. This political schema had its economic variant. Growth and prosperity could best be promoted through reliance on individual initiative. There should be minimum interference by the state in the business of production or exchange. It must be said that the commitment to political liberty proved more elastic than the insistence on free enterprise. Whatever the gap between principle and practice, however, these ideas became the global model. What was good for individual societies might equally contribute to a more harmonious world – the interaction of free peoples through free trade for mutual benefit. If such a world view hardly appears to be the stuff of which crusades are made, its pull is more apparent when ranged against the American understanding of what it would replace – an indifference about the internal arrangements of states, the operation of the balance of power and the economic nationalism of the inter-war years. The crucial perspective, however, was the domestic inheritance. Four lines of thinking, which at various points touch and overlap, help explain the roots and power of America's international idealism.

The first is Frederick Jackson Turner's thesis of the influence of the frontier in American history.[5] The primary purpose of his classic essay published in 1893 was to explain the difference between American and European civilizations. In Turner's interpretation, the difference stemmed from the existence in America of an area of free land westward, with new resources and new challenges, which gave rise to distinctive social ethics and a unique national temperament. The frontier produced a dominant individualism, a resentment of governmental restriction and a democratic tradition of high idealism. It left its stamp both on America's domestic politics and on her foreign policies. Turner's emphasis on the role of environmental factors in shaping American traits has been taken up by later historians. Various aspects have been singled out and developed, the most relevant for our purposes being the significance of the rich natural endowment of the United States. In an incisive study of the American character, David Potter saw the general patterns of American political and economic thought, and especially the ideas about democracy, as heavily influenced by material abundance.[6] The existence of an economic surplus provided fertile conditions for the growth of political democracy in the United States. Yet the extent to which democracy was economically conditioned was little recognized, and the tendency was to equate abundance and freedom. The same myopia contributed to the view that democracy in the American style could take root overseas and that its acceptance was a simple matter of moral choice. Turner himself made a similar point when he commented on the American belief that 'other people had only to will our democratic institutions in order to repeat our own career.'[7] Too often, America's message to the world about the virtues of democracy was preached in places where its economic prerequisites had not been established. Equally, America's message too easily held out to others the prospect of economic sufficiency.

Another school of interpretation has stressed the importance of America's early political experience in shaping the dominant ideas and outlook of the society. The central reference point here is Louis Hartz's book, *The Liberal Tradition in America*.[8] In Hartz's view the outstanding fact of America's history has been the absence of a feudal experience. Without the social antagonisms to which feudalism gave rise, there could be no genuine revolutionary tradition and no tradition of reaction. In this situation liberalism was seen as natural; a moral consensus developed, and was expressed in terms of the American way of life. But Hartz goes on to show that liberalism in America was fundamentally different from liberalism in Europe because it had an absolute quality about it. There was an intolerance of dissent; America's moral unity was such that there could be no sense of relativity or recognition of different paths. Abroad, this meant that the alien was identified with the unintelligible and freedom interpreted only according to political criteria.[9] We are left with the impression that there was almost an inevitability about the way that Americans failed to understand the social dimensions of external conflicts and interpreted the world on the basis of their own political tradition.

Finally, there was the influence of religion on the tenor of American thinking. The circumstances of the migration and settlement of religious sects meant that this influence was predominantly individualistic and democratic. At the same time American political life took on certain religious qualities, most notably the sense of moralistic purpose and an evangelical spirit. Roy Nichols entitled the second part of his book on religion and American democracy 'The Religion of American Democracy'.[10] In Michael Howard's view, the United States has always resembled a secular church, or perhaps a gigantic sect, more than it has the nation states of the Old World.[11] It is of especial interest to note that in its historical context American religious evangelism had an absolutist quality about it. In the seventeenth and eighteenth centuries evangelicals were convinced of the need for obedience. True liberty was to be found only when following God's will: in the words of a Massachusetts cleric of the late eighteenth century, 'O blessed Captivity! no other than perfect liberty'.[12]

Compared with the extensive literature on the nature and roots of American idealism, much less has been written about its significance for specific perceptions and policies in the post-Second World War period. To a degree this is understandable, because idealism represents an orientation to the world which by its nature cannot be weighted, and the influence of which becomes more debatable the more it is analysed in particular situations. Its very generality limits its utility as a guide to thinking and action in concrete circumstances. Yet, at least so far as Asia and Africa are concerned, the evidence suggests that the influence of American idealism was more uneven than much of the literature implies, and that its effects were often very different from the hopes of policy-makers and the American people.

Beneath the high rhetoric of world freedom, American moralism found expression in a number of conceptions which brought together America's self-image with her understanding of the major currents of the epoch. The most important of these conceptions were anti-colonialism, anti-communism, the commitment to the development of the Third World, and, paradoxically, the rise of anti-Americanism within the United States during the latter years of the Vietnam War. What is immediately striking is that, with the partial exception of the commitment to Third World development, the international express-ion of American idealism has been negative: moral purpose has taken political form in opposition to a perceived evil rather than in the pursuit of a positive good.

The first perceived evil to engage America's attention was the colonial system. Almost all analyses of anti-colonialism in recent American history begin with Roosevelt's strong convictions on the colonial question and his commitment to the eventual independence of all colonial territories. Disproportionate attention has probably been paid to his biting criticism of the French record in Indo-China, and his advocacy of some form of international trusteeship for the territory – a solution he held out more generally for the colonial possessions of Italy and Japan. In fact before his death Roosevelt reluctantly abandoned his opposition to the return of the French to Indo-China.[13] It must also be said that Roosevelt's anti-colonialism varied in intensity and application and that there was considerable uncertainty about his ideas regarding international trusteeship. It was inevitable, then, that the President's anti-colonial bias was by no means always reflected in official policy. According to Cordell Hull: 'At no time did we press Britain, France or the Netherlands for an immediate grant of self-government to their colonies.'[14] William Roger Louis has con-cluded that from about 1943 America tended to support rather than break up the British imperial system.[15]

Even the anti-colonial current in American wartime policy cannot be seen simply as an expression of ethical principle, much less as evidence of any positive conception of moral responsibility. Louis comments on the legalistic flavour of morality which characterized the American debate.[16] In a more recent assessment, he has observed that 'The ideology of trusteeship was easily forged into a weapon of American defence.'[17] In some quarters thinking was influenced by hostility to the imperial states. There was the desire to cut Britain down to size and, in the case of other powers, the fear that their very weakness might create conditions outside Europe prejudicial to Amer-ican security. D.C. Watt has drawn attention to what he calls the 'naive populism' of America's approach. He argues that not only were many Americans uninformed about the political conditions in colonial territories, but their assumptions about transferring power to 'the people' were simplistic.[18] British and European critics at the time detected other elements of a more self-seeking nature. Along the lines subsequently to be developed by the revisionist historians, men like De Gaulle saw principle as a pretext for economic ambitions and the expansion of American influence. In the estimate of others, anti-colonialism was in part calculated to appeal to domestic opinion within the United States.

During the period of the Cold War, anti-colonialism surfaced fitfully in American diplomacy, but it was usually something to be weighed alongside wider considerations of international order and the balance of power. In the late forties it is significant that Washington responded differently to nationalism in Indonesia and in Indo-China. The nationalist movement in Indonesia was supported because it was anti-communist and independence was seen as likely to weaken communist elements. In Indo-China, however, America steadily distanced itself from its earlier anti-colonial stance because the nationalist movement was communist. On two important occasions the reluctance to be identified with European imperialism directly affected policy. It was a key consideration in Eisenhower's decision not to intervene in Indo-China in 1954; and it weighed heavily with Eisenhower – and also Dulles – in opposing the Anglo-French invasion of Egypt in 1956. In the former case Eisenhower wrote of the 'incalculable value' of America's standing as an anti-colonial power.[19] In his judgement 'the moral position of the United States was more to be guarded than the Tonkin Delta, indeed than all of Indo-China'.[20] Over Suez, Eisenhower and Dulles were as one in their belief that the United States must make plain its rejection of what smacked of a reassertion of European colonialism.[21]

These cases aside, anti-colonialism was accorded a low priority by American policy-makers preoccupied with the struggle against communism and the need for international stability. Liberals such as Chester Bowles, American Ambassador to India in 1951 and 1952, spoke out against the reluctance to take an anti-colonialist stand. Even if America's need to support France and Britain in Europe muted its own voice, Bowles asked, should not the United States be glad that other countries were prepared to champion nationalist movements?[22] Judging from official pronouncements, the Eisenhower administration was not enthusiastic. In 1953, attempting to deflect criticism of the administration's record, Dulles contended that the United States was pushing for independence more than appeared on the surface. Where restraint was exercised, he explained, it was because 'precipitate action would in fact not produce independence but only transition to a captivity far worse than present dependence.'[23] Five years later, Assistant Secretary of State C. Burke Elbrick warned the Senate Foreign Relations Committee that 'Premature independence and irresponsible nationalism may present grave dangers to dependent peoples.'[24]

No major initiatives appear to have been taken with respect to decolonization in Africa, which at least until the Kennedy administration was viewed very largely as a European concern. America's strategic interests, the importance attached to her relationships with European states, and the fear that rapid decolonization might be destabilizing, ensured that even the rhetorical commitment to self-determination was qualified by the understanding that this process should be evolutionary and the end eventual rather than immediate.[25] Indeed, in the judgement of one recent study, the United States government was content to regard the bulk of the African continent as a colonial appendage of Western Europe.[26] America's voting record on colonial issues at the United Nations discloses frequent abstentions, and a number of cases where the United States actually opposed resolutions initiated by the Third World.[27] Some change of emphasis was evident during the Kennedy years. Much has been made of Kennedy's decision to vote with the Third World in support of self-determination for Angola in 1961, and later in that year to associate the United States with the Declaration on Colonialism. Certainly the style was different and the impact on the Third World substantial, but action was patchy and mixed with a good deal of pragmatism.[28] J.K. Galbraith, American Ambassador to India during the Kennedy period, records his dismay at Dean Rusk's position on Goa shortly before the Indian invasion of the territory. According to Galbraith, Rusk failed to bring any pressure to bear on the Portuguese Foreign Minister – 'No question of anti-colonial principle obtruded.'[29] In his valuable study of Kennedy's African diplomacy, Richard Mahoney contrasts the President's early declarations with his diplomatic record and concludes, in effect, that his African policy was a hostage of the Cold War.[30] On the basis of the available material, it is not possible to assess the extent to which the United States quietly nudged the European powers to relinquish their African territories, but there is little to suggest any strong pressure within the privacy of bilateral relationships.

The ebb in America's anti-colonialism must thus be explained primarily in terms of the priority accorded to anti-communism. Once communism was established as the greater evil, calculations of strategic advantage and alliance solidarity became more compelling than the moral virtues of a post-colonial order. The Soviet Union rapidly assumed the mantle of the leading anti-colonial advocate and the pressures against making common cause with the major adversary for the most part overshadowed America's conception of, her own anti-colonial tradition. Prodding the European states to hasten the transfer of power had now to be weighed in the light of tensions within the Western alliance and the maintenance of the political stability of the metropoles. In his memoirs Eisenhower saw fit to quote a letter from Albert Schweitzer in 1957 warning of the grave consequences if France did not have American support in opposing a resolution at the United Nations calling for Algerian self-determination. In Schweitzer's view, France's defeat could compromise the cause of Europe.[31] There was also a growing disenchantment with the consequences of decolonization. Instability, neutralism and radical rhetoric were not the expected fruits of colonial emancipation. George Ball, Under-Secretary of State in the Kennedy and Johnson administrations, probably summed up the feelings of many American policy-makers when he observed that 'the disintegration of empire created new states to complicate the peace.'[32]

The moral imperative of anti-communism provided a successor to the cause of anti-colonialism, but its influence was enormously greater. Stanley Hoffmann writes of the policy-makers of 1947 and 1948 as the new Founding Fathers, whose task was to save the world from the Soviet Union and, by implication, from itself. Focussing on America's approach to the European states – though his observations apply almost equally to America's approach to Asia at a later stage – he employs the metaphor of the sick and writes of 'their minds diseased by communist parties and unions'.[33] We are thus dealing with an approach much broader and more active than anything envisaged under anti-colonialism, and which brought together on a single canvas the dominant features of the international system and the internal health of states. In the practice of American foreign policy, anti-communism as an expression of moral opprobrium and irrational fear cannot readily be distinguished from *Realpolitik* thinking addressed to the problem of the Soviet Union as an expansive power. Yet if anti-communism as a moral imperative provided the Truman administration with a means of convincing a reluctant Congress and an untutored public that America must establish its own system of overseas power, it came to develop a life of its own.[34] It permeated almost all sections of American society, informing official action as well as shaping popular thinking. In this broader sense anti-communism defined the era.

The impact and implications of anti-communism were far-reaching. It was sufficiently flexible for the enemy to be the Soviet Union, China, monolithic communism or, at a later stage, even Cuba. It might be a combination of a number of these candidates; and, as in the case of Vietnam, it was unnecessary to be specific or to analyse relationships within the enemy camp. David Halberstam writes that for the national security officials, the conflict was 'an ism'; it was defined in ideological, not national, terms.[35] The end result was that the United States was dealing not so much with an adversary as with an evil force, and thus there could be no room for compromise or adjustment of interests – only endless opposition. So, too, the other actors in the system were assigned their value according to how they measured up on the scale of anti-communism. Hence, as Dulles put it, neutralism was immoral. In the Secretary of State's view, it could only be a transitional stage on the way to communist control.[36] Later, the fear of pushing important Afro-Asian states like Indonesia or Egypt into the embrace of the enemy led America to adopt an indulgent approach to radical posturing or local adventurism. Throughout, the criterion of America's interest and beneficence was negative; it was not the freedom vaunted by President Truman that mattered, but where a state or leader stood in the struggle against international communism. In his famous address to Congress in March 1947, Truman had declared that 'it must be the policy of the United States to support free peoples who are resisting attempted subjugation by armed minorities or by outside pressures.'[37] But the key to the Truman Doctrine – at least insofar as it was acted upon – lay in the word 'resisting', and this meant resisting communist subjugation though it was not spelt out. Seven years later, when the United States signed the SEATO treaty, it was more careful to limit its undertaking. An understanding was appended to the treaty that, so far as America was concerned, aggression referred only to communist aggression.[38]

Anti-communism as it developed in the United States was not the result of sectional manipulation or the pleadings of special interest groups, but arose from within the mainstream of American society. Its strength derived from the extent to which it drew on ideas and aspects of a culture rooted in America's past – the belief in American exceptionalism, the claim to universality, the absolutist and even repressive elements in America's political traditions. In no other Western society could McCarthyism have carried so much before it. In his study of the anti-Communist purges, David Caute emphasizes the role of American liberalism in shaping anti-communism both internally and externally. Hostility towards the Soviet Union and American communism became the linchpin of Cold War liberalism; its origins were 'not essentially economic, but rather cultural, idealistic, self-righteous, moral'. It was the liberals who set the United States on course for Vietnam.[39] The consensus began to crack, after the Sino-Soviet split, in the face of the administration's difficulty in explaining the nature and source of the threat, but it was the Vietnam War which played the crucial part in destroying the hold of anti-communism.

The commitment to Third World development and its practical expression, the provision of economic aid, was shaped in part by the anti-communist imperative, but also by the inheritance of idealism and the belief that development was likely to advance the interests of the home economy. Our concern here is with development as a manifestation of American idealism.[40] Accepting the pragmatism which was so frequently associated with development policies, the idea itself represented the most positive if culturally encapsulated expression of moral responsibility to the Third World.

At the core of the doctrines of development was the idea of economic growth. The hope was that Asian and African societies might in time achieve the material standards of the West which had gone before them. Taking up a much longer European tradition, it was believed that the injection of outside skill and capital would initiate self-generating processes of growth. At this point, according to the American version, 'take-off' would occur. Economic development would in turn promote political development, which was understood to mean social stability and democratic government. At times the virtues of political democracy were openly canvassed; if not, they were often implied by referring to the benefits of participation. In the sixties the understanding of development was widened and attention was increasingly directed to the culture and traditions of non-Western societies which were held to impede the processes of economic growth. The message of modernization theory was that if the Third World was to emulate the West economically, it had also to emulate the West in the domain of culture and politics. America's task thus became one of bringing modernity to societies held back by the oppressions of the past. David Apter could write in 1965: 'The work of modernization is the burden of this age. It is our rock. . . . Modernization and the desire for it reaches around the world.'[41]

There can be no doubt that many Americans held sincerely to the conviction that the United States could and should contribute to the advancement of the Third World. In his study of American political development ideas, Robert Packenham states that much of the rhetoric was firmly and widely believed by officials.[42] This was clearly the case with Truman's presentation of the Point Four Programme. Indeed his optimism about what could be accomplished – raising the standard of living of the rest of the world by 2 per cent – can hardly be understood in any other terms. Much later Chester Bowles, Under-Secretary of State during the initial months of the Kennedy administration, genuinely believed that 'Point Four may go down in history as the most important idea of our generation.'[43] The idealism of American thinking appears a good deal less persuasive when account is taken of the influence of Cold War calculations in shaping the direction of economic aid programmes. Yet for the most part, no incompatibility was seen between developmental goals and the pursuit of America's strategic and economic interests. Writing of the various groups interested in the Middle East in the 1950s and 1960s, a critic of American policies noted that all shared a belief that America's national interests were benign and enlightened.[44]

It has become commonplace to observe that American development thinking was cast in an ethnocentric mould and that its optimism was largely ill-founded. There is nothing very surprising about either of these features once it is recognized that America's approach to Third

World development was an outgrowth of its liberal tradition. The key inputs were not only internal but so fully internalized that they were taken for granted by most shades of American opinion. There was the faith that development could be secured through reliance on individual enterprise and the application of technical skills. It was accepted as a matter of course that economic growth and political democracy were mutually self-supporting. The confidence of Americans in their understanding of the bases of their own prosperity welled over and influenced thinking about other societies. Richard Neustadt and Ernest May have drawn attention to the influence of what they call 'can do' beliefs: that anything Americans seek can be accomplished; implementation follows automatically from decision, assuming enough will.[45] In such a climate there was little incentive to take account of international impediments or the different circumstances of Asian and African societies. In short, for most of the period, the moral impulse which sustained the commitment to Third World development can be seen as flowing from a profound satisfaction with the American condition and an assurance that the United States was pacing the course of human improvement.

These themes are forcefully, if unwittingly, illustrated in the fictional writing of William Lederer and Eugene Burdick. *The Ugly American*, published in 1958, constitutes an indictment of the mismanagement in American aid programmes. The message of the book was that policy-makers had failed to grasp the reasons for America's own prosperity. The remedy for Asian backwardness was not lavish and symbolic projects which pandered to the vanities of Asian nationalism, but the establishment of those conditions which had led to development in the United States. What was required, Lederer and Burdick argued, was a grass roots orientation, with the emphasis on small-scale technical assistance and agricultural innovation. In Asia, as in America, national economic development could proceed only on the basis of the expansion of individual production. Moreover, the implementation of aid programmes was hampered by the interference of uninformed bureaucrats, whose values derived from the corporation and big government. The initiative must rest with the man in the field, combining a technical expertise with a rugged individualism.

The Ugly American generated widespread controversy and was sharply criticized for its alleged factual inaccuracies. Senator Fulbright was quoted as saying that the novel contained 'gross exaggeration',[46] while the historian Joseph Buttinger condemned it for 'the flagrant manner in which it distorts, ignores or contradicts' the essential facts.[47] The evidence produced by these and other critics undercut many of the arguments advanced by Lederer and Burdick. Yet what is significant is that for all the rancour the book caused, it remained within the mainstream of American thought about aid and

diplomacy in south-east Asia. Lederer and Burdick accepted the broad
vision of Asian development; they shared the faith in what the United
States could accomplish. Their difference with official policy was not
about ends but about means and execution. Even here, their insistence
on the importance of the 'ordinary' American, the need to make
contact with the people and the priority to be accorded to low-level
technical innovation and modest commercial ventures was distinctively American. It drew on the frontier tradition and the spirit of
individual enterprise which was still influential in rural America,
especially in the western states. In this respect Homer Atkins, the ugly
American, is symbolic. Self-made to the tune of three million dollars,
his fingers black with grease, he is able to develop a simple water
pump and to organize its production at the village level.[48] Certainly
Lederer and Burdick stress that success can come only through
working closely with the local community, which involves learning the
language and being sensitive to the culture. It is noticeable, however,
that cultural differences are assumed to be superficial and hardly affect
the political and economic aspirations thought to be shared by Asians
and Americans alike.

Writing in 1962, Hans Morgenthau drew attention to another
element which in his view influenced the thinking of many Americans
about development assistance – the obligation of the rich to the poor.[49]
The idea of a debt or duty flowing from the very possession of wealth
involves different considerations from generalized notions of altruism
understood to derive from the nature of American society. For most of
the period it was the latter, not the former, which was predominant.
While well-rounded sentiments of obligation no doubt played some
part during the fifties and early sixties, it was not until the late sixties
that this line of thinking came into its own. Then it was often tied to
the idea that there was a causal connection between the affluence of
the West and the poverty of the Third World, and it was said that the
United States must accept some responsibility or even guilt for the
economic backwardness of large parts of the world. By this stage, both
the belief in America as a model and the confidence that the
development of the Third World could be secured had noticeably
waned. Yet as obligation became a theme in American thinking, the
constituency which approached aid and development in moral terms
was becoming smaller and less influential.

At the same time as faith was crumbling in the old formulae of
anti-communism and Third World development, the tides of anti-
Americanism were rising within the United States. These momentous
shifts in belief and thinking were related, though it was never as
simple as the replacement of communism and poverty overseas by the
enemy at home. The connecting rod was the war in Vietnam, but once
opinion had begun to turn, other considerations contributed to a more

general reassessment. The crucial years were the late sixties when the course of the war and its domestic ramifications led to widespread questioning of the purposes of intervention and an impassioned rejection of involvement on the part of vocal sections of American opinion. The moral consensus that America was a force for good in the world was thus shattered as several different currents of thinking met and competed. They came together under the umbrella of the anti-war movement but their coalescence could not survive the end of the Vietnam war – and in any case much of the emotional fervour subsided relatively quickly.

The impact of the war was increasingly to direct attention internally rather than externally – to the values and structures of American society. According to one assessment from the Left, Vietnam focussed 'a diamond light on the internal structure of the rich capitalist societies which compels their negation of the freedom and development of other societies'.[50] The same writer went on to argue that the ideologies of intervention had recoiled on the administration and that the young now drew their examples of dedication and heroism from liberation movements in the Third World. While the whole of the anti-war movement can by no means be characterized in such terms, observers of a decidedly different cast of mind accepted that there had been a fundamental shift in the moral compass of many Americans. In Henry Kissinger's view: 'For too many, a war to resist aggression had turned into a symbol of fundamental American evil.'[51] Likewise, Norman Podhoretz saw anti-Americanism as proceeding on the assumption that the United States was a force for evil in Vietnam.[52]

In large part, popular protest against the war tapped the tradition of American idealism which had earlier worked to sustain the United States' commitment. The central concern was with American society. In Norman Mailer's novel *Why Are We in Vietnam?*, for example, there is no mention of Vietnam until the last page. The arguments against the war were overwhelmingly moral rather than interest-based. The writing on the anti-war movement – and more generally on the protest movements of the sixties – makes plain the degree to which young radicals adhered to many of the values of their parents, anger being directed to the failure of the older generation to live up to its moral precepts. The pattern is one of initial idealism, disillusionment and then the redirection of idealism. In his study of individuals involved in the anti-war campaign, Kenneth Keniston writes that the most impressive feature of the radical commitment was the sense of continuity which most activists felt with their pasts.[53] Their family backgrounds showed a consistent orientation to ethical principles, and radicalism as it developed was fully congruent with the core values of the past.[54]

As the Johnson administration attempted to stave off defeat in

Vietnam by lifting the level of its military involvement, the sense of high moral purpose, long the prerogative of the White House, came to be relocated in the anti-war movement. In Podhoretz's words, New York was replacing Washington as the the source of political legitimacy.[55] For some time, disenchantment with other aspects of America's overseas role had been growing, especially in liberal circles. The ostensible failure of development programmes in the Third World raised new questions about America's aid and trade programmes and the altruism which was claimed by the administration. The rise of dependency theory, which in its cruder formulations postulated that Third World poverty was a function of Western affluence, led in some quarters to a ready acceptance of new orthodoxies about the nature of America's relations with the Third World. The succession of military coups which became a distinctive feature in the political life of the new states in the sixties dashed earlier optimism about the prospects of political democracy in Asia and Africa. Although a general process of re-evaluating America's role could hardly be said to have got under way, significant sections of informed opinion were coming to view the United States as blocking, not advancing, the prospects of the Third World.

What was notable about the new direction of thinking was the strong moral tone of its denunciation of the United States, which was now labelled as imperialist. In the background can also be detected a sense of guilt flowing from the revised interpretation of the historical record. The notion of collective guilt was most fully developed in relation to America's military involvement in Vietnam, but more generally there was a sense of responsibility for the failure of the Third World to fulfil the destiny assigned to it.[56] The idea of guilt stands in sharp contrast to the long tradition of pride in the role of the United States – and the West as a whole – as an instrument of Third World progress. In its most extravagant form, anti-Americanism expressed the conviction that the United States served as an object-lesson in the dangers and failings of industrialism, technology and rational knowledge. Applied science and control over nature, which had once been seen as America's contribution to global advancement, were now cast as barriers to human fulfilment. With the idea that the Third World must avoid the Western model, as exemplified by the United States, the wheel of American idealism had come full circle.

Having examined the way in which the sense of high moral purpose found expression in thinking relating to colonialism, communism, Third World development and American imperialism, we are left with the question of its significance for America's understanding of Asia and Africa. To what extent did moralism influence perceptions and condition policy options? Did it distort American appreciations or rather throw into relief elements and aspects which might otherwise have been missed? It is apparent that assessments here may carry the stamp of cultural bias, and that in practice it is often difficult to disentangle moral considerations from the various other factors which influenced thinking. In his innovative study of the makers of American foreign policy, John Stoessinger explores the role of two basic personality types: crusaders, who are depicted as 'movers', and pragmatists, who are seen as 'players'.[57] Yet the distinction is difficult to sustain when related to specific policy-makers in the real world. According to Stoessinger, Roosevelt combined the qualities of the crusader with those of the pragmatist in equal measure. But how are we to characterize Eisenhower or Johnson? Stoessinger's study offers us few leads.[58] A reminder is also appropriate that the ethical preferences of policy-makers must be considered in the light of the issues and choices as they appeared at the time. It was not until well into the 1960s that radical perspectives on the relationship between the United States and the Third World led to substantial questioning of America's world view. For most of the preceding period the range of political debate was extremely narrow, a fact which led sociologist Daniel Bell to proclaim the end of ideology.[59] The belief that the major problems of American life had been solved had a smothering effect, not only on thinking about domestic issues but also on approaches to the outside world.

In specific forms, the various conceptions spawned by American moralism affected what was seen and what was not seen in Asia and Africa, and how Third World societies were evaluated. To the extent that moralism took the form of anti-colonialism, it tended to attribute the ills of the Third World to the political injustice and economic exploitation of European rule. It carried at least an implicit optimism about the prospects of Asia and Africa once formal independences had been obtained. In 1965 Eisenhower expressed his belief 'that the breaking up of the ties of colonialism will have an effect in the future like that of waves caused by a sizeable stone thrown into the centre of a pond.'[60] Equally, and as European critics frequently pointed out, under the influence of anti-colonialism many Americans passed lightly over the difficulties inherent in the decolonization process – difficulties relating, for example, to the effect of precipitate political change and indigenous ethnic rivalries.

Anti-communism had the effect of distorting America's understanding of the significance of various parts of the Third World, as this criterion overshadowed consideration of the intrinsic importance of a particular region or country, or its relation to specific American interests. Few today would question that Vietnam, and indeed Indo-China as a whole, were given a prominence altogether at variance with their actual international status and value. At the other end of the spectrum was Africa, which was neglected because communism was not an issue. In a speech in May 1950, a senior American official was able simply to express his gratification at finding 'a region of 10 million square miles in which no significant inroads have been made by Communism and to be able to characterize the area as relatively stable and secure'.[61] Similarly, the evaluation of nationalism was skewed by its perceived relationship to international communism. Where nationalism was seen to be anti-communist – as in Indonesia and the Philippines – it was a positive force and won American support. Where it was tainted by communism, it was regarded as profoundly negative and had to be resisted – as in the case of Vietnam, even though in 1954 Eisenhower accepted that in a free election Ho Chi Minh would gather possibly 80 per cent of the vote.[62] Likewise with respect to North Africa, America's fear of communism distorted her understanding of the Algerian nationalist movement and encouraged the view that a true Muslim was a good anti-communist.[63]

The perceived 'truths' of the development model gave American thinking about the nature and prospects of Third World economics a narrow and very particularized bias. Alternative approaches or experimentation within the Third World were either strongly rejected or discounted through neglect. In the former category came the socialist systems of China and North Vietnam and later the centralist planning model of Allende in Chile. The latter category might include early Indian ideas about the revitalization of the village and intermediate technology, and the various attempts by Third World nationalists to limit the economic penetration of external states and to foster self-reliance. So strong was the belief in the Western way forward that, through a process of internalization, the possibilities of other paths to development – perhaps deriving from within indigenous cultures – were largely ruled out or disregarded in the Third World as well as in the United States.

In its more simplistic forms, anti-Americanism very often carried with it the conviction that Third World groups and states which resisted United States involvement held the promise of social justice and economic progress. In much of the literature of the Left, the guerilla fighter was almost by definition a nation-builder. In some quarters of the anti-war movement, the NLF and North Vietnam could do no wrong. According to another line of thinking, the faults and failings of America's enemies were the consequence of America's actions and thus responsibility in the end rested with the United States. What is significant is that anti-Americanism contained within it the tendency to see in America's adversaries the virtues America itself was thought to lack so conspicuously, irrespective of the evidentiary material.[64]

If in these various ways moralism influenced the kind of perceptions Americans had of developments in Asia and Africa, it also left a more

general imprint on the way the United States approached the Third
World. Its categories and reference-points gave a relative sameness to
the diversity of the Third World. Yet its interpretative sweep was of
the broadest kind. American moralism was like a wide-angle lens
which, while enlarging the field of vision, at the same time scales down
the objects in view. Because its categories and reference-points arose
from and remained tied to the American political culture, moralism
obstructed the comprehension of other societies and their different
social patterns and political aspirations. In a fascinating passage
Harold Isaacs suggests that the American belief in social mobility
epitomized by the 'from log cabin to White House' ideal, made the
Indian caste system incomprehensible to Americans and contributed
to the cultural collisions between the two societies.[65]

The assurance of having uncovered basic and universal truths not
only impeded understanding but also limited the interest taken in
Asian and African societies. The incentive to observe and enquire
overseas was lessened by the reliance on America's own experience
and values. During the occupation of Japan, for example, General
MacArthur and his aides viewed with suspicion men who had special
knowledge of Japan and the Far East.[66] Much later, President
Johnson observed: 'Our safest guide to what we do abroad is always
what we do at home . . .'[67] This may help to explain Johnson's habit –
observed by McGeorge Bundy – of treating Third World leaders like
senators.[68] Writing in 1954, George Kennan observed that America
was an exclusive rather than a receptive nation in psychology and in
practice, and he warned of the risk of becoming essentially
provincial.[69] Many of America's critics overseas have expressed
themselves even more sharply. America's lack of cultural empathy is a
recurrent theme in the final novel in Anthony Burgess' Malayan
trilogy, The Long Day Wanes. The professionalism of Americans in
newly-independent Malaya is conceded but it is seen as coming at the
expense of an interest in the people and a sensitivity to their customs –
witness the linguistician who is attempting to develop a local alphabet
without speaking the language.[70]

The most vivid illustration of the neglect of factors external to
American society is provided by some of the writing on the Vietnam
War, specifically what has become known as the 'new journalism'.
Following a route pioneered by Graham Greene in The Quiet
American, writers such as Norman Mailer and Michael Herr chose to
explore the collision in Indo-China through an understanding of the
American psyche and the nature of American society. Although the
new journalists went much further in this direction than Greene, they
were accorded a much easier passage. Whereas Greene was vigorously
criticized for his anti-Americanism, later writers received no such
censure in literary circles. Even more significant, the distortion which

followed from their almost total absorption with self and their own society went largely unnoticed. Norman Mailer presents us with his understanding of the war by writing about a bear hunt in Alaska (*Why Are We in Vietnam?*) and the 1968 march on the Pentagon (*The Armies of the Night*). In the former book, Mailer implies that feelings of sexual frustration and aggression produced by the hold of the corporations on the mental outlook of Americans found their expression in the Vietnam War. In *The Armies of the Night*, Mailer suggests that the push to go into Vietnam came from the American small town. Race riots, Las Vegas, suburban orgies were not enough; Vietnam was needed as an outlet – 'that was where the small town had gone to get its kicks.'[71] American culture is thus the source of the conflict; the Vietnam War the manifestation of its internal frictions.

For Michael Herr also, American culture shapes the perceptions of Vietnam and the military involvement. He reflects pessimistically: '. . . every one of us there a true volunteer'.[72] Beyond this, the meaning of the war can be distilled only through personal experience. At the beginning of his book, *Dispatches*, we are told that an old French map of Vietnam 'wasn't real any more'. By 1967 even the most detailed contemporary maps revealed very little: 'reading them was like trying to read the faces of the Vietnamese, and that was like trying to read the wind.' In his concluding chapter, he refers to a *National Geographic* map of Indo-China but what is significant are his own pencilled marks and the recollections they evoke.[73] The great limitation of Herr's and Mailer's treatment of Vietnam – along with much other American writing of the genre – is that Indo-China is not much more than a stage upon which the authors, as Americans, and the United States itself, act out their parts. International politics are not seen to have much bearing; hence the Vietnam War becomes not simply distinctive but unique. In large part, the conflict in Indo-China is assumed to be incomprehensible; the war insane. America and the individual consciousness are the only realities.

These themes might be given a somewhat different twist by exploring the extent to which the tone of American moralism derives from the need for reassurance. In the previous chapter, insecurity was considered in relation to power politics and it was argued that at least some American leaders felt the need to prove themselves by demonstrating will and resolve overseas.[74] Suggestions have often been made that Americans saw involvement in Asia as an opportunity to test their civilization.[75] According to Hartz, the absolutism which has characterized the American moral ethos reflects an unease with alien things: 'it cannot live in comfort constantly by their side.'[76] Following Morgenthau and Kennan, we thus move towards an explanation of the tendency for America to oscillate between attempting to transform the outside world and retreating into isolation. Senator Fulbright takes us one step further with his reflection that 'lack of self-assurance seems to breed an exaggerated sense of power and mission.'[77]

It is difficult to anchor these thoughts in the empirical and historical material about the evaluation of America's overseas policies. Moreover, unlike the British case considered earlier, American fiction set in Asia in the years before the divisions over the Vietnam war provides few insights into insecurity. The literature of the Cold War era very largely echoes official perspectives, and conveys much the same sense of confidence in American civilization and its overseas destiny. In a few novels there are suggestions that Asia is too old and wily for Americans to understand, let alone change, and doubts as to whether the United States has the will to stand up to the forces of communism.[78] Even so, these doubts and apprehensions seldom stand in isolation and do not constitute broad and continuing themes. A more promising field of enquiry would seem to be the hold of McCarthyism in the early fifties. Clearly, the anti-communist witch-hunts and the ideological extremism associated with Senator McCarthy indicate that America was less sure of itself and more neurotic about its enemies than the diplomatic record would suggest. Generally over the period, attention might profitably be directed to the national mood and to the internal tensions within the United States, in the hope of tracing their influence on overseas perceptions and actions. One largely neglected source would seem to be those fictional works set within the United States which develop themes relating to personal insecurity and alienation. They may well prove to be the more revealing because so often they reject or neglect the political domain.[79]

As America became increasingly ensnared in Vietnam, the subject of insecurity attracted more attention. In the anti-war movement, the idea gained ground of America as a 'sick society' and that external involvement was a symptom of this condition. The notion of America finding 'a release' in Vietnam was an expression both of internal disorder and of the aberrant sexuality of American society. According to Charles Reich, America had suffered a 'loss of self', which stemmed from the sense of individual powerlessness in the face of official rigidity and repression. This pathology of rigidity and repression 'extended outward, to create the Cold War, with its progeny, . . . Vietnam.'[80] In Jerry Rubin's view the problem was much simpler: 'Sexual insecurity results in a supermasculinity trip called imperialism.'[81] Norman Mailer's diagnosis cuts deeper.

> He had come to decide that the center of America might be insane. The country had been living with a controlled, even fiercely controlled, schizophrenia which had been deepening with the years. . . . the foul brutalities of the war in Vietnam were the only temporary cure possible for the condition – since the expression of brutality offers a definite, if temporary, relief to the schizophrenic.[82]

Such thoughts have not been systematically developed – and perhaps cannot be – but they are suggestive, especially when related to the thinking and behaviour of American statesmen.

It is the moralist, rather than the pragmatist, who is prone to perceive issues in overseas policy in highly personalized terms. The record of post-war American diplomacy reveals many instances in which moralism has contributed to behaviour more usually associated with personal than with international relations. Obvious cases are Washington's long-standing attempt to isolate China, and the Eisenhower administration's inability to come to terms with Third World neutralism. According to John Stoessinger, a specific instance where moralism misdirected policy was Dulles' withdrawal of the American offer to finance the Aswan Dam in 1956 because he saw Nasser as attempting to blackmail him by playing the Soviet card. Stoessinger comments: 'A good Calvinist would not be blackmailed by the devil.'[83] While almost certainly Dulles allowed his indignation to colour his judgement, a recent study makes clear that the reversal of American policy was influenced by wider diplomatic considerations and that it was not the sudden decision often assumed.[84] Many will recoil from any characterization of Johnson as a moralist, yet his biographers bring out strong moral strands relating to his vision of Asia's future and his universalization of the Texan dream.[85] What is unquestionable is his personalization of international politics and especially of the conflict in Vietnam. It was 'his' war, American troops became 'his' boys and Walt Rostow 'his' intellectual. The challenge came from Ho Chi Minh; the struggle was a test of wills.[86] By personalizing the war in this fashion, Johnson imparted to it certain aspects of his character and personality.

It would be easy to over-emphasize the links between internal drives and external action. Yet as new material emerges and psycho-analytical insights gain wider currency, it will be surprising if the idea of insecurity does not increasingly inform our understanding of America's moralism – and indeed of her external orientation in general. Writing in 1935, Harold Lasswell predicted that insecurity would play a much larger part in shaping America's outlook on the world as the country became more involved in international politics.[87] It is unfortunate that the main lines of scholarly analysis since then have been more concerned with America's assurance than with its doubts and anxieties.

Nine

ECONOMIC INTEREST III

The literature on America's economic involvement in the Third World since the Second World War is remarkably reminiscent of that on the economics of British imperialism in the period 1870 to 1914. There is the same sharp disagreement between scholars about the priority to be accorded to economic interest. There is a similar preoccupation with explanation at the expense of perception. Many of the categories of analysis and even the lines of argument have a general familiarity. This is less surprising than might at first appear, because in both periods we are dealing with the dominant world power and with policy-makers who played a pre-eminent part in shaping the international economic system. The importance of the subject-matter is thus paralleled by the particular difficulties of interpretation posed by the breadth of policy-makers' concerns and the relationship in their minds between different geographical areas and different kinds of interests. In addition, there has been a tendency for scholars to approach matters of perception and policy in the light of their global characterizations rather than on the basis of the domestic evidentiary material. Not infrequently, assumptions about the determinants of national policy follow almost as a matter of course from the writer's understanding of the nature of the international system of the epoch.

In the recent debate about the place of economic interest in American diplomacy, the running has been made by the revisionist historians, with support being provided by the themes of dependency theorists. It was the revisionists who lifted economic interest from relative obscurity to the forefront of analysis.[1] The course of the war in Vietnam blew open the debate, with the result that revisionist themes received wider circulation and a more sympathetic hearing. In the aftermath of Vietnam a new generation of students approached American involvement in the Third World, with strong presuppositions about the nature and importance of economic considerations and a decided scepticism about both official accounts of American purposes and the interpretations of conventional scholarship. The terrain has thus been marked out by the economic determinism of writers such as Gabriel Kolko and Noam Chomsky, and the more evangelical slant of William Appleman Williams. Subsequent analyses have tended to follow the signposts they have erected or alternatively to argue that these signposts are fundamentally misleading. Either way, the radical critique has been centre-stage. Some consideration must therefore be given to revisionist themes, though a full appraisal would divert attention to issues which extend well beyond the scope of this chapter. Whatever the strengths and weaknesses of revisionist histor-iography, the concerns and approach of these writers are much broader than our focus on the thinking of American policy-makers about the economic importance of Asia and Africa.

This can be demonstrated by briefly referring to certain characteris-tic features of the revisionist case. The fundamental proposition to which all revisionists subscribe is that overseas involvement is rooted in the economic and social structure of the United States and that it has worked to further the economic interests of corporate power. Expansion is thus predetermined by the nature of the corporate economy; American capitalism is a system which organically exerts itself overseas. In evaluating the revisionist structure of thought, it is useful to consider the distinction between function, consequence and intent. In the revisionist conception the crucial category for under-standing American imperialism is function – this is how the system operates, and given the nature of American institutions it cannot do otherwise. On the question of the significance of overseas involvement for the health of the American economy – or corporate capitalism, which is taken to be the same thing since the two are inextricably related – reliance is placed on consequence. Here, revisionists turn to the statistics on overseas trade and investment and stress the import-ance of external outlets at the margin. There is more uncertainty and internal differences with respect to intent: did policy-makers con-sciously perceive the economic underpinning of their actions? Here the purposes of the revisionist have not always been set out clearly; in any case, in terms of the logic of their position, perception and intent are of secondary importance. G. William Domhoff concludes his analysis of the makers of American foreign policy by conceding that he has not proved that they act in the interests of the corporation. He continues:

> However, it is certainly possible to make the beginnings of a case on this on the basis of the economists' assumptions that people tend to act in their self-interest, and the psychologists' and sociologists' finding that people perceive and interpret the world in terms of their individual upbringing, cultural background, and occupational roles.[2]

Joyce and Gabriel Kolko write with far more confidence about the economic objectives of American policy-makers and the deliberateness of their designs. Their analysis of American intentions is couched in terms of a vision, careful calculation and clarity of purpose, but even they find it necessary to point out that 'one cannot divorce principle from its practice and fulfillment.'[3]

It might be argued that revisionist writing is more persuasive when it is directed to function rather than to intent. In the end it is not essential for revisionist purposes to establish that policy-makers knowingly acted on the basis of economic interests, and the trend appears to be that writers on the Left have been increasingly inclined to stress structural factors rather than conscious intent. This is what makes the revisionist literature an unreliable guide for our purposes, all the more so because of the habit of some writers of moving from the needs of the system to the perceptions of policy-makers, secure in their assumption that the two invariably run together.

The concern of this chapter is with the thinking and perceptions of those who made or influenced American overseas policy. What images were held of Asian and African societies as economic units? What future were they seen to have and to what degree could it be shaped by external example or intervention? How far were economic developments in these regions evaluated in the light of the needs and drives of the United States' economy? Thinking at the time by no means always ran in such clear-cut channels. Hindsight lends its own perspective, and what in the eighties appear to have been the central categories and issues were often not seen as such by contemporary opinion. Our initial concern is thus to establish the main lines of American economic thinking during the years of the Cold War. What was the extent and nature of American interest in the economic future of Asia and Africa? What was the relative priority accorded to economic as distinct from political considerations in the approach of policy-makers?

The most important theme to be developed is that in matters of substance there was little that was distinctive about American economic conceptions of Asia and Africa. Progress was the bench-mark and it was seen to follow the same broad course in all societies. The bounds of thinking were set by the commitment to industrial and agrarian growth, and the hope that increased output would be widely if unevenly distributed within the society. Whether material abundance was explicitly held out as the eventual goal or assumed in the analyses of economic processes, there was but one road and a single destination. Although Asia and Africa were certainly seen as economically backward, they were not viewed as different in kind from Western economies at an earlier stage of development. While opinion varied with regard to their potential significance in the international economy or as an adjunct to the domestic economy of the United States, the criteria of evaluation were much the same as those applied to other states and regions. As American interest and knowledge increased from its very low base in the late 1940s, thinking about the Third World became more specialized and theoretical, but the parameters within which it proceeded remained essentially the same. In a sense this was a mark of the ethnocentrism both of American perceptions and of economic analyses. The former proceeded on the assumption that Africa and Asia would fit into or be absorbed by the Western-derived and dominated international economic system. The latter, including both the models and the metaphors they employed, were derived almost exclusively from Western experience – primarily Anglo-America and to a lesser extent European.[4] A clear illustration is provided by W.W. Rostow's seminal work, *The Stages of Economic Growth*, first published in 1960.

It followed that, far from being geographically contained, American economic conceptions proceeded within a global context. Africa and Asia had no meaning as categories in any economic sense – which at one level was after all a fact of life, since for the most part the external linkages of the new states were with the West rather than with their neighbours. The logic of economics was powerfully reinforced by the strategic considerations of the Cold War. The tendency to adopt a global perspective facilitated the transposition of policies designed for one area to another, without much regard for different internal circumstances. It also meant that American thinking about parts of Asia and Africa was approached in the light of the needs and interests of the external states, most notably the European countries and Japan. In the radical view, this global orientation provides the basis for an interpretation of America's overseas economic interests in terms of the interconnectedness of developments almost anywhere in the world. It is conceded that very often America's direct economic stake in a Third World country or region cannot explain the extent of United States involvement. However, the argument runs that account must be taken of the systemic significance attached to local or regional developments. The classic case is America's approach to Vietnam. At various points in the sections which follow we will be concerned to assess the extent to which ideas about global interrelationships influenced American thinking about specific areas, and the degree to which such global perspectives were tied to economic conceptions as distinct from politico-strategic ones.

There is necessarily more uncertainty and conjecture about the approach of American governments to overseas economic issues than to matters of power and strategy, or even questions of moral responsibility. By the very nature of their calling, the picture that most statesmen had of the world was largely political, and their public presentation of issues was most commonly in political terms. It must also be said that the fifties and sixties were a time when international relations were widely understood to revolve around considerations of power politics and international economic questions were regarded as subsidiary. When policy-makers did venture economic arguments and justifications, we face the perennial problem of deciding whether their purpose was to conceal or to reveal. The public record makes clear that for most of the period, American statesmen were not deeply concerned with Asian economic issues and hardly at all with African ones. Further, that insofar as they were concerned, economic development and aid received more attention than resources, investment and trade, though of course all of these were seen to be related.

During and immediately after the Second World War, the belief took shape in Washington that the United States would have to play a key role in establishing a new and more congenial international economic order. Heavily influenced by their reading of the experience of the inter-war years and fearful of the possibility of another depression, a number of key policy-makers outlined their views on post-war international requirements and argued that the United States should take initiatives to restructure the world system. Cordell Hull was probably the most influential advocate of economic reform, but Acheson had firm if more general views on the need for post-war construction. Men such as Henry Morgenthau, Secretary of the Treasury, and William Clayton, Assistant Secretary of State for Economic Affairs, consistently emphasized the importance of international economic arrangements to America's domestic economy. The broad commitment was to a liberal economic system which would prevent economic nationalism by promoting the free movement of capital and commodities and a high level of international interaction. Such a design was believed to be necessary for world recovery and growth, and would provide the foundation for a stable political order. It was on this basis that American leaders approached the Bretton Woods Conference in 1944 to establish a new international monetary system and the projected International Trade Organization which was intended to oversee a liberal international trading system. The United States played a large part in the establishment of the International Monetary Fund and the International Bank for Reconstruction and Development (known as the World Bank), and in fact dominated both institutions until sometime about 1970. American negotiators had much less success in obtaining international agreement for their plan for a new trading system. Eventually, hobbled by Congress, the Truman administration killed the International Trade Organization because it was not sufficiently shaped to fit United States interests, replacing it with the commitment to the more limited GATT (General Agreement on Tariffs and Trade). There can thus be no doubt about the importance the United States attached to restructuring the international economic system during and after the war.

Where the argument sets in is whether America's economic aims overshadowed her broader political objectives.[5]

Developing alongside American thinking about the need to construct a more open economic system was the argument on another plane that it was necessary to close in the Soviet Union. With the emergence of the Cold War, the containment policy triumphed and economic concerns became secondary. In the crucial years of the fifties, when the key decisions were taken about America's role in the Third World, the dominant perceptions were political and military and it was generally accepted that overseas economic considerations followed in their wake. In the first instance thinking was political and strategic, not economic. This conclusion cannot be established on the basis of specific evidence; it is a matter of interpreting the world view of policy-makers and the thrust of their thinking. It is of course challenged by the revisionist historians, both at the general level and with regard to particular regions. It is instructive here to briefly elaborate on the position with respect to south-east Asia in the light of the material made available by the publication of the *Pentagon Papers*.

For the period of the fifties, the *Pentagon Papers* point to the primacy of strategic and power politics considerations. While it is true that there are numerous references to the importance of resources and raw materials, and a few to trade and investment, these mainly slot into a political and military understanding of the area rather than the other way round. This leads Kolko, for example, to assert that the *Pentagon Papers* are 'mediocre as history and partial in documentation', and to censure their limited focus on purpose.[6] The *Pentagon Papers* unmistakably confirm the centrality of the domino theory in American thinking for a period of a decade and a half, and reveal that, with the exception of the CIA, it was never questioned in Washington. The key question for our purposes is whether the domino theory was understood primarily in terms of strategy and political resolve, or whether it was concerned with underlying economic relationships hinging on the argument that the loss of south-east Asian resources and markets would push Japan towards neutralism or more probably into the communist camp. Again it must be said that National Security Council or other documents cannot provide a definitive answer, but the terms and context of argument indicate a politico-military appreciation. The *Pentagon Papers*, like the public speeches of American statesmen, certainly refer to the resources of south-east Asia, but as elements in the power balance and in many cases as elements which contributed to military capability. The economic references are in support of broader arguments; they are not seen as standing alone. Nor are they explored in any detail. This is hardly surprising since, as Robert Tucker observes, south-east Asia could not then be considered vital to the post-war Japanese economy either as a source of raw materials or as a market for Japanese exports.[7]

The revisionist case for an economic understanding of the domino theory involves the assumption that one must go beyond the statements of policy-makers or at least read between the lines. Gabriel Kolko prefaces his statement that 'the domino theory was a counter-revolutionary doctrine' in conjunction with the phrase 'translated into concrete terms'.[8] According to Noam Chomsky, the Pentagon historians do not analyse the implicit content of the theory.[9] John Dower tells us that 'the Pentagon Papers offer largely a tunnel vision of Japan as the ultimate domino'.[10] When it comes to the sixties, the *Pentagon Papers* contain remarkably little evidence of economic thinking on the part of policy-makers. On Peter Dale Scott's account, the explanation must be in terms of distortion, and their very silence 'testifies to the importance of the absent material and the possibility of censorship.'[11]

Thus far the argument has been that, seen through American eyes, the non-European world was an adjunct to the system of economic relations which existed between the developed states; it was expected to follow the same economic path and it was considered to be subject to the same norms of international behaviour. American economic conceptions were therefore global in scope, though this should not be taken to imply that the disruption of one part was seen to threaten the fabric of the entire system. It has been further asserted that the last years of the forties saw emphasis shifting from overseas economic concerns to political ones; that whereas the revisionists have emphasized the continuity of American thinking during and after the war, what is significant is the historical discontinuity. It is now proposed to substantiate and extend these themes by considering the specific lines of thinking with respect to the economics of the non-European world. These will be examined under three heads: development and assistance, resources and strategic materials, and trade and investment.

(i) *Development and Assistance*

The most comprehensive and sustained treatment of the economics of Asia and Africa was contained in the material on development and economic assistance. This was the area about which policy-makers had most to say, because it fell clearly within the domain of official action and it was necessarily the starting-point for broader thinking about the Third World's role. The foundations of America's approach were laid in 1947 with the United States' commitment to the economic recovery of Western Europe. Alongside the immediate economic objectives of the Marshall Plan were three assumptions which had a direct bearing on America's subsequent thinking about aid and development in Asia and Africa. First, Europe was of overwhelming importance in America's conception of its overseas interests. Second, economic development was held to be a condition precedent to political stability and Europe's ability to withstand Soviet aggression. Third, the extension of aid was seen as a means of promoting trade liberalization in Europe and more generally a liberal international order.

Aid and development emerged as an aspect of America's approach to Asia in 1948 when the United States attempted to arrest the economic deterioration of Nationalist China. Assistance was then extended to Korea, Burma and other south-east Asian countries, culminating in the more systematic approach of the Point Four Programme outlined in President Truman's inaugural address of January 1949. Thenceforth, development assistance occupied the attention of successive presidents. It was extensively debated in Congress, and reviewed by various committees and commissions. It thus provides a window through which to view American thinking about Afro-Asia's economic position and potentialities.

The development of the Third World was important in its own right but it was also seen as serving America's diplomatic and commercial purposes. Development and aid were components of the United States' broader overseas policies designed to win advantage in the Cold War and advance the interests of the home economy. The Point Four Program, for example, attempted to advance all three objectives and assumed their complementarity.[12] Much of the internal debate about the level and nature of subsequent economic aid programmes was addressed to the relationship between and priority to be accorded to the various objectives. To some degree, therefore, aid and development give insights into lines of thinking about the contribution Afro-Asia might make to America's own economic welfare, and the efficacy of economic growth as a means of promoting broader political and strategic interests.

The most notable feature of America's approach to development and assistance was the belief that Third World societies could be readily transformed and that the United States had the means. The vision of development was sweeping in scope, yet officials and legislators comfortably assumed that only relatively small quantities of aid were required. When, in 1949, Truman stressed the role aid could play in promoting development and democracy in Korea, the goal of economic self-reliance was believed to be realizable 'within a relatively few years' and a modest $140 million was contributed for the purpose.[13] Such optimism was carried over to the Point Four Program, which was aimed at generating development through the extension of technical assistance. The administration sought $45 million for the first year of what was an extremely ambitious programme which ranged globally. In Truman's view, America's vast reserves of technical knowledge held the key to solving the age-old problems of want and disease.[14] This faith in knowledge and technology remained a consistent feature of official thinking for at least two decades. Technical expertise and organizational skills came to be supplemented by sociological insights and the scientific breakthroughs of the Green Revolution. The widespread optimism about what could be accomplished was therefore much more a testament to America's belief in its own powers than a result of any careful appraisal of Third World potential.

In the case of the Point Four Program, debate in Congress did not focus on the extravagance of the administration's goals but was confined to questions of a more or less instrumental kind.[15] Congressmen did not doubt America's capacity to fulfil the task it had set itself. The worries were rather whether foreign aid programmes heralded too radical a shift from the traditional preference for private economic activity, the advisability of the United States involving itself in multilateral ventures, and the costs of the proposals. These concerns set the tone of Congressional response to foreign assistance policies over a number of years.[16] Congress was mostly hostile, and continually insisted that aid programmes should in some way directly benefit the interests of the United States. In the early fifties there were repeated calls for foreign aid to be terminated at the first opportunity; later, when the fear of global war had receded, Republican administration requests for funds were shaved by an average of 20 per cent. Throughout, Congress showed a strong preference for loans rather than grants. Proposals by Eisenhower and Kennedy that aid policy be determined in the context of longer-term financial plans which would by-pass the annual appropriation process were rejected out of hand.[17]

Implicit in the American approach to development and assistance was the assumption that Third World societies were essentially malleable: that they could be reshaped according to an external formula and through the injection of external resources. The ease with which the principal features of the Marshall Plan were transferred to Asia and later Africa shows the complacency felt on this score. For a time the concept of 'nation-building' was in vogue. More specifically there was the notion that societies could be rebuilt according to the American model. The metaphor of building is not without significance because it indicates that the process of economic change, at least in its initial stages, was seen as mechanical, not organic. The concept of 'take-off' is equally suggestive. Yet if economic growth could be impelled from the outside, it was always seen as having an indigenous component. To attract sceptical American capital, Afro-Asian leaders would have to create an environment conducive to free enterprise. Development would only prove self-sustaining on the basis

of private initiative, rather than through state direction. In 1949
Acheson told the Latin Americans:

> This country has been built by private initiative . . . The preponderance of
> our economic strength depends today as in the past upon the technical and
> financial resources and, even more, upon the abilities and morale of private
> citizens. I venture to say that the same thing is true of the other American
> nations.[18]

Acheson's homily became a theme in America's general approach to
Third World development. Much later Eisenhower emphasized that
development was 'no mere matter of obtaining outside financial
assistance'. What he called 'the national discipline' was an 'indispensable element'.[19]

With the vantage of hindsight, two further aspects of development
thinking appear significant, though both were largely taken for
granted at the time. In the diagnosis of economic backwardness, the
problem was located within Third World societies themselves, emphasis being placed on the cultural and environmental impediments to
change. In terms of prescription, hopes were pinned on the role of a
modernizing elite which would act as the carrier of new skills and
values. Thus change would be introduced from the top. This
conception paralleled the emphasis placed on the Western educated as
the central actors in the development of Afro-Asian nationalism and
the establishment of political democracy along Western lines. These
understandings were challenged in the late sixties; but it was not until
the seventies, with the rise of dependency theory, that conventional
approaches became the subject of wider debate. Then, radical critics
inverted the established orthodoxies, arguing that the causes of
economic backwardness were to be found externally, not internally,
and that if Third World countries were to make economic headway,
change must come from the masses rather than from self-interested
elites.

The intrusion of Cold War considerations gave a more pragmatic
twist to development thinking, and in a number of respects involved a
very different ordering of priorities. The relationship between aid
programmes and America's geopolitical interests had weighed with the
Truman administration in the late forties, but it was not elaborated in
any detail. After the outbreak of the Korean War, development and
aid were increasingly viewed in the context of the global struggle
between the United States and the Soviet Union. In 1951 the
administrative agencies with responsibilities for military and economic
aid were brought together under the Mutual Security Act. The
purpose of this act, which was to govern foreign aid policy until 1961,
was heavily tied to the advancement of United States' security
interests.[20] At the same time the United States embarked on a

programme of military assistance to selected Asian countries. The
expansion of Soviet economic and political relations with Third World
countries after Stalin's death in 1953 provoked some rethinking about
foreign aid. In particular, Eisenhower and Joseph Dodge, Chairman
of the Commission for Foreign Economic Policy, came to the view
that American aid and trade would need to be increased and that the
public sector would have to play a larger role. However, the actual
steps taken were limited and the response of Congress was niggardly.
In view of its assessment that the Cold War had taken an economic
turn, it is paradoxical that the administration did not adopt a more
vigorous and comprehensive approach to development assistance.[21]
As it was, development remained an appendage of rather than an
alternative to the strengthening of military capability, and aid alloca-
tions were concentrated on allies under immediate threat. The result
was that during the Eisenhower period the ratio of military to
economic aid steadily increased, and by the last years of the decade
military aid was heavily predominant.[22] A significant shift away from
narrowly conceived security objectives took place during the Kennedy
presidency. However, the instrumentalist views of the State Department, and Kennedy's own understanding of the more subtle relationship between development and anti-communism, meant that
practice fell short of rhetoric. It has also been argued that the
administration's faint-hearted opposition to the Hickenlooper amendment of 1962 belied its verbal support for structural economic reform
in underdeveloped countries.[23] The Johnson years saw a renewed
emphasis on security considerations plainly conceived. Whatever the
President's predilections about Asian development, his pragmatism
and propensity for short-term analysis, and the impact of Vietnam, led
to an approach stamped with the purposes of the Cold War.

One element in the Cold War approach was the role of foreign
assistance in securing stable supplies of raw materials for the United
States economy. This became of particular concern to policy-makers
with respect to strategic materials in the context of the re-armament
programme of 1950 and 1951. In 1952 the President's Materials Policy
Commission (the Paley Commission) pointed to the likely importance
of Africa and Asia as suppliers of raw materials to the United States,
including minerals essential to Western security. In the view of the
commission, 'if we fail to work for a rise in the standard of living of the
rest of the free world, we thereby hamper and impede the further rise
of our own.'[24] This theme was developed by liberal critics convinced
that a larger and wiser aid programme would produce security
dividends. In the last days of the 1956 presidential campaign, Adlai
Stevenson wrote that aid 'should be a means of keeping essential raw
materials available for the American economy. It should be a means of
checking the Soviet effort to isolate the United States from Asia,

Africa and Latin America.'[25] Another element was the belief that the economic development of Asia and Africa would contribute to the stability of Europe and Japan, both essential to America's global order. A healthy and expanding trading network between Europe and its former colonial possessions, and between Japan and her traditional markets and sources of supply in south-east Asia, were regarded as vital to the economic and thereby military strength of the free world.

A third argument, used to good effect by Kennedy in 1958, was the need to bolster India's development programme in order to offset the image of China in the lead with its 'great leap forward'. With the eyes of the world focussed on the two very different economic models, the idea of China as the hare and India as the tortoise was a major set-back to the anti-communist cause. More generally there was the presumed link between prosperity and peace. In the early post-war period, the inheritance of the thirties inclined policy-makers to present war as a consequence of economic malfunctioning, which in turn was often related to the failure or absence of political democracy. With the development of the Cold War this line of thinking gave way to the reasoning that the appeals of communism paled in the face of growing affluence. Robert McNamara was a vigorous exponent of this viewpoint during his seven years as Secretary of Defence. As he put it subsequently: 'Security is development, and without development there can be no security.'[26]

Reviewing the thinking and debate of the fifties and sixties, it can be seen that there were two competing conceptions of the role of aid in the Cold War struggle. The first was primarily concerned with military aid to counter an immediate threat, and the calculations were in terms of short-term security advantages. The second, which was rooted in the belief that development was a good in itself, drew on a much longer tradition; it stressed the eventual contribution to American security of the emergence of more prosperous and politically stable Third World societies which would be able to resist the machinations and superficial appeals of communism. The first approach was much less concerned with the Third World for its own sake, or with its internal processes. Aid was a tool to promote America's political and strategic interests in the Cold War. In the case of the second approach, America's interests were identified with the consolidation and extension of the liberal capitalist order. Often, arguments which related the provision of aid to the circumstances of the Cold War appear as justifications or rationalizations to win support from a reluctant administration, Congress or the American people.

The need to shore up the case for development assistance provides a partial explanation of the repeated references of policy-makers to the benefits which would accrue to the home economy. Whatever the real concerns, political prudence dictated such a course. President Truman, for example, emphasized that the Point Four Program would stimulate expanded trade with the United States, and that the extension of aid would help solve America's post-war balance of payments surpluses. There can be scarcely any question that at the broadest level most policy-makers accepted that America's prosperity was tied to a vigorous world trade and international economic growth. The debate becomes contentious with regard to the importance attached to Asia and Africa and the extent to which economic aid was geared to producing direct economic benefits. These questions will be considered more fully in section iii, but some observations are relevant here about the way in which aid was approached by sections of domestic opinion within the United States.

Arguments that aid programmes must confer direct economic benefits to the United States were advanced most prominently by Congress and the business sector. Indeed, throughout the period, perceptions in both these quarters were more concerned with the implications and spin-offs for the home economy than the effects on the recipient countries. As has already been noted, Congress persistently saw its role as a watchdog of America's hard interests, and at least on some occasions key elements attempted to tailor aid programmes to advance specific interests.[27] A clear illustration is the approach to PL 480, known as the 'food for peace' programme, which was conceived as a means of relieving the problem of America's agricultural surpluses. The Department of Agriculture played a leading role in formulating the legislation; the State Department exerted little influence. The operation of the act came before the congressional committees on agriculture, the members of which were predominantly representatives from America's larger agricultural states. Most of the witnesses at the hearings were concerned with the problems of domestic agriculture, not overseas aid.[28] In the eyes of its promoters, the purpose of the legislation was twofold: first, to draw off surplus agricultural stocks purchased by the federal government to boost rural incomes. Secondly, by requiring the executive to allocate aid funds to purchase agricultural produce, overseas expenditure on foreign aid would be reduced. Significantly, it was not envisaged that the PL 480 programme would be a permanent feature of America's foreign and agricultural policy.

The American business community, while prepared to accept that military assistance was vital to the national interest, was much less persuaded by the case for economic aid. During the early Eisenhower years, corporations shared the administration's concern with international economic development but believed this could best be accomplished by expanding trade and private investment, not through state action. The claim advanced by under-developed countries that they had a right to economic aid was firmly rejected by the Commission on

Foreign Economic Policy (the Randall Commission) in 1954, which put its trust in trade rather than aid.[29] This approach was sometimes justified by the argument that aid in the form of charity corrupted the relations between donor and recipient country, and led the latter to believe it was being exploited.[30] It was further argued that the export of capital fell clearly within the province of the private sector and that it was this sector which would ensure its most efficient utilization. The state's legitimate role was confined to the application of diplomatic and political pressure directed to the creation of a climate favourable to foreign investment in the Third World. By the late fifties, however, some change in attitude was evident. The fact that Asia and the Middle East had attracted very little private investment led to a greater tolerance of public investment. Indeed the Committee for Economic Development, an organ of liberal business opinion, argued that some governmental action was necessary to promote economic growth in the Third World. The basic needs of developing societies were infra-structural, and thus unattractive to private investment. But private capital would flow into these societies once the foundation for growth had been laid.[31]

Notwithstanding the changed thinking in some quarters on the question of public versus private investment, the broad trend was one of growing hostility to foreign aid. This was reflected in a greater tendency on the part of policy-makers to stress the direct benefits to the United States economy and to adjust aid programmes to accord with Congressional preferences. The increased reliance on 'soft loans' as compared with direct grants can partly be explained in these terms.[32] With the restructuring of aid programmes under Kennedy, aid became tied to the purchase of United States goods and services and all aid commodities were to be shipped in United States vessels.[33] By 1968 William Gaud, an administrator of the Agency for International Development, was able to argue:

> The biggest single misconception about the foreign aid programme is that we send money abroad. We don't. Foreign aid consists of American equipment, raw materials, expert services, and food . . . 96% of AID funds are spent directly in the United States . . .[34]

The notion that aid might represent a barrier to Third World development was scarcely considered before the mid-sixties. Such worries as were expressed arose from classical economic doctrines and related to the shortcomings of charity and the distortions attendant upon relying on public investment. Moreover, to a considerable extent aid was viewed separately from trade, and there was little longer-term thinking and planning.[35] The essential novelty of the revisionist critique attests to the absence of such perspectives in the fifties and early sixties. The point can be illustrated by referring to PL 480. At the time, criticism of the programme was advanced exclusively in terms of the interests of the United States and its allies. The main arguments related to the programme's cost, its failure to address the problem of agricultural overproduction and its impact on the commerce of friendly countries such as Canada and Australia which exported food commodities. Its beneficence was accepted by planners in recipient countries. In 1960 Theodore Schultz, later to be awarded the Nobel Prize for Economics, challenged a number of the programme's central assumptions and questioned the value of PL 480 assistance to the Third World. Some debate ensued but it was not until well into the 1970s that Schultz's critique became the basis of a broad indictment, by radical writers, of PL 480 as detrimental to the interests of recipient countries.

(ii) *Resources and Strategic Materials*

From the early fifties, America's dependence on overseas raw materials was a matter of persistent concern among sections of the policy-making elite and specialized opinion. For some decades industrial expansion had been denting America's traditional self-sufficiency. The process was accelerated by the Second World War. During the war years various measures were taken by the government to ensure adequate supplies of basic materials, and in 1946 the United States began a programme of stockpiling strategic materials. The limited progress made in the late forties led to some concern about America's potential vulnerability in the event of further armed conflict.[36] It was the outbreak of the Korean War, however, which brought the issue into prominence. The fear of shortages of crucial resources was a recurring theme during the war, and the demand for materials such as rubber and tin led to substantial price increases. In addition to the immediate requirements for prosecuting the war it was recognized that the United States' commitment to global leadership would place increasing pressure on supplies in the longer term. Moreover, America's growing population and expanding industrial base would add to requirements, inevitably leading to the depletion of domestic resources and greater dependence on overseas supplies. These considerations induced officials to direct attention to the role the Third World could play in meeting America's resource needs.

A number of reports by official and non-official bodies over the period confirmed that the United States was becoming increasingly dependent upon foreign supplies of raw materials. The Paley Commission, set up by Truman in 1951 to formulate a national policy on resources, concluded that 'The Nation not only is not self-sufficient now, but will become less so as the economy continues to expand and its demands broaden and increase.'[37] In 1954 the Randall Commission advised President Eisenhower that intensified development of foreign sources of deficient raw materials was 'a compelling necessity for the United States'.[38] A more restrained assessment was given in a 1963 study issued under the imprimatur of Resources for the Future, a private research corporation funded by the Ford Foundation. Although finding no cause for alarm, the authors of the study reiterated America's reliance on external resources and thought it clear that this reliance would increase.[39]

Against a background of the conflict in Korea and the fear of general war, the Paley Commission paid particular attention to the feasibility of self-reliance as an objective of United States materials policy. In the view of the Commission, much could be done by way of a more efficient allocation of existing supplies, the development of unutilized domestic reserves and a systematic approach to the production of synthetic materials. In the case of rubber, for example, great hopes were pinned on the expansion of synthetic production. Even so, self-sufficiency was rejected as unfeasible except in limited areas. The United States needed supplies of certain minerals which could neither be manufactured synthetically nor be drawn from domestic reserves. Even where self-reliance was technologically feasible it would be cost-inefficient. With regard to oil, it was noted that domestic reserves were under increasing strain and that petroleum synthetically drawn from shale would probably cost between 25 and 30 per cent more than supplies drawn from crude oil. Technological advances were projected as likely to expand the output of domestic wells and reduce the costs of producing synthetics, but not sufficiently to eliminate dependence on foreign sources.[40]

It was increasingly recognized that many of the overseas resources required by the United States were found in Asia and Africa, often in abundance. The Paley Commission advised that the areas to which the United States must principally look for expansion of its mineral imports were Canada, Latin America and Africa, the Near East, and south and south-east Asia. Together with Latin America, Africa stood first as a potential producer of metals. Asia, it was pointed out, was the world's largest producer of tin and rubber and a supplier of various strategic materials. The benefits to Third World countries of expanding mineral production for export were taken to be substantial. Earnings could finance development programmes, and the inflow of foreign capital and skills would serve wider purposes. Having established the case for the complementarity of the American and Third World economies, the Paley Commission went on to recommend an expanded United States commitment to resource development in the periphery. The Randall Commission was of the same view, although it did not refer specifically to Third World countries. It recommended adopting policies and promoting a climate favourable to private investment overseas, and ensuring that tariff policy toward the required materials should offer reasonably easy access to the United States market.[41]

Despite the assertion of mutual benefit, it was apparent that the United States did not view its dependence on the Third World with comfort. There were the obvious if publicly understated apprehensions about the national security implications of America's increasing reliance on overseas supplies of strategic materials. The possibility of the territories producing these materials being lost to communist aggression and the vulnerability of supply lines in times of war were dangers to be taken into account. If anything, the problem had been accentuated by the changing character of military demand following the development of the jet engine, the gas turbine and the nuclear reactor. In the various policy statements of the National Security Council in the late forties and throughout the fifties, there are frequent references to the importance of south-east Asian materials to United States security. In November 1950 the commission on Foreign Economic policies, headed by Gordon Gray, stressed the need to hold on to such vital regions from 'the force of communist aggression'.[42] The other approach adopted was to expand the national stockpiling programme – though this rapidly developed a life of its own. In some cases stockpiles far exceeded requirements and at times stockpiling was used as a means of regulating the domestic economy.[43]

More generally there was the belief that stable access to raw materials was hostage to internal developments within Asian and African societies, and to their economic and political relations with the West. The growing resentment, in many Third World countries, of continued reliance on the export of raw materials at the expense of industrialization and broadly based development was viewed with anxiety and in some cases hostility. This concern became more acute as the non-aligned movement developed economic doctrines during the 1960s. To counter the rise of radical economic perspectives, the United States government was urged not to adopt too narrow an approach to the development of overseas resources. A balance needed to be struck between America's specific needs and the wider interests of Third World economic advancement.[44] A related concern was the difficulties which many Third World states placed in the way of American private investment. The threat of nationalization, the demand for local participation and the often uncertain legal environment in which to conduct business were all regarded as obstacles to the full and efficient exploitation of resources. Especially from the late fifties, various measures were taken by the American government to make the Third World a more attractive prospect for the private investor. These will be considered in the next section.[45] What needs emphasizing here is that the attitudes of officials and experts towards the importance of Third World resources changed more quickly than those of Americans generally and businessmen in particular. They did not, however, result in governmental initiatives of sufficient scope to yield the desired results.

Surveying American thinking and policy over the years 1945 to 1970, two themes of considerable interest emerged. First, the comfortable assumption of pre-war years that the United States was very largely self-sufficient in terms of resources did not survive the Second World War.[46] Throughout the period it was recognized that America was dependent on overseas and especially Third World resources. This situation was viewed with anxiety when general war seemed a real possibility. Later, the fact of increasing dependence on Third World supplies did not generate the same concern, partly perhaps because of declining resource prices. Second, despite specialist analyses and the recommendations of groups assembled to review the problem, successive administrations were not seized with any urgency, and policy remained surprisingly low-key and incremental. The development of the resources of the Third World was left largely to private investors and individual corporations. Yet, as Mira Wilkins has argued, apart from a minimal interest in iron ore deposits in West Africa, it was only in the case of Middle Eastern oil that American businessmen were prepared to commit capital to resource development in the 1950s.[47] In 1963 the report under the aegis of Resources for the Future observed that policy-makers had made only a limited response to the major events in the resource field and to the recommendations of the various studies such as the Paley Commission.[48] Some years later a former member of the Commission, Edmund Mason, made the same point:

> The commission did indeed make a large number of recommendations but, in the main, these were ignored as the post-war fear of shortages gave way to comfortable complacency.[49]

(iii) *Trade and Investment*

Despite its expansive formulation, America's post-war commitment to a liberal economic order was initially conceived very largely in relation to Europe. The world economy, in essence, meant America together with Europe, to which Japan was added more on account of its prospects than on its immediate performance. Even such vigorous exponents of American economic globalism as J. and G. Kolko concede that the Americans 'did not estimate the potential of Asia, Latin America, or Africa as being of central importance'.[50] It was the strategic dynamic of the Cold War which first led American decision-makers to broaden their conceptions to take account of the significance of the economic potential of these areas.[51]

In 1950 the Gray report on foreign economic policies argued that social and economic progress in the Third World was essential to the security of the free world, and recommended an expanded American involvement.[52] This assessment paralleled that of the Truman administration and remained conventional wisdom throughout the period. The danger was not so much the conversion of Asia and Africa to communism; rather, it was believed that economic stagnation produced political chaos which communists and other extremists could exploit for their own purposes.[53] Account also had to be taken of the need to promote stronger economic links between states which it was considered would contribute to a more stable non-communist system. With respect to the Far East, policy-makers believed that a healthy reciprocal trade was a precondition both of the economic development and internal stability of the Asian states, and of the longer-term vitality of the major power in the region, Japan.[54] Similar arguments were advanced, although less often, with regard to the importance of markets in the former colonial states in Africa to the continuing health of the European economies.[55]

From the late fifties more emphasis was placed on the need to develop economic ties between the United States and Asian countries, as a result of Washington's concern about the expansion of Sino-Soviet trade and aid in the Third World. In 1955 Nikita Khrushchev had told a group of American Congressmen: 'We value trade least for economic reasons and most for political purposes.'[56] The following year, in a major statement to the Twentieth Party Congress, Khrushchev proclaimed in effect that the struggle with the West would be waged in the underdeveloped world and that it would be fought with economic weapons. In the American view, the Soviet offensive was bearing fruit. The economic links forged between the Eastern bloc and the Indo-China states, India, Indonesia and Egypt made American officials acutely conscious of the need to develop stronger ties with vulnerable Asian countries. The influence of this line of thinking on American foreign-aid policies has been noted, but its impact was also felt with respect to official perceptions of the need to strengthen trading and investment ties with Asia.[57]

Cold War considerations were buttressed by references to the direct economic benefits to the United States economy. Investment in Asia and Africa would help to increase the flow of needed raw materials, and there was the more distant prospect of a rising demand in parts of Asia for American machinery and consumer durables. The business sector was less enthusiastic. For the most part, trade and investment opportunities in Asia, let alone Africa, were too marginal and remote to attract sustained interest. In the early sixties the government was criticized by bodies such as the National Foreign Trade Convention for not matching with action its rhetoric about promoting the role of private investment in underdeveloped countries. Yet only a few years before, some business interests had been suspicious of state initiatives. Until the late fifties, for example, sections of corporate opinion were opposed to the investment guarantee programme, fearing it might lead to government regulation of American firms abroad.[58] There was also a concern, expressed by some congressmen, that by contributing to Third World industrialization the United States might be assisting potential competitors.[59] At least until 1962, domestic opinion was suspicious of a liberal trade policy, and powerful producer groups remained committed to tariff protection. Thus assumptions about the longer-term benefits of expanded trade with the Third World, which supposedly would flow from greater specialization, cut little ice with specific interests more concerned with the likely costs. Writing of the trade debate in the period from 1948 to 1961, Robert Pastor observes that Congress behaved 'as if the United States were anything but a global superpower'.[60]

One thing on which there was agreement, however, was that an expanded economic relationship between the United States and the Third World was predominantly a task for the private sector. The Gray Commission recommended that the bulk of the $600 million to $800 million which it envisaged as an annual net outflow to the Third World should come from private sources.[61] This insistence on the primacy of private economic activity was reiterated by the Randall Commission in 1953, and again in 1965 by the Watson Committee on Private Enterprise in Foreign Aid.[62] It applied to both overseas trade and foreign investment, and it characterized opinion within government as well as outside. We thus have the paradox that although policy-makers took the position that America's wider national interests required increased trade with and investment in the underdeveloped world, they never wavered in their belief that the state could not assume responsibility for the attainment of this goal. Although it was appropriate for the government to smooth the way, the development of the economic relationship between the United States and the underdeveloped world fell within the province of the private investor and trader.

To encourage American businessmen to move into underdeveloped countries, successive administrations offered financial and other inducements, and attempted to limit the risks. Indeed, from the late fifties measures were taken to foster investment in underdeveloped rather than developed countries.[63] Overall, however, it is doubtful whether these governmental initiatives were commensurate with the geopolitical significance attached to an invigorated economic relationship between the United States and the Third World. Moreover, action tended to lag well behind political appreciation. Government attempts to negotiate treaties with foreign countries to reduce the likelihood of nationalization and expropriation of investments made least headway where they were most needed.[64] Insurance against expropriation was dependent upon agreement being reached with particular countries, with the result that much of Asia and Africa was not covered. Between 1948 and 1959 insurance issued under the United States investment guarantee programme was approximately ten times greater for Europe than for Asia and Africa.[65] During the 1960s the Agency for International Development extended loans to foreign investors and conducted surveys of investment opportunities in particular regions.[66] Limited taxation concessions were introduced to stimulate overseas economic activity, but they fell well short of the measures advocated by those familiar with the difficulties in the Third World.[67] Initially, government action in support of overseas trade and investment was not directed specifically to the Third World. In the late fifties and in the sixties, however, some inducements – as for example investment guarantees and certain taxation advantages – were offered exclusively to businessmen operating in underdeveloped countries.

Notwithstanding official encouragement, few American corporations were prepared to commit resources to Asia and Africa. The businessman's conception that private commerce rather than government aid held the key to unlocking the economic potential of the Third World remained largely in the realm of theory. The evidence admits no argument on this score. The only major exception was the oil industry. From the early fifties the oil companies invested heavily in the Middle East and were prepared to commit resources to Asia and Africa in circumstances which other corporations would have found far too risky.[68] Such other American investment as took place in Asia and Africa was largely connected with raw material development. In the sixties some funds were also invested in electronics in South Korea, Taiwan and Hong Kong, the aim being to take advantage of low labour costs. Very little private capital went to manufacuring and public utilities.[69]

In the early post-war period, domestic economic opportunities were excellent and there was little incentive for overseas involvement. Later, when the business sector looked overseas, it turned to the politically stable, affluent and industrialized nations of the West. Asia and Africa were unattractive because of their poverty. In the view of corporate decision-makers, poor countries were not consumers of the output of an advanced industrial economy such as that of the United States. Despite the traditional fascination with the China market, post-war business opinion was decidedly cynical about large populations with little purchasing power.[70] The demand for manufactures was likely to be low, and large outputs were required to obtain economies of scale.[71] Moreover, Africa and Asia were unfamiliar to most American businessmen. Corporations preferred to conduct their operations in areas where contact over the years had led to the establishment of working relationships and a fund of local knowledge. Such conservatism lingered throughout the sixties. As Mira Wilkins notes, it is significant that, of all Asian and African less developed countries, United States direct investment in manufacturing between 1955 and 1970 was highest in the Philippines, a country 'known' to Americans.[72]

Above all it was the uncertainty and risk of ventures in the Third World which jaded the outlook of American businessmen. Afro-Asian states were regarded as politically unstable and prone to violence. Economic decision-making was generally considered to be ad hoc and inefficient, if not blatantly corrupt. Complaints ranged from bureaucratic immobility to political discrimination. The failure of many states to provide patent protection was a major disincentive. Even where the environment was congenial, who could say how long it would stay that way? Businesses attracted to a country under one regime often found their assets seized under the next. It has been observed that few American business leaders studied the history of foreign economic involvement in the Third World, so that expropriations came as a surprise and sent shock-waves through the business community.[73] The cumulative effect of these impressions and experiences was to generate a deep scepticism in the corporate mind about economic involvement in the new states.

Reviewing the material on aid, resources, trade and investment, certain themes recur which give the thinking of American policy-makers a consistent texture. The economic images of Asia and Africa were only partially derived from the non-European world, and they drew much of their meaning from non-economic concerns. The understanding of the problems and prospects of Third World economies was largely based on Western experience, and official optimism stemmed directly from beliefs about what could be accomplished through American action. The significance attached to the economic development of Afro-Asian states and to American involvement through trade and investment owed much to Cold War considerations and must therefore be related to the United States' broader political and strategic interests. Herein lies part of the explanation for the neglect of thinking about the economics of Africa. The Afro-Asian economies were also seen as interlocking with the liberal international order, but for the most part their role was considered marginal and more potential than actual.

If, in the outlook of successive administrations, Third World economic issues were frequently approached in the light of wider national purposes, the reliance on private initiatives and capital to advance these purposes was misplaced, at least in the short term. Businessmen were no less concerned than government that the predominant role in overseas economic activity be left to the private sector, but they showed little inclination to act as an instrument of national policy. With the exception of the oil companies and to a lesser extent the mining industry generally, business remained indifferent to the role assigned to it by government – and indeed by the logic of its own ideology. Only very modest investment took place in Africa and Asia. At home, tariff policies, stockpile programmes and subsidies to domestic producers limited the development of trade between the United States and the Third World. Calculations of immediate and direct economic benefit which shaped the thinking of the private sector gave Asia and Africa much lower visibilty than the more general and global perspectives of policy-makers.

CONCLUSION

This book has not been directed to resolving one central problem or answering a single overriding question. Its concern has been less focussed: to analyse Britain's approach to Asia and Africa before the Second World War and America's approach in the years following, and to outline the ideas and images which were most influential in London and Washington. The presupposition has been that understanding is enriched by considering different historical periods and by moving from the case of Britain to that of the United States. Standing back from the detailed material, the book can be seen as an enquiry into the categories of references of the historically dominant power. It may be that hegemony itself has an influence on thinking and helps shape the images held of lesser powers. We are now in a position to review this and other themes developed in individual chapters, to ask whether they are limited by time and national circumstance, and to reflect more generally on the relationship between patterns of thought, national interest and Western domination of the Third World.

It is unnecessary here to dwell on the differences in the position of Great Britain and the United States and the extent to which the international system, and Asia and Africa's place within it, changed from the time of the second expansion to that of the Cold War. In the interchapter the nature of the two imperial systems was contrasted and attention was directed to the difference between Britain and America as world powers. It is apparent that in some respects there is no comparison between the degree and kind of domination exercised by the two states. Yet the same cannot be said of the broad approaches to Asia and Africa adopted by London and Washington and the patterns of thinking which led to domination.

A survey of the century from 1870 makes evident the continuities in the approach of policy-makers and the persistence of basic assumptions about both the West and the non-European world. In many respects the parallels between the period of empire and the Cold War era are striking. The way in which Asia and Africa were subordinated to the requirements of imperial and international politics, and the expansiveness and assurance of the dominant power's conception of its role, stand out despite the obvious differences between the two periods. The years between the wars saw the emergence of new ideas about international politics and economics, and constitute a more distinctive era. Yet in large part the approach of Britain's leaders to Asia and Africa remained anchored in pre-1914 assumptions. There is little to suggest that the Great War represented a watershed in Britain's relations with the non-European world. On the American side, the experiences of the inter-war years – specifically, isolationism and the downgrading of military power – played a powerful part in setting America's post-war course in the Third World. In their years of national ascendancy, there was more congruity between the thinking of British and American policy-makers than might have been expected. A correspondence of approach to the non-European world can be seen in each of the three areas we have considered – power politics, moral responsibility and economic interest. Where substantial differences existed, it is instructive to enquire whether they stemmed from British and American self-conceptions and domestic politics or whether they reflected divergent assessments of the position and potential of Asia and Africa.

The influence of *Realpolitik* guided thinking about the periphery along select channels. During their respective periods of dominance, statesmen and strategists on both sides of the Atlantic linked diplomacy and defence in Asia and Africa to the global balance, with the result that these continents were drawn into the conflicts between the great powers. Because of their weakness, Africa and Asia were open to being used as instruments in the larger power struggle. The understanding of power was such that prestige was accorded an importance in its own right. Positions and possessions in the Third World thus acquired a significance which at times bore little relation to their intrinsic importance. The tendency to see overseas affairs through the lens of power politics led to a view of Asia and Africa which placed disproportionate emphasis on the threats posed by outside powers. In the late nineteenth century much of British thinking about Africa was influenced by fears about French and German ambitions. At different times, India for the British, and Asia as a whole for the Americans, were perceived according to the apprehension of Russian designs. Within Asia and Africa, economic and social processes were often understood as political; equally, internal developments were interpreted in terms of their external significance. It followed that in many cases, perceptions were remote from the realities of the non-European world. The problem was accentuated in the American case, because some statesmen had limited knowledge of Asia and Africa and discounted specialist opinion in favour of global constructs. Reviewing the material we are led to the view that there was a tendency for geopolitics to take on a life of its own.

This tendency was both checked and accentuated by the influence of ideological and economic conceptions. Neither British nor American policy-makers approached Africa and Asia – or overseas affairs generally – with the dispassionate logic of power politics. Using the imagery of a chess-board, it can be said that many of the pieces were invested with a meaning of their own. For Britain, the Empire counted for its own sake. Although it was seen – perhaps too readily – to be a source of power, this hardly explains the bases of Britain's commitment. The Empire existed; it represented a high trust; there was the emotional gratification. These were not matters of rational calculation. For American policy-makers, the understanding of the global struggle with the Soviet Union which developed after the Second World War was overlaid by the ideology of anti-communism. Thinking about the maintenance of a balance of power and the advancement of America's politico-strategic and economic interests was distorted by the broadest conceptions of the moral qualities of the United States itself, its enemies, and the peoples of Asia and Africa.

It is also apparent that behind some of the concern with power and strategy lay assumptions about economic self-interest. Few British or American statesmen took a keen interest in economic questions; much less did they have clear ideas about the benefits to be derived from Asia and Africa. Most, however, had broad notions about the importance of overseas economic interests and their dependence on political conditions. In Britain the need to defend the Empire was couched partly in economic terms. In America a connection was seen between the maintenance of the balance of power and the protection of the capitalist economic order. For both states, therefore, security was seen to encompass economic concerns.

In the case of the dominant power, there is a particular difficulty in establishing the relationship between its specifically national economic interests and its general interest in maintaining the existing international economic order. The same point can be made with respect to political interests and the international political order. Elsewhere in this book, doubts have been expressed about how far *Realpolitik* can offer a guide to action in the real world. These doubts apply with especial force to dominant or global powers.

There was one fundamental difference between British and American approaches to power and strategy in the periphery. Seen through American eyes, the importance of Asia and the relative unimportance of Africa derived from the world struggle. In large part the understanding of developments in these two continents, and America's response, was informed by the appreciation of the central balance and events in Europe. In this respect, American conceptions were more akin to those of the European states before the First World War than to those of Britain. For Britain, the Empire – or at least most of it –

mattered in its own right. Until the thirties, and excepting the war years and those immediately before, Britain's conception of her imperial interests formed the basis of her global view.

There was a much closer correspondence between British and American approaches in other respects. Once an understanding had been reached about Asia and Africa's place in the international politics of the time, neither London nor Washington showed much inclination to reconsider the ends of policy or the interests on which policy was supposedly based. There was also the same geographical sweep of concern and the shared fear that developments at one point, perhaps unimportant in itself, would have repercussions elsewhere. Gladstone's observation, to the effect that the possession of overseas territory is a source of insecurity, carries conviction.[1] When reformulated to cover the obsession with overseas power, it is as applicable to the United States as to Britain.

Similarly, Salisbury's famous remark that if the government's naval and military advisers 'were allowed full scope they would insist on the importance of the moon to protect us from Mars' applies with equal force to the Pentagon as earlier to the British War Office and Admiralty.[2] In fact, in both countries strategists were allowed very substantial scope. In the British case, insistence on the need to defend the Empire's lines of communication acted as a drawstring deepening Britain's involvement in Africa and Asia. It underlaid or reinforced proposals for annexation in parts of Africa and south-east Asia. Over time it burst the distinction between internal and external affairs and inexorably Britain became enmeshed in indigenous politics. It provided the rationale for the establishment of a chain of military bases which created vulnerabilities and political complications as well as security benefits. In the case of the United States, the search for security for the 'free world' led policy-makers to redefine American interests in Asia, misinterpret regional developments, and assert American power. Through the means of security treaties and military intervention, the United States created new tensions and enlarged the sources of conflict. The tendency was for both powers to act assertively, not only because they had the capacity, but also because the risk of appearing weak was seen to threaten their global systems.

In the climate of the 1980s the role of moral conceptions is unlikely to appear as compelling as those about power and strategy. Each age has its own ideals and moral sensibilities, and most have grave difficulties in appreciating those which went before. It seems, moreover, that each age is shorter than its predecessor, and that the stars by which men and women set their sights fade progressively more quickly.[3] Cynicism may also derive from national perspective.[4] Envy, resentment, and a limited understanding of the other culture appear to have contributed to American perceptions of British imperial ideology as a mask for economic exploitation. The same considerations help to explain British and European suspicions, rather later, that American anti-colonialism was a tool by which the United States hoped to lever itself into a position of dominance in Asia. Given such scepticism within the West, it is scarcely surprising that so many Africans and Asians dismiss Anglo-American professions of moral concern as cant.

It has been a central contention of this book that, despite the obvious window-dressing and the need for self-justification, many British and American policy-makers believed what they said, and that moral considerations had an influence on their perceptions and approach. The idea that Britain and the United States had a special moral responsibility for the protection of Asian and African societies and the development of their peoples ran almost unbroken from the establishment of formal empire to the shaping of the post-colonial world. At the end of his term as Viceroy, Lord Curzon counselled his compatriots in India 'to remember that the Almighty has placed your hand on the greatest of His ploughs, in whose furrow the nations of the future are germinating and taking shape'.[5] Over half a century later J.F. Kennedy was to tell the citizens of Dallas: 'We in this country, in this generation, are – by destiny rather than choice – the watchmen on the walls of world freedom.'[6] The conviction that the West had the task of recasting the future of the Third World was shared by many who were critical of official policy – from high-minded Fabians to the down-to-earth fictional characters in *The Ugly American*. It found perhaps its most vulgar expression in the imagery of a senator from Nebraska in 1940: 'With God's help, we will lift Shanghai up and up, ever up, until it is just like Kansas City.'[7]

In both content and sources British and American conceptions had much in common. The commitment to the idea of progress, the ethnocentrism of thinking and the conviction of Western superiority lay at the root of nearly all planning and policies for the Third World. Their form and expression changed over time. Assertions of the innate racial superiority of Europeans, for example, gave way to the phraseology of 'developed' or 'modern' societies, and increased emphasis was placed on the science, skills and social organization of the West. Overtly racial stereotypes were common in Britain before the First World War; cultural and technical categories predominated in America after the Second. In the years between the wars British thinking was in the process of evolving from one to the other. Underlying much of the swagger about the role of the Anglo-Saxon powers were elements of doubt and unease. In Britain the fascination with the exotic and the past led to an ambivalence about modernizing backward societies. In America the personal insecurity of leaders such as Johnson and Nixon contributed to the personalization of overseas politics and the determination to appear tough and unyielding. In both cases imaginative literature and political biography strongly suggest that the need to prove masculinity influenced thinking and action.

It must be doubtful how far either the public arrogance or the private anxieties associated with Britain and America's approach to the Third World can be related to their position as dominant powers. Other Western states had their own conceptions of moral responsibility and the influences appear to be similar. The mono-culturalism and sense of superiority which characterized France's *mission civilisatrice* are immediately apparent. Less so, perhaps, is the extent to which the intensity of feeling can be explained in terms of French insecurity – an insecurity tied to France's defeat in the Franco-Prussian War, her experience in the two world wars, her losses in Indo-China and Algeria, and her eclipse by the Anglo-Saxon powers. Even the Portuguese, with few claims to carry the torch of progress and none to international ascendancy, had their own extravagant conception of overseas mission. In November 1972 the Portuguese Commander-in-Chief in Mozambique justified the war against FRELIMO by claiming it was 'the defence of civilization against the aggression of barbarism.' He continued:

> The war that we are leading and carrying out guarantees, through our success, the consolidation and the development of a multiracial society of religious freedom and melting of cultures which being the solution for Portugal, is also the pilot-solution for the world of today and cannot fail to become the generalized solution for the world of tomorrow.[8]

It would be surprising indeed if this formulation did not reflect an insecurity derived from years of Iberian isolation and economic decline.

The emphasis on the commonality of Anglo-American conceptions of moral responsibility must not obscure the national contrasts. Three were major. First, British ideas and the sense of commitment which underlaid them were sectional rather than national. Sustained interest in Britain's role in Asia and Africa was mainly restricted to the middle and upper classes. For the most part, the imperial ethos was rural, non-intellectual and pre-capitalist. The American sense of mission was more broadly based within the society as a whole. It was evangelical rather than paternalistic, and it had a populist quality characteristic of American political and social life. Second, whereas British conceptions were largely tied to the Empire and derived from the experience of empire, America's approach was in essence non-territorial. Indeed, the Third World was not seen as different in kind from elsewhere, and policies designed for Europe were freely transposed to Asia and Africa. Finally, the United States was decidedly more optimistic about what could be achieved in the Third World and about the role it could play. Experience over time and a much greater familiarity with Asia and Africa had the effect of lowering Britain's sights. There were also more minor differences. Britain made more allowance for Afro-Asian diversity and showed a greater readiness to adjust policies to local circumstances. Almost from the beginning of the imperial undertaking, a sense of guilt about the treatment of Africans and Asians existed in some quarters in Britain. In the United States guilt became significant only in the late sixties, with the impact of the Vietnam War and under the influence of dependency theory and revisionist historiography.

Anglo-American thinking about the economics of Asia and Africa is less amenable to summary treatment than are ideas about power and moral responsibility, because the issues are more diverse and specifics assume a greater importance. The commitment to an open international economic system based on free trade guided Britain's approach until the thirties and America's approach during and after the Second World War. It had its origins in the early nineteenth century and before, and its perspective was global, not regional. No special account was taken of Asia and Africa. Indeed, for most of the period, interest in these continents was limited and derivative. As is well recognized, the commitment to free trade and minimal government interference reflected the interests of the economically dominant powers – a position held by Britain in the nineteenth century (though doctrine outlived dominance) and America at least from the 1940s. What is perhaps less often appreciated is that confidence in economic capability was enhanced by the possession of military and political power. In the nineteenth century Britain's economic superiority was buttressed by her naval supremacy. During and after the Second World War the United States was able to use its great political leverage to advance its conception of a liberal international economic order.

In the light of the correspondence between interests and doctrines, and the close relationship which existed between economic, political and military power, it would be easy to make false assumptions about the approach of the two dominant powers to the economic exploitation and development of Asia and Africa. In fact neither Britain nor the United States was centrally concerned with its economic relations with these continents, and both were unenthusiastic about their short-term potentialities. Britain's stake in India was the one exception to this general proposition. Until the First World War (less so thereafter), India was seen as of undoubted importance to Britain's international economic position. It must be said, however, that thinking about the economic relationship was intertwined with broader conceptions of India's contribution to Britain's international influence and military power. It was recognized, moreover, that there

were strict limits to the extent to which the Indian economy could be
regulated in the interests of the metropole.

In general, British policy-makers were sceptical about the notion of
easy returns from Asia and Africa. Interest was most pronounced
when opportunities elsewhere were drying up, and during periods of
economic downturn at home. Visionaries such as Chamberlain and
Amery relied heavily on non-economic considerations to sustain their
imperial enthusiasm. American policy-makers showed less cynicism
about the economic prospects in Asia and Africa, and less awareness of
the possible costs of involvement than the British, but the level of
their intrinsic interest was markedly lower as well. Europe and Japan
were the predominant concerns. Although the Western economic
system was seen to include Asia and Africa, the part played by these
continents was regarded as marginal – except for the production of oil.
Such official emphasis as was placed on trade and investment in
Afro-Asia was very largely a result of the strategic dimensions of the
Cold War.

Despite dreams of the China market or wistful notions about the
potential of tropical Africa, businessmen were wary about investing in
the underdeveloped world because of the high risks, and they were
mostly luke-warm about trading prospects there because of the
political conditions and the poverty. In Britain the commercial sector
looked to Africa and Asia mainly when tariffs and strong competition
threatened established markets in Europe, America and the Dominions. It is significant that until the thirties, manufacturing and
industrial interests – with a few exceptions – gave little support to the
campaign for an imperial economic system. After the Second World
War American businessmen were even less inclined to move into Asia
and Africa. The Cold War era was a time of economic buoyancy for
the United States. Conditions at home were excellent, while overseas
the opportunities in the developed world appeared decidedly more
attractive than those in the underdeveloped countries.

We are left with the paradox that in Britain, the private sector
looked to government and in America, government looked to the
private sector to take a lead in advancing trade and investment in Asia
and Africa. Especially in the last decades of the nineteenth century,
British businessmen prodded London to become more active in
warding off foreign rivals and establishing appropriate conditions in
the underdeveloped world so that commerce could go forward.
Governmental response was limited because of the continuing hold of
laissez-faire and the belief that the state should not usurp the
functions of commerce and finance, which could only lead to a decline
in entrepreneurship. It was these very considerations which led
United States governments in the 1950s and 1960s to look to the
private sector to deepen American economic involvement in Asia and

Africa as part of its struggle against communism. Here also little response was forthcoming. With limited confidence in business prospects, the private sector was largely indifferent to the idea that it should act as an instrument of national policy.[9]

From the early days of imperial penetration, critics on the Left contended that British economic involvement served a narrow self-interest and ran counter to the interests of African and Asian peoples. This argument was readily endorsed in the United States with regard to European imperialism but, until the mid-sixties, it was seldom related to America's own economic involvement. Indeed, aid was often criticized as an exercise in altruism and concern was expressed about the dangers which charity posted to its recipients. For the most part, policy-makers in both countries felt secure in the belief that the growth of trade and investment, and the provision of economic aid, were mutually beneficial. Theoretical support could be obtained both from the writing of the classical political economists[10] and post-war development theory, but in general, assumptions about the complementarity of interest between the developed and the underdeveloped world were well-rounded and often taken for granted.

In retrospect, what stands out is the extraordinary optimism of Anglo-American thinking. Three aspects are of particular note: the belief that a very small external input was required, the assumption that Third World societies were essentially malleable, and the assurance that market forces could be left to take their own course. Thinking in each of these areas was modified during the inter-war years by British officials and lay authorities. The recognition grew that change would have to be selective, that the process would be much slower than originally envisaged, and that the state would need to play a significant role – for example, to prevent powerful special interests from determining the course of economic change and extracting the benefits. While policy-makers remained confident that Britain could promote economic growth, especially in Africa, it was increasingly accepted that there was no necessary complementarity between the interests of Britain and those of colonial societies, and that the pattern of development would need to be planned, and to some extent controlled, from the centre. The Colonial Office played the key role in this process of reappraisal.

The British experience and the lessons of the inter-war years were largely ignored in the United States. In some respects American thinking after the Second World War, for all its conceptual sophistication, was reminiscent of British thinking before 1914. No doubt America's neglect of the material on colonial development in the twenties and thirties can be explained in part by the limited American interest in history,[11] and the disproportionate influence in the fifties of narrowly economic analyses. It may also have been influenced by the belief in American exceptionalism. These observations suggest a basic difference between British and American approaches to development. At least in the inter-war years, Britain began with particular colonial societies and worked towards a doctrinal formulation (though none was reached before the war). America, on the other hand, began at the level of doctrine and only late in the day, and inadequately then, came to wrestle with the difficulties on the ground. This contrast perhaps reflects the general tendency of Americans to proceed on the basis of doctrine as compared with the British preference for an empirical and historical approach.

Taking a holistic view, the problem must now be faced as to how far the three streams of thinking came together. Did one tend to dominate? It would be straining the material to attempt anything more than the most general answers to these questions. It has been established that the thinking and perceptions of different groups of people and different departments very often followed courses of their own. It is equally apparent that in many cases perspectives were deeply engrained, related to distinctive interests and therefore resistent to change. It can also be argued, though it falls outside the scope of this book, that the process of decision-making did not necessarily break down the compartmentalization of thought and that continuing differences of opinion produced difficulties in the execution and coordination of policy. Bearing these considerations in mind, it must be said that when approaches collided, power politics prevailed. This was indisputably the case with America during the Cold War: it was broadly true of Britain before the First World War; on balance, the proposition holds for Britain in the years between the wars.

This conclusion leaves two things out of account. The first is that approaches by no means always collided or were seen to be in danger of colliding. Imperialism did not present a single face to Asia and Africa; each sphere had a considerable measure of autonomy. For the most part, the Raj and the Colonial Office could act in accordance with their traditions and values. Only on occasions did businessmen feel impelled to link their economic calculations to patterns of international politics. At one and the same time, American statesmen could act in terms of power while the American people thought in terms of ideology. Secondly, there is the extent to which each approach took in elements of the others. Power politics had an economic dimension. Ideas about moral responsibility were predicated on the possession of power and to some extent were an expression of that power. Conceptions of overseas economic opportunities rested on understandings of international politics, as became especially apparent during periods of crisis, for example the 'Great Depression', the depression of the thirties, and the years of the Second World War.

It is clear that the three streams of thinking were more closely related in the United States than in Britain. America's approach to Asia and Africa had a larger unity; the images in each domain were less distinct. The explanation is partly that America's world view was much simpler – even simplistic – and her knowledge of Africa and Asia was more limited. The complexity of issues and events could thus be reduced to a pattern.

This brings us to the question of the nature and content of Anglo-American images of Asia and Africa. A number of generalizations can be made on the basis of the material in this book which corroborate the findings of more specialized studies. The images of Asia and Africa were often facile, their contours being shaped by the prejudices and interests of the dominant society. Some particularistic images, such as the 'lazy native' or the 'childlike' Indian were drawn sharply and derived from the impressions of people on the periphery; others floated more freely and tended to be most strongly held by those with least contact. Images of the richness of tropical resources or Asian nationalism as communism fall into the latter category. It was characteristic of many cultural images to depict Afro-Asia as being the binary opposite of the West. Thus Eastern passivity and feminity was contrasted with the vigour and masculinity of Western civilization, Africa's backwardness with Western progress. In the broadest sense, it was images of this kind which provided the imaginative base upon which the West's role in Africa and Asia was constructed. Edward Said is surely correct when he argues that through such representations, the Orient has helped to define the West's self-identity.[12]

On occasions, one image was inconsistent with another, or even contradictory. Britain's role in India, for example, was seen as time-bound, yet its end could not be envisaged. American views about who was the enemy in Vietnam slid between China, the Soviet Union and world communism. A variety of images was held about how far Asians and Africans would respond to the same economic incentives as Westerners. In a satirical novel about American involvement in south-east Asian politics, an American senator expresses some of the confusion about cultural similarities: 'I'm not sayin' the little Oriental fellow is just like us. He's different all right. But . . . that little man is a lot more like us than he isn't.'[13] The elements of tension and incongruity in these mental pictures can be explained partly by the extent to which ideas endured over time. At their core, the images of Asia and Africa proved remarkably resilient. Even when events led to a major overhaul of existing images, often the underlying assumptions remained constant.[14] This must be attributed to the fact that most images were deeply rooted in the culture of the metropole. The aspects of Afro-Asian people and their societies which caught attention, and so frequently were distorted, were those which touched sensitive nerves in the eyes of the beholder.

When the material is viewed in a comparative perspective, additional themes emerge. Whereas in the British view, India was taken to be the hub of Asia, for America the centre of interest was China. The images of India and China respectively powerfully influenced British and American conceptions of Asia as a whole. Images of Africa usually followed in the wake of those of Asia. They were formed later and in many respects were derivative. In general, American images had less content than British images. Having a limited colonial experience, there was not the same feeling for cultural differences and American self-conceptions probably loomed larger.

There is a widespread tendency to argue or assume that Western approaches to the Third World were functional; that the economic and strategic interest of the metropoles were secured both by the images which prevailed and by the policies which were adopted. There is little in this book to provide support for any such general assumption. Clearly much, though not all, of British and American thinking was guided by considerations of self-interest. Yet in many instances images, approaches and policies diverged from – or even ran counter to – the national interests of Britain and the United States. Policy-making was frequently irrational, short-sighted or excessively ideological. Often information was unreliable and assumptions untenable. Similarly, at times policy-makers acted on assumptions rooted in an earlier era. Britain in the inter-war years took inadequate account of the extent of change in her domestic, imperial and international situation. America in the Cold War, reacting against what were taken to be the errors of the thirties, settled for an indiscriminate globalism. We are left with the thought that in the century from 1870, Asia and Africa were less important to either Britain or America than policy-makers then believed or revisionist historians now contend.

Notes

Introduction

1. Of particular interest are: Kenneth Boulding, *The Logic of Images in International Politics* (University of Michigan Press, Ann Arbor, 1956); John C. Farrell and Asa P. Smith (eds.), *Image and Reality in World Politics* (Columbia University Press, New York, 1967); and Robert Jervis, *The Logic of Images in International Relations* (Princeton University Press, Princeton, New Jersey, 1970).
2. See especially Philip D. Curtin, *The Image of Africa: British Ideas and Action, 1780–1850* (Macmillan, London, 1965); Harold R. Isaacs, *Scratches on Our Minds: American Views of China and India* (M.E. Sharpe, White Plains, New York, 1958, reprinted 1980); Crauford D.W. Goodwin, *The Image of Australia: British Perception of the Australian Economy from the Eighteenth to the Twentieth Century* (Duke University Press, Durham, N.C., 1974); Akira Iriye (ed.), *Mutual Images. Essays in American-Japanese Relations* (Harvard University Press, Cambridge, Mass., 1975); and John G. Stoessinger, *Nations in Darkness: China, Russia and America* (Random House, New York, 3rd edition, 1981).
3. See Maurice Cowling's valuable discussion of this point in *The Nature and Limits of Political Science* (Cambridge University Press, Cambridge, 1963), especially pp. 18–23 and 183–6.
4. G.R. Elton, *Political History* (Allen Lane, Penguin, London, 1970), p. 53.

Chapter One

1. See ch. 7, pp. 166–8.
2. The literature on power politics is, of course, enormous. Among the most useful books are Martin Wight, *Power Politics*, edited by Hedley Bull and Carsten Holbraad (Penguin and RIIA, London, 1979); F.H. Hinsley, *Power and the Pursuit of Peace* (Cambridge U.P., Cambridge, 1963); and Inis L. Claude, *Power and International Relations* (Random House, New York, 1962).
3. A.L. Burns, *Of Powers and Their Politics: A Critique of Theoretical Approaches* (Prentice Hall, Englewood Cliffs, N.J., 1968), pp. 85–6.
4. The best general discussion is Claude, *op. cit*, ch. 2. See also Ernst B. Haas, 'The Balance of Power: Prescription, Concept or Propaganda', *World Politics*, vol. 5 (July 1953), pp. 442–7.
5. Stanley Hoffman, 'Notes of the Elusiveness of Modern Power', *International Journal*, vol. 30 (2) (spring 1975), pp. 183–206.
6. E.H. Carr, *The Twenty Years' Crisis 1919–1939* (Macmillan, London, 1939), ch. 6.
7. This is a central theme of Hedley Bull's, *The Anarchical Society: A Study of*

Order in World Politics (Macmillan, London, 1977). See also Wight, *op. cit.*, ch. 10.

8. Paul Kennedy, *The Realities Behind Diplomacy: Background Influences on British External Policy 1865–1980* (Allen & Unwin, London, 1981), p. 39.

9. Max Beloff, *Imperial Sunset*, vol. 1, *Britain's Liberal Empire 1897–1921* (Methuen, London, 1969), pp. 59–60.

10. See Robert Taylor, *Lord Salisbury* (Allen Lane, Penguin, London, 1975), p. 182, and J.A.S. Grenville, *Lord Salisbury and Foreign Policy: the Close of the Nineteenth Century* (University of London, Athlone Press, London, 1964), pp. 8–9.

11. D.K. Fieldhouse, *Economics and Empire 1830–1914* (Weidenfeld and Nicolson, London, 1973), p. 63.

12. Quoted in Wm. Roger Louis (ed.), *Imperialism: The Robinson and Gallagher Controversy* (New Viewpoints, New York, 1976), p. 27.

13. Among the many accounts of the changing values of the age, part 3 of John U. Nef's *War and Human Progress: An Essay on the Rise of Industrial Civilization* (Russell & Russell, New York, 1968, first published 1950) warrants especial attention.

14. Beust, the Austrian foreign minister, declared as early as 1870: 'I do not see Europe any more.' Quoted in A.J.P. Taylor, *The Struggle for Mastery in Europe 1848–1918* (Clarendon Press, Oxford, 1954), p. 213.

15. Gorden Stables in *Shoulder to Shoulder*, quoted in Patrick A. Dunae, 'Boys' Literature and the Idea of Empire, 1870–1914', *Victorian Studies*, vol. 24 (1) (autumn 1970), pp. 105–21 at p. 111.

16. Carlton J.H. Hayes, *A Generation of Materialism 1871–1900* (Harper, New York, 1941), p. 4.

17. See further Michael Howard, 'The Armed Forces', ch. VIII in F.H. Hinsley (ed.), *The New Cambridge Modern History*, vol. XI, *Material Progress and World-Wide Problems 1870–98* (Cambridge U.P., Cambridge, 1962).

18. Quoted in Nicholas Mansergh, *The Coming of the First World War: A Study in the European Balance 1878–1914* (Longmans, Green & Co., London, 1949), at p. 44.

19. Except in the sense that treaty-making with local emirs, chiefs, etc., was often treated as a serious matter because one European state could better defend its claims against another if it could show that treaties had some basis in local conditions. See Saadia Touval, 'Treaties, Borders, and the Partition of Africa', *Journal of African History*, vol. 7 (2) (1966), pp. 279–92 at pp. 280–81.

20. Quoted in A.L. Kennedy, *Salisbury 1830–1903: Portrait of a Statesman* (John Murray, London, 1953), at p. 224.

21. Quoted in C.J. Lowe, *The Reluctant Imperialists: British Foreign Policy 1878–1902*, vol. 1 (Routledge & Kegan Paul, London, 1967), p. 125.

22. *Ibid.*, p. 129. In more flamboyant style, Bismarck is reported frequently to have said in private that 'the friendship of Lord Salisbury is worth more to me than twenty marshy colonies in Africa'.

23. A.J.P. Taylor, *Germany's First Bid for Colonies 1884–85: A Move in Bismarck's European Policy* (Macmillan, London, 1938).

24. Taylor's sharpest critic has been Henry A. Turner. See his 'Bismarck's Imperialist Venture: Anti-British in Origin?' in Prosser Gifford and Wm. Roger Louis, *Britain and Germany in Africa* (Yale U.P., New Haven, Conn., 1967), ch. 2.

25. On the importance of prestige see Harold Nicolson, *The Meaning of Prestige* (Cambridge U.P., Cambridge, 1937).

26. A.P. Thornton, *The Imperial Idea and Its Enemies* (Macmillan, London, 1959), p. xiv.

27. *op. cit.*, p. 15.

28. See for example F.R. Bridges and Roger Bullen, *The Great Powers and the European States System 1815–1914* (Longman, London, 1980), p. 112.
29. *The Struggle for Mastery in Europe*, p. 256.
30. On the latter case see *ibid.*, pp. 428 and 434.
31. Viscount Grey of Fallodon, *Twenty-five Years, 1892–1916* (Hodder & Stoughton, London, 1925), vol. 1, p. 6.
32. A.J.P. Taylor, 'International Relations', ch. XX in F.H. Hinsley (ed.), *The New Cambridge Modern History*, vol. XI at p. 562.
33. *op. cit.*, p. 62.
34. *op. cit.*, p. 5.
35. See especially Grenville, *op. cit.*; Robert Taylor, *op. cit.*; Lillian Penson, *Foreign Affairs Under the Third Marquis of Salisbury* (Athlone Press, London, 1962); Algernon Cecil, *British Foreign Secretaries 1807–1916: Studies in Personality and Policy* (reissued Kennikat Press, Port Washington, New York, 1971, first published 1927), ch. 6.
36. Robert Taylor, *op. cit.*, p. 11.
37. See William L. Strauss, *Joseph Chamberlain and the Theory of Imperialism* (Howard Fertig, New York, 1971), especially at pp. 81–2.
38. *Twenty-Five Years, 1892–1916*, vol. 1, p. 5.
39. See Keith Robbins, *Sir Edward Grey: A Biography of Lord Grey of Fallodon* (Cassell, London, 1971).
40. W.R. Louis, 'Sir Percy Anderson's Grand African Strategy 1883–1896', *Historical Review* vol. LXXXI (1966), pp. 292–314 at p. 293. See also Zara Steiner, *The Foreign Office and Foreign Policy 1898–1914* (Cambridge U.P., Cambridge, 1969), p. 44.
41. See further ch. 3, pp. 60–66.
42. J.R. Seeley, *The Expansion of England* (Macmillan, London, 1885), p. 7.
43. Quoted in Robert Taylor, *op. cit.*, p. 134.
44. See especially H.J. Mackinder, 'The Geographical Pivot of History', *The Geographical Journal*, vol. XXIII (4) (April 1904), pp. 421–44. Spencer Wilkinson comments on Mackinder's themes at pp. 437–9.
45. Arthur J. Marder, *The Anatomy of British Sea Power: A History of British Naval Policy in the Pre-Dreadnought Era, 1880–1905* (Frank Cass, London, 1964), p. 24. See also p. 30.
46. W.E. Gladstone, 'Aggression on Egypt and Freedom in the East', *Nineteenth Century* (London), vol. 2 (Aug–Dec. 1877), pp. 149–66 at p. 159.
47. Quoted in Denis Judd, *Balfour and the British Empire: A Study in Imperial Evolution 1874–1932* (Macmillan, London, 1968), p. 231.
48. Quoted in Phillip Darby, *British Defence Policy East of Suez 1947–1968* (OUP for RIIA, London, 1973), p. 285.
49. *op. cit.*, p. 108.
50. M. and T. Zinkin, *Britain and India: Requiem for Empire* (Chatto & Windus, London, 1964), pp. 46–7.
51. George Monger, *The End of Isolation: British Foreign Policy 1900–1907* (Nelson, London, 1963), pp. 184–5, 194 and 207.
52. Ian Nish, *The Anglo-Japanese Alliance* (University of London, Athlone Press, London, 1966), p. 231.
53. In 1911 during the second Moroccan crisis it was considered a basic British interest that, in the event of a German infringement of Belgian neutrality, Belgium should call for British assistance. Belgium, however, was distrustful of Britain's motives, a distrust fuelled by Britain's failure to recognize Belgium's annexation of the Congo in 1908. See further Mary E. Thomas, 'Anglo-Belgian Military Relations and the Congo Question, 1911–1913', *Journal of Modern History*, vol. XXV (2) (June 1953), pp. 157–65.

54. V.G. Kiernan, 'Farewells to Empire', originally published in *The Socialist Register* (1964), pp. 259–79. Republished in V.G. Kiernan, *Marxism and Imperialism: Studies* (St Martin's Press, New York, 1975), ch. 2. See p. 83.
55. *Marxism and Imperialism*, pp. 75, 76 and 82. See also Eric Stokes, 'Imperialism and the Scramble for Africa: The New View', in Louis (ed.), *The Robinson and Gallagher Controversy*, pp. 173–95 at pp. 183, 184 and 187.
56. Lord Randolph Churchill, quoted in Kiernan, *op. cit.*, p. 78.
57. *Op.cit.*, pp. 12 and 13.
58. *Op.cit.*, p. 5.
59. See generally Darby, *op. cit.*, p. 2, and K.M. Panikkar, *India and the Indian Ocean* (2nd impr., Allen & Unwin, London, 1962).
60. See further S. Gopal, *British Policy in India 1858–1905* (Cambridge U.P., Cambridge, 1965), and G.J. Alder, *British India's Northern Frontier, 1865–1895* (Longmans, London, 1963).
61. John Marlowe, *Cromer in Egypt* (Elek Books, London, 1970), p. 302.
62. Quoted in *ibid.*
63. See for example Beloff, *op. cit.*, pp. 162–3.
64. Lowe, *op. cit.*, p. 76, and M.E. Chamberlain, *Britain and India: The Interaction of Two Peoples* (David & Charles, Newton Abbot, Devon, 1974), pp. 144–5.
65. Cecil, *op. cit.*, pp. 295–6.
66. Grenville, *op. cit.*, pp. 304, 307–8.
67. See L.K. Young, *British Policy in China 1895–1902* (Clarendon Press, Oxford, 1970), pp. 40–41.
68. On the approach of the British and European governments to the Boxer movement, see George Steiger, *China and the Occident* (Yale U.P., New Haven, Conn., 1927) and Victor Purcell, *The Boxer Uprising: A Background Study* (Cambridge U.P., Cambridge, 1963).

CHAPTER TWO

1. Philip Woodruff (pseudonym for Philip Mason), *The Men Who Ruled India:* vol. 2, *The Guardians* (Cape, London, 1954), at p. 14.
2. *Britain and India. Requiem for Empire*, p. 73.
3. *The Imperial Idea and Its Enemies*, p. x. A.P. Thornton's understanding of the imperial idea is essentially what we label as the conception of moral responsibility.
4. See Paul Scott, *The Towers of Silence* (vol. 3 of *The Raj Quartet*) (Granada, London, 1973), pp. 275–6.
5. See L.H. Gann and Peter Duignan, *The Rulers of British Africa 1870–1914* (Hoover Institution Publications, Croom Helm, London, 1978), pp. 5 and 43.
6. *Op.cit.*, p. 135.
7. Quoted in Beloff, *Britain's Liberal Empire 1897–1921*, p. 142.
8. Quoted in H.C.G. Matthew, *The Liberal Imperialists: The Ideas and Politics of a post-Gladstonian Elite* (Oxford University Press, London, 1973), at p. 153.
9. Winston Churchill, *The River War* (Eyre & Spottiswoode, London, 1951, first published 1899), at p. 10.
10. Joseph Conrad, 'Geography and Some Explorers', in *Last Essays* (J.M. Dent & Sons, London, 1926), p. 25.
11. R.E. Robinson and J. Gallagher, 'The Partition of Africa', ch. XXII in F.H. Hinsley (ed.), *The New Cambridge Modern History*, vol. XI at p. 632.
12. *Marxism and Imperialism: Studies*, p. 69.
13. J.A. Hobson, *Imperialism: A Study* (Allen & Unwin, London, 3rd revised edn

1938, first published 1902), p. 206.

14. The classic work in this area is Albert Memmi, *The Colonizer and the Colonized* (Beacon Press, Boston, 1967, first published 1957).

15. Ashis Nandy, *The Intimate Enemy: Loss and Recovery of Self Under Colonialism* (Oxford University Press, Delhi, 1983), p. ix.

16. See especially *ibid.*, pp. 76–8.

17. See Eric Stokes, *The English Utilitarians and India* (Clarendon Press, Oxford, 1959), and more generally Eric Stokes, *The Political Ideas of English Imperialism* (Oxford University Press, London, 1960).

18. For a stimulating analysis of the literary treatment see Martin Green, *Dreams of Adventure, Deeds of Empire* (Routledge & Kegan Paul, London and Henley, 1980).

19. J.A. Schumpeter, *Imperialism and Social Classes* ed. P.M. Sweezy (Basil Blackwell, Oxford, 1951).

20. On Curzon see Kenneth Rose, *Superior Person* (Weidenfeld & Nicolson, London, 1969); Michael Edwardes, *High Noon of Empire: India Under Curzon* (Eyre & Spottiswoode, London, 1965); and David Dilks, *Curzon in India* (2 vols., Hart-Davis, London, 1969–70). Some interesting material is also to be found in Nigel Nicolson, *Mary Curzon* (Harper & Row, New York, 1977).

21. Viscount Curzon, 'The True Imperialism', *Nineteenth Century and After*, LXIII, (January 1908), pp. 151–65 at pp. 151, 158 and 165.

22. Hannah Arendt, 'The Imperialist Character', *Review of Politics*, 12 (1950), pp. 303–20 at p. 306.

23. Edward Said, *Orientalism* (Routledge & Kegan Paul, London, 1978), p. 121.

24. Soetan Sjahrir, *Out of Exile* (Greenwood Press, New York, 1949), pp. 144 and 146. Letter dated 31 December 1936.

25. Stokes, *The English Utilitarians and India*, p. 300.

26. Quoted in Judd, *Balfour and the British Empire*, p. 287.

27. See M.E. Chamberlain, *Britain and India: The Interaction of Two Peoples*, p. 176.

28. Francis G. Hutchins, *Illusion of Permanence, British Imperialism in India* (Princeton University Press, Princeton N.J., 1967), ch. 8.

29. Herbert Spencer, *Facts and Comments* (Williams & Norgate, London, 1902), p. 112 and following.

30. L.T. Hobhouse, *Democracy and Reaction* (T. Fisher Unwin, London, 1904), especially pp. 47–8.

31. See Milton Singer, 'Passage to More Than India: A Sketch of Changing European and American Images of India', ch. XVII in *Languages and Areas: Studies Presented to George V. Bobrinskoy, 1967* (Division of Humanities, University of Chicago, 1967), pp. 133–6.

32. Nandy, *op. cit.*, p. 6.

33. J.C. Van Leur, *Indonesian Trade and Society: Essays in Asian Social and Economic History* (W. Van Hoeve, The Hague, 1955), p. 289.

34. The most valuable guide is Robert Nisbet, *History of the Idea of Progress* (Heinemann, London, 1980). See also J.B. Bury, *The Idea of Progress: An Enquiry into its Origins and Growth* (Dover, New York, 1955, first published 1920).

35. J.S. Mill, 'On Liberty', in *Three Essays* (World Classics Reprint, OUP, London, 1974), p. 16.

36. Karl Marx, *Capital* (Foreign Languages Publishing House, Moscow, 1954), vol. 1, p. 9. The line is from the Marx's Preface to the First German Edition, originally published as *Das Kapital*.

37. See Herbert Spencer, *Essays: Scientific, Political and Speculative* (Library

Edition, Williams & Norgate, London, 1891), vol. 1, ch. 2.
38. *Orientalism*, p. 3.
39. Quoted in Christine Bolt, *Victorian Attitudes to Race* (London, Routledge & Kegan Paul, 1971), p. 173.
40. For more detailed accounts of European images of non-European cultures see V.G. Kiernan, *The Lords of Human Kind* (Weidenfeld & Nicolson, London 1969); Syed Alatas, *The Myth of the Lazy Native* (Cass, London, 1977) and Said, *op. cit.*.
41. Alatas, *op. cit.*, p. 232.
42. From text in Henry S. Wilson (ed.), *Origins of West African Nationalism* (Macmillan, London, 1969), p. 150.
43. Jawaharlal Nehru, *The Discovery of India* (Anchor Books, Doubleday & Co., New York, 1959, first published 1956), p. 250.
44. Winwood Reade, *The Martyrdom of Man* (Kegan Paul, Trench, Trubner & Co., London, 1917).
45. *Op.cit.*, pp. xi–xii.
46. Quoted in R.J. Moore, *Liberalism and Indian Politics 1872–1922* (Edward Arnold, London, 1966), at p. 82.
47. See Edwardes, *op. cit.*, pp. 143–9.
48. J. Ramsay Macdonald, *The Awakening of India* (Hodder & Stoughton, London, 1910), p. 116.
49. Sir F.D. Lugard, *The Dual Mandate in British Tropical Africa* (Wm. Blackwood, Edinburgh and London, 3rd edition 1926), p. 225.
50. Concern with the bureaucratic structure of empire was fairly general. Milner spoke of sacrificing a little efficiency in administration. Minto thought in terms of greater sympathy.
51. For a perceptive and sympathetic study see Edward Crankshaw, *The Forsaken Idea* (Longmans, Green & Co., London, 1952).
52. John Buchan, *Memory Hold the Door* (Hodder & Stoughton, London, 1940), p. 125.
53. For a fuller treatment of nineteenth-century ideas about race, see Michael Banton and Jonathan Harwood, *The Race Concept* (David & Charles, Newton Abbot, Devon, 1975), and Bolt, *op. cit.*
54. Speech at the Imperial Institute, 11 November 1895, quoted in George Bennett (ed.), *The Concept of Empire: Burke to Attlee 1774–1947* (A. & C. Black, London, 1962), p. 315.
55. Chamberlain, *op. cit.*, p. 156.
56. The stress placed on social distance is most fully explored in Kenneth Ballhatchet, *Race, Sex and Class Under the Raj: Imperial Attitudes and Policies and their Critics 1793–1905* (St Martin's Press, New York, 1980).
57. *Op.cit.*, pp. 39 and 228.
58. See Ballhatchet, *op. cit.*, pp. 139–43.
59. *Op.cit.*, p. 28.
60. B.L. Putnam Weale, *The Conflict of Colour* (Macmillan, London, 1910), p. 127.
61. J.A. Spender, *The Changing East* (Cassell, London, 1926), pp. 153–4.
62. Raghavan Iyer, 'Utilitarianism and All That (The Political Theory of British Imperialism in India)', in *St Antony's Papers* (Chatto & Windus, London, 1960), no. 8, p. 10.
63. Alan Sandison, *The Wheel of Empire. A Study of the Imperial Idea in some late Nineteenth and early Twentieth Century Fiction* (Macmillan, London, 1967), p. 11.
64. Philip Mason, *Patterns of Dominance* (Institute of Race Relations, OUP, London, 1970), pp. 33–5, and *Prospero's Magic*, OUP, London, 1962), ch. 2.
65. See for example Wayland Young, *Eros Denied* (Weidenfeld & Nicolson, London,

1965), and Ronald Hyam, *Britain's Imperial Century 1815–1914 – A Study of Empire and Expansionism* (Batsford, London, 1976), p. 134 and following.
66. *Op.cit.*, ch. 4.
67. Joseph Conrad, *A Personal Record: Some Reminiscences* (J.M. Dent & Sons, London, 1923), uniform edn, vol. 6, p. 112. For a fascinating study of this theme see H.M. Daleski, *Joseph Conrad – The Way of Dispossession* (Faber & Faber, London, 1977).
68. Morton Cohen, *Rider Haggard: His Life and Works* (Hutchinson, London, 1960), pp. 111–14.
69. O. Mannoni, *Prospero and Caliban. The Psychology of Colonization* (Praeger, London, 1964), p. 104.
70. *Op.cit.*, p. 307.
71. *Op.cit.*, p. 218.
72. See Allen J. Greenberger, *The British Image of India. A Study in the Literature of Imperialism 1880–1960* (OUP, London, 1969), p. 39, and Susanne Howe, *Novels of Empire* (Columbia University Press, New York, 1949, reprinted 1971), pp. 27–8.
73. Rudyard Kipling, 'Letters of Marque' (Nov.–Dec. 1887), XIII, in *From Sea to Sea and other Sketches. Letters of Travel* (Macmillan, London, 1900), vol. 1, p. 128.
74. Angus Wilson, *The Strange Ride of Rudyard Kipling. His Life and Works* (Secker & Warburg, London, 1977), pp. 116–17.

CHAPTER THREE

1. A.F. Madden, 'Popular Picture History: The Confessions of a *Soi-disant* 'Consultant', *Journal of Imperial and Commonwealth History*, vol. 1 (2) (January 1973), pp. 352–9 at p. 357.
2. The 'classical political economists' is taken to mean Hume, Smith, Ricardo, Malthus, Torrens, Senior, McCulloch, the two Mills and Bentham. See generally D. Winch, *Classical Political Economy and Colonies* (Bell, London, 1965) and Alan Hodgart, *The Economics of European Imperialism* (Foundations of Modern History, Edward Arnold, London, 1977), ch. 2.
3. The classic study here is Lionel Robbins, *The Theory of Economic Policy in English Classical Political Economy* (Macmillan, London, 1953).
4. J.A. Hobson, *Imperialism. A Study* (Allen & Unwin, London, 3rd revised edition 1938, first published 1902), pp. 227–36.
5. Ronald Robinson, John Gallagher with Alice Denny, *Africa and the Victorians. The Official Mind of Imperialism* (Macmillan, London, 1967), p. 4.
6. See S.B. Saul, *The Myth of the Great Depression 1873–1896*, (Studies in Economic History, Macmillan, London, 1969), and R.C. Floud, 'Britain 1860–1914: a Survey', ch. 1 in Roderick Floud and Donald McCloskey, *The Economic History of Britain Since 1700*, vol. 2, *1860s to the 1970s* (Cambridge University Press, Cambridge, 1981).
7. See Hodgart, *op. cit.*, p. 27.
8. William G. Hynes, *The Economics of Empire: Britain, Africa and the New Imperialism 1870–95* (Longman, London, 1979), ch. 4. The same general point is advanced by A.G. Hopkins, *An Economic History of West Africa* (Longman, London, 1973), pp. 135–7, 154–7, 160–65; Arthur Redford, *Manchester Merchants and Foreign Trade*, vol. 2, *1850–1939* (Manchester University Press, Manchester, 1956), p. 32; and J.S. Galbraith, *Mackinnon and East Africa 1878–1895, A Study in the 'New Imperialism'* (Cambridge University Press, Cambridge, 1972), p. 75.

9. See Hynes, *op. cit.*, ch. 7.
10. Quoted in *ibid.*, pp. 110–11.
11. *Ibid.*, p. 135.
12. See N. Etherington, 'Theories of Imperialism In Southern Africa Revisited', *African Affairs*, 81 (1982), pp. 385–407, and N. Etherington, 'The Capitalist Theory of Capitalist Imperialism', *History of Political Economy*, 15 (1983), pp. 38–62. This section follows the lines of Etherington's analysis.
13. On this point see G.R. Hawke, *Economics for Historians* (Cambridge University Press, Cambridge, 1980), ch. 7.
14. See Etherington, 'The Capitalist Theory of Capitalist Imperialism', *op. cit.*, p. 51, and A.E. Campbell, 'Great Britain and the United States in the Far East, 1895–1903', *Historical Journal*, vol. I (2) (1958), pp. 154–75 at pp. 156–9.
15. Etherington, 'The Capitalist Theory of Capitalist Imperialism', p. 55.
16. Etherington, 'Theories of Imperialism In Southern Africa Revisited', *op. cit.*, pp. 397–98.
17. See Etherington, *ibid.*, p. 398, and Bernard Porter, 'Imperialism and the Scramble', *Journal of Imperial and Commonwealth History*, vol. 9 (1) (1980), pp. 76–81 at p. 77.
18. D.C.M. Platt, *Finance, Trade and Politics in British Foreign Policy 1818–1914* (Clarendon Press, Oxford, 1968), p. xxxiv.
19. See D.A. Wagner, 'British Economists and the Empire I', *Political Science Quarterly*, vol. XLVI (2) (1931), pp. 248–76.
20. Hodgart, *op. cit.*, p. 7.
21. *Africa and the Victorians*, p. 8.
22. See L.C.A. Knowles, *The Economic Development of the British Overseas Empire* (Routledge, London, 1924), vol. 1, pp. 31–2.
23. Hynes, *op. cit.*, pp. 14–15.
24. See Alatas, *The Myth of the Lazy Native*, ch. 8 and conclusion.
25. See S. Ambirijan, *Classical Political Economy and British Policy in India* (Cambridge University Press, Cambridge, 1978), pp. 50–58.
26. Hynes, *op. cit.*, pp. 15 and 16.
27. Ambirajan, *op. cit.*, p. 54.
28. See further *ibid.*, chs. 7 and 8.
29. J.R. Seeley, *The Expansion of England* (Macmillan, London, 1885), p. 193.
30. See Hynes, *op. cit.*, pp. 57–73.
31. A.G. Hopkins, 'Economic Imperialism in West Africa: Lagos, 1880–92', *Economic History Review*, vol. 21 (1968), pp. 580–606.
32. Hynes, *op. cit.*, pp. 77–83.
33. See Analysis of Answers from H.M. Representatives Abroad in the *Final Report of the Royal Commission on Depression of Trade and Industry 1886* Cmnd. 4893, vol. XXIII, pp. 130–37.
34. R.J. Hoffman, *Great Britain and the German Trade Rivalry 1875–1914* (Russell & Russell, New York, 1964), pp. 53–6.
35. Quoted in David McLean, 'Commerce, Finance, and British Diplomatic Support in China, 1885–86', *Economic History Review*, vol. 26 (1973), pp. 464–76 at p. 468.
36. Hoffman, *op. cit.*, p. 56.
37. See Hopkins, *op. cit.*, pp. 600–3.
38. McLean, *op. cit.*, p. 473.
39. See Robinson and Gallagher, *op. cit.*, pp. 395–508 and more generally Strauss, *Joseph Chamberlain and the Theory of Imperialism*.
40. D.C.M. Platt, *op. cit.*, pp. 111–18.
41. *Ibid.*, p. 286.
42. See ch. 1, pp. 25–6. The argument is also advanced by D.C.M. Platt, *op. cit.*,

pp. 256–61, and R. Hyam, 'The Partition of Africa', *Historical Journal*, vol. VII (1964), pp. 154–69.

43. J. Forbes Munro, *Africa and the International Economy 1800–1960. An Introduction to the Modern Economic History of Africa South of the Sahara* (J.M. Dent, London, 1976), p. 73.

44. Quoted in M. Victor Berard, *British Imperialism and Commercial Supremacy* (Longmans, Green & Co., London, 1906), at p. 54.

45. Quoted in B.M. Ratcliffe, 'Commerce and Empire: Manchester Merchants and West Africa, 1873–1895', *Journal of Imperial and Commonwealth History*, vol. VII (1979), pp. 293–320 at p. 306.

46. See Hopkins, *op. cit.*, ch. 4, especially pp. 154–7.

47. See Fieldhouse, *Economics and Empire, 1830–1914*, pp. 312–40.

48. J. Yeats, *Recent and Existing Commerce* (George Philip & Son, London, 1886), p. 338.

49. Sir Alan Pim, *The Financial and Economic History of the African Tropical Territories* (Clarendon Press, Oxford, 1940), p. 111. According to Pim, the opposition was 'only prepared to allow that a trade could be done in Uganda in white donkeys and rat-traps'.

50. Peter Wickins, *An Economic History of Africa from the Earliest Times to Partition* (Oxford University Press, Cape Town, 1981), p. 279.

51. Leonard Woolf, *Empire and Commerce in Africa. A Study in Economic Imperialism* (Allen & Unwin, London, 1920), p. 334. This judgement was perhaps premature.

52. For general accounts of British trade with China during the period, see G.C. Allen and Audrey G. Donnithorne, *Western Enterprise in Far Eastern Economic Development, China and Japan* (Allen & Unwin, London, 1954), part 1, and Francis E. Hyde, *Far Eastern Trade 1860–1914* (A. & C. Black, London, 1973).

53. A.J.H. Latham, *The International Economy and the Undeveloped World 1865–1914* (Croom Helm, London, 1978), p. 81.

54. Hynes, *op. cit.*, pp. 48–50.

55. *Ibid.*, p. 49.

56. N.A. Pelcovits, *Old China Hands and the Foreign Office* (King's Crown Press, New York, 1948); see chapter 2, especially pp. 102–22.

57. Ratcliffe, *op. cit.*, p. 303.

58. Pelcovits, *op. cit.*, pp. 68–71.

59. Campbell, *op. cit.*, pp. 157–8.

60. *Ibid.*, at pp. 159–62.

61. D.C.M. Platt, *op. cit.*, p. 284, and N.A. Pelcovits, *op. cit.*, pp. 264–5.

62. Quoted in Knowles, *op. cit.*, p. 323.

63. See Beloff, *Britain's Liberal Empire 1897–1921*, pp. 31 and 32, but compare Zinkin, *Britain and India: Requiem for Empire*, chapter 8.

64. Robinson and Gallagher, *op. cit.*, p. 11.

65. Latham, *op. cit.*, pp. 77–9.

66. S.B. Saul, *Studies in British Overseas Trade 1870–1914* (Liverpool University Press, Liverpool, 1960), p. 56. For figures for the later years, see pp. 58–60 and 203–4. An Indian scholar has argued that India's contribution to Britain's international trade position was greater than these figures suggest. See A.K. Banerji, *Aspects of Indo-British Economic Relations 1858–1898* (Oxford University Press, Bombay, 1982), p. 19.

67. Beloff, *op. cit*, p. 32.

68. Redford, *op. cit.*, pp. 36–8.

CHAPTER FOUR

1. *Britain's Liberal Empire 1897–1921*, p. 247. See also Max Beloff, *Wars and Welfare. Britain 1914–1945* (Edward Arnold, London, 1984), pp. 58–9.
2. Charles Loch Mowat, *Britain Between the Wars 1918–1940* (Methuen, London, 1972, first published 1955), p. 201. See also A.J.P. Taylor's comment in *English History 1914–1945* (Clarendon, Oxford, 1965), p. 163.
3. See John Darwin, 'Imperialism in Decline? Tendencies in British Imperial Policy Between the Wars', *Historical Journal*, vol. XXIII (3) (1980), pp. 657–79 at pp. 668–72.
4. Gillian Peele, 'Revolt over India', ch. 5 in Gillian Peele and Chris Cook (eds.), *The Politics of Reappraisal 1918–1939* (Macmillan, London, 1975), p. 125.
5. For a full discussion see chapter 5, pp. 102–6.
6. See for example D.C. Watt, *Personalities and Policies* (Longmans, London, 1965), p. 27.
7. See John Connell, *The Office: A Study of British Foreign Policy and its Makers 1919–1951* (Allan Wingate, London, 1958), p. 218.
8. Norton Medlicott, 'The Hoare-Laval Pact Reconsidered', ch. 6 in David Dilks (ed.), *Retreat From Power: Studies in Britain's Foreign Policy of the Twentieth Century*, vol. 1, *1906–1939* (Macmillan, London, 1981), p. 129.
9. Correlli Barnett, *The Collapse of British Power* (Eyre Methuen, London, 1972), p. 238.
10. Medlicott, *op. cit.*, p. 124.
11. The theme is most fully developed in Akira Iriye, *After Imperialism. The Search for a New Order in the Far East 1921–1931* (Harvard University Press, Cambridge, Mass., 1965), ch. 1.
12. See chapter 5, p. 104.
13. B.R. Tomlinson, 'The Contraction of England: National Decline and the Loss of Empire', *Journal of Imperial and Commonwealth History*, vol. XI (1) (Oct. 1982), pp. 58–72 at p. 60.
14. Christopher Thorne, *The Limits of Foreign Policy* (Hamish Hamilton, London, 1972), p. 71.
15. *Op.cit.*, p. 302.
16. See D.C. Watt, *op. cit.*, essay 2.
17. In Max Beloff's view, timidity was the common characteristic of most of Britain's political leaders during the inter-war period. For his explanation see *Wars and Welfare. Britain 1914–1945*, p. 13.
18. A substantial literature developed on the affairs of the British Empire and Commonwealth. See especially the surveys and studies sponsored by the Royal Institute of International Affairs. Curiously, however, this literature tended to remain in a category of its own and was only partly incorporated in the general material on world politics.
19. E.H. Carr, *op. cit.*, pp. 3 and 4.
20. See chapter 6, section ii.
21. Michael Howard, *The Continental Commitment* (Temple Smith, London, 1972), pp. 93–4.
22. *Ibid.*, p. 75.
23. Correlli Barnett, *op. cit.*, p. 232. See part 4, 'An Imperial Commonwealth'.
24. Wm. Roger Louis, *British Strategy in the Far East 1919–1939* (Clarendon, Oxford, 1971), p. 46.
25. *The Mist Procession – The Autobiography of Lord Vansittart* (Hutchinson, London, 1958), p. 523.
26. Christoper Thorne, *Allies of a Kind. The United States, Britain and the War Against Japan* (Hamish Hamilton, London, 1978), p. 7.

27. Hugh Tinker, *Race, Conflict and International Order. From Empire to United Nations* (Macmillan, London, 1974), ch. 2.
28. W.K. Hancock, *Survey of British Commonwealth Affairs*, vol. 1, *Problems of Nationality* (OUP for RIIA, London, 1937), pp. 209–10.
29. See Akira Iriye, *Across the Pacific. An Inner History of American-East Asian Relations* (Harvest/HBJ, New York, 1967), pp. 134–5.
30. Quoted in Louis, *op. cit.*, p. 58.
31. See Wm. Roger Louis, *Great Britain and Germany's Lost Colonies 1914–1919*, (Clarendon, Oxford, 1967), pp. 113–15, and Hancock, *op. cit.*, pp. 211–12.
32. R.F. Holland, *Britain and the Commonwealth Alliance 1918–1939* (Macmillan, London, 1981), p. 31.
33. Hancock, *op. cit.*, p. 492.
34. Quoted in Elizabeth Monroe, *Britain's Moment in the Middle East 1914–1956* (Chatto & Windus, London, 1963), pp. 37 and 38.
35. Louis, *Great Britain and Germany's Lost Colonies 1914–1919*, p. 62.
36. *Ibid.*, p.159.
37. *Ibid.*, pp. 117, 125 and 155, and Beloff, *Britain's Liberal Empire 1897–1921*, pp. 268–70.
38. Jukka Nevakivi, *Britain, France and the Arab Middle East 1914–1920* (University of London, Athlone Press, London, 1969), pp. 105–6.
39. Thomas Jones, *Whitehall Diary*, vol. 1, *1916–1925*, ed. by Keith Middlemas (OUP, London, 1969), p. 181. For the broader context of the Wei-hei-Wei question see Russell H. Fifield, *Woodrow Wilson and the Far East: The Diplomacy of the Shantung Question* (Crowell, New York, 1952), ch. 6.
40. See Wm. Roger Louis, *British Strategy in the Far East 1919–1939*, pp. 19 and 46.
41. James Neidpath, *The Singapore Naval Base and the Defence of Britain's Eastern Empire, 1919–1941* (Clarendon Press, Oxford, 1981), p. 72.
42. Wm. Roger Louis, 'The United States and the African Peace Settlement of 1919: The Pilgrimage of George Louis Beer', *Journal of African History*, vol. 14 (3) (1963), pp. 413–33 at p. 430.
43. Sir Arthur Willert, *Aspects of British Foreign Policy* (Institute of Politics, Yale U.P., New Haven, Conn., 1928), p. 69.
44. Quoted by G.M. Gathorne-Hardy, *A Short History of International Affairs 1920–1939* (OUP for RIIA, London, 4th edn 1952), p. 116.
45. Quoted by A.P. Thornton, *Imperialism in the Twentieth Century* (Macmillan, London, 1978), p. 30.
46. *The Colonial Problem. A Report by a Study Group of Members of the Royal Institute of International Affairs* (OUP for RIIA, London, 1937), p. 28.
47. See Albert Sarraut, *La Mise-en-Valeur des Colonies françaises* (Payot, Paris, 1923).
48. See N.H. Gibbs, *Grand Strategy Vol. 1 – Rearmament Policy*, appendix 2, 'The Defence of India' (HMSO, London, 1976). Also Brian Bond, *British Military Policy Between the Wars* (Clarendon, Oxford, 1980), pp. 102–24.
49. Quoted in Paul Haggie, *Britannia at Bay. The Defence of the British Empire against Japan 1931–1941* (Clarendon, Oxford, 1981), at p. 73.
50. On the Singapore naval base strategy see *ibid.*, and Neidpath, *op. cit.*
51. See Keith Middlemas, *Diplomacy of Illusion – The British Government and Germany 1937–1939* (Weidenfeld & Nicolson, London, 1972), pp. 110–11.
52. See David Dilks (ed.), *The Diaries of Sir Alexander Cadogan 1938–1945* (Cassell, London, 1971), pp. 40–43, also p. 123 and p. 127.
53. Wolfe Schmokel, 'The Hard Death of Imperialism: British and German Colonial Attitudes 1919–1939', in Prosser Gifford and Wm. Roger Louis (eds.), *Britain and Germany in Africa – Imperial Rivalry and Colonial Rule* (Yale U.P., New

Haven, 1967), pp. 317–18. For a contemporary assessment see H.D. Henderson, *Colonies and Raw Materials* (Oxford Pamphlets and World Affairs No. 7, Clarendon Press, Oxford, 1939), p. 5.

54. Barnett, *op. cit.*, parts 4 and 5.
55. Darwin, *op. cit.*, pp. 665–7.
56. Barnett, *op. cit.*, p. 164.
57. Darwin, *op. cit.*, p. 676.
58. John Darwin, *Britain, Egypt and the Middle East: Imperial Policy in the Aftermath of War 1918–1922* (Macmillan, London, 1981), p. 270.
59. Watt, *op. cit.*, p. 27. Lawrence Durrell in his novel *Mountolive* gives insights into the changing attitudes within the Foreign Office in the thirties to the pursuit of power politics. Pursewarden, a representative of the old guard, writes that the Victorians 'were people who believed in *fighting* for the value of their currency; they knew that the world of politics was a jungle. Today the Foreign Office appears to believe that the best way to deal with the jungle is to turn Nudist and conquer the wild beast by the sight of one's nakedness.' Durrell was a Foreign Service press officer in Athens and Cairo, and Press Attache in Alexandria.
60. Quoted in Barnett, *op. cit.*, p. 164.
61. Darwin, 'Imperialism in Decline? Tendencies in British Imperial Policy Between the Wars', p. 673.
62. Anita I. Singh, 'The Origins of the Partition of India 1936–1947' (D. Phil. thesis Oxford, 1981), p. 4.
63. Gowher Rizvi, 'Transfer of Power in India: A Restatement of an Alternative Approach', in R.F. Holland and G. Rizvi (eds.), *Perspectives on Imperialism and Decolonization. Essays in Honour of A.F. Madden* (Cass, London, 1984), pp. 127–44 at p. 127.
64. See for example Barnett, *op. cit.*, pp. 254–8 and 301–2, and Richard Storry, *Japan and the Decline of the West in Asia 1894–1943* (Macmillan, London, 1979), pp. 120–26.
65. Ian H. Nish, *Alliance in Decline – A Study of Anglo-Japanese Relations 1908–23* (University of London, Athlone Press, 1972), p. 381.
66. Peter Lowe, *Great Britain and the Origins of the Pacific War – A Study of British Policy in East Asia 1937–1941* (Clarendon Press, Oxford, 1977), p. 63. The limitations of deterrence theory in the Japanese case are analysed in Bruce Russett, 'Pearl Harbour: Deterrence Theory and Decision Theory', *Journal of Peace Research* (2) (1967), pp. 89–105.
67. Neidpath, *op. cit.*, pp. 45–50.
68. On Vansittart's influence see Medlicott, *op. cit.*, p. 12, and J.A. Cross, *Sir Samuel Hoare: A Political Biography* (Cape, London, 1977), p. 263.
69. Vansittart, *op. cit.*, especially p. 522.
70. James Robertson, 'The Hoare-Laval Plan', *Journal of Contemporary History*, vol. 10 (3) (July 1975), pp. 433–64 at p. 434. In his memoirs, Vansittart records his feeling for 'an over-titled ruler struggling to improve an unruly country seared by barbarous tribes'. *Op.cit.*, p. 522.
71. Keith Middlemas and John Barnes, *Baldwin: A Biography* (Weidenfeld & Nicolson, London, 1969), p. 865.
72. For a fascinating case study of the period 1921–31, see A. Iriye, *After Imperialism*.
73. Quoted in Darwin, 'Imperialism in Decline?', p. 670.
74. Cross, *op. cit.*, p. 155.
75. *Ibid.*, p. 174.
76. Lawrence Durrell, *Mountolive* (Faber & Faber, London, 1979, first published 1958), p. 94.
77. Willert, *op. cit.*, p. 91.

78. Gathorne-Hardy, *op. cit.*, p. 324.
79. Nish, *op. cit.*, p. 300.
80. E.M. Forster, 'Salute to the Orient', *Abinger Harvest* (Penguin, London, 1967), p. 276.
81. Darwin, *Britain, Egypt and the Middle East: Imperial Policy in the Aftermath of War 1918–1922*, p. 132.
82. Daniel Waley, *British Public Opinion and the Abyssinian War 1935–6* (Temple Smith in association with the London School of Economics and Political Science, London, 1975), p. 137.
83. Paul Addison, 'Patriotism Under Pressure: Lord Rothermere and British Foreign Policy', ch. 8 in Peele and Cook, *op. cit.*, p. 202.
84. Howard, *op. cit.*, p. 80.
85. See Max Beloff, 'The Whitehall Factor: the Role of the Higher Civil Service 1919–1939', ch. 9 in Peele and Cook, *op. cit.*, pp. 224–7.

CHAPTER FIVE

1. See *After All: The Auto-biography of Norman Angell* (Hamish Hamilton, London, 1951), pp. 191–7.
2. Partha Sarathi Gupta, *Imperialism and the British Labour Movement, 1914–1964* (Holmes & Meier, New York, 1975), p. 31.
3. *Ibid.*, pp. 32–5.
4. Martin Ceadel, *Pacifism in Britain 1914–1945: The Defining of a Faith* (Clarendon Press, Oxford, 1980), p. 62.
5. Hinsley, *Power and the Pursuit of Peace*, p. 145.
6. Louis, *Great Britain and Germany's Lost Colonies 1914–1919*, pp. 105–106.
7. Gaddis Smith, 'The British Government and the Disposition of the German Colonies in Africa, 1914–1918' in Prosser Gifford and Wm. Roger Louis (eds), *Britain and Germany in Africa*, p. 293.
8. On the mandate system see Phillip Quincy Wright, *Mandates Under the League of Nations* (University of Chicago Press, Chicago, 1930) and H. Duncan Hall, *Mandates, Dependencies and Trusteeship* (Stevens, London, 1948).
9. N. Gordon Levin, *Woodrow Wilson and World Politics* (Oxford University Press, New York, 1968), p. 18.
10. *Mandates, Dependencies and Trusteeship*, p. 23.
11. Louis, *Imperialism at Bay 1941–45*, p. 94.
12. Donald S. Birn, *The League of Nations Union 1918–1945* (Clarendon, Oxford, 1981), p. 95.
13. G. Lowes Dickinson, *The International Anarchy, 1904–1914* (Allen & Unwin, Cambridge, 1926), p. 13. See also Arnold J. Toynbee's comments, *The World After the Peace Conference* (Humphrey Milford, Oxford University Press, London, 1925), p. 89. In 1920 E.D. Morel had conducted a campaign against the behaviour of French colonial troops in Europe in which racism was given free reign. See Beloff, *Wars and Welfare. Britain 1914–1945*, p. 127.
14. R. Palme Dutt, *World Politics 1918–1936*, pp. 137 and 139. Hugh Tinker describes the League of Nations as a European club with a few coloured members. *Race, Conflict and International Order*, pp. 33 and 34.
15. Charles Roden Buxton, 'Inter-continental Peace', ch. 4 in Leonard Woolf (ed.), *The Intelligent Man's Way to Prevent War* (Victor Gollancz, London, 1933) at p. 219.
16. In his book, *A League of Nations* (Headley, London, 1917, 2nd edition), H.N. Brailsford advocated restricting the membership of the Council to great powers, and giving them larger voting rights in other organs than small states.

17. See for example Gathorne-Hardy, *A Short History of International Affairs*, p. 411.
18. Iriye, *After Imperialism*, pp. 21 and 22. D.G.E. Hall has described the Nine Power Treaty as 'based on the illusion that China would gratefully accept the tutelage of western powers'. Part 3 of 'The Western Question in Asia and North Africa', ch. IX in *The New Cambridge Modern History*, vol. XII, *The Era of Violence 1898–1945* (Cambridge University Press, Cambridge, 1960), p. 232.
19. *Op.cit.*, p. 339.
20. Quoted in Michael Pugh, 'Pacifism and Politics in Britain, 1931–1935', *Historical Journal*, vol. XXIII (3) (1980), pp. 641–56 at p. 642.
21. Dorothy Borg, *The United States and the Far Eastern Crisis of 1933–1938* (Harvard University Press, Cambridge, Mass., 1964), pp. 27–9.
22. *Ibid.*, pp. 244–8.
23. Roosevelt's notions seem different in kind from earlier proposals advanced for the neutralization of parts of Africa, some of which were designed to insulate Africa from the play of European power politics. See for example E.D. Morel's proposal for the neutralization of non-colonizable Africa in his booklet, *Africa and the Peace of Europe* (National Labour Press, London, 1917), ch. 6.
24. Duff Cooper, *Old Men Forget* (Rupert Hart-Davis, London, 1954), pp. 192–3. For a detailed analysis of the public outcry and its political impact see Waley, *op.cit.*, ch. 2.
25. Birn, *op.cit.*, p. 166.
26. W.K. Hancock, *Survey of British Commonwealth Affairs*, vol. 1, p. 223.
27. *Ibid.*
28. Earl of Halifax, *Fulness of Days* (Collins, London, 1957), p. 114.
29. Michael Edwardes, *The Last Years of British India* (Cassell, London, 1963), p. 13.
30. Quoted in Thornton, *Imperialism in the Twentieth Century*, p. 176.
31. D.J. Morgan, *The Official History of Colonial Development* vol. 1, *The Origins of British Aid Policy 1924–1945* (Macmillan, London, 1980), p. 14.
32. Lord Hailey, *The Future of Colonial Peoples* (RIIA, Oxford University Press, London, 1943), p. 13.
33. See especially Ronald Robinson, 'Andrew Cohen and the Transfer of Power in Tropical Africa, 1940–1951', ch. 3 in W.H. Morris-Jones and Georges Fischer (eds), *Decolonisation and After – The British and French Experience* (Cass, London, 1980), at pp. 53–4.
34. Robert Heussler, *Yesterday's Rulers – The Making of the British Colonial Service* (Syracuse University Press, Syracuse, New York, 1963), p. 202.
35. See Rudolf von Albertini, *Decolonization – The Administration and Future of the Colonies 1919–1960* (Africana Publishing Co., New York, 1982 ed.), pp. 115–16.
36. Woolf, *op.cit.*. p. 367.
37. W.M. Macmillan, *Africa Emergent. A Survey of Social and Economic Trends in British Africa* (Faber & Faber, London, 1938), p. 395.
38. Louis, *Imperialism at Bay, op.cit.*, p. 94.
39. See Wolfe W. Schmokel, *op.cit.*, in Gifford and Louis (eds), *Britain and Germany in Africa – Imperial Rivalry and Colonial Rule*, pp. 326 and 333–5.
40. Margery Perham, *Colonial Sequence 1930 to 1949* (Methuen, London, 1967), p. 150. See generally Norman Bentwich, 'Colonies, Mandates and Germany', *The New Commonwealth Quarterly*, vol. II (1936–7), pp. 309–16 at p. 315.
41. Hailey, *op.cit.*, pp. 58–61.
42. *Op.cit.*, p. 13.
43. This theme is developed in R.J. Moore, *The Crisis of Indian Unity 1917–1940* (Clarendon Press, Oxford, 1974).
44. Thus in 1921 King George V had proclaimed 'My determination ever to maintain

unimpaired the privileges rights and dignities of the Princes of India. The Princes may rest assured that this pledge remains inviolate and inviolable.' Quoted in R.J. Moore, *Escape from Empire. The Attlee Government and the Indian Problem* (Clarendon Press, Oxford, 1983), p. 335.

45. This conclusion was reached by the Butler Committee, which in 1928 inquired into the relationship between the states and the paramount power. See V.P. Menon, *The Story of the Integration of the Indian States* (Longmans, Green & Co., London, 1956), pp. 21–5.

46. Moore, *Escape from Empire*, p. 9 and Rizvi, *op.cit.*, p. 141.

47. For a detailed account of the Labour Government's strategy in 1946 and 1947 see Anita Inder Singh, 'Decolonization in India: The Statement of 20 February 1947', *The International History Review* (Simon Fraser University), vol. 6 (2) (May 1984), pp. 191–209. There is also much relevant material in Moore, *Escape from Empire*, especially pp. 319–26. With respect to Britain's residual moral responsibility for India's defence see Darby, *British Defence Policy East of Suez 1947–1968*, ch. 1.

48. See ch. 2, pp. 43–4 and 51–2.

49. Charles Allen (ed.), *Tales from the Dark Continent. Images of British Colonial Africa in the Twentieth Century* (Andre Deutsch & British Broadcasting Corporation, London, 1979), p. 34.

50. Gupta, *op.cit.*, p. 51.

51. *The Colonial Problem* (1937), p. 235.

52. *Op.cit.*, p. 34.

53. The best general guide is Kenneth Robinson, *The Dilemmas of Trusteeship: Aspects of British Colonial Policy Between the Wars* (OUP, London, 1965). Some useful material is to be found in Penelope Hetherington, *British Paternalism and Africa 1920–1940* (Cass, London, 1978), especially ch. 3.

54. See Morgan, *op.cit.*, pp. 44–6 and Albertini, *op.cit.*, pp. 103–5, and for a detailed consideration, Stephen Constantine, *The Making of British Colonial Development Policy 1914–1940* (Cass, London, 1984), ch. 7.

55. D.A. Low, *Lion Rampant: Essays in the Study of British Imperialism* (Cass, London, 1973), p. 70. See generally his observations on the 'development fever', pp. 70–72.

56. *Ibid.*, p. 72.

57. Rita Hinden, *Empire and After – A Study of British Imperial Attitudes* (Essential Books, London, 1949), pp. 127–8, and Hetherington, *op.cit.*, p. 90.

58. See Morgan, *op.cit.*, pp. 28–31 and Hetherington, *op.cit*, pp. 100–3.

59. Lord Hailey, *An African Survey: A Study of Problems Arising in Africa South of the Sahara* (issued by the Committee of the African Research Survey under the auspices of the RIIA; OUP, London, 1938).

60. The material in the following section, although primarily addressed to the moral issues of British imperialism, also touches on themes developed in the previous chapter. It would be artificial to attempt to separate those aspects of the literature which relate to moral responsibility and those which relate to power.

61. Susanne Howe, *Novels of Empire*, p. 79.

62. 'Shooting an Elephant', in Sonia Orwell and Ian Angus (eds), *The Collected Essays, Journalism and Letters of George Orwell*, vol. 1, *An Age Like This 1920–1940* (Secker & Warburg, London, 1968), pp. 235–42 at p. 239.

63. The point comes from Raymond Williams, *Orwell* (Fontana, London, 1971), p. 19.

64. For a perceptive discussion see M.M. Mahood, *Joyce Cary's Africa* (Methuen, London, 1964), p. 76.

65. Paul Scott, *A Division of the Spoils* (Granada, London, 1977), p. 105.

CHAPTER SIX

1. (RIIA, Oxford University Press, London).
2. 'Keith Hancock and Imperial Economic History: A Retrospect Forty Years On', ch. 7 in Frederick Madden and D.K. Fieldhouse (eds), *Oxford and the Idea of Commonwealth* (Croom Helm, London, 1982), p. 151. See also Ronald Robinson, 'Oxford in Imperial Historiography', ch. 2, *ibid.*, pp. 39–41.
3. See ch. 7, pp. 147–50 and ch. 9, pp. 195–6. There is room for argument about the character of Britain's approach to Asia and Africa after the Second World War. The evidence makes it clear that the Attlee government was deeply concerned to extract economic returns from the Empire. Later, and especially under Harold Macmillan, there was anxiety about the costs of economic development in Africa and the strains which might be placed on the British economy through continued political involvement. On the other hand, residual notions of moral responsibility and world power status had a considerable impact on thinking.
4. Ian M. Drummond, *Imperial Economic Policy 1917–1939, Studies in Expansion and Protection* (Allen & Unwin, London, 1974), p. 422.
5. Macmillan, *Africa Emergent*, p. 389. On at least one occasion some years earlier Lionel Curtis, with Dominion interests in mind, urged Macmillan not to 'rock the boat'. He was later led to reconsider his neglect of the colonial Empire. See Lucy S. Sutherland, 'William Miller Macmillan: An Appreciation', ch. 1 in Kenneth Kirkwood (ed.), *St Antony's Papers, No. 21; African Affairs No. 3* (Oxford University Press, London, 1969), pp. 16 and 17.
6. See Charles P. Kindleberger's general comments, *The World in Depression 1929–1939* (Allen Lane, London, 1973), pp. 23–4.
7. See W.K. Hancock's observations, *Survey*, vol. 2, part 1, p. 290 and also those of Drummond, *op.cit.*, p. 283.
8. For a detailed study of the ideology and composition of the various imperial societies see A.D. Turrell, *The Struggle for Imperial Unity: Imperial Societies and their Relation to British Politics and Business Interests, 1916–1932* (Ph.D. thesis, Cambridge, 1982).
9. A.J.P. Taylor, *Beaverbrook* (Hamish Hamilton, London, 1972), p. 274.
10. *Ibid.*, pp. 276–7.
11. Ch. 3, p. 67.
12. B.R. Tomlinson, *The Political Economy of the Raj 1914–1947. The Economics of Decolonization in India* (Macmillan, London, 1979), p. 90.
13. Viscount Swinton, *I Remember* (Hutchinson & Co., London, 1948), p. 65.
14. Cyril Ehrlich, 'Building and Caretaking: Economic Policy in British Tropical Africa, 1890–1960', *Economic History Review*, vol. 26 (1973), pp. 649–67 at p. 653.
15. See *The Leo Amery Diaries*, vol. 1, *1896–1929*, edited by John Barnes and David Nicholson (Hutchinson, London, 1980), p. 552.
16. See Ian M. Drummond, *British Economic Policy and the Empire, 1919–1939* (Allen & Unwin, London, 1972), p. 124.
17. This bald statement hardly indicates the complexities of the issues and the shifts in thinking. For detailed analyses see Tomlinson, *op.cit.*, and A.K. Bagchi, *Private Investment in India 1900–1939* (Cambridge University Press, Cambridge, 1972).
18. See Hancock's observations, *op.cit.*, vol. 2, part 1, p. 106.
19. See further H. Martin Leake, *Land Tenure and Agricultural Production in the Tropics* (W. Heffer & Sons, Cambridge, 1927), pp. 8–9.
20. See Hancock's comments on the ideas of the Empire Resources Development Committee in *Survey*, vol. 2, part 1, pp. 106–10.

21. L.H. Amery, *A Plan of Action* (Faber & Faber, London, 1932), p. 4.
22. Gregory Blaxland, *J.H. Thomas: A Life for Unity* (Frederick Muller, London, 1964), p. 170.
23. See W. Arthur Lewis's observations, *Economic Survey 1919–1939* (Allen & Unwin, London, 1949), pp. 59–60.
24. See Hancock, *op.cit.*, vol. 2, part 1, pp. 137–42 and 198–200.
25. Quoted in Margery Perham, *Lugard*, vol. 2, *The Years of Authority 1898–1945* (Collins, London, 1960), p. 568.
26. Quoted in *ibid.*, p. 573. For a full statement of Lugard's views in this area see *The Dual Mandate in British Tropical Africa*, pp. 273–9 and his article 'The Crown Colonies and the British War Debt', *The Nineteenth Century*, vol. LXXXVIII (August 1920).
27. Hancock's *Survey* remains the classic exposition. In his two studies cited earlier, Ian M. Drummond provides a detailed account of economic policies on the basis of archival sources, though the political background is rather neglected. For the period down to 1932 there is much interesting material in A.D. Turrell, *op.cit.*.
28. Hancock, *Survey*, vol. 2, part 1, p. 200.
29. Hancock, *Survey*, vol. 2, part 1, pp. 94–110. For developments in the immediate post-war period see pp. 111–26.
30. See for example Drummond, *British Economic Policy and the Empire 1919–1939*, p. 42, and D.J. Morgan, *The Official History of Colonial Development*, vol. 1, ch. 5.
31. Thomas Jones, *Whitehall Diary*, vol. 1, p. 260. See also pp. 252, 261–2.
32. Thomas Jones, *Whitehall Diary*, vol. 2, edited by Keith Middlemas (Oxford University Press, London, 1969), p. 235.
33. *Op. cit.*, p. 214.
34. Drummond, *British Economic Policy and the Empire 1919–1939*, p. 95.
35. *Ibid.*, p. 114.
36. Hancock, *op. cit.*, vol. 2, part 1, p. 229.
37. This of course was partly an effect of the 1932 general tariff.
38. Generally on the retreat from Ottawa see Hancock, *op. cit.*, vol. 2, part 1, pp. 230–92, and Drummond, *op. cit.*, part 1, ch. 3.
39. Robert Skidelsky, *Politicians and the Slump: The Labour Government of 1929–1932* (Macmillan, London, 1967), pp. 248–9.
40. W.A.S. Hewins, *The Apologia of an Imperialist*, vol. 2 (Constable & Co., London, 1929), p. 302.
41. *Plan of Action*, p. 162.
42. *Ibid.*, p. 178.
43. Swinton, *op. cit.*, p. 74.
44. Drummond, *British Economic Policy and the Empire, 1919–1939*, p. 137.
45. See for example Lewis, *op. cit.*, p. 119.
46. Hancock, *Survey*, vol. 2, part 1, pp. 94–126.
47. Originally India was included in the Committee's proposals but it was later dropped. *Ibid.*, p. 107.
48. See Charles Wilson, 'The Economic Role and Mainsprings of Imperialism' in Peter Duignan and L.H. Gann (eds), *Colonialism in Africa 1870–1960*, vol. 4, *The Economics of Colonialism* (Cambridge University Press, Cambridge, 1975), ch. 2, at p. 86.
49. Gupta, *Imperialism and the British Labour Movement, 1914–1964*, p. 71.
50. See Forbes Munro, *Africa and the International Economy 1800–1960*, pp. 128–9, and Constantine, *The Making of British Colonial Development Policy 1914–1940*, ch. 6.
51. Gupta, *op. cit.*, p. 59. According to Gupta, Amery spoke of the need to develop sources of supply from that part of the colonial Empire which was on a sterling

exchange. It seems unlikely, however, that there was any full-blown recognition of a sterling exchange in a cabinet meeting of 1925. The system was analysed (by Keynes) for India before the First World War, but is otherwise usually traced to an article by A.H. Tocker in *The Economic Journal* of 1924. It became widely recognized only after the floating of sterling in the 1930s. See also above, p. 131.

52. Kathleen M. Stahl, *The Metropolitan Organization of British Colonial Trade: Four Regional Studies* (Faber & Faber, London, 1951), p. 100. In 1937, for example, Malaya's exports to the United States were valued at £45.5 m. compared with United Kingdom exports of £42 m.

53. See Hancock's discussion in *Survey*, vol. 2, part 1, pp. 113–22.

54. See further Swinton, *op. cit.*, pp. 75–8 and Drummond, 'The British Empire Economics in the Great Depression', *op. cit.*, pp. 227–9.

55. See Forbes Munro, *op. cit.*, pp. 157–64.

56. See for example Stahl's comments on the establishment of the Tin Producers' Association and the International Tin Control Scheme, *op. cit.*, pp. 119–20.

57. Swinton, *op. cit.*, p. 76.

58. Drummond, *Imperial Economic Policy 1917–1939*, p. 443.

59. *Plan of Action*, p. 228.

60. Hancock, *op. cit.*, vol. 2, part 1, pp. 184–5.

61. This theme is most fully developed by Constantine, *op. cit.*, chs. 5 and 6.

62. Blaxland, *op. cit.*, p. 225.

63. Tomlinson, *op. cit.*, p. 141.

64. *Ibid.*, p. 105.

65. Drummond, 'The British Empire Economics in the Great Depression', *op. cit.*, p. 225.

66. Drummond, *Imperial Economic Policy 1917–1939*, pp. 444.

67. B.R. Tomlinson, 'The Contraction of England: National Decline and the Loss of Empire', *Journal of Imperial and Commonwealth History*, vol. XI (1) (Oct. 1982), pp. 58–72 at p. 67.

68. See further B.R. Tomlinson, 'Britain and the Indian Currency Crisis, 1930–2', *Economic History Review*, vol. XXXII (1) (Feb. 1979), pp. 88–99, especially, p. 96.

69. Quoted in Gupta, *op. cit.*, p. 216.

70. See Stahl, *op. cit.*, p. 146–7.

71. The 'open economy' is a standard economic concept and refers to an economy in which international trade is possible. It is understood that actual economies vary in their openness for reasons of tariffs, transports costs and so on. A.G. Hopkins uses the concept in a more specific way in his study of West Africa, being concerned with the nature of trade – in the particular case, substantial exports of a limited range of primary products in exchange for imports of manufactures. An open economy has free trade or low tariffs. See Hopkins, *An Economic History of West Africa*, pp. 168–70.

72. One modified line of free trade thinking accepted the need to protect infant industries during their early years. This position was consistent with the basic Ricardian argument for free trade on the basis of comparative advantage, and it was endorsed by John Stuart Mill. Most economists accepted the broad line of reasoning, though the usual judgement was that infant industries which in the fullness of time could survive without protection were rare.

73. Knowles, *The Economic Development of the British Overseas Empire*, pp. 204, 217 and 219.

74. See Constantine, *op. cit.*, especially at pp. 288–9.

75. See for example, *ibid.*, pp. 94–8.

76. See ch. 5, pp. 112–13.

77. See Tomlinson, *The Political Economy of the Raj*, pp. 61–2.

78. *Ibid.*, p. 102.
79. Vera Anstey, *The Economic Development of India* (Longmans, Green & Co., London, 3rd edn 1936), p. 477.
80. Tomlinson, *The Political Economy of the Raj*, pp. 88–90.
81. *Ibid.*, p. 57.
82. *Ibid.*, p. 131.
83. Rudolf von Albertini, *European Colonial Rule, 1880–1940: The Impact of the West on India, Southeast Asia and Africa* (Clio Press, Oxford, England, 1982), p. 40.
84. Hopkins, *op. cit.*, ch. 7, especially pp. 260–67.
85. See for example W.M. Macmillan, *Africa Emergent, op. cit.*, p. 221.
86. Leonard Barnes, *The Duty of Empire* (Victor Gollancz Ltd., London, 1935), pp. 19–20.
87. Herbert Frankel, *Capital Investment in Africa: Its Course and Effects* (Oxford University Press for RIIA, London, 1938), p. 427.
88. See *Private Enterprise in British Tropical Africa*, Cmnd 2016 (January 1924), but note the minority report of Sir Edwin Stockton who argued the case for development 'on purely business lines' (p. 22).
89. Constantine, *op. cit.*, pp. 63, 84, 120–21 and 181.
90. See Morgan, *The Official History of Colonial Development*, ch. 10, Constantine, *op. cit.*, pp. 257–61, and J.M. Lee's comments in *Colonial Development and Good Government* (Clarendon, Oxford, 1967), p. 111. The best account of the background to the 1940 Act is given by Constantine, *op. cit.*, at pp. 227–57.
91. See for example Frankel, *op. cit.*, p. 8, and Macmillan, *op. cit*, p. 241.
92. Anstey, *op. cit.*, p. 3.
93. Knowles, *op. cit.*, p. 451.
94. Constantine, *op. cit.*, p. 286.
95. See Drummond, *Imperial Economic Policy 1917–1939*, pp. 440–42, and Cross, *Sir Samuel Hoare: A Political Biography*, p. 116.
96. See Simon E. Katzenellenbogen, 'The Miner's Frontier, Transport and General Economic Development', ch. 10 in Peter Duignan and L.H. Gann (eds), *Colonialism in Africa 1870–1960*, vol. 4, *The Economics of Colonialism* (Cambridge University Press, Cambridge, 1975).
97. Frankel, *op. cit.*, p. 210.
98. See for example W.M. Macmillan's observations, *op. cit*, pp. 231–40.
99. C.C. Wrigley, *Crops and Wealth in Uganda* (East African Studies no. 12, East African Institute of Social Research, Kampala, 1959), p. 16.
100. See further *ibid.*, p. 32, and Hancock *Survey*, vol. 2, part 2, pp. 192–94.
101. See Hancock, *op. cit.*, vol. 2, part 2, pp. 188–200.
102. For details see Kindleberger, *op. cit.*, pp. 190–91, and Forbes Munro, *op. cit.*, pp. 150–52.
103. Ian M. Drummond, 'The British Empire Economies in the Great Depression', in Herman Van Der Wee, *The Great Depression Revisited: Essays on the Economics of the Thirties* (Martinus Nijhoff, The Hague, 1972), pp. 212–35 at p. 220.
104. See p. 129.
105. Quoted in RIIA, *The Colonial Problem, op. cit.*, p. 156.
106. See Forbes Munro, *op. cit.*, pp. 155–7 and von Albertini, *op. cit.*, p. 154.
107. See G.B. Masefield, *A History of the Colonial Agriculture Service* (Clarendon Press, Oxford, 1972), pp. 67–9.
108. See Ehrlich's comments, *op. cit.*, pp. 661, but compare Hancock, *op. cit.*, vol. 2, part 2, p. 237.
109. Wrigley, *op. cit.*, p. 63.
110. Masefield, *op. cit.*, p. 70.

111. W.M. Macmillan, *Warning from the West Indies* (Penguin Special, London, 1938), p. 140.
112. Hancock, *op. cit.*, vol. 2, part 2, p. 200. See also p. 237.

INTERCHAPTER

1. Other reasons why it was judged appropriate to exclude Latin America are given in the Introduction, p. 5.
2. The 'Monroe Doctrine', proclaimed by President James Monroe in 1823, declared that the United States would resist European colonization in the Western hemisphere. The American republics, it was argued, operated on the basis of different political precepts from those of the European powers, and the United States was determined to maintain their distinctive traditions.
3. Isaacs, *Scratches on Our Minds*, p. 37.
4. The one exception, it could be argued, was the occupation of Japan under America's only real proconsul, General MacArthur.
5. Denis W. Brogan, 'The Illusion of Omnipotence', *Harper's Magazine*, 205 (December 1952), pp. 21–8. See also his comments in the introduction to Ronald Steel, *Pax America* (Hamish Hamilton, London, 1968).
6. By convention the State Department is the principal executive body in the foreign policy process but in the post-war years its stature and influence have declined.
7. In 1958 an independent Bureau of African Affairs was set up within the State Department. See Peter Duignan and L.H. Gann, *The United States and Africa: A History* (Cambridge University Press, Cambridge, and Hoover Institution, 1984), p. 288.

CHAPTER SEVEN

1. See Phillip Darby, 'The West, Military Intervention and the Third World', *Brassey's Annual. Defence and the Armed Forces 1971*, edited by Maj.-Gen. J.L. Moulton (Wm. Clowes & Sons, London, 1971), pp. 65–79 at pp. 67–70.
2. John Lewis Gaddis, *Strategies of Containment. A Critical Appraisal of Postwar American National Security Policy* (OUP, New York, 1982), p. 4.
3. Louis, *Imperialism at Bay*, pp. 6, 19, 108 and 485.
4. Wendell Willkie's book *One World*, published in 1943, sold over one million copies in that year.
5. Ernest R. May, *'Lessons' of the Past. The Use and Misuse of History in American Foreign Policy* (OUP, New York, 1978), pp. 22–31.
6. Here Truman followed the recommendations of his principal advisers, Dean Acheson, James Forrestal and Robert Patterson. In their view, the ramifications of Soviet action in Turkey might even extend to India and China. See *ibid.*, p. 39.
7. Gaddis, *op. cit.*, pp. 30–31 and 55.
8. See Robert M. Blum, *Drawing the Line. The Origin of the American Containment Policy in East Asia* (Norton, New York, 1982), pp. 108–24.
9. This theme is developed by Blum, *ibid.*, especially pp. 214–15.
10. See especially David P. Mozingo, 'Containment in Asia Reconsidered' *World Politics*, vol. 19 (3) (April 1967), pp. 361–77, and Seyom Brown, *The Faces of Power: Constancy and Change in United States Foreign Policy From Truman to Johnson* (Columbia University Press, New York, 1968), p. 59.
11. See Hans J. Morgenthau, 'The American Tradition in Foreign Policy', in Roy C. Macridis (ed.), *Foreign Policy in World Politics* (2nd edition, Prentice-Hall, N.J., 1962), pp. 201–24 at pp. 201–2.

12. Robert Endicott Osgood, *Ideals and Self-Interest in America's Foreign Relations* (University of Chicago Press, Chicago, 1953), p. 364.
13. *Ibid.*, p. 429.
14. See Joyce and Gabriel Kolko, *The Limits of Power. The World and United States Foreign Policy, 1945–1954* (Harper & Row, New York, 1972), ch. 1; and Harry Magdoff, *The Age of Imperialism. The Economics of U.S. Foreign Policy* (Monthly Review Press, New York, 1969).
15. Bruce M. Russett, *No Clear and Present Danger. A Skeptical View of the United States Entry into World War II* (Harper & Row, New York, 1972), pp. 84–5. At p. 84 there is a representative sample of quotations from leading American policy-makers equating Stalin with Hitler.
16. Quoted in Lance Morrow, 'JFK After 20 Years, the question: How good as President?', *Time*, 14 November 1983), p. 49.
17. Arthur H. Vandenberg Jr. (ed.), *The Private Papers of Senator Vandenberg* (Victor Gollancz, London, 1953), p. 1.
18. David Halberstam, *The Best and the Brightest* (Fawcett Publications, Greenwich, Conn., 1973, first published 1969), p. 14.
19. Reinhold Niebuhr, *Moral Man and Immoral Society* (Charles Scribner's Sons, New York, 1932), p. xx.
20. For a fuller discussion of the movement of scholarly opinion in the thirties and later, see Osgood, *op. cit.*, ch. 16, and Kenneth W. Thompson, 'American Approaches to International Politics', in *The Yearbook of World Affairs 1959* (Stevens & Sons, London, 1959), pp. 205–35.
21. Henry Kissinger, *The White House Years* (Hodder & Stoughton, Sydney, 1979), p. 59.
22. Quoted in Richard E. Neustadt, *Presidential Power. The Politics of Leadership with Reflections on Johnson and Nixon* (John Wiley & Sons, New York, 1976 edition) at p. 118. According to Neustadt, the remark was representative of views Truman expressed while he was President.
23. For accounts of Acheson's presentation see Richard J. Barnet, *Intervention and Revolution: The United States in the Third World* (Meridian, New York, 1968), pp. 114–16, and Seyom Brown, *op. cit.*, pp. 39–41.
24. Gaddis, *op. cit.*, pp. 141–5.
25. Halberstam, *op. cit.*, p. 135. For a fuller discussion of anti-communism and its influence on American diplomatic thinking see chapter 8, pp. 176–8.
26. Bernard Brodie, *Strategy in the Missile Age* (Rand Corporation, Princeton University Press, N.J., 1959), ch. 7.
27. See for example Blum, *op. cit.*, p. 166.
28. It has been argued, however, that the degree to which the military could imprison their political superiors by such means has been exaggerated by some writers. It happened more under Eisenhower than later. See Richard K. Betts, *Soldiers, Statesmen, and Cold War Crises* (Harvard University Press, Cambridge, Mass., 1977), p. 42.
29. See Glenn H. Snyder, 'The "New Look" of 1953' in Warner H. Schilling, Paul Y. Hammond and Glenn H. Snyder, *Strategy, Politics and Defense Budgets* (Columbia University Press, New York and London, 1962), pp. 379–524.
30. See for example Colin S. Gray, 'The Rise and Fall of Academic Strategy', *Journal of the Royal United Services Institute for Defence Studies*, vol. CXVI (662) (June 1971), pp. 54–7.
31. Alexander L. George and Richard Smoke, *Deterrence in American Foreign Policy: Theory and Practice* (Columbia University Press, New York and London, 1974).
32. *Ibid.*, ch. 21.
33. See for example Gaddis, *op. cit.*, p. 84.

34. Following T.E. Lawrence, this theme is developed in Ken Booth, *Strategy and Ethnocentrism* (Croom Helm, London, 1979), pp. 26–7.
35. J. William Fulbright, *The Arrogance of Power* (Penguin Books, Harmondsworth, 1970, first published 1966), at p. 31. On pp. 21 and 22 Fulbright ponders on the reasons why Americans abroad sometimes act as though they 'own the place'. He relates this behaviour to Americans' consciousness of their power and wealth. It is curious that he does not go further and raise the issue of insecurity: that ignorance of the local language and unfamiliarity with the culture may have contributed to the behaviour he describes. This interpretation would have accorded with the general theme of his book.
36. The fear of men like General MacArthur and Senator Robert Taft was that America's overseas role would so increase expenditure and concentrate power at the centre as to cause internal stresses and a process of social corrosion. See Paul Seabury, *The Rise and Decline of the Cold War* (Basic Books, New York, 1967), pp. 91–3.
37. See David Riesman with Nathan Glazer and Reuel Denney, *The Lonely Crowd. A Study of the Changing American Character* (Doubleday & Co., New York, n.d., first published 1950).
38. Robert Dallek, *The American Style of Foreign Policy. Cultural Politics and Foreign Affairs* (Mentor, New American Library, New York, 1983), pp. 172–3. It cannot be said that Dallek is altogether successful in sustaining his thesis that very often foreign policy was less a reaction to events abroad than to conditions at home.
39. Richard D. Mahoney, *J.F.K. Ordeal in Africa* (OUP, New York, 1983), pp. 30–31.
40. Bruce Mazlish in the Foreword to Nancy Gager Clinch, *The Kennedy Neurosis: A Psychological Portrait of an American Dynasty* (Grosset & Dunlap, New York, 1973), p. xiii.
41. For material on Kennedy's personality and background see Arthur Schlesinger Jr., *A Thousand Days, John F. Kennedy in the White House* (Andre Deutsch, London, 1965); T.M. Mongar, 'Personality and Decision-Making: John F. Kennedy in Four Crisis Decisions', *Canadian Journal of Political Science*, vol. 2 (2) (June 1969), pp. 200–25; Clinch, *op. cit.*; and Garry Wills, *The Kennedy Imprisonment: A Meditation on Power* (Little Brown, Boston, 1982).
42. See for example George Ball, 'A Policy-Maker's View: Experience Vs. Character', *Psychology Today* (March 1975), pp. 40–42 at p. 42.
43. Clinch, *op. cit.*, especially chs. 5 to 8.
44. Neustadt, *op. cit.*, pp. 32–3.
45. Quoted in Merle Miller, *Lyndon – An Oral Biography* (G.P. Putnam's Sons, New York, 1980) at p. 420. More generally see Philip Geyelin, *Lyndon B. Johnson and the World* (Praeger, New York, 1966); Eric F. Goldman, *The Tragedy of Lyndon Johnson*, (Alfred A. Knopf, New York, 1969); and Doris Kearns, *Lyndon Johnson and the American Dream* (Andre Deutsch, London, 1976).
46. Quoted in Halberstam, *op. cit.*, p. 643.
47. Larry L. King, 'Machismo in the White House: LBJ and Vietnam', *American Heritage*, vol. 27 (5) (1976) pp. 8–13, 98–101 at p. 99.
48. James David Barber quoted in J.L. Dubbert, *A Man's Place: Masculinity in Transition* (Prentice-Hall, Englewood Cliffs, N.J., 1971), pp. 278–9. For other analyses of Nixon's insecurity see James David Barber, *The Presidential Character: Predicting Performance in the White House* (Prentice-Hall, Englewood Cliffs, N.J., 1972); Bruce Mazlish, *In Search of Nixon. A Psycho-historical Inquiry* (Basic Books Inc., New York, 1972); and Rowland Evans and Robert D. Novak, *Nixon in the White House: The Frustration of Power* (Vintage Books, New York, 1972).

49. Quoted in Aaron Wildavsky, 'Was Nixon Tough? Dilemmas of American Statecraft', *Society* (formerly *Transaction*), vol. 16 (1) (Nov./Dec. 1978), pp. 25–35 at p. 27.
50. The idea of 'Eurafrica' was that Africa remained a semi-dependency of Europe and the United States should not intrude. See William Attwood, *The Reds and the Blacks* (Hutchinson, London, 1967), p. 290.
51. Arthur Gavshon, *Crisis in Africa – Battleground of East and West* (Penguin, Harmondsworth, 1981), p. 234.
52. *Ibid.*, p. 157.
53. Quoted in Arthur M. Schlesinger, *The Bitter Heritage – Vietnam and American Democracy 1941–1966* (Andre Deutsch, London, 1966), p. 22.
54. Eisenhower, *Waging Peace, 1956–61*, p. 265.
55. William J. Pomeroy, 'The Philippines: A Case History of Neocolonialism', in Mark Selden (ed.), *Remaking Asia. Essays on the American Use of Power* (Pantheon Books, New York, 1974), pp. 157–99 at p. 177.
56. For an analysis of changing perceptions of guerilla warfare see Chalmers Johnson, *Autopsy on People's War* (Quantam Books, University of California Press, Berkeley, 1973).
57. Townsend Hoopes, *The Devil and John Foster Dulles* (Andre Deutsch, London, 1974), pp. 141–2. Hoopes goes on to describe Dulles as 'the sole intellectual wellspring of conception and action in foreign policy during his period in office'. *Ibid.*, p. 143. This claim cannot be sustained. Robert A. Divine, in *Eisenhower and the Cold War* (OUP, New York, 1981) has shown that Eisenhower determined the main lines of his foreign policy and that Dulles' influence was more limited than was thought at the time. Richard Neustadt makes a similar judgement in *Alliance Politics* (Columbia University Press, New York, 1970), pp. 103–6. According to Neustadt, during the Suez crisis (including the cancellation of the Aswan Dam), Dulles cleared every move with Eisenhower in advance: '. . . Eisenhower was no 'patsy' in this process. Far from it, he was laying down the law . . .' *Ibid.*, p. 105.
58. Halberstam, *op. cit.*, p. 326–7.
59. John C. Donovan, *The Cold Warriors: A Policy Making Elite* (D.C. Heath & Co., Lexington, Mass., 1974), p. 275.
60. *Ibid.*, p. 276.
61. Quoted in Tony Smith, *The Pattern of Imperialism. The United States, Great Britain and the late-industrializing world since 1815* (Cambridge University Press, Cambridge, 1981), at p. 199.
62. See Hoopes, *op. cit.*, pp. 405–8, especially at p. 407.
63. Gavshon, *op. cit.*, p. 157.
64. John Donovan has developed this point. *Op. cit.*, p. 275.
65. For a fuller discussion see Isaacs, *Scratches on Our Minds*, pp. 212–18.
66. George and Smoke, *op. cit.*, p. 327.
67. Isaacs, *op. cit.*, p. 217.
68. *Ibid.*, pp. 218–36.
69. Said, *Orientalism*, p. 285. In his later book, *Covering Islam. How the Media and the Experts Determine How We See the Rest of the World* (Routledge & Kegan Paul, London, 1981), Edward W. Said considers the approach of the media to Islam and gives an account of the media's treatment of the Iranian hostage crisis. But see the review by M.E. Yapp, 'The Revival Misrepresented', in *Times Literary Supplement*, 9 October 1981, p. 1160.
70. Quoted in W. Macmahon Ball, *Japan – Enemy or Ally?* (John Day Company, New York, 1949), p. 11.
71. For a detailed account see Selig S. Harrison, *The Widening Gulf – Asian Nationalism and American Policy* (Free Press, New York, 1978), part 3.

72. *Ibid.*, p. 253.
73. In 1964, W.P. Bundy, chairman of the NSC Working Group on south-east Asia, justified the US commitment to the defence of South Vietnam and Laos on the basis of 'national prestige, credibility, and honor with respect to world-wide pledges'. *The Pentagon Papers. The Defence Department History of United States Decision-making on Vietnam* (Senator Gravel edn, Beacon Press, Boston, 1971), vol. 3, pp. 622–3. Secretary of State Dean Rusk echoed this assessment on 9 August 1965, when he equated America's national security with the honour and integrity of her commitment to Vietnam. *Ibid.*, vol. 4, p. 636.
74. *Ibid.*, vol. 3, p. 695.
75. *The Limits of Power*, pp. 706–7.
76. *Ibid.*, p. 707.
77. Raymond Aron, *The Imperial Republic – The United States and the World 1945–1973* (Prentice-Hall, Englewood Cliffs, N.J., 1974), p. 2.
78. For a full discussion see Robert L. Rothstein, *Alliances and Small Powers* (Columbia University Press, New York, 1968) and Robert L. Rothstein, *The Weak in the World of the Strong* (Columbia University Press, New York, 1977), especially, ch. 4.
79. See Seabury, *op. cit.*, p. 56.
80. *Imperialism At Bay*, p. 69.

Chapter Eight

1. Quoted in Osgood, *Ideals and Self-Interest in America's Foreign Relations*, at p. 297.
2. From Commencement Address at Catholic University, 6 June 1965, in *Public Papers of the Presidents*, Lyndon B. Johnson, 1965, Book 2 (US Govt. Printing Office, Washington, 1966), p. 641.
3. Reprinted in Jane L. Scheiber and Robert C. Elliot, *In Search of the American Dream* (Meridian, New York, 1974), p. 286.
4. 'Utilitarianism and All That', *St Antony's Papers*, p. 50.
5. Frederick Jackson Turner, *The Frontier in American History* (Holt, Rinehart & Winston, New York, 1962).
6. David Potter, *People of Plenty. Economic Abundance and the American Character* (University of Chicago Press, Chicago, 1954).
7. Turner, *op. cit.*, p. 244.
8. Louis Hartz, *The Liberal Tradition in America* (Harcourt, Brace & World, New York, 1955).
9. *Ibid.*, ch. 11, especially pp. 285 and 306.
10. Roy Nichols, *Religion and American Democracy* (Louisiana State University Press, Baton Rouge, 1959).
11. Michael Howard, *War and the Liberal Conscience* (Temple Smith, London, 1978), p. 116.
12. Quoted in Philip Greven, *The Protestant Temperament. Patterns of Child-Rearing, Religious Experience and the Self in Early America* (Knopf, New York, 1977), p. 103.
13. D. Cameron Watt, *Succeeding John Bull. America in Britain's Place 1900–1975* (Cambridge University Press, Cambridge, 1984), p. 217. Chapter 10 provides a searching account of the diplomacy between Britain and America over Indo-China, 1942–5.
14. Cordell Hull, *The Memoirs of Cordell Hull*, vol. 2 (Hodder & Stoughton, London, 1948), p. 1599.
15. *Imperialism at Bay*, p. 567.

16. *Ibid.*, p. 475.
17. William Roger Louis, 'American Anti-colonialism and the Dissolution of the British Empire', *International Affairs* (London), vol. 61 (3) (summer 1985), pp. 395–420 at p. 397.
18. Watt, *op. cit*, ch. 11, especially at p. 250.
19. Dwight D. Eisenhower, *The White House Years,* volume 1, *Mandate for Change 1953–1956* (Heinemann, London, 1963), pp. 373–4.
20. First draft of Eisenhower's memoirs, quoted in Norman Podhoretz, *Why We Were in Vietnam* (Simon & Schuster, New York, 1982), p. 36.
21. See Louis, 'American Anti-colonialism and the Dissolution of the British Empire', pp. 414–16.
22. Chester Bowles, *Ambassador's Report* (Harper & Bros., New York, 1954), pp. 259–60.
23. Quoted in Rupert Emerson, *Africa and United States Policy* (Prentice-Hall, Englewood Cliffs, N.J., 1967), p. 23.
24. Quoted in Mahoney, *J.F.K. Ordeal in Africa,* p. 35.
25. This understanding was spelt out in a speech on the colonial problem by Assistant Secretary of State Henry A. Byroade in 1953. See Emerson, *op. cit.*, p. 5.
26. Gann and Duignan, *Colonialism in Africa, 1870–1960*, p. 285.
27. See Davidson Nicol, 'Africa and the USA in the United Nations', *Journal of Modern African Studies*, vol. 16 (3) (1978), pp. 365–95, and Ernst B. Haas, *Tangle of Hopes – American Commitments and World Order* (Prentice-Hall, Englewood Cliffs, N.J., 1969), ch. 8.
28. In the view of some British officials involved in African affairs, the appointment of G. Mennen 'Soapy' Williams, a former Governor of Michigan, to the position of Assistant Secretary of State for African Affairs began a period in which the hope for rapid and peaceful decolonization counted for more than any realistic understanding of the African situation. Adlai Stevenson was regarded as a more effective critic of colonialism because of his recognition that responsibility must lie somewhere.
29. John Kenneth Galbraith, *Ambassador's Journal. A Personal Account of the Kennedy Years* (Hamish Hamilton, London, 1969), pp. 283–4.
30. Mahoney, *op. cit.*, p. 222 and pp. 244–8.
31. Eisenhower, *Waging Peace 1956–1961*, p. 106.
32. George W. Ball, *The Past Has Another Pattern. Memoirs* (W.W. Norton & Co., New York, 1982), p. 176.
33. Stanley Hoffman, *Gulliver's Troubles, Or the Setting of American Foreign Policy* (McGraw Hill for the Council on Foreign Relations, New York, 1968), pp. 96–7. I have taken a certain liberty in reformulating Hoffmann's point without, I hope, changing its meaning.
34. See our earlier discussion, ch. 7, pp. 153–4.
35. *The Best and the Brightest*, p. 134.
36. Hoopes, *The Devil and John Foster Dulles*, p. 316.
37. Harry S. Truman, *Memoirs*, vol. 2, *Years of Trial and Hope 1946–53* (Signet Books, New York, 1956), p. 129.
38. For the text see George Modelski, *SEATO – Six Studies* (Cheshire for the Australian National University, Melbourne, 1962), pp. 291–2.
39. David Caute, *The Great Fear – The Anti-Communist Purge Under Truman and Eisenhower* (Simon & Schuster, New York, 1978), pp. 21, 22 and 51.
40. Arguments that Third World development would help stem communism and that it would advantage the United States economy are considered in ch. 9.
41. David E. Apter, *The Politics of Modernization* (University of Chicago Press, Chicago, 1965), p. 1.
42. Robert A. Packenham, *Liberal America and the Third World* (Princeton Uni-

versity Press, Princeton, N.J., 1973), p. xix.

43. Ball, *op. cit.*, p. 170.

44. Amos Perlmutter quoted in Packenham, *op. cit.*, p. 303.

45. Richard E. Neustadt and Ernest R. May, *Thinking in Time. The Uses of History for Decision-Makers* (Free Press, New York, 1986), p. xx.

46. Quoted in Joseph Blotner, *The Modern American Political Novel* (University of Texas Press, Austin, 1966), p. 351.

47. Joseph Buttinger, 'Fact and Fiction on Foreign Aid. A Critique of "The Ugly American"', *Dissent*, vol. 6 (1959), pp. 317–67 at p. 322.

48. In Lederer's and Burdick's later novel, *Sarkhan* (1965), it is significant that figures such as Homer Atkins have disappeared. By the time of its publication much of the earlier optimism had evaporated, and economic and political change in Asia seemed less feasible. The tone of *Sarkhan* is sombre, and the issues with which the authors are concerned are international and military, rather than social.

49. Hans Morgenthau, 'A Political Theory of Foreign Aid', *American Political Science Review*, vol. 56 (2) (June 1962), pp. 301–9 at pp. 301–2.

50. Goran Therborn, 'From Petrograd to Saigon', *New Left Review*, no. 48 (March–April 1968), pp. 3–11 at p. 6.

51. Kissinger, *The White House Years*, p. 56.

52. Podhoretz, *op. cit.*, p. 103.

53. Kenneth Keniston, *Young Radicals – Notes on Committed Youth* (Harcourt Brace & World, New York, 1968), p. 35.

54. *Ibid.*, pp. 66 and 113. More generally see Kenneth Keniston, *Youth and Dissent: The Rise of a New Opposition* (Harcourt Brace Jovanovich, New York, 1971).

55. Podhoretz, *op. cit.*, p. 107.

56. See P.T. Bauer, *Dissent on Development: Studies and Debates in Development Economics* (Weidenfeld & Nicolson, London, 1971) and *Equality, the Third World and Economic Delusion* (Harvard University Press, Cambridge, Mass., 1981).

57. John G. Stoessinger, *Crusaders and Pragmatists – Movers of Modern American Foreign Policy* (Norton, New York, 1979).

58. Eisenhower is not discussed at length, and Stoessinger avoids any attempt to characterize Johnson according to the typology he has set up. For his judgement on Roosevelt see p. 53.

59. Daniel Bell, *The End of Ideology: On the Exhaustion of Political Ideas in the Fifties* (Free Press, New York, 1960).

60. *Waging Peace 1956–1961*, p. 657.

61. Quoted in Emerson, *op. cit.*, p. 22.

62. Eisenhower, *Mandate for Change 1953–56*, p. 372.

63. See Paul J. Zingy, 'The Cold War in North Africa: American Foreign Policy and Postwar Muslim Nationalism 1945–1962', *Historian*, vol. 39 (1) (1976), pp. 40–61, especially at pp. 50–52.

64. See generally Peter Berger's thought-provoking article, 'Indochina and the American Conscience', *Commentary* (Feb. 1980), pp. 29–39.

65. *Scratches on Our Minds*, pp. 387–9.

66. William L. Neumann, *America Encounters Japan. From Perry to MacArthur* (John Hopkins Press, Baltimore, 1963), p. 295.

67. Quoted in Dallek, *The American Style of Foreign Policy*, at p. 216.

68. See William J. Burns, *Economic Aid and American Policy Toward Egypt 1955–1981* (State University of New York Press, Albany, 1985), pp. 152, 202 and 203.

69. George Kennan, *Realities of American Foreign Policy* (Oxford University Press, London, 1954), pp. 107 and 109.

70. Anthony Burgess, 'Beds in the East' in *The Long Day Wanes* (Penguin, Harmondsworth, 1972), pp. 544–53. *Beds in the East* was first published in 1959.
71. Norman Mailer, *The Armies of the Night* (Penguin, Harmondsworth, 1968), p. 164.
72. Michael Herr, *Dispatches* (Picador, London, 1978, first published 1977), p. 24.
73. The references to the various maps are at pp. 11 and 203–4. See also John Hellmann, 'The New Journalism and Vietnam: Memory as Structure in Michael Herr's *Dispatches*', *The South Atlantic Quarterly*, vol. 79 (2) (1980), pp. 141–51.
74. See chapter 7, pp. 155–8.
75. See for example James C. Thomson, Peter W. Stanley and John C. Perry, *Sentimental Imperialists – The American Experience in East Asia* (Harper & Row, New York, 1981), pp. 18–19, and Philip W. Quigg, *America the Dutiful – An Assessment of U.S. Foreign Policy* (Simon & Schuster, New York, 1971), p. 30.
76. Hartz, *op. cit.*, p. 286.
77. Fulbright, *The Arrogance of Power*, p. 32.
78. See for example Robert Shaplen, *A Forest of Tigers* (Alfred A. Knopf, New York, 1956) and John P. Marquand, *Stopover: Tokyo* (Collins, London, 1956).
79. Some relevant material is to be found in Ruth Prigozy, 'The Liberal Novelist in the McCarthy Era', *Twentieth Century Literature*, vol. 21, pp. 253–63, and Douglas T. Miller and Marion Nowak, *The Fifties: The Way We Really Were* (Doubleday & Co., Garden City, New York, 1977), ch. 14, 'Beyond Alienation: Fiction in the Fifties'.
80. Charles A. Reich, *The Greening of America* (Penguin, Harmondsworth, 1971, first published 1970), pp. 16, 179–80.
81. Jerry Rubin, *Do it!* (Simon & Schuster, New York, n.d.), p. 111.
82. Mailer, *op. cit.*, p. 210.
83. *Crusaders and Pragmatists*, p. 113.
84. See Burns, *op. cit.*, especially pp. 76, 105 and 203.
85. See Eric F. Goldman, *The Tragedy of Lyndon Johnson* (Knopf, New York, 1969), p. 519; Merle Miller, *Lyndon – An Oral Biography*, pp. 456–66; and Doris Kearns, *Lyndon Johnson and the American Dream*, pp. 266–9. See also George Ball's comments in *The Past Has Another Pattern*, pp. 318–20.
86. King, 'Machismo in the White House', pp. 98–9.
87. Harold D. Laswell, *World Politics and Personal Insecurity* (Free Press, New York, 1956, first published 1935), p. 163.

CHAPTER NINE

1. The major revisionist writers include Gabriel Kolko, David Horowitz, Noam Chomsky, William A. Williams, Walter La Faber, Harry Magdoff, Paul A. Baran and Paul H. Sweezy.
2. G. William Domhoff, 'Who Made American Foreign Policy 1945–1963?', in David Horowitz (ed.), *Corporations and the Cold War* (Monthly Review Press for the Bertrand Russell Peace Foundation, New York, 1969), pp. 25–70 at pp. 63–4.
3. *The Limits of Power*, p. 18.
4. See Howard J. Wiarda, 'The Ethnocentrism of the Social Science Implications for Research and Policy', *Review of Politics*, vol. 43 (2) (April 1981), pp. 163–97.
5. The primacy of America's economic objectives is argued by Gabriel Kolko in *The Politics of War. The World and United States Foreign Policy, 1943–1945* (Vintage

Books, New York, 1970), ch. 11. See Robert Tucker's refutation in *The Radical Left and American Foreign Policy*, (Washington Center of Foreign Policy Research, John Hopkins Press, Baltimore, Maryland, 1971), pp. 94–5.

6. Gabriel Kolko, 'The American Goals in Vietnam', ch. 1, in *The Pentagon Papers*, vol. 5, *Critical Essays*, edited by Noam Chomsky and Howard Zinn (The Senator Gravel Edn, Beacon Press, Boston, 1972) at pp. 14 and 2. Along similar lines see Noam Chomsky's comments in ch. 11, 'The Pentagon Papers as Propaganda and History', *ibid*.

7. Robert Tucker, *op. cit.*, pp. 116–17.

8. Quoted in Noam Chomsky, *The Backroom Boys* (Fontana/Collins, Bungay, Suffolk, 1973), p. 29.

9. *Ibid*.

10. John W. Dower, 'The Superdomino in Postwar Asia: Japan In and Out of the Pentagon Papers', ch. 8 in *The Pentagon Papers*, vol. 5, (Senator Gravel Edn), p. 103.

11. Peter Dale Scott, 'The Vietnam War and the CIA – Financial Establishment', in Mark Selden (ed.), *Re-making Asia. Essays on the American Uses of Power* (Pantheon Books, New York, 1974), pp. 91–154 at p. 116.

12. See W. Reitzel, M. Kaplan and C. Coblenz, *United States Foreign Policy 1945–1955* (Brookings Institution, Washington, 1956), pp. 134–6.

13. Packenham, *Liberal America and the Third World*, p. 37.

14. See Truman, *Memoirs*, vol. 2, *Years of Trial and Hope 1946–1952*, pp. 268–76.

15. Packenham, *op. cit.*, p. 47.

16. For a full account of the role of Congress in US foreign assistance policy see Robert A. Pastor, *Congress and the Politics of U.S. Foreign Economic Policy 1929–1976* (University of California Press, Berkeley and Los Angeles, 1980), part 3, ch. 9.

17. David A. Baldwin, *Economic Development and American Foreign Policy 1943–62*, (University of Chicago Press, Chicago, 1966), p. 217. Baldwin's book gives a detailed account of changing Congressional attitudes to foreign aid.

18. Quoted in *ibid.*, p. 78.

19. Quoted in *ibid.*, p. 193.

20. Packenham, *op. cit.*, p. 49.

21. This theme is developed at some length in W.W. Rostow, *Eisenhower, Kennedy, and Foreign Aid* (University of Texas Press, Austin, 1985), especially ch. 7 and pp. 196–201. See also James P. Warburg, 'United States Postwar Policy in Asia', *The Annals of the American Academy of Political and Social Science*, vol. 318 (July 1958), pp. 72–82, and Russell H. Fifield, *Southeast Asia in United States Policy* (Council on Foreign Relations, Praeger, New York, 1963), pp. 251–61.

22. Packenham, *op. cit.*, p. 49.

23. Charles Lipson, *Standing Guard. Protecting Foreign Capital in the Nineteenth and Twentieth Centuries* (University of California Press, Berkeley, L.A. and London, 1985), p. 210. The Hickenlooper amendment required the suspension of bilateral aid to foreign countries which failed to provide prompt compensation to US companies which suffered expropriation or discriminatory treatment. It is significant that expropriation was understood as an aspect of global communism. For an excellent analysis of the politics of the Hickenlooper amendment see Lipson, *op. cit.*, ch. 6.

24. *President's Materials Policy Commission, Resources for Freedom*, vol. 1 (Government Printing Office, Washington, 1952), p. 3. See also the observations on pp. 17 and 19.

25. Adlai E. Stevenson, *The New America* (Rupert Hart-Davies, London, 1957), p. 71.

26. Robert S. McNamara, *The Essence of Security. Reflections in Office* (Hodder &

Stoughton, London, 1968), p. 149.
27. It should not be assumed that the role of Congress was simply negative. Indeed one scholar has argued that its impact on policy has been beneficial and that collective interests have largely prevailed over particular interests. See Pastor, *op. cit.*, pp. 4 and 5, 281–4.
28. See for example US Congress, Senate Committee on Agriculture and Forestry, *Farm Demand and Price Situation and Administration of the Agricultural Trade Development and Assistance Act of 1954*, 84th Congress, first session (19 Jan. 1955), and US Congress, Senate Committee on Agriculture and Forestry, *The Operation and Administration of the Agricultural Trade Development and Assistance Act of 1954, and its Relationship to Foreign Policy*, 85th Congress, first session (June–July 1957). See generally Baldwin, *op. cit.*, pp. 154–8.
29. *Commission on Foreign Economic Policy. Report to the President and the Congress, January 1954* (US Government Printing Office, Washington, 23 January 1954), p. 9.
30. See for example the report of a study group sponsored by the Woodrow Wilson Foundation and the National Planning Association (Wm. Y. Elliott, chairman), *The Political Economy of American Foreign Policy. Its Concepts, Strategy, and Limits* (Henry Holt, New York, 1955), pp. 315–16.
31. Thomas V. DiBacco, 'American Business and Foreign Aid – The Eisenhower Years', *Business History Review*, vol. XLI (1967), pp. 21–35 at p. 30.
32. Baldwin, *op. cit.*, pp. 249–51, and Pastor, *op. cit.*, p. 267. A 'soft loan' has elements of a grant but is so packaged as to make the grant less obvious.
33. Michael Hudson, *Super Imperialism – The Economic Strategy of American Empire* (Holt, Rinehart & Winston, New York, 1968), p. 152.
34. Quoted in Mira Wilkins, *The Maturing of the Multinational Enterprise: American Business Abroad from 1914 to 1970* (Harvard University Press, Cambridge, Massachusetts, 1974), p. 328n.
35. Baldwin, *op. cit.*, p. 272.
36. For an overview of the situation in the early post-war years and some historical background see Percy W. Bidwell, *Raw Materials. A Study of American Foreign Policy* (Council on Foreign Relations, Harper & Row, New York, 1958), chs. 1 and 3.
37. *Op. cit.*, vol. 1, p. 157.
38. *Commission on Foreign Economic Policy, op. cit.*, p. 40.
39. Hans H. Landsberg, Leonard L. Fischman and Joseph L. Fischer, *Resources in America's Future: Patterns of Requirements and Availabilities 1960–2000* (Resources for the Future Inc., John Hopkins Press, Baltimore, 1963). See especially pp. 45 and 53.
40. See generally Paley Commission, *op. cit.*, vol. 1, pp. 10 and 108, and R.H.K. Victor, 'The Synthetic Liquid Fuels Program: Energy Politics in the Truman Era', *Business History Review*, LIV (1980), pp. 1–34.
41. *Commission on Foreign Economic Policy, op. cit.*, p. 40.
42. Report to the President on Foreign Economic Policies, 10 November 1950, by Gordon Gray, in Raymond Dennett and R.K. Turner (eds), *Documents on American Foreign Relations*, vol. XII (1950) (published for the World Peace Foundation by Princeton University Press, New York, 1951), ch. VII at p. 270.
43. See Bidwell, *op. cit.*, pp. 46–54.
44. See for example Paley Commission, *op. cit.*, vol. 1, p. 62, and the Brookings Institution publication, *Major Problems of United States Foreign Policy 1952–1953* (Geo. Banta, Menasha, Wisconsin, 1952), pp. 339–40.
45. See pp. 209–10.
46. In 1937 Eugene Staley, in his study of America's raw materials needs in time of war, confidently concluded that there was no materials problem as such.

E. Staley, *Raw Materials In Peace and War* (Council on Foreign Relations, New York, 1937).

47. Wilkins, *op. cit.*, pp. 305–6 and 314–24.
48. H. Landsberg *et al., op. cit.*, p. 42. Bidwell, *op. cit.*, reaches the same broad conclusion. See especially p. 339.
49. E.S. Mason, 'Resources in the Past and for the Future', in C.J. Hitch (ed.), *Resources for an Uncertain Future* (John Hopkins Press, Baltimore, 1978), p. 5.
50. *The Limits of Power*, p. 14.
51. With respect to Latin America the position was more complex, because of America's pre-eminence in the region and the pressures arising from the economic dependence and political instability of so many of the regional states. Even so, America's economic thinking and policies were heavily influenced by the belief that it was necessary to stem Latin American interest in the Soviet Union. Key developments here were the Guatemala crisis of 1954 and the Cuban revolution in 1959. For a broad overview see R. Harrison Wagner, *United States Policy Towards Latin America. A Study in Domestic and International Politics* (Stanford University Press, California, 1970), ch. 1. Although Latin America falls outside the scope of this study, it should be recognized that US thinking about its economic relationship with Asia and Africa was often influenced by its experience in Latin America. This was particularly the case regarding investment and attitudes to expropriation and insurance.
52. Report to the President on Foreign Economic Policies, 10 November 1950, *op. cit.*, pp. 270, 273–4.
53. See Peter B. Kenen, *Giant Among Nations: Problems in United States Foreign Economic Policy* (Rand McNally, Chicago, 1960), pp. 10 and 11.
54. See for example President Eisenhower's address at the Gettysburg College Convocation on 4 April 1959, in *The Pentagon Papers. The Defense Department History of United States Decision-making in Vietnam Volume 1* (Senator Gravel Edition, Beacon Press, Boston, 1972), p. 627. Also see more generally Dower, *op. cit.*, pp. 105–10.
55. See for example Harry R. Rudin, 'Past and Present Role of Africa in World Affairs', *The Annals of the American Academy of Political and Social Science*, vol. 298 (March 1955), p. 37.
56. Quoted in Emerson, *Africa and United States Policy*, at p. 253.
57. See for example the address by Douglas Dillon, Deputy Under-Secretary for Economic Affairs on 8 Jan. 1958, printed under the title 'Foreign Investment and Economic Development', in *The Department of State Bulletin*, vol. XXXVIII (970) (27 Jan. 1958), pp. 139–43. The same issue contains a State Department summary of the Soviet economic offensive in less developed areas (pp. 144–9).
58. Lipson, *op. cit.*, pp. 231–5.
59. Kenen, *op. cit.*, p. 13.
60. Pastor, *op. cit.*, p. 189.
61. Report to the President on Foreign Economic Policies, 10 November 1950, *op. cit.*, pp. 273–4.
62. See generally Jack. H. Behrman, 'The Case of the Cautious Matchmaker', in Benjamin J. Cohen (ed.), *American Foreign Economic Policy* (Harper & Row, New York, 1968), ch. 26.
63. Wilkins, *op. cit.*, p. 331.
64. See Behrman, *op. cit.*, pp. 400–1 and Kenen, *op. cit.*, pp. 125–8.
65. Kenen, *op. cit.*, p. 126.
66. Behrman, *op. cit.*, pp. 404–5.
67. See for example the 1951 suggestion of the International Development Advisory Board, chaired by Nelson Rockefeller: Kenen, *op. cit.*, pp. 122–3. Also the recommendation of the Randall Commission, *Commission on Foreign Economic*

Policy, pp. 18–22.
68. See Wilkins, *op. cit.*, pp. 314–24.
69. Kenen, *op. cit.*, pp. 116–17.
70. In March 1950 Dean Acheson attempted to put the 'loss of China' in economic perspective by observing:

> In the period 1946–48 the United States supplied over fifty per cent of China's imports and bought approximately one quarter of China's exports. Yet those same exports from America were less than 5% of our total exports and our purchases from China were a mere 2% of all we bought abroad.

> *State Department Bulletin*, vol. XXII (1950), p. 470.
71. Kenen, *op. cit.*, pp. 128–9.
72. Wilkins, *op. cit.*, pp. 363–4n.
73. *Ibid.*, p. 351.

CONCLUSION

1. See ch. 1, p. 24.
2. Quoted by Michael Howard in 'The Armed Forces', ch. 8 in *The New Cambridge Modern History*, vol XI, at p. 223.
3. Alvin Toffler's *Future Shock* (Bodley Head, London, 1970) is suggestive here, especially part 1.
4. D.C. Watt makes some comments on the influence of national culture on the historian in *Succeeding John Bull. America in Britain's Place 1900–1975*, p. 158.
5. Curzon's comment was made in a speech at a farewell dinner in Bombay, 16 November 1905. See Bennett, *The Concept of Empire*, p. 315.
6. From the text of the speech to have been delivered 22 November 1963. Quoted in Ronald Steel, *Pax Americana* (Hamish Hamilton, London, 1967), at p. 3.
7. Quoted in Dallek, *The American Style of Foreign Policy*, at p. 117.
8. 'The Eight Points of General Kaulza de Arriaga', *Press Release of the High Command of the Armed Forces in Mocambique* (Nampula, Mozambique, Nov. 1972).
9. For an exploration of the relationship between private interests and national policies in the economic sphere see Eugene Staley, *War and the Private Investor: A Study in the Relations of International Politics and International Private Investment* (University of Chicago Press, Chicago, 1935).
10. On this point see H. Myint, 'The "Classical Theory" of International Trade and the Underdeveloped Countries', *The Economic Journal*, vol. 68 (June 1958), pp. 317–37.
11. In their recent important study of the uses of history for decision-makers, Richard Neustadt and Ernest May argue that a general knowledge of history is increasingly less characteristic of American decision-makers and their aides. Neustadt and May, *Thinking in Time*, p. 245.
12. Said, *Orientalism*, pp. 1 and 2.
13. Thomas B. Streissguth, *Tigers in the House. A Satirical Novel of American 'Do-Good-Ism' in Indochina* (Exposition Press, New York, 1958), p. 79.
14. American images of China and Japan during the Cold War are cases in point. On images of China see Isaacs, *Scratches on Our Minds*, pp. 209–38. On images of Japan see Nathan Glazer, 'From Ruth Benedict to Herman Kahn: The Postwar Japanese Image in the American Mind', ch. 7 in Akira Iriye (ed.), *Mutual Images. Essays in American-Japanese Relations*.

SELECT BIBLIOGRAPHY

This guide to sources is restricted to works of broad relevance. Specialized studies, memoirs, biographies and imaginative literature have been omitted, and for these the reader is referred to the chapter notes. The list of books and articles has been arranged in three sections: those of a general nature, those relating primarily to Britain, and those relating primarily to the United States.

GENERAL

Alatas, Syed, *The Myth of the Lazy Native* (Cass, London, 1977).

Albertini, Rudolf von, *Decolonization – The Administration and Future of the Colonies 1919–1960* (Africana Publishing Co., New York, 1982 edn).

Arendt, Hannah, 'The Imperialist Character', *Review of Politics*, 12 (1950), pp. 303–20.

Bolt, Christine, *Victorian Attitudes to Race* (Routledge & Kegan Paul, London, 1971).

Booth, Ken, *Strategy and Ethnocentrism* (Croom Helm, London, 1979).

Bridges, F.R. and Roger Bullen, *The Great Powers and the European States Systems 1815–1914* (Longman, London, 1980).

Bury, J.B., *The Idea of Progress: An Enquiry into its Origins and Growth* (Dover, New York, 1955, first published 1920).

Carr, E.H., *The Twenty Years' Crisis 1919–1939* (Macmillan, London, 1939).

Etherington, Norman, 'The Capitalist Theory of Capitalist Imperialism', *History of Political Economy* 15 (1983), pp. 38–62.

Etherington, Norman, 'Theories of Imperialism In Southern Africa Revisited', *African Affairs* 81 (1982), pp. 385–407.

Green, Martin, *Dreams of Adventure, Deeds of Empire* (Routledge & Kegan Paul, London and Henley, 1980).

Hayes, Carlton J.H., *A Generation of Materialism 1871–1900* (Harper, New York, 1941).

Hinsley, F.H., *Power and the Pursuit of Peace* (Cambridge University Press, Cambridge, 1963).

Hobson, J.A., *Imperialism: A Study* (Allen & Unwin, London, 3rd revised edition 1938, first published 1902).

Hodgart, Alan, *The Economics of European Imperialism* (Foundations of Modern History, Edward Arnold, London, 1977).

Iriye, Akira, *After Imperialism. The Search for a New Order in the Far East 1921–1931* (Harvard University Press, Cambridge, Mass., 1965).

Kiernan, V.G. *The Lords of Human Kind* (Weidenfeld & Nicolson, London, 1969).

Kiernan, V.G., *Marxism and Imperialism: Studies* (St. Martin's Press, New York, 1975).

Laswell, Harold D., *World Politics and Personal Insecurity* (Free Press, New York, 1965, first published 1935).

Latham, A.J.H., *The International Economy and the Undeveloped World 1865–1914* (Croom Helm, London, 1978).

Mannoni, O., *Prospero and Caliban. The Psychology of Colonization* (Praeger, London, 1964).

Mansergh, Nicholas, *The Coming of the First World War: A Study in the European Balance 1878–1914* (Longmans, Green & Co., London, 1949).

Memmi, Albert, *The Colonizer and the Colonized* (Beacon Press, Boston, 1967, first published 1957).

Munro, J. Forbes, *Africa and the International Economy 1800–1960. An Introduction to the Modern Economic History of Africa South of the Sahara* (J.M. Dent, London, 1976).

Nandy, Ashis, *The Intimate Enemy: Loss and Recovery of Self Under Colonialism* (Oxford University Press, Delhi, 1983).

Nisbet, Robert, *History of the Idea of Progress* (Heinemann, London, 1980).

Said, Edward, *Orientalism* (Routledge & Kegan Paul, London, 1978).

Sandison, Alan, *The Wheel of Empire. A Study of the Imperial Idea in some late Nineteenth and early Twentieth Century Fiction* (Macmillan, London, 1967).

Smith, Tony, *The Pattern of Imperialism. The United States, Great Britain and the late-industrializing world since 1815* (Cambridge University Press, Cambridge, 1981).

Storry, Richard, *Japan and the Decline of the West in Asia 1894–1943* (Macmillan, London, 1979).

Taylor, A.J.P., *The Struggle for Mastery in Europe 1848–1918* (Clarendon Press, Oxford, 1954).

Thorne, Christopher, *The Limits of Foreign Policy* (Hamish Hamilton, London, 1972).

Thornton, A.P., *Imperialism in the Twentieth Century* (Macmillan, London, 1978).

Watt, D. Cameron, *Succeeding John Bull. America in Britain's Place 1900–1975* (Cambridge University Press, Cambridge, 1984).

Winch, Donald, *Classical Political Economy and Colonies* (G. Bell, & Sons for the London School of Economics, London, 1965).

BRITAIN

Allen, Charles (ed.), *Plain Tales from the Raj* (Futura/Macdonald & Co., London, 1982, first published 1975).

Allen, Charles (ed.), *Tales from the Dark Continent. Images of British Colonial Africa in the Twentieth Century* (Andre Deutsch & British Broadcasting Corporation, London, 1979).

Ambirijan, S., *Classical Political Economy and British Policy in India* (Cambridge University Press, Cambridge, 1978).

Ballhatchet, Kenneth, *Race, Sex and Class Under the Raj: Imperial Attitudes and Policies and their Critics 1793–1905* (St. Martin's Press, New York, 1980).

Barnes, Leonard, *The Duty of Empire* (Victor Gollancz Ltd, London, 1935).

Barnett, Correlli, *The Collapse of British Power* (Eyre Methuen, London, 1972).

Beloff, Max, *Imperial Sunset*, vol. 1, *Britain's Liberal Empire 1897–1921* (Methuen, London, 1969).

Beloff, Max, *Wars and Welfare – Britain 1914–1945* (Edward Arnold, London, 1984).

Bennett, George (ed.), *The Concept of Empire: Burke to Attlee 1774–1947* (Adam & Charles Black, London, 1962).

Berard, M. Victor, *British Imperialism and Commercial Supremacy* (Longmans, Green & Co., London, 1906).

Chamberlain, M.E., *Britain and India: The Interaction of Two Peoples* (David & Charles, Newton Abbot, Devon, 1974).

Constantine, Stephen, *The Making of British Colonial Development Policy 1914–1940* (Cass, London, 1984).

Crankshaw, Edward, *The Forsaken Idea* (Longmans, Green & Co., London, 1952).

Curtin, Philip D., *The Image of Africa: British Ideas and Action, 1780–1850* (Macmillan, London, 1965).

Curzon, Lord, 'The True Imperialism', *Nineteenth Century and After*, LXIII (January 1908), pp. 151–65.

Darby, Phillip, *British Defence Policy East of Suez 1947–1968* (Oxford University Press for RIIA, London, 1973).

Darwin, John, *Britain, Egypt and the Middle East: Imperial Policy in the Aftermath of War 1918–1922* (Macmillan, London, 1981).

Darwin, John, 'Imperialism in Decline? Tendencies in British Imperial Policy Between the Wars', *Historical Journal* 23 (3) (1980), pp. 657–79.

Dilks, David (ed.), *Retreat From Power. Studies in Britain's Foreign Policy of the Twentieth Century* vol. 1 *1906–1939* (Macmillan, London, 1981).

Drummond, Ian M., *British Economic Policy and the Empire, 1919–1939* (George Allen & Unwin, London, 1972).

Drummond, Ian M., *Imperial Economic Policy 1917–1939, Studies in Expansion and Protection* (Allen & Unwin, London, 1974).

Duignan, Peter and L.H. Gann (eds.), *Colonialism in Africa 1870–1960*, vol. 4, *The Economics of Colonialism* (Cambridge University Press, Cambridge, 1975).

Edwardes, Michael, *High Noon of Empire: India Under Curzon* (Eyre & Spottiswoode, London, 1965).

Ehrlich, Cyril, 'Building and Caretaking: Economic Policy in British Tropical Africa, 1890–1960', *Economic History Review* 26 (1973), pp. 649–67.

Gann, L.H. and Peter Duignan, *The Rulers of British Africa 1870–1914* (Hoover Institution Publications, Croom Helm, London, 1978).

Gifford, Prosser and Wm. Roger Louis, *Britain and Germany in Africa* (Yale University Press, New Haven, Conn., 1967).

Gladstone, W.E., 'Aggression on Egypt and Freedom in the East', *Nineteenth Century* (London) 2 (Aug–Dec. 1877), pp. 149–166.

Greenberger, Allen J., *The British Image of India. A Study in the Literature of Imperialism 1880–1960* (Oxford University Press, London, 1969).

Grenville, J.A.S., *Lord Salisbury and Foreign Policy: The Close of the Nineteenth Century* (University of London, Athlone Press, London, 1964).

Gupta, Partha Sarathi, *Imperialism and the British Labour Movement, 1914–1964* (Holmes & Meier, New York, 1975).

Haggie, Paul, *Britannia at Bay. The Defence of the British Empire Against Japan 1931–1941* (Clarendon, Oxford, 1981).

Hailey, Lord, *An African Survey: A Study of Problems Arising in Africa South of the Sahara* (Issued by the Committee of the African Research Survey under the auspices of the RIIA, Oxford University Press, London, 1938).

Hailey, Lord, *The Future of Colonial Peoples* (RIIA, Oxford University Press, London, 1943).

Hancock, W.K., *Survey of British Commonwealth Affairs*, vol. 1, *Problems of Nationality* (Oxford University Press for RIIA, London 1937); vol. 2, *Problems of Economic Policy* (*Part 1*, 1940, *Part 2*, 1942).

Hetherington, Penelope, *British Paternalism and Africa 1920–1940* (Frank Cass,

London, 1978).

Heussler, Robert, *Yesterday's Rulers – The Making of the British Colonial Service* (Syracuse University Press, Syracuse, New York, 1963).

Holland, R.F. and G. Rizvi (eds.), *Perspectives on Imperialism and Decolonization. Essays in Honour of A.F. Madden* (Cass, London, 1984).

Hutchins, Francis, G., *Illusion of Permanence, British Imperialism in India* (Princeton University Press, Princeton, N.J., 1967).

Hyam, Ronald, *Britain's Imperial Century 1815–1914 – A Study of Empire and Expansionism* (Batsford, London, 1976).

Hynes, William G., *The Economics of Empire: Britain, Africa and the New Imperialism 1870–95* (Longman, London, 1979).

Iyer, Raghavan, 'Utilitarianism and All That (The Political Theory of British Imperialism in India)' in *St. Antony's Papers*, No. 8 (Chatto & Windus, London, 1960).

Judd, Denis, *Balfour and the British Empire: A Study in Imperial Evolution 1874–1932* (Macmillan, London, 1968).

Kennedy, Paul, *The Realities Behind Diplomacy: Background Influences on British External Policy 1865–1980* (Allen & Unwin, London, 1981).

Knowles, L.C.A., *The Economic Development of the British Overseas Empire*, volume 1 (Routledge, London, 1924).

Louis, William Roger, *British Strategy in the Far East 1919–1939* (Clarendon, Oxford, 1971).

Louis, William Roger, *Great Britain and Germany's Lost Colonies 1914–1919* (Clarendon, Oxford, 1967).

Louis, William Roger, *Imperialism at Bay. The United States and the Decolonization of the British Empire, 1941–1945* (Oxford University Press, New York, 1978).

Louis, William Roger (ed.), *Imperialism: The Robinson and Gallagher Controversy* (New Viewpoints, New York, 1976).

Low, D.A., *Lion Rampant: Essays in the Study of British Imperialism* (Frank Cass, London, 1973).

Lowe, C.J. *The Reluctant Imperialists: British Foreign Policy 1878–1902*, vol. 1 (Routledge & Kegan Paul, London, 1967).

Lugard, Sir F.D., *The Dual Mandate in British Tropical Africa* (Wm. Blackwood, Edinburgh and London, 3rd edition 1926, first published 1922).

Macdonald, J. Ramsay, *The Awakening of India* (Hodder & Stoughton, London, 1910).

Macmillan, W.M., *Africa Emergent, A Survey of Social and Economic Trends in British Africa* (Faber & Faber, London, 1938).

Madden, Frederick and D.K. Fieldhouse (eds.), *Oxford and the Idea of Commonwealth* (Croom Helm, London, 1982).

Marder, Arthur J., *The Anatomy of British Sea Power: A History of British Naval Policy in the Pre-Dreadnought Era, 1880–1905*, (Frank Cass, London, 1964).

Marlowe, John, *Cromer in Egypt* (Elek Books, London, 1970).

Matthew, H.C.G., *The Liberal Imperialists: The Ideas and Politics of a post-Gladstonian Elite* (Oxford University Press, London, 1973).

Monger, George, *The End of Isolation: British Foreign Policy 1900–1907* (Nelson, London, 1963).

Monroe, Elizabeth, *Britain's Moment in the Middle East 1914–1956* (Chatto & Windus, London, 1963).

Moore, R.J., *Escape from Empire. The Attlee Government and the Indian Problem* (Clarendon Press, Oxford, 1983).

Moore, R.J., *Liberalism and Indian Politics 1872–1922* (Edward Arnold, London, 1966).

Morgan, D.J., *The Official History of Colonial Development*, vol. 1, *The Origins of*

British Aid Policy 1924–1945 (Macmillan, London, 1980).

Morris-Jones, W.H. and Georges Fischer (eds.), *Decolonization and After – The British and French Experience* (Cass, London, 1980).

Mowat, Charles Loch, *Britain Between the Wars 1918–1940* (Methuen, London, 1972, first published 1955).

Neidpath, James, *The Singapore Naval Base and the Defence of Britain's Eastern Empire, 1919–1941* (Clarendon Press, Oxford, 1981).

Nish, Ian H., *Alliance in Decline – A Study of Anglo-Japanese Relations 1908–23* (University of London, Athlone Press, 1972).

Nish, Ian H., *The Anglo-Japanese Alliance* (University of London, Athlone Press, London, 1966).

Pelcovits, N.A., *Old China Hands and the Foreign Office* (King's Crown Press, New York, 1948).

Perham, Margery, *Colonial Sequence 1930 to 1949* (Methuen, London, 1967).

Platt, D.C.M., *Finance, Trade and Politics in British Foreign Policy 1818–1914* (Clarendon Press, Oxford, 1968).

Ratcliffe, Barrie M., 'Commerce and Empire: Manchester Merchants and West Africa, 1873–1895', *Journal of Imperial and Commonwealth History* VII (1979), pp. 293–320.

Redford, Arthur, *Manchester Merchants and Foreign Trade*, vol. 2, *1850–1939* (Manchester University Press, Manchester, 1956).

Robinson, Kenneth, *The Dilemmas of Trusteeship: Aspects of British Colonial Policy Between the Wars* (Oxford University Press, London, 1965).

Robinson, Ronald and John Gallagher with Alice Denny, *Africa and the Victorians. The Official Mind of Imperialism* (Macmillan, London, 1967, first published 1961).

Seeley, J.R., *The Expansion of England* (Macmillan, London, 1885).

Steiner, Zara, *The Foreign Office and Foreign Policy 1898–1914* (Cambridge University Press, Cambridge, 1969).

Stokes, Eric, *The English Utilitarians and India* (Clarendon Press, Oxford, 1959).

Stokes, Eric, *The Political Ideas of English Imperialism* (Oxford University Press, London, 1960).

Strauss, William L., *Joseph Chamberlain and the Theory of Imperialism* (Howard Fertig, New York, 1971).

Thorne, Christopher, *Allies of a Kind. The United States, Britain and the War Against Japan* (Hamish Hamilton, London, 1978).

Thornton, A.P., *The Imperial Idea and Its Enemies* (Macmillan, London, 1959).

Tomlinson, B.R., 'The Contraction of England: National Decline and the Loss of Empire', *Journal of Imperial and Commonwealth History*, XI (1) (October 1982), pp. 58–72.

Tomlinson, B.R., *The Political Economy of the Raj 1914–1947. The Economics of Decolonization in India* (Macmillan, London, 1979).

Waley, Daniel, *British Public Opinion and the Abyssinian War 1935–6* (Temple Smith in association with the London School of Economics and Political Science, London, 1975).

Woodruff, Philip (pseudonym for Philip Mason), *The Men Who Ruled India:* vol. 2, *The Guardians* (Cape, London, 1945).

Yeats, J., *Recent and Existing Commerce* (George Philip & Son, London, 1886).

Young, L.K., *British Policy in China 1895–1902* (Clarendon Press, Oxford, 1970).

Zinkin, Maurice and Taya, *Britain and India: Requiem for Empire* (Chatto & Windus, London, 1964).

AMERICA

Baldwin, David A., *Economic Development and American Foreign Policy 1943–62* (University of Chicago Press, Chicago, 1966).

Barnet, Richard J., *Intervention and Revolution: The United States in the Third World* (Meridian, New York, 1968).

Bidwell, Percy W., *Raw Materials. A Study of American Foreign Policy* (Council on Foreign Relations, Harper & Row, New York, 1958).

Blum, Robert M., *Drawing the Line. The Origin of the American Containment Policy in East Asia* (Norton, New York, 1982).

Brown, Seyom, *The Faces of Power: Constancy and Change in United States Foreign Policy From Truman to Johnson* (Columbia University Press, New York, 1968).

Burns, William J., *Economic Aid and American Policy Toward Egypt 1955–1981* (State University of New York Press, Albany, 1985).

Caute, David, *The Great Fear – The Anti-Communist Purge Under Truman and Eisenhower* (Simon & Schuster, New York, 1978).

Commission on Foreign Economic Policy. Report to the President and the Congress, January 1954 (US Government Printing Office, Washington, 23 January 1954).

Dallek, Robert, *The American Style of Foreign Policy. Cultural Politics and Foreign Affairs* (Mentor, New American Library, New York, 1983).

Donovan, John C., *The Cold Warriors: A Policy Making Elite* (D.C. Heath & Co., Lexington Mass., 1974).

Duignan, Peter and L.H. Gann, *The United States and Africa: A History* (Cambridge University Press, Cambridge, and Hoover Institution, 1984).

Emerson, Rupert, *Africa and United States Policy* (Prentice-Hall, Englewood Cliffs, New Jersey, 1967).

Fifield, Russell H., *Southeast Asia in United States Policy* (Council on Foreign Relations, Praeger, New York, 1963).

Fulbright, J. William, *The Arrogance of Power* (Pelican, Penguin Books, Harmondsworth, 1970, first published 1966).

Gaddis, John Lewis, *Strategies of Containment. A Critical Appraisal of Postwar American National Security Policy* (Oxford University Press, New York, 1982).

George, Alexander L. and Richard Smoke, *Deterrence in American Foreign Policy: Theory and Practice* (Columbia University Press, New York and London, 1974).

Halberstam, David, *The Best and the Brightest* (Fawcett Publications, Greenwich, Connecticut, 1973, first published 1969).

Harrison, Selig S., *The Widening Gulf – Asian Nationalism and American Policy* (The Free Press, New York, 1978).

Hoopes, Townsend, *The Devil and John Foster Dulles* (Andre Deutsch, London, 1974).

Iriye, Akira, *Across the Pacific. An Inner History of American-East Asian Relations* (Harvest/H.B.J., New York, 1967).

Iriye, Akira (ed.), *Mutual Images. Essays in American-Japanese Relations* (Harvard University Press, Cambridge, Mass., 1975).

Isaacs, Harold R., *Scratches on Our Minds: American Views of China and India* (M.E. Sharpe, White Plains, New York, 1958, reprinted 1980).

Kenen, Peter B., *Giant Among Nations: Problems in United States Foreign Economic Policy* (Rand McNally, Chicago, 1960).

Kennan, George, *Realities of American Foreign Policy* (Oxford University Press, London, 1954).

Kolko, Joyce and Gabriel, *The Limits of Power. The World and United States Foreign Policy, 1945–1954* (Harper & Row, New York, 1972).

Landsberg, Hans H., Leonard L. Fischman and Joseph L. Fischer, *Resources in America's Future: Patterns of Requirements and Availabilities 1960–2000* (Resources for the Future Inc., John Hopkins Press, Baltimore, 1963).

Lipson, Charles, *Standing Guard. Protecting Foreign Capital in the Nineteenth and Twentieth Centuries* (University of California Press, Berkeley, Los Angeles and London, 1985).

Mahoney, Richard D., *J.F.K. Ordeal in Africa* (Oxford University Press, New York, 1983).

May, Ernest R., *'Lessons' of the Past. The Use and Misuse of History in American Foreign Policy* (Oxford University Press, New York, 1978).

Neustadt, Richard E. and Ernest R. May, *Thinking in Time. The Uses of History for Decision-Makers* (Free Press, New York, 1986).

Osgood, Robert Endicott, *Ideals and Self-Interest in America's Foreign Relations* (University of Chicago Press, Chicago, 1953).

Packenham, Robert A., *Liberal America and the Third World* (Princeton University Press, Princeton N.J., 1973).

Pastor, Robert A., *Congress and the Politics of U.S. Foreign Economic Policy 1929–1976* (University of California Press, Berkeley and Los Angeles, California, 1980).

The Pentagon Papers. The Defence Department History of United States Decision Making on Vietnam, vols. 1–4 (Senator Gravel edn, Beacon Press, Boston, 1971) and vol. 5, *Critical Essays*, edited by Noam Chomsky and Howard Zinn (1972).

President's Materials Policy Commission, Resources for Freedom, 5 volumes (Government Printing Office, Washington, 1952).

Rostow, W.W., *Eisenhower, Kennedy, and Foreign Aid* (University of Texas Press, Austin, 1985).

Russett, Bruce M., *No Clear and Present Danger. A Skeptical View of the United States Entry into World War II* (Harper & Row, New York, 1972).

Schilling, Warner H., Paul Y. Hammong and Glenn H. Snyder, *Strategy, Politics and Defense Budgets* (Columbia University Press, New York and London, 1962).

Schlesinger, Arthur Jnr., *A Thousand Days, John F. Kennedy in the White House* (Andre Deutsch, London, 1965).

Selden, Mark (ed.), *Remaking Asia. Essays on the American Use of Power* (Pantheon Books, New York, 1974).

Staley, Eugene, *Raw Materials in Peace and War* (Council on Foreign Relations, New York, 1937).

Steel, Ronald, *Pax Americana* (Hamish Hamilton, London, 1967).

Stoessinger, John G., *Crusaders and Pragmatists – Movers of Modern American Foreign Policy* (Norton, New York, 1979).

Thomson, James C., Peter W. Stanley and John C. Perry, *Sentimental Imperialists – The American Experience in East Asia* (Harper & Row, New York, 1981).

Tucker, Robert, *The Radical Left and American Foreign Policy* (The Washington Center of Foreign Policy Research, The John Hopkins Press, Baltimore, Maryland, 1971).

Wilkins, Mira, *The Maturing of the Multinational Enterprise: American Business Abroad from 1914 to 1970* (Harvard University Press, Cambridge, Mass., 1974).

INDEX

Abyssinian crisis (1935) 81, 84, 94–5, 99, 105–6
Acheson, Dean 154, 166, 194, 199
Allen, Charles: *Plain Tales from the Raj* and *Tales from the Dark Continent* 51, 111
Amery, L.S. 122, 123, 132–3
Anderson, Sir Percy 22
Angell, Norman 102
Anglo-Japanese Alliance (1902) 14, 21, 28, 85, 93
Asquith, Lord 33
Australia 63, 85, 87, 96, 126

Baldwin, Stanley 93, 95, 125
Balfour, Arthur 88–9, 103
Ball, George 177
Baring, Sir Evelyn *see* Cromer
Barnes, Leonard 108
Beaverbrook, Lord 120, 125–6
Beer, George 90
Berlin Act (1885) 104
Berlin Conference (1884) 19, 143
Bismarck, Prince 13, 17–18, 20; aphorisms 14, 15, 226n
Bowles, Chester 151, 175, 179
Boxer uprising (1900) 21, 28, 228n
Bretton Woods Conference (1944) 194
Britain (1870–1914):
colonial literature and imperialism 36, 49–52; Colonial Office 32, 222; commercial pressure for political support 63–6, 71; economic perceptions of Asia/Africa 58–60, 62, 66–74, 220–1; and Egypt 16, 20, 24, 25; ethnocentrism 37, 42–5, 52, 217; and Europe 15–20, 24–5, 27–9, 227n; faith in free trade 54–8, 60–2, 65, 219; faith in progress 40–3, 217; ideologies of empire 35–9, 45; imperial diplomacy 16–21, 24–30; and India:
economic perceptions 62, 71–3, 219–20; moral responsibility 31–2, 36–9; perceptions of 36–9, 43, 224; special position of 24, 29, 61–3
and indirect rule 43–4; international decline 23, 63–6; and Japan 14, 21, 28, 85, 93; jingoism 33, 48; 99; military strength 21–3, 26, 219; moral responsibility 30, 31–52, 216–19; needs of the home economy 55–60; perceived role of state in the economy 54–5, 59, 63–6, 220; policy-makers and public opinion 12–13; and power politics 21–4, 26–7, 29, 214–16, 222; racism 45–8, 52, 217, 223; and settlement colonies 57, 61–3

Britain (inter-war years):
Abyssinian crisis 94–5, 99, 105; attitudes to military power 82, 97–8; colonial literature and imperialism 115–17; Colonial Office 77, 83, 130, 133, 135–9, 221–2; commodity management 129–30; and the Dominions 83–4, 96, 119, 122–3; economic decline 122, 127, 224
economic perceptions of Asia/Africa 121–32, 215, 220–1; aspects of trusteeship 132–40, 222; ignorance of colonial economies 120–1
European concerns 78, 94–5; faith in free trade 122–4, 132–4, 219; and Far East 93–4; Foreign Office 80, 84, 90, 95; 'Great Commercial Republic' 121, 123; Great Depression 125–6, 138; imperial preference/protectionism 123–8, 134; imperial system 79, 88–9, 95, 119
and India 83–4, 86, 97, 109–11; devolution 77, 93, 97, 110; economic constraints 119, 122, 131–3; Government of India Act (1935) 92–3; Indian Army 90, 93, 131; nationalism 93, 97, 106–7, 132; strategy 92–3
insecurity of Empire 90–1, 93–4, 114–17, 216; and League of Nations 80, 89, 92, 95, 99, 104; and Middle East 77, 92–3, 97; moral responsibility 101–17, 216–19; perceptions of Asia/Africa 77–8, 89, 91–7, 101, 106–17, 119, 223–4; perceptions of Empire 82–4, 90, 100, 106–9, 112–14, 215; power politics 87–100, 214–16, 222; public opinion as political force 99, 101; racism 84–6, 100, 104, 136, 217; realist/moralist dichotomy 79–82, 100; relations with US 82, 107, 126; role of state in colonial development 112–14, 129–30, 135–6, 139, 221; ten-year rule (1919) 82
Bruce, Stanley 122
Buchan, John 49, 50
Burgess, Anthony: *The Long Day Wanes* 186

Canada 61–2, 126
Carr, E.H:
International Relations Between the Wars 77; *The Twenty Years Crisis 1919–39* 79–80
Cary, Joyce:
An American Visitor 117; *Mr Johnson* 49, 115–16
Ceylon 132
Chamberlain, Joseph 22, 46; economic perceptions 58, 65–7, 122

Chamberlain, Neville 97
Chatfield, Admiral Sir E. 91
China:
    economic images of 57, 59, 64–5, 69–71,
    127; perceptions of 15, 86, 89–90, 105; rise
    of nationalism 82, 97; US perceptions of
    145, 149, 160–1, 163–4, 167, 170, 189, 224
Churchill, Winston 34, 77, 88–9, 97, 151–2
Clayton, William 194
Clifford, Sir Hugh 138
Colonial Development Act (1929) 135
Colonial Development Fund 112
Colonial Development and Welfare Act (1940)
    112, 130, 135
Colquhoun, A.R. 70
commodity management 129–30
Concert of Europe 11
Congo Basin 25, 63, 66, 68, 128
Conrad, Joseph 49, 51
Craigie, Sir Robert 94
Creech Jones, Arthur 113
Cripps, Stafford 114
Cromer, Lord 16, 24, 26–7, 32, 89
Crowther, Bishop Samuel 41
Cunliffe-Lister, Sir Philip 120–1, 123, 128
Curtis, Lionel 83
Curzon, Lord 16, 85–6, 89; and imperialism
    37–8, 43, 47, 66, 89, 217; and India 24, 26,
    37–9

Dickinson, G. Lowes 104
Disarmament Conference (1932) 105
Disraeli, Benjamin 18, 42, 46
Dodge, Joseph 200
Dominions, inter-war relations with Britain
    83–4, 96, 123, 126; *see also* settlement
    colonies
Dual Alliance (1879) 14
Dulles, J.F. 154, 162–3, 166, 247n; moral
    attitudes 175, 177–8, 189
Durrell, Lawrence: *Mountolive* 98
Dutch East Indies *see* Indonesia
Dutt, R. Palme: *World Politics 1918–36* 77–8,
    104

Earle, Edward Meade 152
East Africa 17, 63, 67–9, 85–6, 91, 107, 128,
    130–1, 137
Egypt 16, 20, 24–5, 92–3, 97, 178, 189, 208
Eisenhower Doctrine (1957) 159, 162–3
Eisenhower, Dwight 156, 163, 184, 198–200;
    anti-communism 160, 175, 185
Elbrick, C. Burke 175
Empire Crusade 120, 125–6
Empire Economic Union 130
Empire Resources Development Committee
    128
Esher, Lord 12
Europe (1870–1914):
    Asia/Africa in European diplomacy 13–21,

226n; commercial penetration overseas
    63–6, 71; Eurocentrism 41, 44–5; nation-
    alism 13–14, 16; power perspectives 14–21;
    racial attitudes 19
Europe (inter-war years):
    Eurocentrism 102–5; European system
    78–9; and League of Nations 81; and man-
    date system 103–4; realist/moralist
    dichotomy 79–81

Fitzjames Stephen, Sir J. 38, 39
Forrestal, James 151, 154, 167
Forster, E.M. 98, 114, 116
Fulbright, Senator W. 156, 180, 187–8,
    245–6n

Galbraith, J.K. 176
Gallatin, Albert 170
Galsworthy, John: *Flowering Wilderness* 116
Gandhi, Mahatma 107
Gaud, William 203
Gladstone, W.E. 24
Government of India Act (1935) 92
Gray Commission (1950) 206, 208–9
Grey, Sir Edward 22, 33, 89

Haggard, Rider 50
Hailey, Lord 107, 109, 111, 114
Halifax, Lord 107
Hancock, Sir Keith: *Survey of British
    Commonwealth Affairs ... 1918–39* 83,
    85–6, 107, 118, 124–8, 130, 139
Hankey, Maurice 87
Hartz, Louis: *The Liberal Tradition in
    America* 172–3, 187
Henderson, Arthur 89
Herr, Michael: *Dispatches* 186–7
Hewins, W.A.S. 38, 122–3, 127
Hoare-Laval plan (1935) 94–5, 105
Hoare, Sir Samuel 80, 97
Hobson, J.A. 35, 55, 102
Ho Chi Minh 158, 162, 185, 189
House, Colonel Edward 103
Hughes, W.M. 85
Hull, Cordell 174, 194

Imperial Economic Conference (1932) 119,
    122, 126
India (1870–1914):
    Indian Army 18; nationalism 42–3, 73;
    relative autonomy 26, 57, 222; special posi-
    tion 24, 29, 61–3
India (inter-war years):
    demands for self-government 106–7, 110;
    fiscal autonomy convention 122, 133–4;
    Government of India Act (1935) 92–3;
    Indian Army 90, 93, 131; nationalism 93,
    97, 106, 132; protectionism 122; *see also*
    Britain (inter-war years)

indigenous peoples:
acceptance of racial stereotypes 45; and imperial system 13, 36, 38–9, 41; *see also* nationalism
Indo-China 149, 162, 174–5; 184, 187
Indonesia/Dutch East Indies 129, 165, 178, 185, 208

Japan (1870–1914):
Anglo-Japanese Alliance (1902) 14, 21, 28, 85, 93; economic penetration overseas 71; rise to power 28
Japan (inter-war years):
expansion 79, 81–2, 89, 91, 96, 128; invasion of Manchuria 81, 84, 94, 98; perceptions of 86; Twenty-One Demands (1915) 87
Japan (Cold War era)
US perceptions of 159, 164, 195–6, 207–8
Johnson, Lyndon 151, 169, 186, 189, 200; insecurity 157–8

Kellogg Pact (1928) 89
Kennan, George 149, 151–2, 169, 186
Kennedy, J.F. 143, 156, 160–1, 176, 217; and aid programmes 198, 200–1; insecurity 157–8
Kerr, Philip 108
Khrushchev, Nikita 160, 208
Kidd, Benjamin 46, 55
Kipling, Rudyard 36, 38, 49–51
Kissinger, Henry 160, 163, 182
Korea/South Korea 197, 210
Korean War 150, 199, 204–5

Lansdowne, Lord 22
Latin America 5, 143
Lawrence, T.E. 50
League of Nations 45, 80–1, 85, 102–3; Eurocentric imperative 104; *see also* Woodrow Wilson
League of Nations Union 103–5
Lederer, W. & Burdick, E: *The Ugly American* 180–1
Lever, William 128
Leys, Norman 108
Livingstone, David 42
Lloyd George, David 85, 87, 125
Lugard, Lord 37, 43–4, 111, 133; and imperial trusteeship 109, 124, 138

MacArthur, General Douglas 164, 186, 244n, 246n
Macdonald, Ramsay 43, 89, 126
Macmillan, W.M. 108–9, 119, 139
McNamara, Robert 201
McNaughton, John 162, 165
Magsaysay, Ramon 161
Mahan, Captain A. 18, 23

Mailer, Norman:
Armies of the Night 187; *Why Are We in Vietnam*? 182, 186–8
Malaya/Malaysia 129–30, 138, 165, 186
Mallett, Sir Louis 70
'man-bap' 32
Manchurian crisis (1931) 81, 84, 94
mandate system 88, 103–4, 107, 109
Marshall Plan 153–4, 196, 198
Marx, Karl 40, 41–2
Mason, Edmund 207
Massey, W.F. 85
Mill, J.S. 40, 41, 61
Milner, Lord 24, 38, 45, 83, 108; and imperial future 122, 133
Minto, Lord 37
Monroe Doctrine (1823) 143, 159, 244n
moral responsibility, concept of 31–2
Morel, E.D. 102, 238n
Morgenthau, Hans 150, 152, 169, 181
Morgenthau, Henry 194
Morley, Lord 37, 43
Mutual Security Act (US) (1951) 199

Nasser, Gamal Abdel 160, 189
nationalism (1870–1914):
Asian 28, 42–3, 73; European 13–14, 16
nationalism, Afro-Asian (inter-war years) 82, 93, 96–7, 101, 106, 132
nationalism, Afro-Asian, US perceptions of 160–3, 175, 185
Nehru, Jawaharlal 41
New Guinea 18
New Zealand 85, 87, 96, 126
Niebuhr, Reinhold 152, 169
Nixon, Richard 157–8, 161

Orwell, George: *Burmese Days* 114–16

Pakistan 164–5
Paley Commission (1952) 200, 204–7
Paris Peace Conference 79, 83, 88, 90, 103
Perham, Dame Margery 109
Permanent Mandates Commission 103
Persian Gulf 26
Philippines 143, 144, 161, 165, 185, 211
Point Four Program 179, 197–8, 201–2
power:
balance of 10; military capability and 11
power politics:
economic factors and 10, 19; fundamentals of 9–13, 81; moral considerations and 11; *see also* Britain; Europe; United States

racism:
(1870–1914) 45–8, 52, 217, 223; (inter-war years) 84–6, 100, 104, 136, 217; in United States (Cold War era) 163–4, 217, 223
Randall Commission (1954) 200, 202–3, 205–6

Roberts, Field Marshal Lord 27
Robertson, Sir James 111–12
Roosevelt, F.D. 83, 105, 148–9, 238n; anti-colonialism 149, 174
Rosebery, Lord 22, 24
Rostow, W.W: *The Stages of Economic Growth* 193
Round Table movement 83, 119
Runciman, Walter 126, 128
Rusk, Dean 160, 162, 176, 248n
Russo-Japanese War 20, 21

Salisbury, Lord 12, 27, 54, 216; and Asia/Africa 13, 17, 46, 64–5; colonial diplomacy 17, 19, 22–3, 27–8
Samoa 17
Sarraut, Albert 90
Say's Law 56
Schultz, Theodore 204
Schuster, Sir George 134
Schweitzer, Albert 176–7
Scott, Paul:
  The Day of the Scorpion 116; *A Division of the Spoils* 117
Seeley, Sir John 63
settlement colonies 57, 61–2, 63; *see also* Dominions
Siam *see* Thailand
Singapore naval base 91, 94, 99
Sjahrir, Soetan 38–9
Smith, Adam 60–1
Smoot Hawley Tariff Act (US) (1930) 125
Smuts, Field Marshal J.C. 85–6, 114
Social Darwinism 45–6
South Africa 85–6, 87, 96, 114
south-west Africa 18
Soviet Union:
  Cold War era 150, 152, 160; US perceptions of 152–5, 159–61, 208; *see also* Europe (1870–1914)
Spencer, Herbert 39, 40–1
Stanley, H.M. 68
Stevenson, Adlai 160, 200–1, 249n
Stimson, Henry 167
Sudan 21, 33, 128
Suez Canal 24, 26
Swinton *see* Cunliffe-Lister
Sykes-Picot Agreement (1916) 87

Thailand/Siam 57, 165
Thomas, J.H. 123, 130–1
Toynbee, Arnold 90
Treaty of London (1915) 87
Truman Doctrine 178
Truman, H.S. 149, 151, 153–4, 156, 178–9; and aid programmes 197–8, 201–2
Turner, F.J. 172

Union of Democratic Control 102–3
United States (1870–1914):
  isolationist policy 28; protectionism 63
United States (inter-war years):
  anti-colonialism 103, 107, 217; confusion over national interests 81, 96; isolationism 105, 151; protectionism 125; racism 85, 217; relations with Britain 82, 107, 126
United States (Cold War era):
  aid programmes 180–1, 197–204, 209, 221, 252n; anti-Americanism within the US 174, 181–3, 185; anti-colonialism 143, 146, 173–6, 184, 217; anti-communism 156, 161, 173, 175–8, 184–5, 188, 215; attitudes to Asia/Africa 159–67, 173–89, 217, 223–4; attitudes to military force 150, 154–5, 158; and China 145, 149, 161, 163–4, 167, 170, 189, 224; commitment to Third World development 173–4, 178–80, 185, 194, 207–12, 220–1; containment strategy 148–66, 195; domino theory 159, 165, 195–6; economic dimension of power politics 168, 215, 222; economic perceptions of Asia/Africa 192–4, 196–212; ethnocentrism 170–2, 179–81, 193, 198, 217; evangelism 171, 173, 218; exceptionalism 170, 178, 221–2
    globalism 143–4, 147–65, 215, 224; and economic conceptions 193, 196, 204
  idealism 169–74; ideological preconceptions 153–4, 162–5, 223; ignorance of Asia/Africa 142–3, 145, 160, 163, 166–7, 176, 214–15, 221–3; imperialism 144
    insecurity 155–6, 187–9, 245–6n of leaders 156–8, 217–18
  insensitivity to Asian/African issues 144, 155, 162–3, 206, 216; and Japan 159, 164, 195–6, 207–8; liberalism 172–3; literature 180–1, 182, 186–9, 223; and Middle East 159, 162–4; Monroe Doctrine (1823) 143, 159, 244n; and nationalism 160–3, 175, 185; and post-war international economic order 194–5, 207, 219; *Pentagon Papers* 154, 165, 195–6; perceptions of Soviet Union 152–5, 159–61, 208; Point Four Program 179, 197–8, 201–2; position of Congress 145, 154, 201–2, 209; power politics 148–68, 195, 214–16, 222; protectionism 209; racism 163–4, 217, 223; sensitivity to public opinion 144–6, 171; and south-east Asia 149, 159, 175, 195–6, 197, 206; strategic materials acquisition 200, 204–7, 208; Vietnam War 156–8, 165–6, 178, 181, 186–7, 190, 247–8n; anti-war movement 181–3, 188

Vandenberg, Senator Arthur 151, 154
Vansittart, Lord 80, 84, 91, 95, 97
Victoria, Queen 46

Vietnam War 156–8, 165–6, 178, 181, 186–7, 190, 247–8n; anti-war movement 181–3, 188

Wallace, Henry 151
Washington Conference (1921–2) 89, 105
Waugh, Evelyn: *Black Mischief* 115

West Africa 20, 43–4, 63, 66, 68–9, 91, 112, 128, 138, 207
Williams, G. Mennen 249n
Willkie, Wendell 148
Wilson, Hugh 105
Wilson, Woodrow 86, 96, 103, 169; and Paris Peace Conference 79, 83, 88
Woolf, Leonard 69, 108